THE FATHERS
OF THE CHURCH

A NEW TRANSLATION

VOLUME 6

THE FATHERS OF THE CHURCH

A NEW TRANSLATION

EDITORIAL BOARD

HERMIGILD DRESSLER, O.F.M.
Quincy College
Editorial Director

ROBERT P. RUSSELL, O.S.A.
Villanova University

THOMAS P. HALTON
The Catholic University of America

WILLIAM R. TONGUE
The Catholic University of America

SISTER M. JOSEPHINE BRENNAN, I.H.M.
Marywood College

FORMER EDITORIAL DIRECTORS

LUDWIG SCHOPP, ROY J. DEFERRARI, BERNARD M. PEEBLES

WRITINGS OF SAINT JUSTIN MARTYR

SAINT JUSTIN MARTYR

THE FIRST APOLOGY

THE SECOND APOLOGY

DIALOGUE WITH TRYPHO

EXHORTATION TO THE GREEKS

DISCOURSE TO THE GREEKS

THE MONARCHY
or
THE RULE OF GOD

by

THOMAS B. FALLS, D.D., Ph.D.
St. Charles Seminary
Overbrook, Pennsylvania

THE CATHOLIC UNIVERSITY OF AMERICA PRESS
Washington, D.C.

NIHIL OBSTAT:

JOSEPH A. M. QUIGLEY
Censor Librorum

IMPRIMATUR:

✠ D. CARDINAL DOUGHERTY
Archiepiscopus Philadelphiensis

October 5, 1948

The *nihil obstat* and *imprimatur* are official declarations that a book or pamphlet is free of doctrinal or moral error. No implication is contained therein that those who have granted the *nihil obstat* and *imprimatur* agree with the content, opinions, or statements expressed.

Library of Congress Catalog Card No.: 65-18317
ISBN 8132-0006-7
ISBN: 978-0-8132-1552-5 (pbk)

Copyright © 1948 by
THE CATHOLIC UNIVERSITY OF AMERICA PRESS, INC.
All rights reserved
Second Printing 1965
Third Printing 1977
First paperback reprint 2008

CONTENTS

FOREWORD 9
THE FIRST APOLOGY
   Introduction 23
   Text 33
THE SECOND APOLOGY
   Introduction 115
   Text 119
DIALOGUE WITH TRYPHO
   Introduction 139
   Text 147
EXHORTATION TO THE GREEKS
   Introduction 369
   Text 373
DISCOURSE TO THE GREEKS
   Introduction 427
   Text 431
THE MONARCHY or THE RULE OF GOD
   Introduction 439
   Text 443
INDEX 457

FOREWORD

ST JUSTIN MARTYR is known as the outstanding apologist[1] of the second century. While the Apostolic Fathers[2] like St. Clement of Rome, St. Ignatius of Antioch, and St. Polycarp had addressed their letters and admonitions to communities and members within the Christian fold, St. Justin is considered to be the first prominent defender of the Christian faith against non-Christians[3] and the enemies[4] of the Church.

The chief sources for the uncertain and meager chronological data of Justin's life are his own writings, the two *Apologies* and the *Dialogue with Trypho*. The circumstances leading up to his conversion are recorded in the first eight chapters of the *Dialogue,* and the events surrounding his death are reported in the *Acta SS. Justini et Sociorum,* an authentic source of the latter part of the second century.

Historians place his birth in the beginning of the second century (*ca.* 100-110 A.D.) at Flavia Neapolis[5] (today Nablûs) in Samaria. Although St. Epiphanius[6] calls him a

---

1 For Christian Apologists, cf. R. Arbesmann in Foreword to Vol. 1 of *The Writings of Tertullian* in this series.
2 *The Apostolic Fathers* is a collective name, in use since the seventeenth century, for a group of Christian writers who either were or were believed to be disciples of the Apostles. Cf. K. Bihlmeyer, *Die apostolischen Väter* (Tübingen 1924) VIIf. A translation *of The Apostolic Fathers* by F. X. Glimm, J.-F. Marique and G.G. Walsh is found in the first volume of this series.
3 Cf. his *Dialogue with Trypho* pp. 147-366 below.
4 Cf. his two *Apologies* pp. 33-135 below.
5 Cf. 1 *Apol.* 1. It was called Flavia in honor of Flavius Vespasian who had built this city on the ruins of Sichem, formerly the capital of Samaria.
6 Cf. *Haereses* 46.

Samaritan, and he himself refers to his people as Samarians,[7] Justin was not a Jew either by race or religion.[8] His family was rather of pagan and Greco-Roman[9] ancestry. They had come as colonists to Flavia Neapolis during the reign of Titus (79-81 A.D.), the son of Flavius Vespasian (69-79), who had built this city and had granted its inhabitants the privileges of Roman citizens.

Obviously, the parents of Justin had considerable means and could afford to give their son an excellent education in the pagan culture of the day. Young Justin had a keen mind, was inquisitive by nature and endowed with a burning thirst for learning. He tried to broaden his knowledge further by extensive travels. Driven by an inner urge and a profound inclination for philosophy,[10] he subsequently frequented the schools of the Stoics, the Peripatetics, the Pythagoreans,[11] and the Platonists. He set out to reach the truth; to gain a perfect knowledge of God was his greatest and only ambition. Dissatisfied with the Stoics and Peripatetics, he tells us of finding temporary peace in the philosophy of the Platonists: 'the perception of incorporeal things quite overwhelmed me and

---

7 Cf. *Dial. with Tr.* 120.
8 According to *Dial. with Tr.* 29, he was not circumcised.
9 F. Cayré, *Patrologie et Histoire de Théologie* (3rd ed. Paris 1938) 110, states that Justin 'probably' was of Roman origin only; B. Altaner, *Patrologia* (Roma 1940) 69, that he was a Greek. The Latin name of his father and the Greek name of his grandfather suggest a mixed ancestry. Cf. Smith and Wace, *Dict. of Christ. Biog.*
10 Cf. *Dial. with Tr.* 2f.: 'Philosophy is indeed one's greatest possession. It is most precious in the sight of God, to whom it, alone, leads us and to whom it unites us. They are really holy men who have devoted themselves to philosophy.' For Justin, philosophy comprises both the search for the truth and Truth itself which is God; since 'God is the Being having the same nature in the same manner and is the cause of existence of all else, . . . therefore it is philosophy that alone produces happiness.'
11 The extensive acquaintance with music, astronomy, and geometry, required as a preliminary step, as well as personal reasons, made him quit this school after a very short time.

the Platonic theory of ideas added wings to my mind, so that in a short time I imagined myself a wise man. So great was my folly that I fully expected immediately to gaze upon God.'[12]

One day, being in such frame of mind and desiring absolute solitude for contemplation, he took a walk to an isolated spot near the seashore. Here, he was accosted by a 'respectable old man of meek and venerable mien' who had noticed his occupied and pensive look.[13] When Justin told him that he was trying to form a perfect idea of God and praised the excellency of the philosophy of the Platonists, the stranger answered: 'a long time ago, long before the time of those reputed philosophers, there lived blessed men, just and loved by God, men who spoke through the inspiration of the Holy Spirit and predicted events that would come to pass in the future, which events are now taking place. We call those men Prophets. Their writings are still extant, and whoever reads them with proper faith will profit greatly and his knowledge of the origin and the end of things, and of any other matter that a philosopher should know. Thus, above all, you should beseech God to open to you the gates of light, for no one can perceive or understand these truths unless he has been enlightened by God and His Christ.'

After the venerable man had left, 'my spirit was immediately set on fire, and an affection for the Prophets and for those who are friends of Christ took hold of me; while pondering on his words, I discovered that his was the only sure and useful philosophy.'[14]

Justin relates another, practical reason for becoming a Christian. For quite some time he had observed and admired the steadfastness and heroism of the Christians in the face of

---
12 *Dial. with Tr.* 2.
13 *Dial with Tr.* 3.
14 *Dial. with Tr.* 7f.

grave punishment and death; 'when I heard,' he writes, 'the Christians misrepresented and watched them stand fearless in the face of death, I realized that they could not possibly live in sinful pleasure.'[15]

Justin became a Christian about 130˚ A.D.,[16] probably at Ephesus,[17] as Rauschen[18] and others hold. From this time on he dedicated his life and all his energy to the defense and dissemination of the Christian faith.

After his baptism, little is known about the chronological events of his life, except that during the Jewish uprising against the Roman invaders in 132-135, he encountered Trypho,[19] a Jew in the city of Ephesus, with whom he had a debate on the relative merits of Christianity and Judaism. Eusebius and Jerome inform us that, after he had become a Christian, Justin continued to wear the pallium or philosopher's cloak.[20] St. Epiphanius refers to him as 'a great ascetic who lived an austere and holy life.' It is almost certain that Justin never became a priest, as Tillemont and Dom

---

15 2 *Apol.* 12.
16 According to Eusebius, *Historia ecclesiastica* 4.8, it was after 182 A.D.; others, like Maran, think his conversion occurred as late as 137. Cf. also A. Butler, *The Lives of the Primitive Fathers, Martyrs*, under St. Justin, June 1st.
17 While Cave holds that he was converted at Nablûs and Maran at Alexandria, according to Cayré (*loc. cit.* 110) it was 'more probably' at Caesarea.
18 Foreword to *Frühchristliche Apologeten* (Bibl. d. Kirchenväter, 1913).
19 Cf. *Dial. with Tr.* 3. According to Eusebius (*Hist. eccl.* 4.18.6) and Jerome (*De viris illust.* 23), Trypho was one of the best known Hebrews of his time. However, other historians, such as O. Bardenhewer (*Geschichte der altkirchlichen Literatur* [1913] I² 229), doubt the historical existence of Trypho. For his probable identification with the famous Rabbi Tarphon, see Th. Zahn, 'Dichtung und Wahrheit in Justins Dialog mit dem Juden Tryphon' *Zeitschrift für Kirchengeschichte* 8 (1885-1886) 37-66.
20 So did Aristides of Athens, after becoming a Christian, and Heracles even when he had become Bishop of Alexandria.

Maran[21] think; that he had been a deacon[22] is only a matter of conjecture. Most of the historians agree with Ceillier that Justin was always a layman who, in a philosopher's mantle, wandered about and tried to converse with people of every walk of life, putting into practice the words he addressed to Trypho: 'I am now [after his conversion] a philosopher, and it is my wish that everyone would be of the same sentiment as I and never spurn the Savior's words; for they have in themselves such tremendous majesty that they can instill fear into those who have wandered from the path of righteousness, whereas they ever remain a great solace to those who heed them. Thus, if you have any regard for your own welfare and for the salvation of your soul, and if you believe in God, you may have the chance, since I know you are no stranger to this matter, of attaining a knowledge of the Christ of God and, after becoming a Christian, of enjoying a happy life.'[23]

Some time after his conversion Justin went to Rome,[24] where he stayed for a while. He opened a philosophical school, and Tatian became the most outstanding of his pupils. Wherever he had an opportunity, he freely and fearlessly engaged in intellectual discourses and apologetic controversies.[25] One is recorded, that with Crescens the Cynic, 'the lover not of wisdom but of false opinions,'[26] 'who disregarded that praiseworthy remark of Socrates:[27] "No man must be

---
21 Migne, *P.G.* 6.113f.
22 Cf. A. Butler, *loc. cit.*
23 Cf. *Dial. with Tr.* 8.
24 Cf. Eusebius, *Hist. eccl.* 4.11.
25 The most famous is the *Dial. with Tr.* at Ephesus. Cf. Joach. Perionius, O.S.B.: . . . *praestantissimum se et acerrimum Christiani nominis ac religionis propugnatorem . . . omnibus in locis* . . . Cf. below, note 45.
26 *2 Apol.* 3.
27 Cf. Plato, *Republic* 10.595C.

honored before the truth."' Although Justin had exposed the Cynic's utter ignorance of the Christian teachings in a public debate and declares: 'I *expect* to be the victim of a plot and to be affixed to the stake . . . perhaps even by Crescens, that lover of fanfare and ostentation,'[28] and in spite of Tatian's words: 'Crescens who made himself a nest in Rome, while professing to despise death, proved his fear of it by scheming to bring Justin and myself to death as to an evil thing,[29] it is not at all certain that the Cynic was the direct instigator[30] of Justin's execution. At least, neither Crescens nor any particular person is mentioned in the *Acta Sancti Justini*, although in them we find a very detailed report of Justin's examination and sentence by Rusticus the prefect of Rome. Probably, the fact that Justin, with a determination that knows no compromise, challenged the state authorities for calumniating the blameless life and character of the Christians and protested openly and fearlessly against their prosecution is responsible for his decapitation (*ca.* 165).

According to the *Acta*,[31] Rusticus sentenced six other holy martyrs[32] to die with Justin: 'Let those who have refused to sacrifice to the gods and to obey the command of the Emperor be scourged, and led away to suffer the punishment of decapitation according to the laws.'[33] However, for Justin[34] and his companions, death did not mean punishment; the hour of death was their hour of glory, and an hour of triumph for the Christian faith.

---

28 2 *Apol. 3.*
29 *Oratio* 32; cf. Eusebius, *Hist. eccl.* 4.16.
30 Cf. F. Cayré, *loc. cit.* 112.
31 *Acta* 5.
32 Chariton, Charito, Euelpistus, Hierax, Paeon, Liberianus.
33 Justin was then in Rome for the second time; Cf. *Acta* 2.
34 Cf. Justin's proud words in 1 *Apol.* 2: 'You may be able to kill us [Christians], but you cannot harm us.'

Of the works Justin composed in his very active life, several, as so many of other early Christian writers, have unfortunately not been preserved for us. Among those that have perished, perhaps the most important is the *Syntagma against all the Heresies,* to which Justin[35] himself referred; it probably was made up in part by his treatise *Against Marcion,* cited by St. Irenaeus.[36] As the only authentic[37] works of the apologist that are still extant can be considered his two *Apologies* and the *Dialogue with Trypho.*

Eusebius (265-340 A.D.) in his *Ecclesiastical History*[38] attributes also to Justin: *The Discourse to the Greeks, The Admonition to the Greeks, On the Divine Monarchy, The Psalmist* and *On the Soul.* While the two latter seemingly have been lost,[39] critics assign the origin of the three former to the end of the second or the beginning of the third century.

In addition to these five works, the editions of Prud. Maran [40] and J. C. Th. von Otto[41] list the following spurious titles amongst the writings of Justin: *The Exposition of True Faith, Letter to Zena and Serenius,*[42] *Refutation of Some Aristotelian Dogmas, Answers to the Orthodox, Christian Questions to the Gentiles,* and *Questions to the Gentiles.* How-

---

35 1 Apol. 26.
36 *Adversus haereses* 4.6.2.
37 According to G. Rauschen, *loc. cit.* 4, F. Cayré, *loc. cit.* 112, and others also, the fragments *On the Resurrection* are really from the hand of Justin. That the *Letter to Diognetus,* attributed to Justin up to the seventeenth century, for many reasons, is not Justin's, is today considered a matter of fact.
38 4.18.
39 Cf. Bardy, *D.T.C.* 8. 2238ff.
40 *S.P.N. Justini philosophi et martyris opera quae extant omnia* (Paris 1742), reprinted in J. P. Migne, *Patrologia Graeca* 6.
41 *Corpus Apologetarum Christianorum saeculi secundi* (Jena 1877) I 23.
42 Batiffol conjectures this Letter to be written by Sisinnius, the Novation Bishop of Constantinople (*ca.* 400 A.D.); cf. *Revue Biblique* 5 (1896) 114ff.

ever, in the opinion of the historians, they did not issue from the pen of Justin and are attributed by different scholars to different later authors.[43] The first edition of Justin's writings in the original Greek printed by R. Stephanus,[44] as well as the first Latin edition with the commentary by Joach. Perionius carrying the imprint of Jac. Dupuys,[45] do not list: *The Discourse to the Greeks, The Psalmist,* and *On the Soul.* In addition to the collections already mentioned, later, more critical editions are extant for individual works.

Justin's authentic writings will remain forever[46] a treasure in the history of Christian literature. They may invite criticism from the strict literary viewpoint,[47] for Justin did not always adhere to a strictly logical sequence of ideas; he indulged in digressions[48] and placed sometimes unnecessary emphasis on less important thoughts, losing sight of the original topic. However, his style and structure are redeemed by a simplicity of expression, a warmth of feeling and a love for truth and righteousness that are so characteristic of him. For Justin, 'sound reason demands that the lover of truth must choose, in every possible way, to do and say what is right, even when threatened by death, rather than save his own life . . .'[49] Thus, historians will always regard him as a most trustworthy witness of the events of his day. With a passionate objectivity

---

43 A.Harnack ascribes these five works to Diodorus of Tarsus (d. 391-392); F.X.Funk thinks that the *Exposition of True Faith* was written in the fifth century and ascribes the *Answers to the Orthodox* to the pen of Theodoret of Cyrus (d. *ca.* 455). Cf. J. Tixeront, *Patrology* (1920) 40.
44 Paris 1551
45 Paris 1554.
46 Cf. G. Rauschen, *loc. cit.* 9.
47 Cf. Otto, *loc. cit.* 1. lxiv.
48 Cf. *Dial. with Tr.* 30-40; 63-66, 79-83; 1 *Apol.* 27-29, 43-44; 2 *Apol.* 3-9.
49 1 *Apol.* 2.

his writings shed light on the relationship of Christians and non-Christians, on the worship of the early followers of Christ, their community life, their persecution by irrational and biased State authorities, their sufferings and their heroism.

From the theological point of view, also, the works of Justin are of exceptional value.[50] If his use of rare words[51] and imperfect terminology sometimes gave rise to not entirely correct statements, it should be borne in mind that Justin wrote at a time when theological terms were not universally and precisely fixed. Of course, like the other apologists of the second century, Justin was, in his theology, to a great extent influenced by, and dependent upon, Greek philosophy.[52] In fact, he was not only the first Christian writer to apply the categories and to utilize a philosophical terminology in Christian thought, but he was also one of the first to attempt to reconcile faith with reason. He fortunately subordinated reason to faith, and therefore avoided the pitfalls of Gnosticism. In combining Plato's[53] world of ideas with the Word-concept of the Holy Scripture, he became the origin-

---

50 F. Cayré, *loc. cit.* 115, concurs with M.-J. Lagrange, [*Saint Justin* (Paris 1914)] that St. Justin merits well the title of a Doctor of the Church.
51 Cf. Otto, *loc. cit.*
52 Cf. Photius, *Bibliotheca* cod. 125: 'He is a man who has climbed the heights of philosophy, Greek as well as foreign; he is overflowing with much learning and the riches of knowledge.' Early Christian writers already referred to him as 'St. Justin Martyr and Philosopher' (cf. Anastasius) or 'St. Justin Philosopher and Martyr' (cf. John of Damascus).
53 Cf. J. M. Pfättisch, *Der Einfluss Platos auf die Theologie Justins des Märtyrers. Eine dogmengeschichtliche Untersuchung nebst einem Anhang über die Komposition der Apologien Justins* (Paderborn 1910); J. Thümer, *Über den Platonismus in den Schriften des Justin Martyr* (Glochau-Programm 1880); C. Weizsäcker, 'De l'influence du Timée de Platon sur la Théologie de Justin Martyr,' *Bibliothèque de l'Ecole des Hautes Etudes. Sciences religieuses* VII (Paris 1896).

ator of the philosophical[54] exposition of the Logos.[55] While others like Origen[56] did not appreciate the merits of this great achievement, 'it remained for St. Augustine to trace the basic patterns that were to serve St. Thomas Aquinas in the composition of the *Summa Theologica*; however, the modest precursor [Justin Martyr] should not be forgotten,'[57] 'who in virtues [and heroism] was not far removed from the Apostles.'[58]

---

54 For the development of the Logos-concept in philosophy, cf F. Cayré, *loc. cit.* 115ff.
55 Cf. 1 *Apol.* 46: 'We have been taught that Christ was First-begotten of God [the Father] and we have indicated above that He is the Word of whom all mankind partakes. Those who lived by reason are Christians . . . ,' and 2 *Apol.* 13 where Justin expounds on the *Verbum Divinum* (*Verbum Perfectum*) and *verbum seminale* (human reason); cf. Lagrange, *loc. cit.* 134-144; also, *Letter to Diognetus* 7.
56 Cf. F. Cayré, *loc. cit.* 119.
57 M.-J. Lagrange, *loc. cit.* 156.
58 Photius, *Bibliotheca* cod. 234.

SELECT BIBLIOGRAPHY

B. Altaner, *Patrologia* (Roma 1940).
B. Aubé, *Saint Justin philosophe et martyr* (Paris 1861).
O. Bardenhewer, *Geschichte der altkirchlichen Literatur* (Freiburg i.B. 1913) 1².
G. Bardy, '[Saint] Justin,' *Dict. theol. cath.* 8.2238ff.
P. Batiffol, *Ancienne littérature chrétienne grecque* (Paris 1901).
A. Bery, *Saint Justin, sa vie, sa doctrine* (Paris 1911).
F. Cayré, *Patrologie et Histoire de la Théologie* (3rd ed. Paris 1938).
A. Ehrhard. *Die altchristliche Literatur und ihre Erforschung* (Freiburg 1884/1900)
Ch. E. Freppel, *Saint Justin* (Paris 1885).
A. Harnack, *Geschichte der altchristlichen Literatur bis Eusebius* (Leipzig 1893).
H. Jordan, *Geschichte der altchristlichen Literatur* (Leipzig 1911).
M.-J. Lagrange, *Saint Justin* (Paris 1914).
J. Leblanc, 'Le Logos de Saint Justin,' *Annales de philosophie chrétienne* 3 série, II (1904) 191ff.
J. Lebreton, *Théories du Logos au début de l'ère chrétienne* (Paris 1906).
C. C. Martindale, *St. Justin the Martyr* (N. Y. 1921).
R. Otto, 'Zur Charakteristik des heiligen Justinus des Philosophen Märtyrers,' *Kaiserl. Akad. der Wissensch. Philos. Hist. Cl. Sitzungsber.* Bd. 8, (1852) 164ff.
J. M. Pfättisch, 'Der Einfluss Platos auf die Theologie Justins des Märtyrers. Eine dogmengeschichtliche Untersuchung nebst einem Anhang über die Komposition der Apologien Justins,' *Forschungen zur christl. Literatur und Dogmengeschichte.* Bd. 10, Heft 1 (Paderborn 1910).
C. Semish, *Justin der Märtyrer* (Breslau 1840-1842).
W. Smith and H. Wace, *A Dictionary of Christian Biography* (London 1882) 3. 561ff.
J. Springl, 'Die Theologie des hl. Justinus des Märtyrers,' *Linzer Theol. prakt. Quartalschrift* 37 (1884) 283ff.
J. Tixeront, *Handbook of Patrology* (St. Louis and London 1920).
J. Thümer, *Über den Platonismus in den Schriften des Justin Martyr* (Glauchau—Programm, 1880).

THE FIRST APOLOGY

INTRODUCTION

JUSTIN'S *First Apology* is one of the earliest extant in the annals of Christianity. Right from the start the reader cannot but admire its author's courage, his firmness of purpose, his love for truth, righteousness, and wisdom.

The petition is addressed to the Emperor, the Emperor's sons, the sacred Senate and the whole Roman people. The petitioner is 'Justin, the son of Priscus and grandson of Bacchius of the city of Flavia Neapolis in Syria-Palestine.'[1] He is just 'one of those men of every race[2] who are unjustly hated and mistreated.'

He fearlessly states that his discourse contains neither words of flattery nor a request for favors. The purpose of his petition is to prove that truth and right are equal for all men and to demand that all should be treated equally; that the guardians of justice and lovers of wisdom must dispassionately base their judgment on truth, and truth alone, rather than on irrational impulse or evil rumors. Not without a flair of satire he states: 'Common sense dictates that they who are truly pious men and philosophers [such as state authorities should be] must honor and cherish what is true, . . . rulers should pass judgment not through force and tyranny, but in accordance with piety and philosophy.' He demands that, in every individual case, 'the accusations against the Christians receive unbiased examination, and if proved true, they should be punished as any guilty person', . . . 'sane reason, on the other hand,'

---
1 Justin was apparently a Roman citizen, cf. Foreword p. 10
2 Refers to the Catholicity of Christianity.

he declares, 'does not allow that injustice is done to innocent men just because of mischievous rumors'; no one should be condemned unheard for merely carrying a name [Christian]; for, a name without supporting deeds is but an empty shell. 'As far as we [Christians] are concerned,' he states, 'we believe that no evil can befall us unless we be proved to be criminals and sinful persons,' adding the proud words, 'you, indeed, may be able to kill us, but you cannot harm us.'

Some scholars like O. Bardenhewer[3] and G. Rauschen[4] do not find a strict sequence and clear exposition of thoughts in this *Apology*. Others like T. H. Wehofer[5] and A. Erhard[6] hold that Justin had composed his petition according to a preconceived plan.[7] Even if we concede that the material brought forth by Justin is not arranged in an exact order, one may see three sets[8] of ideas developed in its sixty-eight chapters.

In Chapters 1-20, he describes clearly the principals in his discourse: the state authorities on one side, and the Christians on the other. He expounds then on the principles upon which their relationship should be based, in order that 'both rulers and subjects fare well.' He shows that the precepts of Christ are bare of impiety and all unjust ambition. Christians do not strive for earthly power, but for a heavenly kingdom. They obey the state authorities in all civil matters and lead holy and virtuous lives. He brands the charges of atheism, anthro-

---

3 *Geschichte der altkirchlichen Literatur* (Freiburg i B. 1913) 1².
4 'Die formale Seite der Apologien Justin,' *Theol. Quartalschrift* (Tübingen 1899) 188ff.
5 'Die Apologie Justins des Philosophen und Märtyrers in literarhistorischer Beziehung zum erstenmal undersucht,' *Röm. Quartalschrift* 6, Suppl. Heft. (Rom. 1897) 2.
6 *Die altchristliche Literatur und ihre Erforschung* (Freiburg 1884-1900).
7 Cf. J. M. Pfättisch, *loc cit.*, who refers to the different opinions.
8 Cf. F. Cayré, *loc. cit.* 114f.

pophagy, and incest, held against the Christians, as untrue and baseless. Their belief in the immortality of the soul is, even according to the pagans, neither incredible nor against reason.

In Chapters 21-60, the superiority of Christianity over paganism is demonstrated. He shows that many prophecies of the Old Testament were fulfilled by Christ and explains the difference between the wonders of Jesus Christ and the tricks of the heathen magicians. The Gentiles, especially the pagan philosophers, including Plato himself, borrowed from the Bible.

In Chapters 61-68, Christian practices are explained: particularly the ceremony of initiation into the Christian fold (baptism),[9] the sacrament of the Holy Eucharist, the Sunday assembly of the Christians, their fastings, prayers, and care for less fortunate brethren.

At the end, Justin attached a copy of Hadrian's Rescript [69] written in favor of the Christians. Other scribes, at a later date, added[10] the Letter of Antoninus Pius to the Assembly of Asia [70] and the Letter of Marcus Aurelius to the Senate [71].

Apparently this *Apology* was written at Rome. Basing their opinions on internal evidence, historical events and tradition,[11] historians have set for its composition various dates,[12] from 138 to 156 A.D. Justin himself professes[13] to be writing one-hundred-and-fifty years after the birth of Christ. Eusebius

---
9 Cf. p. 100 n.5.
10 These two Letters are also contained in the first original edition (1551) and the first Latin translation (1554). Cf. above, notes 44 and 45.
11 Cf. the detailed analysis in W. Smith and H. Wace *loc. cit.* 3, 563.
12 Cf. W. Moeller, *History of the Christian Church* (London 1892) 174. K. Hubík, *Die Apologien des St. Justinus, des Philosophers und Märtyrers* (Wien 1912) 121ff. and 298f.
13 1 *Apol.* 46.

in his *Chronicon* assigns it to the year 141, the fourth year of the reign of Antoninus (137-161 A.D.). Tillemont, and later the Benedictine editors in the preface of their edition of Justin's works, place the date at about 150 A.D., and it seems that 'without very positive evidence against it, the year 148—i.e., Justin's 150 A.D.—should be taken as the approximate date.'[14]

This *Apology* has been preserved in two manuscripts,[15] in which, however, it is preceded by the *Second Apology*. The same sequence is found in the original Greek edition[16] and in the first Latin translation.[17] Eusebius[18] also refers, sometimes, to what we call the first as the second. Some critics reckon that the *Second Apology* is a preface to the first, others that it is just an appendix to the first.[19] However, since, in the *Second Apology,* Justin alludes[20] to the *First Apology*, there is great merit in the opinion that Eusebius erroneously confused the two apologies and that those we have now are two distinct works.[21] G. Krüger writes: 'There are no sufficient grounds for the assumption that the two apologies were originally one, and consequently that the one which Eusebius calls the second has been lost (Harnack). Similarly, the second is not to be regarded as a mere supplement to the first (Zahn).'[22]

---

14 Cf. W. Smith and H. Wace, *loc. cit.*
15 The *Codex Regius*, of the year 1364, at the National Library of Paris, and the *Codex Claromontanus* of the year 1541, at Cheltenham, England.
16 Printed by R. Stephanus (Paris 1551) pp. 135-163; *the Second Apology* is on pp. 129-134.
17 With a commentary by Joach. Perionius O.S.B., printed by Jac. Dupuys (Paris 1554). pp. 13-44. The *Second Apology* is on pp. 5-12.
18 *Hist. eccl.* 4.16.
19 Cf. Smith and Wace, *loc. cit.*, and M. Dods, *The Writings of Justin Martyr and Athenagoras*, 5 (Edinburgh 1867).
20 2 *Apol. 4,6,8.*
21 J.M. Pfättisch. *loc cit.*, and also G. Rauschen, *loc. cit.*
22 *History of Early Christian Literature* (New York 1897), p. 108.

In addition to those listed in the Select Bibliography, the following editions—without great variations in the text—are, among others, extant: by G. Krüger with an introduction (4th ed. Jena 1914), A.W.F. Blunt with a new text-analysis (Cambridge 1911) and J.M. Pfättisch with a commentary in German (Münster 1912f.). This translation is based on that of Prud. Maran; those of J.C.Th.v. Otto and G. Rauschen were consulted.

SELECT BIBLIOGRAPHY

Texts and Translations:

Prud. Maran, *S. P. N. Justini philosophi et martyris opera quae extant omnia* (Paris 1742), reprinted in J. P. Migne, *Patrologia Graeca 6.*

J. C. Th.v. Otto, *Corpus Apologetarum Christianorum saeculi secundi* (Jena 1877) I 2³.

G. Rauschen, *S. Justini apologiae duae* (Florilegium Patristicum, fasc. 2, Bonnae 1904).

W. B., *The Apologies of Justin Martyr, Tertullian, and Minucius Felix* (London 1709).

T. Chevallier, *A Translation of the Epistles of Clement of Rome, Polycarp, and Ignatius; and of the Apologies of Justin Martyr and Tertullian* (Cambridge 1833).

M. Dods and G. Reith, *The Writings of Justin Martyr and Athenagoras* (Edinburgh 1867).

L. Pautigny, *Les Apologies* (Textes et Documents, Paris 1904).

G. Rauschen, 'Des heiligen Justins des Philosophen und Märtyrers zwei Apologien' *(Frühchristliche Apologeten*—Bibl. d. Kirchenväter, Bd. I, 1913).

G. J. Goodspeed, *Die ältesten Apologeten* (Göttingen 1915).

Secondary Works:

P. Allard, *Le christanisme et l'empire romain* (Paris 1897).

G. Bardy, '[Saint] Justin,' *Dict. theol. cath.* 8.2238ff.

O. Bardenhewer, *Geschichte der altkirchlichen Literatur* (Freiburg i. B. 1913) 1².

A. Casamassa, Gli Apologisti e i Polemisti Del II Secolo (Roma 1935).
F. Cayré, *Patrologie et Histoire de la Théologie* (3rd. ed. Paris 1938).
J. Geffcken, *Zwei griechische Apologeten* (Leipzig 1917).
A. Harnack, *Die Überlieferung der griechischen Apologeten des zweiten Jahrhunderts* (Leipzig 1882).
K. Hubík, *Die Apologien des hl. Justins des Philosophen und Märtyrers* (Wien 1912).
G. Krüger, *History of Early Christian Literature* (New York 1897).
M.-J. Lagrange, *Saint Justin* (Paris 1914).
J. M. Pfättisch, 'Der Einfluss Platos auf die Theologie Justin des Märtyrers. Eine dogmengeschichtliche Untersuchung nebst einem Anhang über die Komposition der Apologien Justins,' *Forschungen zur christl. Literatur und Dogmengeschichte*, Bd. 10, Heft 1, (Paderborn 1910).
G. Rauschen, 'Die formale Seite der Apologien Justins,' *Theol. Quartalschrift*, (Tübingen 1899) 180ff.
J. Rivière, *St. Justin et les Apologistes du 2me Siècle* (Paris 1907).
W. Smith and H. Wace, *A Dictionary of Christian Biography* (London 1882).
Th. Wehofer, 'Die Apologie Justins des Philosophen und Märtyrers in literarhistorischer Beziehung zum erstenmal untersucht,' *Röm. Quartalschrift* 6, Suppl. Heft (Rome 1897) 2.

CONTENTS

Chapter	Page
1 Address	33
2 Justin asks for justice	34
3 Justin demands a fair trial	34
4 Christians condemned because of their name	36
5 Persecution of Christians instigated by demons	37
6 Christians are not atheists	38
7 The crime must be proved	39
8 Christians would rather die than lie	40
9 Pagan gods made by lustful men	41
10 Christians observe proper worship of God	42
11 The kingdom of heaven	43
12 God sees all	43
13 Jesus Christ our Teacher	45
14 Beware of the demons	46
15 The teaching of Christ	47
16 Of Christian patience	50
17 Christians respect civil authority	52
18 Immortality	52
19 Resurrection	54
20 Where paganism parallels Christianity	55
21 Pagan analogies to the life of Christ	56
22 Pagan analogies to the Sonship of Christ	57
23 What we intend to prove	58

Chapter	Page
24 Pagans worship inanimate objects and animals	59
25 Christians have abandoned paganism	60
26 Simon Magus	61
27 Christians consider it wicked to expose children	63
28 Divine Providence	64
29 Christian continence	65
30 Christ was not a magician	66
31 The Jewish Prophets	66
32 Moses foretold Christ	68
33 Isaias foretold the manner of Christ's birth	70
34 Micheas foretold the place of Christ's birth	71
35 The Crucifixion foretold	72
36 Various modes of prophecy	73
37 God the Father speaks	73
38 God the Son speaks	74
39 God the Holy Ghost speaks	75
40 David foretold the coming of Christ	76
41 David foretold the Crucifixion	78
42 Prophets speak of future as past	78
43 Man responsible for his actions	79
44 Prophets taught free will of man	80
45 Christ's ascension and glory foretold	82
46 Christ is the Logos	83
47 Fall of the Jews foretold	84
48 Christ's miracles and death foretold	85
49 Jews' repudiation of Christ foretold	85

Chapter	Page
50 Christ's suffering predicted by Isaias	86
51 Isaias foretold the majesty of Christ	88
52 Future prophecies will certainly be fulfilled	88
53 Calling of Gentiles foretold	90
54 Fables, imitations of prophecies	91
55 The Cross	93
56 Demoniacal influence	94
57 Christians persecuted by demons	95
58 Marcion	96
59 Plato's debt to Moses	97
60 Plato's doctrine of the Son and Cross	97
61 Baptism of the Christians	99
62 Christian baptism imitated	101
63 God the Son spoke to Moses from a fiery bush	101
64 Demons invented fables of Proserpine and Minerva	104
65 The Holy Eucharist	104
66 Further explanation of the Eucharist	105
67 The Sunday Assembly	106
68 Concluding appeal	107
[69] Letter of Adrian to Minucius Fundanus in behalf of the Christians	108
[70] Letter of Antoninus Pius to the General Assembly of Asia	109
[71] Letter of Marcus Aurelius to the Senate	110

THE FIRST APOLOGY

Chapter 1

TO THE EMPEROR Titus Aelius Adrianus Antoninus Pius Augustus Caesar; to his son Verissimus[1] the philosopher; to Lucius the philosopher, by birth son of Caesar and by adoption son of Pius,[2] an admirer of learning; to the sacred Senate and to the whole Roman people; in behalf of those men of every race[3] who are unjustly hated and mistreated: I, one of them, Justin, the son of Priscus and grandson of Bacchius, of the city of Flavia Neapolis[4] in Syria-Palestine,[5] do present this address and petition.

---

1 Marcus Aurelius Antoninus, whose name, before his adoption by Antoninus Pius, was Marcus Annius Verus. Because of the connotation of this last name ('true'), which fitted his lifelong quest for philosophical truth, Hadrian used to call him emphatically Verissimus.

2 Lucius Ceionius Commodus, who afterwards will share the imperial honors with Marcus Aurelius. His father, Lucius Aelius Caesar, who had been adopted by the Emperor Hadrian, died before Hadrian. Afterwards, when Hadrian adopted Antoninus Pius, he obliged him in turn to adopt Marcus Annius Verus (Marcus Aurelius) and Lucius Ceionius. The title 'philosopher' was given to both adopted sons of Antoninus.

3 A proof of the rapid and vast propagation of Christianity at this early date.

4 The city built by the Romans on the ancient ruins of Sichem (modern Nablûs). Named in honor of the Emperor Flavius Vespasian, it was colonized by the Romans.

5 'Palaestina' is originally an adjective added to Syria, meaning the Philistine or southern part of Syria. After the suppression of the rebellion under Hadrian, Judaea was called as a Roman province Syria Palaestina.

Chapter 2

Common sense dictates that they who are truly pious men and philosophers[1] should honor and cherish only what is true, and refuse to follow the beliefs of their forefathers, if these beliefs be worthless. For, sound reason not only demands that we do not heed those who did or taught anything wrong, but it requires that the lover of truth must choose, in every way possible, to do and say what is right, even when threatened with death, rather than save his own life. You hear yourselves everywhere called pious men and philosophers, guardians of justice and lovers of learning: whether you really deserve this reputation will now become evident. Indeed, we have come not to flatter you with our writings or to curry your favor with this discourse, but to ask that, after an accurate and thorough examination, you hand down a decision that will not be influenced by prejudice or by the desire to please superstitious men; a decision that will not be the result of an irrational impulse or of an evil rumor long persistent, lest it become a judgment against yourselves. As far as we [Christians] are concerned, we believe that no evil can befall us unless we be convicted as criminals or be proved to be sinful persons. You, indeed, may be able to kill us, but you cannot harm us.

Chapter 3

Lest anyone consider this an absurd and rash statement, we demand that the accusations against them [the Christians] be probed, and, if these be shown to be true, they be punished,

---

1 An allusion to the surnames of the addressees.

as any guilty persons should be.¹ If, however, no one has any way of proving these accusations, sane reason does not allow that you, because of a mischievous rumor, do an injustice to innocent men; [in this case] you rather do an injustice to yourselves when you choose to impose punishment² not by fair judgment but by passion. Every reasonable person will agree that the only proper and just proposition is this: let the subjects render a blameless account of their life and doctrine; likewise, let the rulers pass judgment, not through force and tyranny, but in accordance with piety and philosophy. In this way both rulers and subjects would fare well. In fact, one of the ancients has somewhere stated: 'Unless the rulers and their subjects become philosophers, it is impossible for states to become happy.'³ It is our duty, therefore, to give everyone a chance of investigating our life and doctrines, lest we should pay the penalty for what they commit in their blindness, they who persist in being ignorant of our ways.⁴ As for you, sound reason makes it your duty to prove yourselves good judges after you hear [our defense]. Hereafter, you will be without excuse before God, if you know the truth, yet do not act in accordance with justice.

---

1 The words *mâllon dè kolázein* of the Paris manuscript have caused considerable discussion as to the proper meaning and translation of this passage. Thirlby, Otto, Krüger and others think that the words were originally a marginal note that was later incorporated into the text, suggesting an active infinitive (*kolázein*) for the passive *kolázesthai*: 'better read *kolázein*'. Again, Maran and others emended the text to read: *állon de kolázein*, 'let them be punished as it is proper to punish another.' I have followed the conjectural reading, *dlontas kolázein*, adopted by Otto's 3rd ed. and Rauschen.
2 *prágmata epágein*, 'to cause harm, vexation.' Cf. Rauschen.
3 A loose but fitting quotation of Plato, *Republic* 5.18, for it was a favorite one of the emperors to whom the apology was addressed.
4 I.e., we ourselves would be responsible for the sin of our accusers if we kept them in darkness.

Chapter 4

Nothing good or evil is included in the mere use of a name, apart from the actions which are associated with that name. We, if you judge from the name we are accused of, are most excellent persons.[1] Now, we do not think it right to ask for acquittal because of a name, if we be convicted as criminals. Likewise, if we be found to have done no wrong, either as regards the use of our name or our conduct as citizens, you must be careful lest, by unjustly punishing the unconvicted, you justly incur punishment yourselves. Indeed, neither praise nor punishment can rightly arise from a name, unless some good or bad action can be proved. For, you do not punish those of your own people who are accused, before they are proved guilty, yet with us you accept the name alone as proof against us.[2] But so far as a name is concerned, you ought rather to punish our accusers. We are accused of being Christians, yet to hate what is good[3] is not just. Then, too, if any of the accused should deny verbally to be what the name implies, you acquit him, as though having no proof that he did wrong. But, if anyone confesses to be [a Christian], because of that confession you punish him. You ought rather to investigate the life of both the one who makes the admission and of the one who denies, so that the character of each might become known from his actions. Some, who learned from Christ the Master not to deny Him, when they are questioned, give encouragement to others

---

1 Justin here indulges in paronomasia to play upon the words *Christós, Christianoí* (Christ, Christians) and *chrestós, chrestótatoi* (excellent, most excellent). Cf. Theophilus of Antioch, *Ad Autolycum* 1.1; Lactantius, *Inst. div.* 4.7.
2 To be a Christian was then illicit. From the time of Nero the cry was: *Christianos esse non licet.* Just to be known as a Christian was then sufficient cause for persecution.
3 Cf. note 1.

thereby;[4] they who lead evil lives equally encourage all those who rashly accuse all Christians of impiety and injustice. This, too, is not just. Some persons, too, assume the name and attire[5] of philosophers and do nothing worthy of their profession. You know that those of the ancients who held and taught opposing opinions are all called by the one name of philosophers; some of them taught that there are no gods. Even your poets denounce the licentiousness of Jupiter with his children. But those who follow these teachings are not checked by you; on the contrary, you bestow rewards and honors on them for insulting your gods with sweet-sounding words.

Chapter 5

What, then, can all this mean? Although, in our case, we promise to do no evil, and to hold no such atheistic opinions, you do not investigate the charges made against us. Instead, led by unreasonable passion and at the instigation of wicked demons,[1] you punish us inconsiderately without trial. But the truth shall be told, for the wicked demons from ancient times appeared and defiled women, corrupted boys, and presented such terrifying sights to men that those who were not guided by reason in judging these [diabolical] acts were

---

4 Pfättisch and Rauschen understand the verb *parakeleúontai* ('they exhort, give encouragement') in the passive voice: 'they are led to . . .' and supply 'denial'—thus changing the entire meaning ('although they learned . . . not to deny him, they are led, when questioned, to denial').

5 The philosophers of Justin's time wore a distinctive garb. Even after his conversion to Christianity, Justin continued to wear his philosopher's robe.

1 Demoniacal influence in general and demoniacal instigation of persecutions in particular were favorite themes of Justin. In fact, demons are mentioned in over a dozen chapters in this apology. The same theme returns later in Tertullian, *Apol.* 27 and Lactantius, *Instit. div.* 5.21. Justin uses the word *daimon* (which meant a god to the pagans) to signify an evil spirit who was the offspring of a bad angel and a human (Cf. 2 *Apol.* 5).

panic-stricken. Seized with fear and unaware that these were evil demons, they called them gods and greeted each by the name which each demon had bestowed upon himself. But, when Socrates attempted to make these things known and to draw men away from the demons by true reason and judgment, then these very demons brought it about, through men delighting in evil, that he be put to death as an atheist and impious person, because, they claimed, he introduced new divinities.[2] And now they endeavor to do the very same thing to us. And not only among the Greeks were these things through Socrates condemned by reason [*logos*],[3] but also among the non-Hellenic peoples by the Logos Himself, who assumed a human form and became man, and was called Jesus Christ. Through our belief in Him we not only deny that they who did these things are good deities,[4] but claim that they are evil and ungodly demons, whose actions should not be compared with those of virtue-seeking men.

Chapter 6

Thus are we even called atheists.[1] We do proclaim our-

---

2 Cf. Plato, *Apology* 24B.
3 Justin distinguishes between the seminal word (*lógos spermatikós*) and the Perfect Word (*ho pás lógos*) which is the Word of God. The seminal word (human reason) is implanted as a seed in every man and by a wise use of it a man, e.g., Socrates, could acquire a partial knowledge of the Perfect Logos. Only Christians, by Revelation, can attain a full knowledge of the Divine Logos. The greater one's knowledge of the Logos, the more severe was the demons' persecution.
4 In this sentence Justin uses the same word (*daímonas*) for deities and demons.

---

1 A common charge against the early Christians, based on the fact that Christians refused to offer sacrifice or acts of reverence to the pagan idols and imperial statues. They also stayed away from the temples and pagan religious festivities. They were called atheists, therefore, because they showed no respect for the State gods and for the State religion.

selves atheists as regards those whom you call gods, but not with respect to the Most True God, who is alien to all evil and is the Father of justice, temperance, and the other virtues. We revere and worship Him and the Son who came forth from Him and taught us these things, and also the legion of good angels[2] who attend Him and reflect His virtues, and the Prophetic Spirit, and we pay homage to them in reason and truth, and pass His doctrine on intact to everyone who wishes to learn it.

Chapter 7

Someone will object that some Christians have already been arrested and convicted as criminals. Indeed, you often condemn many persons after an individual investigation into the lives of the accused, but you do not condemn them because of other persons previously convicted.[1] On the whole, we admit one thing: among the Greeks those who announce

---

2 Literally: 'and the other good angels.' Two difficulties arise from this passage. (1) Justin seems to imply that Christ, too, is one of the angels; but 'other' (*állos*) is in Greek often used pleonastically for the second of two separate subjects, meaning no more than 'in addition.' Cf. also French *nous autres citoyens*, 'we citizens.' (2) The passage would commit Justin to the worship of angels. That this was not his teaching is clear from Chapters 13, 16, and 61. Various attempts at another translation of the passage have been made by making the words, 'the legion of other good angels,' in one or the other way contingent upon the verb 'taught.' The translation would then be, 'taught these things to us and to the legion of other good angels,' or, still differently: 'taught us about these things, and about the legion of other good angels.' A third explanatory translation would refer the word 'revere' to the angels and the word 'worship' to the Holy Trinity.

---

1 The *Codex Paris.* reads *prolechthéntas*, 'those mentioned before,' which has been referred by some to the sincere Christians (Otto), by others, to the demons of Ch. 5 (Trollope). I have followed Maran, Rauschen, and others, who preferred the word *proelechthéntas*, 'those previously convicted.'

their own particular theories are all addressed by the one name of 'philosophers,' even though they hold contrary opinions; so, among the non-Hellenic peoples, those who are and those who seem to be wise all have the one common name—they are all named Christians. Hence, we ask that the actions of all those denounced to you be judged, so that whoever is convicted may be punished as an offender, not as a Christian. If it is apparent that a man is innocent, let him be dismissed as a Christian who has committed no crime. We will not ask you to punish the accusers,[2] for they are sufficiently punished by their present iniquity and ignorance of fine and noble things.

Chapter 8

You can be sure that we have spoken these things for your benefit, since we, when on trial, can always deny [that we are Christians]. But we do not desire to live by lying. We are desirous of an eternal and good life; we strive for the abode of God, the Father and Creator of all; we make haste to profess our faith; we believe with firm conviction that they can attain these things who have shown God by their works that they follow Him and love to make their home with Him where there is no sin to cause disorder. In brief, this is what we look for and what we have learned from Christ and in turn teach to others. Plato also stated[1] that Rhadamanthus and Minos would punish the wicked who came before them. We declare that the very same thing will take place, but that it will be Christ who will assign the punishment to sinners.

---

2 Under the Roman criminal law in general, and by the rescript of Hadrian (which Justin added at the end of this apology), Christians could have asked for the punishment of their false accusers.

---

1 Plato, *Gorg.* 523E.

And in their very bodies, reunited to their souls, they will endure the pangs of torment eternally, and not only for a period of one thousand years as Plato said.[2] If anyone shall say that this is incredible or impossible, this 'error' still is ours and of no concern to anybody else, as long as we are not convicted of having committed any wicked deed.

Chapter 9

We do not worship with many sacrifices and floral offerings the things men have made, set in temples, and called gods. We know that they are inanimate and lifeless and have not the form of God (for we do not think that God has that form which some say they reproduce in order to give honor to Him)—but have the names and shapes of those evil demons who have appeared [to men]. Why should we tell you, who already know, into what different shapes the workmen fashion their material, by carving, cutting, molding, and hammering? From vessels destined for vile purposes, by merely changing their shape and by skillfully giving them a new form, they often make what they call gods.[1] Thus, His name is applied to corruptible things that need constant care. This, we think, is not only stupid but also disrespectful to God, who is of ineffable glory and form. You are well aware of the fact that their skilled artisans are licentious men and, not to enter into details, are experienced in every known vice; they even defile the girls who work with them. What stupidity, that lustful men should carve and reshape gods for your veneration, and that such men should be appointed the guards of the temples wherein the gods are set up, not realizing that it is

---

[2] Cf. Plato, *Phaedrus* 249A; *Republic* 10, 615A.

[1] A favorite theme of the early Christian Apologists. Cf. also Athenagoras, *Suppl.* 26.

forbidden to declare or even think that men are the keepers of the gods.

Chapter 10

But we have learned from tradition that God has no need of the material gifts of men, since we see that He is the Giver of all things.[1] We have been taught, are convinced, and do believe that He approves of only those who imitate His inherent virtues, namely, temperance, justice, love of man, and any other virtue proper to God who is called by no given name. We have also been instructed that God, in the beginning, created in His goodness everything out of shapeless matter[2] for the sake of men. And if men by their actions prove themselves worthy of His plan, they shall, we are told, be found worthy to make their abode with Him and to reign with Him, free from all corruption and pain. Just as in the beginning He created us when we were not, so also, we believe, He will consider all those who choose to please Him, because of their choice, to be worthy of eternal life in His presence. Our creation was not in our own power. But this —to engage in those things that please Him and which we choose by means of the intellectual faculties He has bestowed on us—this makes our conviction and leads us to faith. Indeed, we think it is for the good of all men that they are not prevented from learning these things, but are even

---
1 Cf. Acts 17.25.
2 These words of Justin should be interpreted in the light of a similar but clearer statement in 2 *Apol.* 5. There he states that the Son of God existed before all things and that God the Father, through the Son, created and arranged in order all things. The two actions, *viz.*, *creatio ex nihilo* and the adornment of the created matter, are definitely stated. Therefore, when Justin states here that God created all things out of 'shapeless matter' he does not deny *creatio ex nihilo*, as Plato did, but he merely had in mind the adornment of the created matter.

urged to consider them. For, what human laws were unable to effect, the Divine Word would have accomplished, had not the evil demons enlisted the aid of the various utterly evil inclinations, which are in every man by nature, and scattered many false and ungodly accusations—none of which, however, applies to us.

Chapter 11

When you hear that we look forward to a kingdom, you rashly assume that we speak of a human kingdom,[1] whereas we mean a kingdom which is with God. This becomes evident when, being questioned, we openly profess to be Christians, although we know well that for such a profession of faith the punishment is death. If we expected a human kingdom, we would deny that we are Christians, that we might not be put to death, and we would try to hide from you, that we might attain what we expect. But, because we do not place our hope in the present, we do not mind when men murder us, since death is inevitable anyhow.

Chapter 12

We, more than all other men, are truly your helpers and allies in fostering peace, since we believe that it is impossible for the wicked or the avaricious, or the treacherous, and the virtuous alike to hide from the sight of God, and that each man receives eternal punishment or salvation according to the merits of his actions. If everyone realized this, no one would prefer to be in sin even for a little while, knowing that he would incur the pains of eternal fire, but he would

---

1 One of the accusations against the Christians was that of owing allegiance to another kingdom. This, it was claimed, made the Christians guilty of treason and prevented them from being good citizens.

by all means control himself and adorn himself with virtue, in order to gain the favor of God and escape His punishments. It is not[1] because of the laws and penalties you fix that men try to hide from you when they break the law, but they disobey the law knowing that it is possible to elude you, since you are mere men. If, however, they learned and were convinced that nothing, whether in their actions or in their thoughts, can be hidden from the knowledge of God, they would live a completely orderly life, if only because of the threatened punishments, as you yourselves will admit. But you seem to dread lest all men become just and you no longer have any left to punish. Such might be the worry of public executioners, but it should not be the concern of righteous rulers. As we said before, we believe that these things have been instigated by the evil demons who claim sacrifices and veneration even from those who do not live according to reason. But we do not presume that you who strive for piety and philosophy will act against reason. Still, if you, too, like thoughtless men, respect custom rather than truth, then do what is in your power. Rulers who prefer popular opinion to truth have as much power as robbers in the desert. That you will not succeed[2] is testified to by the Word, and we know no ruler more kingly or just than He except God [the Father] who begot Him.[3] For, just as all men try to avoid inheriting the poverty, misery, and dishonor of their fathers, so will the

---

1 'Not' (*ou*); others read the article *hoi* (cf. Rauschen, *ad loc.*): 'For those who try, because of the laws and penalties you fix, to hide from you when they break the laws, disobey the law knowing' etc.
2 Namely, the rulers will not succeed in their persecution of the Christians, because the latter have the support of Christ, and because they are encouraged by the knowledge that their trial and sufferings are but the fulfilments of His prophecies.
3 This seems to imply the error of subordinationism which teaches that the Father is greater than the Son; cf. also Ch. 2 *Apol.* 13; *Dial.* 56 (Cf. Rauschen, *ad loc.*, and Altaner, *Patrologia*).

man of reason refuse to choose whatever the Word forbids him to choose. That all these things should happen was foretold, I say, by our Teacher, Jesus Christ, who is the Son and Apostle[4] of God, the Father and Ruler of all, and from whom we have received our name of Christians. Hence, we are convinced of the truth of all the things He taught us, because whatever He foretold would happen is actually happening; this, indeed, is the practice of God, to speak of something before it takes place and then to show it taking place just as He predicted.

We might stop here and add nothing more, since we plead for what is just and true. But, since we know how difficult it is to change over a mind trained in ignorance, we have decided to add a few observations to convince all lovers of truth, for we know that it is not impossible to dispel ignorance by setting truth against it.

Chapter 13

What sensible person will not admit that we are not atheists, since we worship the Creator of this world and assert, as we have been taught, that He has no need of bloody sacrifices, libations, and incense. But we praise Him to the best of our power by prayer and thanksgiving for all our nourishment.[1] We have been instructed that the only worship worthy of Him is not to consume by fire those things that He created for our sustenance, but to employ them for the good of ourselves and the needy, and, with thankful voices, to offer Him

---

4 Cf. the same expression in St. Paul, Heb. 3.1.

1 Literally: 'for all things we consume.' Others translate: 'in all things we offer,' i. e. in our sacrifices. The verb *prosphéresthai* may mean both 'to consume' and 'to offer.'

solemn prayers and hymns[2] for our own creation, for the preservation of our health, for the variety of things, and for the changes of the seasons, and to beseech Him in prayer that we may rise to life everlasting because of our faith in Him. Our Teacher of these things is Jesus Christ, who was born for this end, and who was crucified under Pontius Pilate, procurator of Judea, in the reign of Tiberius Caesar. We shall prove that we worship Him with reason, since we have learned that He is the Son of the living God Himself, and believe Him to be in the second place, and the Prophetic Spirit in the third.[3] For this they accuse us of madness, saying that we attribute to a crucified man a place second to the unchanging and eternal God, the Creator of all things, but they are ignorant of the mystery which lies herein. To this mystery we entreat you to give your attention, while we explain it to you.

Chapter 14

Indeed, we warn you to be careful lest the demons, previously accused by us, should mislead you and turn you from reading and understanding thoroughly what we have said. They strive to make you their slaves and servants. They ensnare, now by apparitions in dreams, now by tricks of magic, all those who do not labor with all their strength for their

---

2 *Pompàs kaì húmnous.* Some, like Grabe, considered *pompàs* to be the solemn prayers that were recited aloud, especially in the celebration of the Sacraments. Others, like Maran (in Migne), interpret the word to mean the rites and ceremonies practiced in the celebration of the Sacraments. I have followed the first interpretation in my translation of 'solemn prayers.' Justin prefaces *pompà* by *dià lógou* to show that the Christian *pompaí* were different from the pagan *pompaí* of the temples, arenas, theatres, etc. The *húmnous* would indicate not only the psalms of David, but also the strictly Christian hymns.
3 On Justin's subordinationism, see above, Ch. 12, n. 3.

own salvation—even as we, also, after our conversion by the Word have separated ourselves from those demons and have attached ourselves to the only unbegotten[1] God, through His Son. We who once[2] reveled in impurities now cling to purity; we who devoted ourselves to the arts of magic now consecrate ourselves to the good and unbegotten God; we who loved above all else the ways of acquiring riches and possessions now hand over to a community fund what we possess, and share it with every needy person; we who hated and killed one another and would not share our hearth with those of another tribe because of their [different] customs, now, after the coming of Christ, live together with them, and pray for our enemies, and try to convince those who hate us unjustly, so that they who live according to the good commands of Christ may have a firm hope of receiving the same reward as ourselves from God who governs all. But, lest we seem to quibble, we think it fitting to recall a few of the teachings of Christ, before giving our proofs;[3] it is up to you, as mighty emperors, to consider whether we have been taught and do teach the truth. His sayings were brief and concise, for He was not a sophist, but His word was the power of God.

Chapter 15

Thus did He speak concerning chastity: 'Whoever looks with lust at a woman has already committed adultery with

---

1 By this word Justin distinguishes God the Father both from the begotten Son, the Logos, and from the many begotten gods of pagan polytheism.
2 This sudden change in morality after conversion to Christianity was often cited by the early Apologists as a proof of the divine origin of the Christian Church. In fact, this theme has been called 'The triumphal song of the Apologists.'
3 *Viz.*, the proofs, promised in Ch. 13, 'that we worship Him with reason.' These proofs begin in Ch. 30, below.

her in his heart before God.'¹ And, 'If thy right eye is an occasion of sin to thee, pluck it out for it is better for thee to enter into the kingdom of Heaven with one eye, than, having two eyes, to be cast into everlasting fire.'² And, 'Whosoever marries her who has been divorced from another husband, commits adultery.'³ And, 'There are eunuchs who were born so; and there are eunuchs who were made so by men; and there are eunuchs who have made themselves so for the kingdom of Heaven's sake; not all however can receive this saying.'⁴ As all who, according to the human law, contract a second marriage⁵ are sinners in the eyes of our Master, so are those who look upon a woman with lustful eyes. Not only he who actually does commit adultery, but also he who wishes to do so, is repudiated by God, since not only our actions, but even our inner thoughts, are manifest to Him. Many men and women who were disciples of Christ from childhood remain pure at sixty or seventy years of age; I am proud to say that I can cite examples from every nation. Why should we mention here the countless throng of those who turned from intemperance to learn our teaching? Christ came, indeed, to call to repentance not the just or the pure, but the impious, the incontinent, and the unjust, for He said: 'I came not to call the just, but the sinners to repentance.'⁶

---

1 Matt. 5.28.
2 Matt. 5.29.
3 Matt. 5.32.
4 Matt. 19.12.
5 Maran claims that by this word, *digamias*, Justin wanted to forbid bigamy, and not two successive marriages (one after the death of a first partner). Justin could also mean a second marriage after the divorce (but not the death) of the former partner, for he had just quoted Matt. 5.32: 'Whosoever marries her who has been divorced from another husband, commits adultery.' If this interpretation be accepted, Justin did not follow the rigid tendency of some early Christians against second marriages after the death of the consort.
6 Matt. 9.13.

The Heavenly Father wishes the repentance of a sinner, rather than his punishment. Concerning the love we should have for all, Christ thus taught: 'If you love those who love you, what new thing do you do? For even the fornicators do this.[7] But I say unto you, pray for your enemies, love them that hate you, bless them that curse you, and pray for them who insult you.'[8] He taught to share our goods with the needy and to do nothing for our own personal glory, when He said: 'Give to everyone who asks of you, and do not turn your back on him who would borrow;[9] for if you lend to them who you hope will repay you, what new thing do you do? Even the publicans do this.[10] Do not lay up for yourselves treasures on earth where rust and moth consume, and where thieves break in; but lay up for yourselves treasures in heaven, where neither rust nor moth consumes.[11] For what does it profit a man to gain the whole world, and lose his own soul? Or what shall a man give in exchange for his soul?[12] Store up treasures, therefore, in heaven, where neither rust nor moth consumes.'[13] And, 'Be kind and merciful as your Heavenly Father also is kind and merciful,[14] who makes His sun to rise on sinners, and on the just and the wicked.[15] Be not anxious about what you shall eat, or how you shall dress; for are you not better than the birds and the beasts? And yet God feeds them. Therefore be not anxious about what you shall eat, or how you shall dress, for your Heavenly Father knows that you have need of these things. But seek the king-

---

7 Matt. 5.46.
8 Luke 6.27, 28.
9 Matt. 5.42.
10 Luke 6.34.
11 Matt. 6.19,20.
12 Luke 9.25.
13 Matt. 6.20.
14 Luke 6.36.
15 Matt. 5.45.

dom of God, and all these things shall be added unto you.'¹⁶ For where the treasure is, there also is the mind of man.'¹⁷ And, 'Do not these things to be gazed at by men; otherwise you shall have no reward from your Father who is in Heaven.'¹⁸

Chapter 16

With the following words He taught us that we should be patient, and be willing to submit to everyone, and never give way to anger: 'To him who strikes you on the one cheek, offer the other also; and hinder not him who takes away your cloak or coat.¹ Whoever is given to anger is subject to the fire of hell.² And everyone who forces you to go with him a mile, go with him two.³ Let your good deeds shine before men, that they, seeing them, may glorify your Heavenly Father.'⁴ We should not be contentious, nor does He want us to imitate the wicked, but He rather urges us to draw all men from dishonor and desire of evil by our own patience and mildness. We can show that this has happened in the case of many of those who were of your side and turned from a life of violence and tyranny, because they were conquered either by the constancy of their neighbors' lives, or by the strange patience they noticed in their injured associates, or by experiencing their honesty in business matters. With these words He commanded us never to swear, but always to tell the truth: 'Do not swear at all, but let your yes be yes, and your no, no; for whatever is beyond these comes from

---
16 Matt. 6.25,26,33.
17 Matt. 6.21.
18 Matt. 6.1.

1 Matt. 5.39,40.
2 Matt. 5.22.
3 Matt. 5.41.
4 Matt. 5.16.

the evil one.'⁵ He convinced us that only God is to be worshipped, when He said: 'The greatest commandment is this: "Thou shalt adore the Lord thy God, and Him only shalt thou serve, with all thy heart, and with all thy strength, the Lord God who made thee," '⁶ and when a certain man came to Him and said: 'Good Master,' He replied: 'There is none good but God alone who made all things.'⁷ May they who are not found living according to His teachings know that they are not Christians, even though they profess with their tongues the teaching of Christ, for He said that not those who only profess His doctrines, but those who put them into practice, shall be saved.⁸ Indeed, He said: 'Not everyone who says to Me, "Lord, Lord," shall enter into the kingdom of heaven; but he who does the will of My Father who is in Heaven. For whosoever hears Me and does what I say, hears Him who sent Me. And many will say to Me, "Lord, Lord, have we not eaten and drunk, and done wonders in your name?" And then will I say to them: "Depart from Me, you workers of evil."'⁹ Then there shall be weeping and gnashing of teeth, when the just shall shine as the sun, and the wicked are sent into everlasting fire.¹⁰ For many shall come in My name, dressed outwardly in sheep's clothing, but who inwardly are ravenous wolves. By their works you shall know them. Every tree that does not bring forth good fruit, shall be cut down and cast into the fire.'¹¹ And we ask that you also punish all those who call themselves Christians, but are not living according to His teachings.

---

5 Matt. 5.34,37.
6 Mark 12.30.
7 Matt. 19.16,17.
8 Faith without works not sufficient.
9 Matt. 7.21-23.
10 Matt. 13.42,43.
11 Matt. 7.15,16,19.

Chapter 17

As we have been instructed by Him, we, before all others, try everywhere to pay your appointed officials the ordinary and special taxes. For in His time some people came to Him and asked if it were necessary to pay tribute to Caesar, and He replied: 'Tell Me, whose likeness does this coin bear?' They said: 'Caesar's.' And He again replied: 'Render therefore to Caesar the things that are Caesar's, and to God, the things that are God's.'[1] Wherefore, only God do we worship, but in other things we joyfully obey you, acknowledging you as the kings and rulers of men, and praying that you may be found to have, besides royal power, sound judgment. If you do not heed us, though we beseech you and clearly explain our position, it will by no means harm us, for we believe (rather, we are absolutely sure) that every man will pay the penalty of his misdeeds in the everlasting fire, and that every one will give an account in proportion to the powers he received from God, as Christ made known to us when He said: 'To whom God has given more, of him more shall be required.'[2]

Chapter 18

Look back on the end of each of the past emperors, and consider how they died the death common to all men, which, if it led to a state of insensibility, would be a godsend[1] for all sinners. But, since a state of sensibility does await all those who were alive and since eternal punishment awaits the

---
1 Matt. 22.20 21.
2 Luke 12.48.

---
1 *Hérmaion*, a find on the wayside; reputed by the ancients to be a gift from the god Hermes.

wicked, be convinced and believe that these statements are true. Indeed, let the oracles of the dead and the sorcery you perform through innocent children,[2] and the invoking of the souls of the dead,[3] let those whom the magicians call dream-sending and familiar spirits,[4] and let whatever else is performed by those skilled in such arts convince you that even after death souls remain in a state of sensibility. Be convinced, likewise, by those possessed and tormented by the souls of the deceased, whom everyone calls demoniacs and madmen,[5] and by what you call the oracles of Amphilochus, Dodona, Apollo, and of others like them, and by the teaching of the writers Empedocles and Pythagoras, Plato and Socrates, and by the ditch of Homer,[6] and by the descent of Ulysses to see the dead, and by those who told similar stories. Treat us, therefore, in a similar manner as you treat them, for we believe in God not less, but more than they do, since we expect that our own bodies, even though they should be

---

2 Eusebius (*Hist. eccl.* 7.10) describes the pagan method of divination performed by 'cutting the throats of wretched boys and sacrificing children of hapless parents and opening up the entrails of new-born babes.' But Tertullian (*Apol.* 23) mentions children who were used in some way to utter oracles. Justin probably refers to this second use of children in pagan divination.
3 Spiritistic seances were not unknown to the ancients. In his *Dialogue* (Ch. 105) Justin gives as a proof of the immortality of the soul the invocation of Samuel by the witch of Endor.
4 *Oneiropompoí* and *páredroi* were the magicians' helping spirits: the first (*oneiropompoí*) were sent to inspire the subjects with dreams that could tell them something of the future; and the second (*páredroi*) were sent to men to sit by their side and shield them from illness or misfortune.
5 The identification of demoniacs and madmen and the possession of both by the spirits of departed men are not stated as Justin's own teaching, but as pagan doctrine. For here Justin is collecting examples from pagan lore to prove the immortality of the soul.
6 In the *Odyssey* 11.24,25, Ulysses is portrayed digging a pit with his sword and filling it with blood to attract to that place the souls of the dead.

dead and buried in the earth, will be revived; for we claim that nothing is impossible with God.

Chapter 19

And what would seem more incredible to a thinking person that if we were not in a body and someone were to affirm that from a little drop of the human seed it were possible to shape bones, muscles and flesh into the human form we now see? Now let us make this supposition: If you yourselves had not the form you now have, and were not born of parents like yours, and someone were to show you the human seed and the painted picture of a man, and were to affirm that from such a seed such a being could be produced, would you believe him before you saw the actual production? No one would dare to deny [that you would not]. In like manner, because you have never witnessed a dead person rise again to life, you refuse to believe. But as in the beginning you would not have believed it possible that from a little sperm such persons could be produced, and yet you actually see that they are, so now realize that it is not impossible that human bodies, after they are dead and disseminated in the earth like seeds, should at the appointed time, at God's command, arise and assume immortality. We cannot imagine what power worthy of God is attributed to Him by those who say that everything returns to that from which it was produced, and that not even God can do anything more than this. But this we clearly know, that they would not have believed it possible that from such matter they could ever have been such as they now perceive themselves and the whole world to be. We have learned that it is better to believe what is impossible to our own nature and to men than, like other men, to be unbelievers, for we know that our Teacher, Jesus Christ, has said: 'What is impossible with men, is possible with God.'[1] And again: 'Fear not them who kill you, and after that can do you no harm; but fear him who after death is able to cast both soul and body into hell.'[2] Hell, in truth, is the place of punishment for those who lived wickedly and refused to believe what God taught through Christ will take place.

Chapter 20

Indeed, Sibyl[1] and Hystaspes[2] foretold that all corruptible things are to be destroyed by fire. And the so-called Stoic philosophers teach that even God is to be transformed into fire, and they claim that after this evolution the world is to be made over again. We, on the contrary, believe that God, the Maker of all things, is superior to changeable things. If, therefore, we agree on some points with your honored poets and philosophers, and on other points offer a more complete and supernatural teaching, and if we alone produce proof of our statements, why are we unjustly hated beyond all others? When we say that God created and arranged all things in this world, we seem to repeat the teaching of Plato;[3] when we announce a final conflagration [of the world], we utter the doctrine of the Stoics; and when we assert that the souls of the wicked, living after death, will be sensibly

---

1 Matt. 19.26.
2 Matt. 10.28.

1 There were many Sibyls in heathen legendary history. The most famous Greek Sibyl was located at Marpessus (near Troy), while the Cumaean Sibyl was most respected by the Romans, who kept her oracles in the temple of Jupiter Capitolinus at Rome. In times of great danger the Senate ordered the Sibylline oracles to be consulted.
2 He was the Greek counterpart of the Persian Vishtaspa, a semi-legendary king praised by Zoroaster and noted for prophetic sayings.
3 In *Timaeus, passim.*

punished, and that the souls of the good, freed from punishment, will live happily, we believe the same things as your poets and philosophers. In claiming that we should not worship the work of men's hands, we agree with the comic poet Menander and other writers like him, for they have declared that the creator is greater than his work.

Chapter 21

When, indeed, we assert that the Word, our Teacher Jesus Christ, who is the first-begotten of God the Father, was not born as the result of sexual relations, and that He was crucified, died, arose from the dead, and ascended into Heaven, we propose nothing new or different[1] from that which you say about the so-called sons of Jupiter. You know exactly the number of sons ascribed to Jupiter by your respected writers: Mercury, who was the interpretative word and teacher of all; Aesculapius, who, though himself a healer of diseases, was struck by a thunderbolt and ascended into heaven; Bacchus, who was torn to pieces; Hercules, who rushed into the flames of the funeral pyre to escape his sufferings; the Dioscuri, the sons of Leda; Perseus, the son of Danaë; and Bellerophon, who, though of human origin, rose to heaven on his horse Pegasus.[2] And what can we say of Ariadne and those like her, who are said to be placed among

---

1 This manner of argumentation seems strange and distasteful to us today, but Justin and the other apologists of his time were ready to meet the pagans on their own ground and match them story for story, with the intention of proving that the Christian story was not a fable or a myth. This position of those early apologists was aptly expressed by Tertullian (*Apol.* 21): *Recipite interim hanc fabulam, similis est vestris, dum ostendimus quomodo Christus probetur.*

2 Maran, Sylburg, and others read *eph hippou* (as in Ch. 54 of this Apology) instead of *uph hippou*. Justin is not exactly correct here, for it seems that Bellerophon did not actually reach heaven. *See* Pindar, *Isthm.* 7.63 and Horace, *Odes* 4, 11, 25ff.

the stars? And what about the emperors who die among you, whom you think worthy to be deified,[3] and for whom you lead forth a false witness to swear that he saw the burning Caesar rise from the funeral pyre and ascend to heaven?[4] Nor is it necessary to relate to you, who know them already, what kind of actions are imputed to those so-called sons of Jupiter, except to add that they have been recorded for the profit and instruction[5] of young students; for everyone considers it a good thing to imitate the gods. But may such a thought concerning the gods be far from every sound mind, as to believe that Jupiter himself, whom they consider the ruler and creator of all things, was a parricide and the son of a parricide, and that, seized by a lust of evil and shameful pleasures, he descended upon Ganymede and the many women whom he violated, and that his sons were guilty of similar actions. But, as we stated above, the wicked demons have done these things. We, however, have been taught that only they will have eternal bliss who live a holy and virtuous life close to God; we believe that they who live an evil life and do not repent will be punished in everlasting fire.

Chapter 22

Furthermore, the Son of God who is called Jesus, even if

---

3 The apotheosis, or deification, of Roman rulers was quite common after the time of Julius Caesar. Some of the Roman emperors so honored were: Augustus, Claudius, Vespasian, Titus, Nerva, Trajan, Hadrian, Antoninus Pius, Marcus Aurelius, Commodus, Septimius Severus, and Caracalla.
4 There are three such examples: of Romulus (Tertullian, *Apol.* 21), Augustus (Suetonius, *Aug.* 100), and Claudius (Seneca, *Apocolocyntosis* 1).
5 *Diaphoràn kai protropèn*, profit and instruction. Justin evidently meant to use these words in a sarcastic manner. Because they claim that such a mode of expression was not common in the writings of Justin, some have changed the text to *diaphthoràn kai paratropèn*, corruption and ruin. This seems unnecessary.

He were only a man by common generation, is because of His wisdom, worthy to be called the Son of God, for all your writers[1] call God the Father of men and gods. And if we declare that the Word of God was begotten of God not in the ordinary, but in an extraordinary,[2] manner, as we stated above, this may be compared to your claim that Mercury is the announcing word of God. And should any one object that He [Christ] was crucified, this indignity may be compared to that of Jupiter's sons, as you call them, who suffered as indicated above.[3] Their sufferings at death are said to have been, not all similar, but different, so that not even His unusual manner of suffering was inferior to theirs. But, as we have promised and will prove as our discourse progresses (or rather, as we have already proved), He is their superior also in this regard, for one is proved superior by his actions. If we state that He was born of a Virgin, this may be comparable to what you admit of Perseus.[4] When we say that He cured the lame, the paralytics, and those blind[5] from birth, and raised the dead to life, we seem to attribute to Him actions similar to those said to have been performed by Aesculapius.

Chapter 23

To make this clear to you, we shall present the following

---

1 E.g., Homer. Cf. *Cohortatio ad Graecos* 2.
2 Cf. *Dialogue* 61, 128. Justin is referring here to the begetting of the Word before all time.
3 Arnobius, *Adversus nationes* 1.41, mentions Bacchus, Aesculapius, and Hercules.
4 In Greek mythology it is related that King Actisius was warned by the oracle that he would perish at the hand of his daughter's son. Accordingly, he imprisoned his only daughter, the virgin Danaë, in an underground vault. But Zeus visited her in a shower of gold, and thereafter Perseus was born to Danaë.
5 The text has *poneroùs*, the 'evil' or 'infirm,' but some editors prefer the reading *pērous*, 'blind,' which is repeated in this *Apology* (Ch. 60) and also in the *Dialogue* 69.

arguments[1] to prove: [first] that whatever statements we make, because we learned them from Christ and the Prophets who preceded Him, are alone true, and are older than all writers, and that we should be believed, not because we speak the same things as the writers, but because we speak the truth; [second] that Jesus Christ alone is properly the Son of God, since He is His Word, First-begotten, and Power, and that, having become man by His will, He taught us these doctrines for the conversion and restoration of mankind; [third] that, before He assumed human nature and dwelt among men, some,[2] namely, those previously mentioned demons, foretold through the poets as if already accomplished those things which they invented, just as they caused to be imputed to us slanderous and impious actions, of which they can produce neither witness nor proof.

Chapter 24

In the first place [we wish to say] that, although we hold teachings similar to the Greeks, we alone are hated because of the name of Christ, and, though we commit no crime, we are excuted as criminals, while other men in other coun-

---

1 Justin here promises to prove three things: (1) that the Christian teachings are alone true, and are to be accepted because of their own value, and not because of their similarity to the teachings of the poets and philosophers (Chs. 24-29); (2) that Jesus Christ is the Son of God and He became Man for our sake (Chs. 30-53); (3) that, prior to His Incarnation, the demons learned something of His future mission and then instigated the poets and others to invent myths that would anticipate the Incarnation and thus keep men away from Christ (Ch. 54ff.). In the development of these themes Justin is guilty of many digressions.
2 Literally, 'Some, through the fore-mentioned evil demons, foretold, through the poets, as if already accomplished, those things which they invented.' I have followed Maran's emendation of the text (Migne, *PG* 6.364).

tries worship trees and rivers,[1] mice, cats, crocodiles, and many other irrational animals;[2] nor do all worship the same beings, but in one place they worship one, in another place another, so that all are considered impious by one another, because they do not all venerate the same objects. And this is the sole charge you lodge against us, that we do not worship the same gods as you do, offer to the dead libations, fats, crowns for their statues,[3] and sacrificial victims. For you know well[4] that the very same animals are considered gods by some people, wild beasts by others, and sacrificial victims by still others.

Chapter 25

In the second[1] place [we wish to observe] that we who, from every nation, once worshipped Bacchus, the son of Semele, and Apollo, the son of Latona (who in their lusts for men practiced things too disgraceful even to mention), and Proserpine and Venus (who were thrown into a frenzy for love of Adonis, and whose mysteries you also celebrate), and Aesculapius, or any one of the other so-called gods, now, through Jesus Christ, even under the threat of death, hold these in contempt, while we consecrate ourselves to the unbegotten and impassible God, who, we know, never de-

---

1 E.g., the Persians.
2 E.g., the Egyptians.
3 *En graphaís stephánous*: Some would read *en taphaís* (on the tombs) instead of *en graphaís* (on the pictures). Others interpret the text as the equivalent of *stephánous gegramménous* (painted crowns), but Maran (PG 6.365) proves that *graphḕ* can signify not only a picture, but also a statue.
4 The Mss. have *hóti gàr ou*, but I have followed Maran (PG 6.365) in omitting *ou* or reading *hóti gàr hoûn*.

---

1 This second argument is based on the purity of the one God worshipped by the Christians even under the threat of death.

THE FIRST APOLOGY   61

scended with sexual desire upon Antiope, or other such women, or Ganymede; nor was He liberated by that hundred-handed giant[2] whose assistance Thetis obtained; nor was He solicitous, in return for such aid, that Achilles, the son of Thetis, because of his concubine Briseis, should slaughter so many Greeks. We feel sorry for those who believe these things, but we know that the real instigators are the demons.

Chapter 26

In the third[1] place [we wish to state] that, after the Ascension of Christ into Heaven, the demons produced certain men who claimed to be gods, who were not only not molested by you, but even showered with honors. There was a certain Simon,[2] a Samaritan, from the village called Gitta, who, in the time of Emperor Claudius, through the force of the demons working in him, performed mighty acts of magic in your royal city of Rome, and was reputed to be a god. And as a god he was honored by you with a statue, which was erected [on an island] in the Tiber River, between the two bridges,

---
2 Briareus.

---
1 The third argument is that truth only is persecuted. Even those heretics whom the demons urged to corrupt the Christian teachings were not persecuted for their beliefs alone.
2 Simon Magus of Samaria was baptized by Philip the Deacon about the year 36. Shortly afterwards, he offered St. Peter money in exchange for spiritual powers. Rebuked by St. Peter for his sin of *simony*, he became his avowed enemy. Because he was the earliest adversary of the Church, he is considered the patriarch of heretics. Indeed, his doctrine contained the seed whence later grew Gnosticism.

with this Roman inscription: 'To Simon, the holy God.'[3] Almost every Samaritan, and even a few from other regions, worship him and call him the first God. And they call a certain Helena, who was his traveling companion at that time, and had formerly been a prostitute, the first idea generated from him. And we know, too, that a certain Menander,[4] also of Samaria, of the town of Capparetaea, a disciple of Simon, and likewise inspired by the demons, deceived many by his tricks of magic while he was at Antioch. He even convinced his followers that they would never die, and there are some alive today who, inspired by him, still believe this. Then there is a certain Marcion of Pontus,[5] who even now still teaches his disciples to believe in another and greater god than the Creator. Assisted by the demons, he has caused many men of every country to blaspheme, and to deny that God is the Creator of the universe, and to proclaim another god to

---

[3] The Latin inscription would have been, according to Justin, *Simoni Sancto Deo*. This story was repeated by Euseb., *Hist. eccl.* 2.13; Irenaeus, *Adv. haer.* 1.23,4; Tertullian, *Apol.* 13. In the year 1574, excavators found on the island of the Tiber a column with an inscription whose first part reads: *Semoni Sanco Deo Fidio Sacrum*. Scholars immediately claimed that this was the pedestal of the statue mentioned by Justin and that Justin misread the inscription, for, they say, it was dedicated not to *Simoni Sancto Deo*, but to *Semoni Sanco*—a Sabine god. But there is no proof that the pedestal found in 1574 belonged to the same statue mentioned by Justin back in the second century. The identity of the two statues has been presumed, yet it is not beyond the realm of probability that there were two statues in the city of Rome where all sorts of pagan superstitions had their statues and altars. It has not been definitely proved, therefore, that Justin was mistaken in saying that the Romans considered Simon Magus a god and honored him with a statue.

[4] Menander, a disciple and successor of Simon Magus, also had Messianic delusions. He introduced baptism among his followers and told them it would keep them eternally young and free from death.

[5] He was born at Sinope in Pontus. About the year 140, he went to Rome. There his teaching was condemned and he then joined the Gnostic Cerdo and later founded his own sect based on a system of dualism.

be greater and to have done greater deeds than He. All who follow these men are, as we said above, called Christians, just as those who do not share the same doctrines share among philosophers the name of philosophy. We do not know whether they are guilty of those disgraceful and fabulous deeds, the upsetting of the lamp, promiscuous intercourse, and anthropophagy,[6] but we do know, that you neither molest nor execute them, at least not for their beliefs. We have a treatise written against all the heresies that have arisen, which, if you wish to read, we will give to you.

Chapter 27

Lest we molest[1] anyone or commit sin ourselves, we have been taught that it is wicked to expose even newly-born children,[2] first, because we see that almost all those who are exposed (not only girls, but boys) are raised in prostitution. As your forefathers are said to have raised herds of oxen,

---

6 The pagans, after hearing only vague reports (due to the *Disciplina Arcani*) of the activities at the Christian assemblies—reports of the eating of someone's flesh and the drinking of his blood; of the exchange of the kiss of peace among the Christians who called one another brother and sister—reconstructed the scene in this way: the neophytes were given clubs with which to beat a huge lump of dough in which an infant had been concealed. After the infant was killed, its blood and its flesh were consumed by those present. This was followed, they thought, by the extinguishing of the lights and every sort of immorality. Thus arose the stock accusations against the Christians: infanticide, cannibalism (Thyestean feasts), and incest (Oedipodean intercourse). Cf. Athenagoras, *Suppl.* 3; Tertullian, *Apol.* 7; Minucius Felix, *Octavius* 9.

1 *Diókomen*, 'molest.' There is no need to read *adikómen*, for Justin's meaning is that Christians consider it unlawful to expose children, because by doing so they would be doing wrong to the children in case they were not found and sheltered, or, if found, they might be educated in evil practices.
2 The custom was then not uncommon of abandoning unwanted infants along the hillside or roadside.

or goats, or sheep, or grazing horses,³ you now raise children only for this same disgraceful purpose, for in every country there is a throng of females, hermaphrodites, and degenerates, ready for this evil practice. And you, who should eradicate them from your land, instead accept wages, tribute, and taxes from them.⁴ Anyone who consorts with them, besides being guilty of a godless, impious, and shameful action, may by some chance be guilty of intercourse with his own child, or relative, or brother. There are some who make prostitutes even of their own children and wives; for purposes of sodomy, some are publicly known to have been mutilated; and they impute these secret cults to the mother of the gods, and beside each of those whom you consider gods is painted a serpent,⁵ as a great symbol and mystery. In truth, what is publicly done and honored by you, as if the divine light were overturned and extinguished, you hold against us. This, of course, does not harm us who refuse to do such evil things, but it does harm those who practice them and those who falsely accuse us.

Chapter 28

As you may learn by examining our writings, the chief of the wicked demons we call the serpent, Satan, the devil, and Christ foretold that he with his army of demons, and the men who follow him, will be cast into the fire [of Hell] to be punished for endless ages. The cause of God's delay in doing this is his regard for mankind, for in His foreknowledge He sees that some will be saved by repentance, some who are, perhaps, not yet in existence. Indeed, in the beginning

---

3 Cf. Tatian, *Oratio ad Graec.* 28; Clemens Alex., *Paed.* 3, 4, 26.
4 Taxes for prostitution were first imposed by Caligula (cf. Suetonius, *Cal.* 40) and were not abolished until the time of Justinian.
5 A familiar figure in pagan religions as the symbol of eternity, power, and wisdom.

when He created man, He endowed him with the power of understanding, of choosing the truth, and of doing right; consequently, before God no man has an excuse if he does evil, for all men have been created with the power to reason and to reflect. If anyone does not believe that God takes an interest in these things, he will by some artifice imply either that God does not exist, or that though He does exist, He takes delight in evil, or that He is [as unmoved] as stone, and that neither virtue nor vice is a reality, but that things are considered good or bad only in the opinion of men: this indeed would be the height of blasphemy and injustice.

Chapter 29

Still [another reason against exposing children is], lest some of them would not be [discovered and] taken home, but die, and we would then be murderers. But either we marry, in the first place, in order to raise children, or, refusing to marry, we live in continence for the rest of our lives. Recently, one of us Christians, to convince you that promiscuous intercourse is not one of our practices, presented a petition to Felix, the Prefect of Alexandria, asking that a surgeon be allowed to make him a eunuch, for the physicians in that place said that without the prefect's permission it was forbidden[1] to do this. When Felix positively refused to grant the permission, the youth remained unmarried and continent, and he was satisfied with the approval of his own conscience and that of his fellow believers. And we do not consider it out of place here to mention Antinous,[2] who

---
1 By a law dating back to the Emperor Nerva (96-98).
2 Antinous, a favorite of the Emperor Hadrian, drowned in the Nile River. After his death Hadrian ordered divine honors bestowed upon him.

was alive until recently, and whom everyone reverently began to worship as a god, even though they all knew who he was and whence he came.

Chapter 30

Lest anyone should object and ask, 'What prevents us from supposing that He whom we call Christ was a man born of men, and has worked what we term miracles through the art of magic,[1] and thus appeared to be the Son of God,' we now present proof that such was not the case.[2] We shall do so not by trusting in mere statements [without proof], but by necessarily believing those who predicted these things before they happened, for we are actual eye-witnesses of events that have happened and are happening in the very manner in which they were fortold. This, we are sure, will appear even to you the greatest and truest proof.

Chapter 31

Indeed, there were certain men among the Jews who were Prophets of God, through whom the Prophetic Spirit predicted events, that were to happen, before they actually took place. The successive kings of Judea carefully kept their prophetic sayings in their possession, as they were worded at the time of their utterance in their Hebrew language, and as they were arranged in books by the Prophets themselves. When Ptolemy,[1] King of Egypt, was forming a library, and attempt-

---

1 A common accusation cited and answered by Arnobius, *Adv. nat.* 1.43: *Magus fuit, clandestinis artibus omnia illa perfecit.*
2 Justin now begins his proof that Christ 'was the Son of God.

---

1 I.e., Ptolemy Philadelphus, who in the third century before Christ had the Hebrew Scriptures translated into Greek at the Museum in Alexandria. This is the famous Septuagint version.

ing to collect the writings of every nation, he heard about these prophetic writings and he sent to Herod,[2] then King of the Jews, asking that he send the prophetic books to him. King Herod did send them, written, as we said, in the Hebrew language. But when the Egyptians could not understand these writings, he again sent and asked for some persons[3] to translate them into the Greek tongue. After this was accomplished, the books remained in the possession of the Egyptians from that day to this, as they are also in the possession of every Jew, wherever he be. But these Jews, though they read the books, fail to grasp their meaning, and they consider us as their enemies[4] and adversaries, killing and punishing us, just as you do, whenever they are able to do so, as you can readily imagine. In the recent Jewish war, Bar Kocheba,[5] the leader of the Jewish uprising, ordered that only the Christians should be subjected to dreadful torments, unless they renounced and blasphemed Jesus Christ. In the books of the Prophets, indeed, we found Jesus our Christ foretold as coming to us born of a virgin, reaching manhood, curing every disease and ailment, raising the dead to life, being hated, unrecognized, and crucified, dying, rising from the dead, ascending into Heaven, and being called and actually being the Son of God. And [we found predicted also] that He would send certain persons to every nation to make known these things, and that the former Gentiles rather [than Jews]

---

2 Justin is here guilty of an anachronism, for Herod was not then King of the Jews. Grabe, Maran, and others lay the blame on the scribe, who should have written *basileúonti hierei* instead of *basileúonti heróde*. In fact, Philo (*De vit. Mos.* 2) claims that the high priest (viz., Eleazar) to whom Ptolemy sent his request was also King of the Jews.
3 Justin, like Philo and Josephus, here follows the account of Aristeas on the seventy-two translators of the Bible.
4 Jewish hostility to Christianity is mentioned often by Justin.
5 Leader in the Jewish war of insurrection against the Roman power (132-135).

would believe in Him. He was foretold, in truth, before He actually appeared, first five thousand years before,[6] then three thousand, then two thousand, then one thousand, and, finally, eight hundred. For, in succeeding generations new Prophets rose time and again.

Chapter 32

Indeed, Moses, the first of the Prophets, spoke literally in these words: 'The sceptre shall not be taken away from Juda, nor a ruler from his thigh, until He come for whom it is reserved; and He shall be the desire of nations, tying His foal to the vine, washing His robe in the blood of the grape.'[1] It is up to you to make a thorough investigation and to learn up to what time the Jews had their own ruler and king. [They had a ruler] until the coming of Jesus Christ our Teacher, and Expounder of the prophecies that were not then understood, as the divine and holy Prophetic Spirit predicted through Moses: 'The ruler will not depart from Juda, until He come, for whom the kingdom is reserved.' For Juda was the forefather of the Jews, and from him they derive their name; and after He [Christ] appeared you started to rule the Jews, and have become masters of their whole country. But the prophecy, 'He shall be the desire of nations,' meant that people from all nations would look for His second coming, as you yourselves can see with your own eyes and be convinced by factual evidence; for men of every nation look for Him who was crucified in Judea, after whose coming the country of the Jews was immediately given over to you as booty of war. And the words, 'tying His foal

---

6 Some claim that Adam is here meant; others, Enoch. Justin, in Ch. 42, places David at 1500 B.C.

1 Gen. 49.10.

to the vine, and washing His robe in the blood of the grape,' allegorically signified the things that would befall Christ, and the deeds that He would perform. For the foal of a donkey stood tied to a vine[2] at the entrance to a village, and He ordered His disciples to lead it to Him, and when this was done, He mounted and sat upon it, and entered Jerusalem, where was located the greatest Jewish temple, which you later destroyed. After this He was crucified, in order that the rest of the prophecy be verified, for the words, 'washing His robe in the blood of the grape,' were a forewarning of the passion He was to endure, purifying with His blood those who believe in Him. For, what the Divine Spirit called through the prophet 'His robe' are those believers in Christ, in whom dwells the seed[3] of God, namely, the Word. And the saying, 'the blood of the grape,' means that He who was to appear would have blood, though not through the seed of man, but through the power of God. The first power after God the Father and Lord of all things is the Word, who is also His Son, who assumed human flesh and became man in the manner which we shall presently explain. For, just as God, not man, made the blood of the grape, so was it indicated also that this blood would not arise from human seed, but from the power of God, as we stated above. Another Prophet, Isaias, expressing the thoughts in different language, spoke thus: 'A star shall rise out of Jacob, and a flower shall spring from the root of Jesse, and in His arm shall nations trust.'[4] Indeed, a brilliant star has arisen, and a

---

2 The Synoptics (Matt. 21.2; Mark 11.2; Luke 19.30) make no mention of the vine.
3 Justin here speaks of the seminal word (which is in every man and is his reason), as distinct from the Perfect Word who is in the faithful only.
4 Num. 24.17.

flower has sprung up from the root of Jesse—this is Christ. For, by God's power He was conceived by a virgin who was a descendant of Jacob, who was the father of Juda, the above-mentioned father of the Jewish race; and Jesse was His forefather according to this prophecy, and He was the son of Jacob and Juda according to lineage.

Chapter 33

And, again, hear how it was expressly foretold by Isaias that He was to be born of a virgin; here is the prophecy: 'Behold, a virgin shall conceive, and bear a son, and His name shall be called Emmanuel' [i.e., God with us].[1] For, what man has deemed incredible and impossible, God foretold through the Prophetic Spirit as about to take place, so that, when they did take place, they should not be denied, but believed because they had been foretold. But, lest some who do not grasp the meaning of this prophecy should accuse us of the very things of which we accused the poets who said that Jupiter approached women for the sake of sensual pleasure, let us attempt to explain the words of the prophecy. The words, 'Behold, a virgin shall conceive,' therefore mean that the virgin shall conceive without intercourse. For, if she had had intercourse with anyone whomsoever, she was then no longer a virgin, but, the power of God descending upon the virgin overshadowed her, and caused her, while still a virgin, to conceive. And the angel of God, who was then sent to that same virgin, carried the glad news to her when he said: 'Behold, thou shalt conceive in thy womb of the Holy Ghost, and shalt bring forth a Son, and He shall be called the Son of the Most High, and thou shalt call His

---

[1] Isa. 7.14; (Matt. 1.23).

name Jesus, for He shall deliver His people from their sins.'[2] This happened as related by the recorders of all the acts of our Savior, Jesus Christ, whom we believed, and through the above-mentioned Isaias the Prophetic Spirit foretold that He should be born in the manner we stated above. It is not right, therefore, to understand the Spirit and the power of God as anything else than the Word, who is also the First-begotten of God, as Moses,[3] the previously mentioned Prophet, has stated. And it was this Spirit who came upon the virgin, overshadowed her, and brought it about that she became pregnant, not by sexual intercourse, but by divine power. Jesus is a name in the Hebrew tongue which means Savior in the Greek; thus, the angel said to the virgin: 'And thou shalt call His name Jesus, for He shall deliver His people from their sins.' I think that even you will concede that the Prophets are inspired by none other than the Divine Word.

Chapter 34

And hear in what part of this earth He was to be born, as it was foretold by another Prophet, Micheas, who spoke thus: 'And thou, Bethlehem, land of Judah, art not the least among the princes of Judah; for out of thee shall come forth a Ruler, who shall feed my people.'[1] Now, this [Bethlehem] is a certain village in the land of the Jews, distant thirty-five stadia from Jerusalem, where Jesus Christ was born, as you can learn by consulting the census taken by Quirinius, your first procurator in Judea.[2]

---
2 Luke 1.31.
3 Many would substitute the name Isaias for Moses in this passage because, they claim, it would better agree with the context. But I follow Maran (*PG* 6.381) in retaining the Mss. reading, for Justin, in his *Dialogue* 52, cites Moses to prove that Christ was the First-begotten.

---
1 Mich. 5.2; (Matt. 2.6).
2 Actually, he was a legate of Syria.

Chapter 35

Hear also how it was foretold that, after His birth, Christ should escape the notice of other men until He reached the age of maturity, and this also took place. Here are the words of the prophecy: 'A child is born to us, and a young man is given to us, and the government is upon His shoulders.'[1] This signifies the power of the cross, which, at His crucifixion, He placed on His shoulders, as shall be demonstrated more clearly as we proceed in this discourse. And again the same Prophet Isaias, inspired by the Prophetic Spirit, said: 'I have stretched out my hands to an unbelieving and contradicting people, who walk in a way that is not good.[2] They now ask judgment from Me, and dare to approach God.'[3] Again [the Prophetic Spirit] says, in other words, through another Prophet: 'They have pierced My hands and My feet, and have cast lots for My clothing.'[4] David, however, the king and prophet who spoke these words, endured none of these sufferings, but Jesus Christ stretched out His hands when He was crucified by the Jews who contradicted Him and denied that He was the Messiah. And, as the Prophet said, they placed Him in mockery on the judgment seat, and said: 'Judge us.'[5] And the words, 'They have pierced My hands and My feet,' refer to the nails which transfixed His hands and feet on the cross. And, after He was crucified, they cast lots for His clothing, and His crucifiers divided it among themselves. That these things really happened, you can ascertain from the Acts of Pontius Pilate. We shall now cite the predictions of another Prophet, Sophonias, to prove

---
1 Isa. 9.6.
2 Isa. 65.2.
3 Isa. 58.2.
4 Ps. 21.17-19.
5 Cf. Matt. 27.26-30.

that it was foretold that He was to enter Jerusalem sitting upon the foal of an ass. Here are the words of the prophecy: 'Rejoice greatly, O daughter of Sion, shout for joy, O daughter of Jerusalem; behold thy King cometh to thee, gentle and riding upon an ass, and upon a colt the foal of an ass.'[6]

Chapter 36

However, when you listen to the prophecies, spoken as in the person [of someone], do not think that they were spoken by the inspired Prophets of their own accord, but by the Word of God who prompts them. For, sometimes He asserts, in the manner of a Prophet, what is going to happen; sometimes He speaks as in the name of God, the Lord and Father of all; sometimes, as in the name of Christ; sometimes, as in the name of the people replying to the Lord, or to His Father. So it may be observed even in your own writers, where one person writes the entire narrative, but introduces different persons who carry on the conversation. The Jews, who possess the writings of the Prophets, did not understand this; not only did they not recognize Christ when He came, but they even hate us who declare that He has come, and who show that He was crucified by them, as it was foretold.

Chapter 37

In order that this truth may also be clear to you, there were uttered in the name of the Father, through the forementioned Prophet, Isaias, the following words: 'The ox knoweth his owner, and the ass his master's crib; but Israel hath not known Me, and My people hath not understood.

---

6 The quotation is not from Sophonias, but from Zacharias (9.9).

Woe, sinful nation, people laden with iniquity, wicked seed, lawless sons, ye have forsaken the Lord.'¹ And again, in another passage, when the same Prophet again speaks in the name of the Father: 'What is this house that you will build unto Me? saith the Lord. Heaven is My throne, and the earth is My footstool.'² And yet again, in another passage: 'My soul hateth your new moons and your sabbaths; I cannot bear the great day of the fast and your idleness; nor will I heed you, if you come to be seen by Me. Your hands are full of blood. And if you bring fine flour [or] incense, it is an abomination to Me; the fat of lambs and the blood of bulls, I desire not. For who hath required these things from your hands?³ But loose every bond of iniquity, tear apart the knots of contracts made by violence, shelter the homeless and naked, deal thy bread to the hungry.'⁴ You can now understand what things were taught through the Prophets in the name of God [the Father].

Chapter 38

When the Prophetic Spirit speaks in the name of Christ, these are His words: 'I stretched forth My hands to a rebellious and contradicting people, who walk in a way that is not good.'¹ And again: 'I have extended My back to the scourges and My cheeks to the blow; I have not turned My face away from the shame of spittings; and the Lord was My helper, therefore I was not confounded; but I set My face like a hard rock, and I knew that I would not be put

---
1 Isa. 1.3,4.
2 Isa. 66.1.
3 Isa. 1.11-15.
4 Isa. 58.6,7.

---
1 Isa. 65.2.

to shame, for He is near that justifieth Me.'² And again, when He says: 'They have cast lots for My clothing, and they have pierced My feet, and My hands.'³ 'I have slept and have taken My rest, and I have risen up, because the Lord hath protected Me.'⁴ And yet again, when He says: 'They have spoken with their lips and have wagged their heads, saying, "Let Him deliver Himself." '⁵ That all the above-mentioned things happened to Christ at the hands of the Jews you can easily learn, for, as He lay crucified on the cross, they wagged their heads and sneered as they exclaimed: 'Let Him who raised the dead to life save Himself.'⁶

Chapter 39

But when the Prophetic Spirit speaks, as foretelling what is going to happen, His words are the following: 'For the law shall come forth from Sion, and the word of the Lord from Jerusalem. And He shall judge the Gentiles, and rebuke many people; and they shall turn their swords into ploughshares, and their spears into sickles; nation shall not lift up sword against nation, neither shall they be exercised any more in war.'¹ That this prophecy, too, was verified you can readily believe, for twelve illiterate men, unskilled in the art of speaking, went out from Jerusalem into the world, and by the power of God they announced to the men of every nation that they were sent by Christ to teach everyone the word of God; and we, who once killed one another, [now] not only do not wage war against our enemies, but,

---
2 Isa. 50.6.
3 Ps. 21.17-19.
4 Ps. 3.5.
5 Ps. 21.8.
6 Matt. 27.39.

---
1 Isa. 2.3,4.

in order to avoid lying or deceiving our examiners, we even meet death cheerfully, confessing Christ. In this case we might well follow that saying: 'The tongue has sworn, but the mind is unsworn.'[2] But, if the soldiers enrolled and sworn in by you prefer the allegiance they owe to you rather than their own life, their parents, their country, and all their relatives, though you cannot offer them anything immortal as reward, it would be ridiculous if we who long for immortality should not bear all things patiently, in order to attain what we hope for from Him who has the power to grant it.

Chapter 40

Now hear what was predicted of those who preached His doctrine and announced His coming, for thus spoke the fore-mentioned prophet and king through the inspiration of the Prophetic Spirit: 'Day to day uttereth speech, and night to night showeth knowledge. There are no speeches nor languages, where their voices are not heard. Their sound hath gone forth into all the earth, and their words unto the ends of the world. He hath set His tent in the sun, and He, as a bridegroom coming out of his wedding chamber, shall rejoice as a giant to run his course.'[1] To these we have thought it proper and appropriate to add some other prophecies of David, from which you may know how the Prophetic Spirit invites men to live, and how He predicted the plot formed against Christ by Herod, king of the Jews, and the Jews themselves, and Pilate, your procurator of the Jews, with his soldiers; and how men from every nation would believe in Him, and how God [the Father] calls Him His Son, and

---

2 Euripides, *Hippol.* 607. Cicero (*De Off.* 3.29) gives a Latin version: *Iuravi lingua, mentem iniuratam gero.*

---

1 Ps. 18.3-6.

has announced that He shall subject all His enemies to Him; and how the demons do their utmost to escape the power both of God, the Father and Lord of all, and of Christ Himself; and how God calls everyone to repent before the day of judgment arrives. His [David's] words were these: 'Blessed is the man who hath not walked in the counsel of the ungodly, nor stood in the way of sinners, nor sat in the chair of pestilence; but his will is in the law of the Lord, and on this law he shall meditate day and night. And he shall be like a tree planted near running waters, which shall bring forth its fruit in due season; and his leaf shall not fall off, and whatsoever he shall do shall prosper. Not so the wicked, not so; but they are like the dust which the wind driveth from the face of the earth. Therefore the wicked shall not rise again in judgment nor the sinners in the council of the just. For the Lord knoweth the way of the just; and the way of the wicked shall perish.[2] Why have the Gentiles raged, and the people devised vain things? The kings of the earth stood up, and the princes met together against the Lord, and against His Christ, saying: "Let us break their bonds asunder, and let us cast away their yoke from us." He that dwelleth in Heaven shall laugh at them, and the Lord shall deride them. Then shall He speak to them in His anger, and trouble them in His rage. But I am appointed king by Him over Sion, His holy mountain, preaching His commandment. The Lord hath said to Me: "Thou art My Son, this day have I begotten Thee. Ask of Me and I will give Thee the Gentiles for Thy inheritance, and the utmost parts of the earth for Thy possession. Thou shalt rule them with a rod of iron, and shall break them in pieces like a potter's vessel." And now, O ye kings, under-

---
2 Ps. 1.1-6.

stand, receive instruction, you that judge the earth. Serve ye the Lord with fear, and rejoice unto Him with trembling. Embrace discipline, lest at any time the Lord be angry, and you perish from the just way, when His wrath is suddenly kindled; blessed are all they that trust in Him.'[3]

Chapter 41

In yet another prophecy, the Prophetic Spirit, revealing through the same David that Christ would reign after His crucifixion, spoke thus: 'Sing ye to the Lord, all the earth, and show forth His salvation from day to day. For the Lord is great, and exceedingly to be praised; He is to be feared above all gods. For all the gods of the Gentiles are idols of demons; but God made the heavens. Glory and praise are before Him, strength and glorying are in His sanctuary. Give glory to the Lord, the Father everlasting; receive grace, and enter His presence, and worship in His holy courts. Let all the earth be fearful before His face, and be well established and not be shaken. Let them rejoice among the Gentiles, saying: "The Lord hath reigned from the tree." '[1]

Chapter 42

Now we will explain why the Prophetic Spirit speaks of what is about to take place as if it had already happened (as may be seen in the above-quoted passages), so that our readers will have no excuse [for remaining in error]. The

---

[3] Ps. 2.1-13.

[1] Ps. 95.1-13. Justin (*Dialogue* 73) wrongly accused the Jews of expunging from their text the words: 'from the tree.' These words appear neither in the Hebrew nor the Septuagint text, but Tertullian knew them; they are an early Christian addition (Cf. *Letter of Barnabas* 8).

things which He certainly knows will come to pass He foretells as if they have already come to pass. You must give your full attention to these prophecies to realize that they must be accepted as such. David uttered the words quoted [in the preceding chapter] fifteen hundred[1] years before Christ the Incarnate was crucified, and no one before Him or after Him occasioned joy among the Gentiles by being crucified. Yet, our Jesus Christ, after His crucifixion and death, arose from the dead and, after ascending into Heaven, ruled there; through the tidings announced by the Apostles in His name to the people of every nation, joy is given to those who look forward to the immortality promised by Him.

Chapter 43

Now, lest some persons conclude from what we have just stated that whatever takes place must necessarily do so by force of destiny, because of the prediction of things foreknown, we make answer to this, too. Through the Prophets we have learned, and we profess as true, that punishments, and torments, and wonderful rewards are distributed according to the merit of each man's actions. If such were not the case, but everything were to happen by fate,[1] no choice would be in our power at all. For, if fate decrees that this man is to be good and this other man evil, neither the former is praiseworthy, nor the latter blameworthy. Furthermore, if man does not have the free faculty to shun evil and to choose good, then, whatever his actions may be, he is not responsible for them. But we will now prove that

---

[1] Grabe claims that this was not Justin's mistake, but the scribe's, who should have written *dr* (1,100) instead of *dph* (1,500).

[1] A teaching of Stoic philosophy, the favorite philosophy of the emperor and princes to whom this apology is addressed.

only by free will does man act rightly and wrongfully. We observe a man in pursuit of opposite things; if, however, he were destined to be either evil or good, he would not be able to attain both opposites nor would he change his mind so often. Nor would some men be good and others evil, for then we would have to affirm fate to be the cause of good and evil and to act in opposition to itself; or what has been declared above would seem to be true, namely, that neither virtue nor vice is any thing real, but things are considered either good or bad by opinion only—which, as sound reason shows, is the greatest impiety and injustice. This, however, we say is inevitable fate, that they who choose good have merited rewards, just as those who prefer the contrary have appropriate punishments. God did not create man like the other beings, trees and quadrupeds, for example, which can do nothing by free choice. For, neither would he deserve reward or praise if he did not choose good of his own accord, but were created precisely for this purpose; nor, if he were sinful, would he deserve punishment, since he would not be such of himself nor able to be other than what he was born.

Chapter 44

Indeed, the Holy Prophetic Spirit taught us this when He informed us through Moses that God spoke the following words to the first man: 'Behold, before thy face are good and evil, choose the good.'[1] And again, through Isaias, another Prophet, as from God the Father and Lord of the universe, the following words were spoken in the same vein: 'Wash yourselves, be clean; banish sin from your souls, learn to do well; judge for the fatherless, and defend the widow; and then come and let us reason together, saith the Lord:

---

1 Deut. 30.15.19.

And if your sins be as scarlet, I will make them white as wool; and if they be red as crimson, I will make them white as snow. And if you be willing and will hearken to Me, you shall eat the good things of the land; but if you will not hear Me, the sword shall devour you. For thus has spoken the mouth of the Lord.'[2] The words, 'The sword shall devour you,' do not mean that the disobedient will be put to death by swords, but that the sword of God is the fire of which those who choose to do evil shall be made the fuel. Therefore, He says: 'The sword shall devour you: for thus has spoken the mouth of the Lord.' If, however, He had meant a sword that cuts and immediately destroys, He would not have used the expression, 'shall devour.' Plato, too, when he stated: 'To him who chooses belongs the guilt, but in God there is no guilt,'[3] borrowed the thought from the Prophet Moses. Indeed, Moses is more ancient than all the Greek authors, and everything the philosophers and poets said in speaking about the immortality of the soul, or retribution after death, or speculation on celestial matters, or other similar doctrines, they took from the Prophets as the source of information, and from them they have been able to understand and explain these matters. Thus, the seeds of truth seem to be among all men, but that they did not grasp their exact meaning is evident from the fact that they contradict themselves. So, if we declare that future events have been predicted, by that we do not claim that they take place by the necessity of fate. But, since God has foreknowledge of what all men will do, and has ordained that each man will be rewarded in accordance with the merit of his actions, foretells through the Prophetic Spirit that He Himself will reward them in accord-

---
2 Isa. 1.16-20.
3 *De Repub.* 10.617E.

ance with the merit of their deeds, ever urging men to reflection and remembrance, proving that He both cares and provides for them. But at the instigation of the wicked demons, the punishment of death has been decreed[4] against those who read the books of Hystaspes, or the Sibyl, or the Prophets, in order that they may, through fear, stop prospective readers from acquiring a knowledge of fine things, and keep them as their own slaves; which they were not completely able to do. For, not only do we read those books without fear, but, as you see, we offer them to you to inspect, confident that their contents will please everyone. Even if we persuade only a few, we shall obtain very great rewards, for, like good laborers, we shall receive recompense from the Master.

Chapter 45

That God the Father of the universe would bring Christ to Heaven after His resurrection from the dead, and would keep Him there until He struck His enemies, the demons, and until the completion of the quota of those whom He foreknows to be good and virtuous, because of whom He has always delayed the consummation of the world, listen to the words spoken through David the Prophet: 'The Lord said to My Lord: Sit Thou at My right hand, until I make Thine enemies Thy footstool. The Lord shall send to Thee the sceptre of power out of Jerusalem; and rule Thou in the midst of Thine enemies. With Thee is the government in the day of Thy power, in the brightness of Thy saints. From

---

[4] Perhaps the degree cited in Jul. Paul. *Sentent. recept.* 5, 21, 3: *qui de salute principis vel de summa rei publicae mathematicos, hariolos, haruspices, vaticinatores consulit cum eo qui responderit capite punitur. . . . Non tantum divinatione quis, sed ipsa scientia eiusque libris melius fecerit abstinere.*

the womb have I begotten Thee before the morning star.'[1] The words, 'He shall send to Thee the sceptre of power out of Jerusalem,' signified the powerful teaching which the Apostles, going out from Jerusalem, preached everywhere. And although death is determined for those who teach, or even profess, the name of Christ, we everywhere both accept and teach it. But, if you also should read these words with hostile mind, you can do nothing more, as we already stated, than kill us, which does no real harm to us, but does bring the eternal punishment of fire to you and to all who unjustly hate and do not repent.

Chapter 46

Lest some should unreasonably assert, in order to turn men from our teaching, that we affirm that Christ was born one hundred and fifty years ago[1] under Quirinius, and then afterward, under Pontius Pilate, taught what we claim He did, and should accuse us as if [we said] all men born before the time of Christ were not accountable for their actions, we shall anticipate and answer such a difficulty. We have been taught that Christ was First-begotten of God [the Father] and we have indicated above that He is the Word of whom all mankind partakes. Those who lived by reason are Christians, even though they have been considered atheists: such as, among the Greeks, Socrates, Heraclitus, and others like them; and among the foreigners, Abraham, Elias, Ananias,

---

1 Ps. 109.1-3.

1 Justin probably used round numbers here, otherwise the date of this *Apology* would have to be placed, at the latest, in the year 147. But Felix the Prefect of Alexandria (mentioned in Ch. 29), has been identified as Munacius Felix, Prefect of Alexandria from 148 to 154. The *Apology*, therefore, must have been written after 147.

Azarias, Misael,[2] and many others whose deeds or names we now forbear to enumerate, for we think it would be too long. So, also, they who lived before Christ and did not live by reason were useless men, enemies of Christ, and murderers of those who did live by reason. But those who have lived reasonably, and still do, are Christians, and are fearless and untroubled. From all that has been said an intelligent man can understand why, through the power of the Word, in accordance with the will of God, the Father and Lord of all, He was born as a man of a virgin, was named Jesus, was crucified, died, rose again, and ascended into Heaven. But, since the proof of this topic is not necessary at this time, we shall now proceed to the proof of more urgent matters.

Chapter 47

Listen, also, to what the Prophetic Spirit said concerning the future devastation of the land of the Jews. His words were spoken as if in the name of the people who wondered at what had happened. These are the words: 'Sion has been made a wilderness, Jerusalem has become a desolation; the house, our sanctuary has become a curse; and the glory which our fathers praised is burned with fire; and all its glorious things have fallen in ruins. And Thou refrainest Thyself at these things, and hast held Thy peace, and hast humbled us greatly.'[1] And you know full well that, as it was foretold to come to pass, Jerusalem has been destroyed. That it would be destroyed and that no one would be allowed to dwell therein was thus foretold by the Prophet

---

[2] These last three are also known as Sidrach, Abdenago, and Misach, the three children who were unharmed by the flames of the fiery furnace (Dan. 1.7; 3.20-93).

[1] Isa. 64.10-12

Isaias: 'Their land is desolate, and their enemies consume it before them, and none of them shall dwell therein.'[2] And you are fully aware that it was guarded by you, lest anyone should dwell in it, and that a death penalty was decreed for any Jew caught entering it.

Chapter 48

Concerning the prophecy that our Christ should cure all diseases and raise the dead to life, hear what was spoken. Here are the exact words of the prophecy: 'At His coming the lame shall leap like a stag, and the tongue of the dumb shall be clear; the blind shall see, and the lepers shall be cleansed, and the dead shall rise and walk about.'[1] That Christ did perform such deeds you can learn from the Acts of Pontius Pilate. Hear, also, the following words of Isaias, which tell how the Prophetic Spirit foretold that Christ and those men who trusted in Him should be put to death: 'Behold how the Just One perisheth, and no one takes it to heart; and how just men are slain, and no one gives it a thought. The Just One is snatched from the face of evil, and His burial shall be in peace, He is taken from our midst.'[2]

Chapter 49

Consider, too, how this same Isaias foretold that the Gentiles, who did not look forward to the Messiah, should worship Him, but the Jews, who were always awaiting His arrival, should not recognize Him when He did arrive. These are his words spoken as in the name of Christ Himself: 'I

---

2 Isa. 1.7.

1 Isa. 35.5,6.
2 Isa. 57.1,2.

was manifest to those who did not ask for Me; I was found by those who did not seek Me. I said, "Behold Me" to a nation that did not call upon My name. I stretched out My hands to an unbelieving and contradicting people, who walk along a way that is not good, but follow after their own sins; a people who provoke Me to anger before My face.'[1] The Jews, in truth, who had the prophecies and always looked for the coming of Christ, not only did not recognize Him, but, far beyond that, even mistreated Him. But the Gentiles, who had never even heard anything of Christ until His Apostles went from Jerusalem and preached about Him and gave them the prophecies, were filled with joy and faith, and turned away from their idols, and dedicated themselves to the Unbegotten God through Christ. That these slanders which were to be directed against those who confess Christ were foreknown, and how they who slander Him and who claim that it is well to retain the ancient customs would be afflicted, listen to these few words of Isaias: 'Woe unto those who call sweet bitter, and bitter sweet.'[2]

Chapter 50

Listen, also, to the prophecies that foretold how, after He became man for us, Christ, submitted to suffering and dishonor, and how He shall come again in glory. Here are the prophecies: 'Because they delivered His soul unto death, and He was reputed with the wicked, He hath borne the sins of many, and shall pray for the transgressors.'[1] 'For, behold, My servant shall understand, and shall be exalted and greatly glorified. As many shall be astonished at Thee, so

---
1 Isa. 65.1-3.
2 Isa. 5.20.

---
1 Isa. 53.12.

shall Thy form be inglorious before men, and Thy glory shall be hidden from before men; so shall many nations wonder, and kings shall shut their mouths at Him. For they to whom it was not told concerning Him and they who have not heard about Him, will understand.'² 'O Lord, who hath believed our report? And to whom is the arm of the Lord revealed? We have spoken in His sight as a child, as a root in dry ground; there is no beauty in Him, nor glory, and we have seen Him, and He had no form or beauty, but His form was dishonored and despised beyond that of men. He was a Man of sorrows, who knew how to endure infirmity, for His face was turned away; He was despised and not of good repute. He Himself bears our sins, and suffers for us; and we have thought Him to be in distress, under blows, and affliction. But He was wounded for our iniquities, and He was bruised for our sins. The chastisement of our peace was upon Him; by His bruises we are healed. Like sheep we have all gone astray; every man has wandered in his own way. And He delivered Him for our sins, and throughout His afflictions He opened not His mouth. He was led as a sheep to the slaughter, and He remained dumb as a lamb before its shearer, so He opens not His mouth. In His humiliation His judgment was taken away.'³ Thus, after His Crucifixion, all His close followers deserted His cause and even denied Him. Afterwards, when He arose from the dead, and appeared to them, and taught them to read the prophecies in which all the above happenings were predicted as about to take place, and after they had seen Him ascending into Heaven, and had believed, and had received the power He thence sent to them, they went forth to every nation to teach these things, and they were called Apostles.

---

2 Isa. 52.13-15.
3 Isa. 53.1-8.

Chapter 51

Furthermore, in order to make known to us that He who suffered these things had an indescribable origin, and rules over His enemies, the Prophetic Spirit spoke thus: 'Who shall declare His generation? For His life is taken away from the earth; for their sins is He led to death. And I will give the wicked for His burial and the rich for His death, for He has done no wrong nor has any deceit been found in His mouth; and the Lord is pleased to cleanse Him of the blow. If He shall be given over for sin, your soul shall see His seed prolonged. And the Lord desires to free His soul of sorrow, and to show Him light, and form Him with knowledge, to justify the Just One who administers well to many. And He shall bear our sins; for this He shall inherit many, and shall divide the spoils of the strong; because His soul was consigned to death, and He was reputed with the wicked, and He has borne the sins of many, and because of their sins He was delivered up.'[1] Hear, too, the prophecy of how He was to ascend into Heaven. Thus was it spoken: 'Lift up the gates of Heaven, and be ye opened, that the King of Glory may enter. Who is this King of Glory? The Lord strong, and the Lord mighty.'[2] And hear what the Prophet Jeremias said about how He was to come again from Heaven in glory. These are his words: 'Behold, as the Son of Man He comes upon the clouds of heaven, and His angels with Him.'[3]

Chapter 52

Now, since we show that all those things that have happened had been foretold by the Prophets before they hap-

---
1 Isa. 53.8-12.
2 Ps. 23.7,8.
3 This passage is not found in Jeremias, but in Daniel 7.13.

pened, it must of necessity also be believed that those things which were likewise foretold, but are yet to happen, shall with certainty come to pass. For, just as those things which have already happened took place as they were foretold, or have remained unrecognized, so future events, even if they are not known or believed, shall come to pass. The Prophets have foretold two comings of Christ: the one, which already took place, was that of a dishonored and suffering man; the other coming will take place, as it is predicted, when He shall gloriously come from Heaven with His angelic army, when He shall also raise to life the bodies of all the men that ever were, shall cloak the worthy with immortality, and shall relegate the wicked, subject to sensible pain for all eternity, into the eternal fire together with the evil demons. We will now show how these things also have been predicted as yet to happen. Thus spoke the Prophet Ezechiel: 'Joint shall be placed against joint, and bone against bone. And flesh shall grow again,[1] and every knee shall bend before the Lord, and every tongue shall acknowledge Him.'[2] Listen, also, to what was foretold concerning the suffering and torment the wicked will endure; here are the words of the prophecy: 'Their worm shall not rest, and their fire shall not be quenched.'[3] Then shall they repent when it will avail them nothing. What the tribes of the Jews will say and do when they see Him coming in glory has been thus foretold by Zacharias the Prophet: 'I will order the four winds to collect together the scattered children; I will command the north wind to carry them, and the south wind not to strike against them. And then there shall be great lamentation in Jerusalem, not the lamentation of mouths or of lips, but

---
1 Ezech. 37.7.
2 Isa. 45.24.
3 Isa. 66.24.

the lamentation of the heart; and they shall tear not their clothing, but their thoughts; they shall lament tribe by tribe, and then they shall look upon the One whom they pierced, and they shall exclaim: "Why, O Lord, have You made us wander from Your way? The glory which our fathers blessed has for us become a shame." [4]

Chapter 53

We could produce many other prophecies, but we refrain from doing so, since we think that those above-mentioned are sufficient to convince those who have ears to hear and understand, and we assume that these persons are also capable of perceiving that we do not make bare statements, such as the fables of the supposed sons of Jupiter, without being able to prove them. Why should we believe a crucified Man that He was the First-begotten of an Unbegotten God, and that He will pass judgment on the entire human race, unless we had found testimonies concerning Him foretold before He came and was made Man, and unless we had seen events happen just as foretold, namely, the devastation of the Jewish land, and men of every race believing through the teaching of His Apostles, and turning away from old customs which they had practised in error; indeed, perceiving ourselves amongst them, and realizing that the Christians from the ranks of the Gentiles are more numerous and more faithful than those from amongst the Jews and Samaritans? All other nations the Prophetic Spirit calls Gentiles, whereas the Jewish and the Samaritan people are called Israel and the House of Jacob. And we can present the prophecy in which it was foretold that the Gentile converts should be more numerous than the Jewish and Samaritan converts. Here

---

4 Zach. 2.6; 12.10-12; Joel 2.13; Isa. 63.17; 64.11.

it is: 'Rejoice, O thou barren, that didst not bear; break forth and cry aloud, thou that didst not travail; for many more are the children of the desolate, than the children of her who hath a husband.'[1] All the Gentiles were desolate of the true God, worshipping the works of their own making, but the Jews and Samaritans, having been given the word of God by the Prophets, and having always awaited the coming of Christ, did not recognize Him when He did come, except a few, who were to be saved, as the Prophetic Spirit foretold through Isaias, who thus spoke in their name: 'Except the Lord had left us seed, we should have been as Sodom and Gomorrah.'[2] Now, Moses related that Sodom and Gomorrah were cities, filled with impious men, which God burned and devastated with fire and brimstone, none of the dwellers therein being spared except a certain stranger, Chaldaean by birth, Lot by name; and this man's daughters were also saved. Those who so desire may view their whole countryside even now desolate, scorched, and sterile. To prove that the Gentile converts were foreknown as more faithful and more believing we will quote the words of Isaias the Prophet, which are as follows: 'Israel is uncircumcised in heart, but the Gentiles are uncircumcised in the flesh.'[3] Truly, then, such self-evident truths should convince and lead to faith those who accept the truth, and who are not vainglorious, or slaves of their passions.

Chapter 54

On the other hand, those who pass down the myths fabricated by the poets give no proof of their truth to the youths who learn them, yet we can now show that these myths

---
1 Isa. 54.1.
2 Isa. 1.9.
3 This quotation is not from Isaias, but from Jeremias 9.26.

were first related through the instigation of evil demons to deceive and seduce all men.¹ For, having heard the Prophets announce the coming of Christ and the punishment of sinful men by fire, they produced many who were reputed to be sons of Jupiter, thinking that they would be able to put the suspicion in men's minds that those things foretold of Christ were fabulous tales, just as were those related by the poets. And these stories were promulgated both among the Greeks and among all other peoples wheresoever they [the demons] heard the Prophets say that Christ would especially be accepted. We will also prove that the demons did not clearly grasp the meaning² of what they heard said by the Prophets, but, like erring men, mimicked what was said of Christ. Moses the Prophet was, as we have already stated, older than all writers, and through him, as we also stated above, it was thus prophesied: 'A prince shall not fail from Juda, nor a ruler from his thighs, until He comes for whom it is reserved; and He shall be the expectation of the Gentiles, tying His foal to the vine, washing His robe in the blood of the grape.'³ When the demons heard this prophetic saying, they proclaimed that Bacchus was the begotten son of Jupiter and that he discovered the vine (so they place wine⁴ in his mysteries), and taught that, after he was torn apart, he ascended into heaven. Now, the prophecy of Moses did not expressly define whether He who was to come was the Son of God, and whether, seated on the foal, He would

---

1 The third of the three things Justin promised (Ch. 23) to prove.
2 An oft-repeated statement of the early Apologists. Cf. Lactantius, *Inst. div.* 2.14.
3 Gen. 49.10.
4 The Mss. have *oînon* (wine) and the reading corresponds well to the context, as Maran (*PG* 6.409) ably proves. Others, like Sylburg, Grabe, Thirlby, Otto and Trollope, change the text to read *ónon*, 'ass,' since Justin's line of reasoning would require mention of an ass.

remain on earth or ascend into Heaven; further, the word 'foal' could mean either the foal of an ass or the foal of a horse. [The demons], uncertain whether He who was foretold would bring the foal of an ass or of a horse as a sign of His coming, and not knowing, as mentioned above, whether He was the Son of God or of man, proclaimed that Bellerophon himself, a man born of man, ascended into Heaven upon his horse Pegasus. And when they heard it foretold by another Prophet, Isaias, that He was to be born of a virgin, and would, by His own power, ascend into Heaven, they pretended that it was Perseus who had done so. And when they realized that it was stated, as we already said, in the prophecies written long before: 'He is strong as a giant to run His course,'[5] they announced that Hercules was strong and had traversed the entire earth. Then, too, when they found out that it had been prophesied that He would cure every illness and raise the dead to life, they brought forward Aesculapius.

Chapter 55

However, not in one instance, even for any of the so-called sons of Jupiter, was the crucifixion[1] imitated. Indeed, this did not occur to them, for, as was proved above, everything concerning the crucifixion was said symbolically. This[2] is the greatest sign of His power and dominion, as predicted by

---
5 Ps. 18.6.

---
1 The arguments expressed in this chapter would not seem very forceful to the Christian mind today, but it must be remembered that Justin addressed his words to pagans who considered nothing more vile than the cross. He wanted to show them how irrational was their hatred of the cross which was so much a part of their daily life. Even an astute writer like Tertullian will use the same argument. Cf. *Apol.* 16; *Ad. nat.* 12.
2 I.e., the crucifixion as symbolized by the cross.

the Prophet, and as is shown by all that is visible. For, ponder on all the things in this universe [and judge] whether they could be regulated or be interrelated without this figure [of the cross]. The sea, for instance, cannot be plowed unless the 'token of victory' which is called a sail be securely attached to the ship; the earth, too, is not plowed without it; diggers and artisans do all their work with tools of this shape. And man's form differs from that of irrational animals precisely in this, that it stands erect, with hands extended, and has on its face extended from the forehead what we call a nose, through which the living creature breathes, and this is exactly the figure of the cross. Hence the Prophet said: 'The breath before our face is Christ the Lord.'[3] The very symbols on your own banners[4] and trophies which you use in all your processions show the power of this sign, and you, though unwittingly, use these as signs of your dominion and power. After the death of your emperors you put their images upon this figure and you call them gods in your inscriptions. Thus, since we have tried to the best of our ability to convince you, both by word and by an obvious symbol, we are certain that henceforth we are without blame, even if you should not believe, for our task is now completely accomplished.

Chapter 56

It was not enough for the evil demons to proclaim, before the coming of Christ, that the so-called sons of Jupiter were really born to him. But after Christ appeared and

---

3 Lam. 4.20.
4 The word for 'banners' is not complete in the Greek text, for only the letters *llomen* are given. In the claromontane text, a later hand corrected it to read: *bixillomen*. This, Maran (*PG* 6.412) claims, was a Greek transliteration of the Latin *vexillorum*.

lived among men, and after they learned that He had been announced by the Prophets, and realized all nations believed in Him and expected Him, they once more, as stated above, produced other men, such as Simon and Menander of Samaria, who by mighty deeds of magic misled, and still mislead, many. As we stated before,[1] this Simon lived in your midst in the imperial city of Rome during the reign of Claudius Caesar, and amazed the sacred Senate and Roman people to such an extent that he was deemed a god and was honored with a statue, like the others whom you venerate as gods. For this reason we beseech that you join with the sacred Senate and Roman people as judges of this our petition, so that whoever is ensnared by Simon's teaching may know the truth and escape error. And, if you will, destroy his statue.

Chapter 57

Nor can the evil demons convince men that there will be no hell fire to punish sinners,[1] just as they could not keep Christ unknown after His appearance on earth. The only thing they could do was to cause us to be hated and be put to death by unreasonable living men, who were taught to indulge their passions in evil ways. Not only do we not hate such men, but, as is evident, we pity them and would like to bring about their conversion. We, indeed, have no dread of death, for it is an admitted fact that one day we must certainly die; nor is there anything new, but the same things follow the same routine, and, if the monotony of these things an-

---

1 Cf. notes to Ch. 26, above.

1 This seems to be Justin's line of reasoning: There is hope that Simon's followers will be converted, because the demons cannot convince them that there will be no future punishment for the wicked. This future punishment will frighten them into avoiding evil.

noys those who indulge in them even for the space of one year, they should turn their minds to our teachings, in order to have eternal life free from pain and privation. If they do not believe there is anything after death, but affirm that the dead lapse into a state of insensibility, then they do us a favor by releasing us from the sorrows and wants of this life, though in reality they show themselves to be evil, inhuman and prejudiced, for they put us to death, not to give us freedom, but to strip us of life and its joys.

Chapter 58

As previously stated,[1] the evil demons also introduced Marcion of Pontus who even now urges men to deny that God is the Creator of all things in heaven and on earth, and that the Christ foretold by the Prophets is His Son, and he proclaims another god besides the Maker of all things, and likewise another son. Many have believed this man, as though he were the sole possessor of truth, and they ridicule us, even though they do not prove their assertions, but are foolishly snatched away, like lambs by a wolf; they are victimized by the demons and their atheistic teachings. These spirits whom we call demons strive for nothing else than to alienate men from God their Creator, and from Christ, His first-begotten. Indeed, they have clamped down those who are powerless to lift themselves above earthly conditions, and they still clamp them down to earthly things, and to manufactured idols. Besides, they even try to trip those who rise to the contemplation of divine things, and, unless such persons are wise in their judgments and pure and passionless in their life, the demons will force them into ungodliness.

---
1 Cf. Chapter 26.

Chapter 59

To help you know that Plato plagiarized from our teachers[1] when he affirmed that God changed shapeless matter and created the world, listen to the authentic words of Moses, who was mentioned above as the first of the Prophets and older than the writers of Greece,[2] and through whom the Prophetic Spirit uttered the following words to show how and from what God first created the world: 'In the beginning God created heaven and earth. And the earth was invisible and empty, and darkness was upon the face of the deep; and the spirit of God moved over the waters. And God said: "Be light made." And light was made.'[3] Thus, Plato, his followers, and we, too, have learned, as you yourselves can also be assured, that God by His word created the whole world out of matter,[4] of which Moses had already spoken. We also know that Moses had already mentioned what the poets call Erebus.[5]

Chapter 60

Plato likewise borrowed from Moses when, while inquiring into the nature of the Son of God in his *Timaeus*, he states, 'He placed him in the universe in the manner of the letter *X*.'[1] For, in the writings of Moses it is stated that,

---

1 I.e., from the teaching of the Prophets.
2 Cf. Chapter 44.
3 Gen. 1.1-3.
4 Cf. Chapter 10, n.1.
5 *Erebos* is the name given to the darkness that prevailed in the western region where the sunless Cimmerian land and Hades were located.

---

1 Here (*Timaeus*, 36B.C.) Plato is not speaking of the Son of God, but of the soul of the universe. He says that the entire compound of the universe was divided by God lengthwise into two parts, which He joined together at the center like the Greek letter *Chi* (X), and bent them into an inner and outer circle, cutting each other near the point of contact. Justin refers this to the Son of God in the sense that at the creation of the universe the Son was extended in the form of the cross (the letter X). Thus, as does the cross (the letter X), so does the Son extend to every part of the world.

at the time when the Israelites left Egypt and were living
in the desert, they encountered poisonous beasts, vipers, asps,
and every sort of serpent which brought death to the people,
and that Moses, through the inspiration and impulse of God,
took some brass, shaped it into the figure of a cross,[2] placed
it over the holy tabernacle, and announced to the people:
'If you gaze upon this figure and believe, you shall be saved
thereby.'[3] He related that, after this was done, the serpents
perished, and tradition has it that the people of Israel were
thus saved from death. When Plato read this, he did not
clearly understand it, for, not perceiving that the figure
of the cross was spoken of, he took it for the form of the
letter X, and said that the power next to the first God was
placed in the universe in the form of the letter X. Plato's
mention of a third [subsistence] also originated, as we already stated, from his reading of Moses, who said: 'The
Spirit of God moved over the waters.'[4] He gives the second
place to the Word who is with God, who, as he stated, is
placed in the universe in the form of the letter X, and the
third place he attributes to the Spirit who was said to have
been borne over the waters, affirming: 'The Third about
the Third.'[5] And hear the Prophetic Spirit foretelling through
Moses the future conflagration; these are His words: 'An

---

[2] Num. 21.9: 'Moses therefore made a brazen serpent, and set it up for a sign.' In his *Dialogue* 94, Justin refers to this incident just as it is described above, but here Justin states: 'Moses... took some brass, shaped it into the figure of a cross, placed it over the holy tabernacle ...' In Numbers, no mention is made of a cross or of a tabernacle. In the Septuagint, the word for a sign is *semeion*, which Justin, as did many writers of the time, interpreted as the figure of the cross. According to Maran (*PG* 6.418), Justin used the word tabernacle as an image of the universe. Thus, the cross was placed in the universe, as Plato intimated.
[3] Num. 21.8.
[4] Gen. 1.2.
[5] Pseudo-Plat., *Epist.* 2.312E; Cf. Athenagoras, *Suppl.* 23.

everlasting fire shall descend and shall devour to the pit below.'[6] Thus, it is not that we hold the same opinion as others, but that they all imitate and re-echo ours. You can hear and learn these things from persons among us who do not even know the letters of the alphabet, who are uncultured and rude in speech, but wise and believing in mind; some, too, have been disabled and have lost their eyesight. So you can readily see that things are not the result of human wisdom, but are the pronouncements of the power of God.

Chapter 61

Lest we be judged unfair in this exposition, we will not fail to explain[1] how we consecrated ourselves to God when we were regenerated through Christ. Those who are convinced and believe what we say and teach is the truth, and pledge themselves to be able to live accordingly, are taught in prayer and fasting to ask God to forgive their past sins, while we pray and fast with them. Then we lead them to a place where there is water, and they are regenerated in the same manner in which we ourselves were regenerated. In the name of God, the Father and Lord of all, and of our Savior, Jesus Christ, and of the Holy Ghost,[2] they then receive the washing with water. For Christ said: 'Unless you be born again, you shall not enter into the kingdom of heaven.'[3] Now, it is clear to everyone how impossible it is for those who have been born once to enter their mothers' wombs again. Isaias the Prophet explained, as we already stated, how those who have

---

6 Deut. 32.22.

1 In this Chapter, and again in Chapters 65, 66, and 67, Justin ignored the *Disciplina arcani* to explain some Christian practices. This was unusual at that time.
2 The Trinitarian formula; Cf. Matt. 28.19.
3 John 3.3. Justin did know St. John's Gospel.

sinned and then repented shall be freed of their sins. These are his words: 'Wash yourselves, be clean, banish sin from your souls; learn to do well: judge for the fatherless and defend the widow; and then come and let us reason together, saith the Lord. And if your sins be as scarlet, I will make them white as wool; and if they be red as crimson, I will make them white as snow. But if you will not hear me, the sword shall devour you: for the mouth of the Lord hath spoken it.'[4] And this is the reason, taught to us by the Apostles, why we baptize the way we do. We were totally unaware of our first birth, and were born of necessity from fluid seed through the mutual union of our parents, and were trained in wicked and sinful customs. In order that we do not continue as children of necessity and ignorance, but of deliberate choice and knowledge, and in order to obtain in the water the forgiveness of past sins, there is invoked over the one who wishes to be regenerated, and who is repentant of his sins, the name of God, the Father and Lord of all; he who leads the person to be baptized to the laver calls him by this name only. For, no one is permitted to utter the name of the ineffable God, and if anyone ventures to affirm that His name can be pronounced, such a person is hopelessly mad. This washing is called illumination,[5] since they who learn these things become illuminated intellectually. Furthermore, the illuminated one is also baptized in the name of Jesus Christ, who was crucified under Pontius Pilate, and in the name of the Holy Spirit, who predicted through the Prophets everything concerning Jesus.

---
4 Isa. 1.16-20.
5 *Photismós*: illumination, commonly used in ancient times as a synonym for baptism.

Chapter 62

After hearing of this baptism which the Prophet Isaias announced, the demons prompted those who enter their temples and come to them with libations and burnt offerings to sprinkle themselves also with water; furthermore, they cause them to wash their whole persons, as they approach the place of sacrifice, before they go to the shrines where their [the demons'] statues are located. And the order given by the priests to those who enter and worship in the temples, to take off their shoes, was imitated by the demons after they learned what happened to Moses, the above-mentioned Prophet. For at this time, when Moses was ordered to go down into Egypt and bring out the Israelites who were there, and while he was tending the sheep of his mother's brother[1] in the land of Arabia, our Christ talked with him in the shape of fire from a bush. Indeed, He said: 'Put off thy shoes, and draw near and hear.'[2] When he had taken off his shoes, he approached the burning bush and heard that he was to go down into Egypt and bring out the people of Israel who were in that land; and he received great power from Christ who spoke to him under the form of fire, and he went down and brought out the people after he performed great and wondrous deeds. If you wish to know about these deeds you may learn them clearly from his writings.

Chapter 63

Even now, all Jews teach that the ineffable God spoke to Moses. Wherefore, the Prophetic Spirit, censuring the Jews

---
[1] Maran (*PG* 6.422) thinks that Justin was here guilty of a slip of the memory, writing mother's brother, instead of father-in-law. Thirlby, on the other hand, claims that he confused the somewhat similar events in the lives of Moses and Jacob.
[2] Exod. 3.5.

through Isaias, the above-mentioned Prophet, said: 'The ox knoweth his owner, and the ass his master's crib; but Israel hath not known Me, and My people hath not understood Me.'[1] Because the Jews did not know the nature of the Father and the Son, Jesus Christ likewise upbraided them, saying: 'No one knows the Father except the Son; nor does anyone know the Son except the Father, and those to whom the Son will reveal Him.'[2] Now, the Word of God is His Son, as we have already stated, and He is called Angel and Apostle; for, as Angel He announces all that we must know, and [as Apostle] He is sent forth to inform us of what has been revealed, as our Lord Himself says: 'He that heareth Me, heareth Him that sent Me.'[3] This will be further clarified from the following words of Moses: 'And the Angel of God spoke to Moses in a flame of fire out of the midst of a bush and said, "I AM WHO AM, the God of Abraham, the God of Isaac, and the God of Jacob, the God of your fathers; go down into Egypt, and bring forth My people." '[4] If you are curious to know what happened after this, you can find out by consulting these same Mosaic writings, for it is impossible to recount everything in this work. What has been written has been here set down to prove that Jesus Christ is the Son of God and His Apostle, being of old the Word, appearing at one time in the form of fire, at another under the guise of incorporeal beings [i. e., as an angel], but now, at the will of God, after becoming man for mankind, He bore all the torments which the demons prompted the rabid Jews to wreak upon Him. Although it is explicitly stated in the Mosaic writings: 'And the Angel of God spoke to

---

1 Isa. 1.3.
2 Matt. 11.27.
3 Luke 10.16.
4 Exod. 3.2,14-15.

Moses in a flame of fire out of the midst of a bush and said, "I AM WHO AM, the God of Abraham, the God of Isaac, and the God of Jacob," [5] the Jews assert that it was the Father and Maker of all things who spoke thus. Hence, the Prophetic Spirit reproaches them, saying: 'Israel hath not known Me, and My people hath not understood Me.'[6] And again, as we have already shown, Jesus, while still in their midst, said: 'No one knows the Father except the Son, nor does anyone know the Son except the Father, and those to whom the Son will reveal Him.'[7] The Jews, therefore, always of the opinion that the Universal Father spoke to Moses, while in fact it was the very Son of God, who is styled both Angel and Apostle, were justly reproached by both the Prophetic Spirit and by Christ Himself, since they knew neither the Father nor the Son. For, they who claim that the Son is the Father are reproached for knowing neither the Father nor that the Father of all has a Son, who, as the First-born Word of God, is also God. He once appeared to Moses and the other prophets in the form of fire and in the guise of an angel, but now in the time of your reign, after He became man by a virgin, as we already stated, by the design of God the Father, to effect the salvation of those believing in Him, He permitted Himself to be an object of contempt and to suffer pain, so that by dying and arising from the dead He might conquer death. But what was proclaimed to Moses from the bush: 'I AM WHO AM, the God of Abraham, and the God of Isaac, and the God of your fathers,'[8] meant that those who had died were still in existence, and belonged to Christ Himself. For they were the first of all to occupy themselves in searching for

---

5 *Ibid.*
6 Isa. 1.3.
7 Matt. 11.27.
8 Exod. 3.14-15.

God; Abraham being the father of Isaac, and Isaac the father of Jacob, as was written by Moses.

Chapter 64

From what has already been stated you can readily perceive how the demons, imitating what Moses said, instigated men to erect at the fountain-heads a statue of her who was called Kore,[1] and claimed that she was the daugther of Jupiter. For, as we stated previously, Moses said: 'In the beginning God created heaven and earth. And the earth was invisible and empty, and the Spirit of God moved over the waters.'[2] In imitation of the Spirit of God who was said to be borne over the waters, therefore, they [the demons] said that Kore was the daughter of Jupiter. They likewise viciously affirmed that Minerva was the daughter of Jupiter, not by sexual union, but, well knowing that God conceived and created the world by the Word, they state that Minerva was the first conception; which we consider most ridiculous, to present the female form as the image of conception. Their deeds likewise condemn the others who are called sons of Jupiter.

Chapter 65

After thus baptizing the one who has believed and given his assent, we escort him to the place where are assembled those whom we call brethren, to offer up sincere prayers in common for ourselves, for the baptized person, and for all other persons wherever they may be, in order that, since we have found the truth, we may be deemed fit through our actions to be esteemed as good citizens and observers of

---

1 *Cora,* maiden or daughter, i.e., Proserpine.
2 Gen. 1.1-3.

the law, and thus attain eternal salvation. At the conclusion of the prayers we greet one another with a kiss.[1] Then, bread and a chalice containing wine mixed with water[2] are presented to the one presiding over the brethren. He takes them and offers praise and glory to the Father of all, through the name of the Son and of the Holy Spirit, and he recites lengthy prayers of thanksgiving to God in the name of those to whom He granted such favors. At the end of these prayers and thanksgiving, all present express their approval by saying 'Amen.' This Hebrew word, 'Amen,' means 'So be it.' And when he who presides has celebrated the Eucharist, they whom we call deacons permit each one present to partake of the Eucharistic bread, and wine and water; and they carry it also to the absentees.[3]

Chapter 66

We call this food the Eucharist, of which only he can partake who has acknowledged the truth of our teachings, who has been cleansed by baptism for the remission of his sins and for his regeneration, and who regulates his life upon the principles laid down by Christ. Not as ordinary bread or as ordinary drink do we partake of them, but just as, through the word of God, our Savior Jesus Christ became Incarnate and took upon Himself flesh and blood for our salvation, so, we have been taught, the food which has been

---

[1] The pagans, who misinterpreted the kiss of peace, must not have realized that it was a form of greeting confined to persons of the same sex.

[2] *Potérion húdatos kaì krámatos*, a chalice of water and wine mixed with water. It seems, however, that *kráma* is here used as a synonym for wine.

[3] Maran (*PG* 6.427) points out that, although Justin wrote his *Apology* at Rome he describes the Eucharist according to the rite of the Eastern Church rather than of the Western Church. For instance, in the Western Church the kiss of peace immediately preceded communion and the deacons distributed only the chalice.

made the Eucharist by the prayer of His word,[1] and which nourishes our flesh and blood by assimilation, is both the flesh and blood of that Jesus who was made flesh. The Apostles in their memoirs, which are called Gospels, have handed down what Jesus ordered them to do; that He took bread and, after giving thanks, said: 'Do this in remembrance of Me; this is My body.' In like manner, He took also the chalice, gave thanks, and said: 'This is My blood';[2] and to them only did He give it. The evil demons, in imitation of this, ordered the same thing to be performed in the Mithraic mysteries.[3] For, as you know or may easily learn, bread and a cup of water, together with certain incantations, are used in their mystic initiation rites.

Chapter 67

Henceforward, we constantly remind one another of these things. The rich among us come to the aid of the poor, and we always stay together. For all the favors we enjoy we bless the Creator of all, through His Son Jesus Christ and through the Holy Spirit. On the day which is called Sunday we have a common assembly of all who live in the cities or in the outlying districts, and the memoirs of the Apostles or the writings of the Prophets are read, as long as there is time. Then, when the reader has finished, the president of the assembly verbally admonishes and invites all to imitate such

---

1 *Di' euchḗs lógou toû par' autoû*: by the prayer of His word. The word *lógou* does not refer to the Word of God, but to the words of Christ—the words of consecration: 'This is My Body; this is My Blood.' Indeed, Justin quotes these words of Christ to prove to the pagans why Christians believe that the bread and wine become the Body and Blood of Christ.
2 Cf. Luke 22.19; Matt. 26.26-27; Mark 14.22.
3 Cf. Tertullian, *De praesc. haer.* 40. The worship of the Persian sun-god became popular during the reign of Hadrian (A.D. 117-138). Julian the Apostate made Mithras his god.

examples of virtue. Then we all stand up together and offer up our prayers, and, as we said before, after we finish our prayers, bread and wine and water are presented. He who presides likewise offers up prayers and thanksgivings, to the best of his ability, and the people express their approval by saying 'Amen.' The Eucharistic elements are distributed and consumed by those present, and to those who are absent they are sent through the deacons. The wealthy, if they wish, contribute whatever they desire, and the collection is placed in the custody of the president. [With it] he helps the orphans and widows, those who are needy because of sickness or any other reason, and the captives and strangers in our midst; in short, he takes care of all those in need. Sunday, indeed, is the day on which we all hold our common assembly because it is the first day on which God, transforming the darkness and [prime] matter, created the world;[1] and our Savior Jesus Christ arose from the dead on the same day. For they crucified Him on the day before that of Saturn, and on the day after, which is Sunday, He appeared to His Apostles and disciples, and taught them the things which we have passed on to you also for consideration.

Chapter 68

If you think our statements are in accordance with reason and truth, respect them; if they seem silly, despise them as such. But do not impose the death penalty against those who have done no wrong, as you would against your enemies. For, we forewarn you that you shall not elude the future judgment of God, if you continue to be unjust; and we will exclaim: 'Let God's will be done.' Although on the basis of the letter of the greatest and most illustrious Emperor Adrian,

---
1 Cf. Ch. 10, n.1.

your father, we could have asked that you command judgment to be made according to our petition, yet, not because of Adrian's decree, but because we know what we ask is just, have we appealed to you with this address and explanation. We have appended a copy of Adrian's letter that you may see that even in this matter we speak the truth. This is the copy:

[Chapter 69][1]

I received the letter sent to me by your most illustrious predecessor, Serenius Granianus. It does not seem to me that this report can be passed over without an investigation, lest [blameless] persons be upset and false accusers be given an opportunity to engage in their wicked practices. If, therefore, the subjects of your province can back up their complaint against the Christians, so as to accuse them in court, I do not object to their doing so, but I cannot allow them to proceed solely by noisy demands and shouts.[2] It is far more appropriate, if anyone wishes to make an accusation, that you decide [the question]. So, if anyone accuses the Christians and proves that they broke the law, you must assign the punishment in accordance with the gravity of the crime. On the other hand, by Hercules, be very careful that, if anyone shall accuse these persons [the Christians] merely to calumniate them, you arrest him for villainy and inflict penalties against his guilt.

---

1 The famous Rescript of Hadrian to Minucius Fundanus, the Proconsul of Asia. Eusebius (*Hist. eccl.* 4.8) states that Justin presented to the Antonines a copy of the original Latin letter, which Eusebius himself translated into Greek. Rufinus has preserved the original Latin form.

2 *Axiósesin* . . . . *boats,* an allusion to the popular cry in the theatres: *Christianos ad leonem.* Cf. Tertullian, *Apol.* 40.

[Chapter 70][1]

The Emperor Caesar Titus Aelius Adrianus Antoninus Augustus Pius, Supreme Pontiff, in the fifteenth year of his Tribuneship, the third time Consul, father of his country, to the General Assembly of Asia, greetings. I should have thought that the gods would have seen to it that such persons [the Christians] should not escape. For, if they were able, they would much rather punish those who refuse to worship them. But you plague these people, charging them with atheistic opinions and with other things which we cannot prove. It would be to their advantage to have the reputation of suffering death because of your accusations, and they overwhelm you by being prodigal of their own lives rather than do what you demand of them. Nor is it proper for you to remind me of the earthquakes that have taken place, and are still taking place, for you who lose hope when they do occur should compare your conduct with that of the Christians who are much more trustful in God than you are. At such a time you appear to ignore the gods, you disregard the temples, and you have no understanding of the worship of God. And so you are envious of those who do worship Him, and harass them unto death. Certain other governors of the provinces had written to my father, of sacred memory, concerning these persons. He replied that they should not annoy such persons, unless it was evident that they were plotting against the Roman government. Many have written to me, too, about them, and I have replied to them in the same fashion by following my father's judgment. If, how-

---

1 This letter of Antoninus to the General Assembly of Asia is found in Eusebius (*Hist. eccl.* 4.13), who appeals to Melito of Sardis as authority for its authenticity. In all probability, it was added to Justin's *Apology* by someone else, for Justin makes no mention of it; furthermore, had he known of its existence, he certainly would have used it in his appeal to Antoninus, instead of the letter of Hadrian.

ever, anyone has a charge to bring against a person of this class, merely because he is such, let the accused be absolved of the charge, even if it is clear that he was one of the class; but the accuser shall pay the penalty.

[Chapter 71][1]

The Emperor Caesar Marcus Aurelius Antoninus Germanicus Parthicus Sarmaticus, to the people and the Sacred Senate of Rome, salutation: I have informed you of my grand plan, and what results I achieved at the border of Germany, when, with resultant toil and suffering, I was hemmed in by the enemy and bottled up in the city of Carnutum by seventy-four enemy regiments, about nine miles away. When these forces were so near at hand, both the scouts and our general Pompeianus told us what we already knew, namely, that the enemy had massed nearby a mixed throng of 977,000 soldiers (and I was shut up by this huge savage mob, while I had only a mixed regiment made up of part of the first, tenth, double and marine legions). When I compared myself and my troops with the vast number of the barbaric enemy troops, I hastened to beseech our country's gods in prayer. When I received no reply from them and when I perceived how far my power had been reduced, I summoned those whom we call Christians. On investigation, I discovered how vast was their number, and I then boiled with rage against them, which was not proper, as I later realized when I perceived their power. They do not begin by preparing their weapons, or shields, or trumpets, for this is hateful to them because of the God they bear in their conscience. Thus, very probably, they whom we consider atheists have God freely enclosed in

---

1 This letter of the Emperor Marcus to the Senate was also added later by someone else, for Justin had already suffered martyrdom before the events described in the letter took place.

their conscience. Falling to the ground, they prayed not only for me, but for the whole standing army, that they might be relieved of the present thirst and famine. We had not taken water for five days, because none could be obtained; we were in the midst of Germany, on enemy soil. As soon as they fell to the ground and prayed to God, whom I knew not, rain fell from the heavens; upon us it was most cool, but upon the enemies of Rome it was a hail of fire. And immediately after this prayer was felt the presence of God, as of One invincible and indestructible. Because of this, let us permit such persons to be Christians, lest by their prayers they acquire a similar weapon against us. I therefore decree that such a person shall not be accused simply because he is a Christian. But, if anyone be found to accuse a Christian of being a Christian, I want it made clear that he who is charged with being a Christian, and admits that he is one, is accused of nothing other than this, that he is a Christian; but the accuser shall be burnt alive. Nor shall the Governor of the province compel the Christian who confesses and shows he is a Christian to retract; neither shall he imprison him. I desire that these regulations be confirmed by a decree of the Senate, also, and, in order that it might be read, I command this edict of mine to be displayed in the Forum of Trajan. Vitrasius Pollio, the Prefect, will see to it that a copy be sent to all the surrounding provinces, and that no one who desires to use and possess a copy be prevented from obtaining it from the documents which I now make public.

THE SECOND APOLOGY

INTRODUCTION

EUSEBIUS in his *Ecclesiastical History*[1] states that Justin's *Second Apology* was addressed to Marcus Aurelius when he was sole emperor (169-180). But modern critics assign both apologies to the latter part of the reign of Antoninus Pius (i.e., 147-161), and some conjecture that its addressees are the same as those of the *First Apology*.[2]

The *Second Apology* came down to us in two manuscripts,[3] in which it precedes the *First Apology*. In the original Greek edition[4] as well as in the first Latin translation[5] this sequence is preserved. However, it was pointed out above[6] that the second followed the first, not as an appendix but as an independent petition, although it may have been written only shortly after the first. This would place its composition between 155 and 160, at Rome.

This short address of fifteen chapters was provoked through the execution of three Christians by Urbicus, the prefect of Rome. Because they had been condemned to death *only* because they were Christians, Justin opens his address by accusing the Romans of injustice.

---

1 4.15.18.
2 Cf. below, p. 121 nn.2 and 3.
3 Cf. above, p. 26 n. 15.
4 Cf. above, p. 26 n.16.
5 Cf, above, p. 26 n.17.
6 Cf. above, p. 25f.

Then he goes on to answer these two sarcastic questions: (1) If the Christians desire so earnestly to see God, why do they not commit suicide and save their enemies the trouble of killing them? (2) If their God has the power to help Christians, why does He permit their enemies to oppress and punish them?

In answer to the first query, Justin explains that man is not master of his own life. In replying to the second question, he shows that the persecution of the Christians is due not only to man's free will, but also, and this especially, to the hatred of the demons. After proving the superiority of Christianity over paganism, Justin brings the Apology to a close by exhorting the rulers to show justice in their treatment of Christians.

The reader will do well in reading the introduction to the *First Apology* and consult the *Select Bibliography* on page 27 of this volume.

CONTENTS

Chapter		Page
1	Preface	119
2	Three Christians executed by Urbicus	120
3	Crescens the Cynic	122
4	The reasons why Christians do not commit suicide	123
5	The bad angels	124
6	The meaning of the Divine Names	125
7	Christians are the cause of the preservation of the universe	126
8	Participation in the Word a cause of persecution	127
9	Eeternal punishment by fire	128
10	Christ the Logos	129
11	Vice and virtue	130
12	The Christians' attitude toward death proves their innocence	132
13	The seminal word	133
14	A request that the petition be published	134
15	Conclusion	134

THE SECOND APOLOGY OF JUSTIN TO THE ROMAN SENATE IN BEHALF OF THE CHRISTIANS

Chapter 1

THE THINGS that have lately[1] taken place in your city under Urbicus,[2] and the evil deeds that are likewise being perpetrated without reason by your governors, have forced me to compose this address for you Romans who are men of feelings like ours and are our bethren,[3] even though you fail to realize it or refuse to admit it because of your pride in your so-called dignities. Everywhere, indeed, whoever is chastened by father, or neighbor, or child, or friend, or brother, or husband, or wife for any shortcoming, such as being stubborn, and pleasure-loving, and difficult to urge to good (except those who believe that the wicked and sensual shall suffer the punishment of eternal fire, but that the virtuous and Christ-like, *i. e.*, those who have become Christians, shall live with God free from all pain)—these and the wicked demons who hate us so, and have as their slaves and worshippers such men as the above-mentioned judges, compel them, like rulers under demoniacal influence, to put us to death. That you may clearly understand the reason for all that took place under Urbicus I will now tell you just what happened.

1 *Kaì tà chthès dè kaì próen*: 'both yesterday and the day before,' a Homeric expression.
2 Urbicus was consul and prefect of Rome under the Emperor Antoninus Pius.
3 Tertullian (*Apol.* 39) aptly expressed this thought: *Fratres autem etiam vestri sumus, iure naturae matris unius, etsi vos parum homines, quia mali fratres.*

Chapter 2

There was a certain woman who lived with an unchaste husband, and she, too, had once been unchaste. After learning the doctrines of Christ, she became a self-controlled person and she tried to effect a similar change in her husband, explaining the Christian teachings and warning him of the eternal punishment by fire reserved for those who live without chastity or right reason. But by clinging to the same shameful conduct he lost his wife's affections, and she desired a divorce from him because she considered it sinful to live any longer with a husband who sought in every way those means of sensual pleasure contrary to the law of nature and in violation of every right. However, she forced herself to stay with him after her friends convinced her that it was advisable to remain with him in the hope that at some future time he might change his ways. But when her husband went to Alexandria and the report reached her that his conduct was worse than ever, she, in order not to participate in his sinful and impious acts by continuing to live with him by sharing his table and his bed, gave him what you term a bill of divorce[1] and left him. But that gallant and gentlemanly husband—instead of being delighted that those evil actions which she used to commit so recklessly with servants and employees in those days when she took pleasure in drunkenness and every wicked action, she had now discontinued, and wanted him to do the same—when she left him against his will, brought a charge against her, claiming that she was a Christian. And she presented a petition to you, O Emperor, asking that she might be permitted first to set her household affairs in order, and then, after that was done she

---

[1] *Rhepoúdion*: a transliteration of the Latin *repudium*, a bill of repudiation.

would defend herself against the accusation. You gave your permission. When her former husband could not answer her, he thus turned his attack on a certain Ptolemaeus, who had instructed her in Christian doctrine, in the following way. He induced his personal friend, a centurion, to summon Ptolemaeus and ask him just one question: Was he a Christian? And Ptolemaeus, being of a truthful and not deceitful or mendacious nature, confessed that he was a Christian, and was therefore placed in chains by the centurion and mistreated in prison for a long time. At length, when he appeared before Urbicus for judgment, he was again asked this one question: Was he a Christian? And again, being aware of the benefits he had gained through the teaching of Christ, he confessed to be a member of the school of divine virtue. For he who denies anything, either does so because he condemns the thing itself, or he avoids confessing it because he deems himself unworthy of and alien to it; neither of which applies to the true Christian. When Urbicus ordered him to be led away to execution, a certain Lucius, also a Christian, realizing how unreasonable the sentence was, said to Urbicus: 'What is the reason for this sentence? Why have you punished this man who is not an adulterer, or fornicator, or murderer, or thief, or robber, nor in a word convicted of any crime at all, but only confesses that he bears the name of Christian. Your judgment, Urbicus, does not become the Emperor Pius,[2] nor the Philosopher,[3] son of Caesar, nor the sacred Senate.' The only answer he made to Lucius was this: 'You also seem to be one [of this class].' And when Lucius replied, 'I certainly am,' he ordered him also to be led away to execution. And Lucius expressed his thanks, since he knew that he would soon be freed from such evil rulers,

---

2 'To call Marcus Aurelius "Pius" would be utterly unprecedented.' D. C. B. 3.564
3 To give Lucius 'the name of a philosopher would be profoundly meaningless.' Cf. D. C. B. 3.564, where it is argued that the addressees here are the same as those of the *First Apology*.

and would go to the Father and King of Heaven. A third Christian also came forward, and was likewise condemned to punishment.

Chapter 3[1]

I also expect to be the victim of a plot and to be affixed to the stake by those just mentioned, or perhaps even by Crescens,[2] that lover of fanfare and ostentation.[3] For that man does not deserve the name of lover of wisdom, since he accuses us publicly in matters of which he is ignorant, claiming that Christians are atheists and irreligious, and doing this just to please and to gain the support of the deceived mob. If, indeed, he attacks us without studying the teachings of Christ, he is positively wicked, and far worse than illiterate—persons are generally careful not to argue or lie about matters of which they are ignorant. On the other hand, if he has studied them [the teachings of Christ] and has not grasped their grandeur, or, if he has and acts as he does in order not to appear to be a Christian, he is much more vile and evil, because he is then inferior even to a slave in popular and unreasonable opinion and fear. I want you to know that I put certain questions to him on this matter and I learned most assuredly that he truly knows nothing. And to show that I speak the truth, I am prepared, if our debate has not already been reported to you, to repeat it in your presence. Such a permission would be an act worthy of a royal ruler.

---

1 In the Mss., this chapter is found after the end of Chapter 8, but Maran inserted it here because that is how it is found in Eusebius, and because it fits in better.
2 The Cynic philosopher who was Justin's most bitter enemy.
3 Justin here plays with the words *philopsóphou*, and *philokómpou*, which sound so much like *philosóphou*, but are so different in meaning.

But if my questions and his replies were brought to your attention, it is evident to you that he knows nothing of our teachings, or, if he does know them, but, through fear of his hearers, dares not utter them, as Socrates would have, then he proves himself to be, as I said before, not a lover of wisdom, but a lover of false opinions,[4] who disregards that praiseworthy saying of Socrates: 'But no man must be honored before the truth.'[5] However, it is impossible for a Cynic like Crescens, who considers the last end to be indifferent, to recognize any good but indifference.

Chapter 4

Lest any one should say to us, 'All of you, go, kill yourselves and thus go immediately to God, and save us the trouble,' I will explain why we do not do that, and why, when interrogated, we boldly acknowledge our faith. We have been taught that God did not create the world without a purpose, but that He did so for the sake of mankind; for we have stated before[1] that God is pleased with those who imitate His perfections, but is displeased with those who choose evil, either in word or in deed. If, then, we should all kill ourselves we would be the cause, as far as it is up to us, why no one would be born and be instructed in the divine doctrines, or even why the human race might cease to exist; if we do act thus, we ourselves will be opposing the will of God. But when we are interrogated we do not deny our faith, for we are not conscious of having done any wrong, but we do consider it ungodly always not to tell the truth, which we also realize is pleasing to God; and we also now want to free you from an unfair prejudice.

---

4 Another play on the words *philósophos* and *philódoxos*.
5 Cf. Plato, *Republic* 10.595C.

1 Cf..1 *Apol.* 10.

Chapter 5

But if anyone should think that, if we profess God to be our protector, we should not, as we admit, be overpowered and molested by unjust persons[1]—this difficulty, too, I will remove. When God made the universe and put all earthly things under man's dominion, and arranged the heavenly bodies for the increase of fruits and the change of seasons, and decreed a divine law for these, which He apparently also created for man's sake, He appointed His angels, whom He placed over mankind, to look after men and all things under heaven. But the angels violated their charge, fell into sin with women and begot children who are called demons.[2] Moreover, they subsequently subjected the human race to themselves, partly by magic writings, partly by the fear they instilled into them and the punishments they inflicted upon them, and partly by instructing them in the use of sacrifices, incense, and libations, which they really needed after becoming slaves of their lustful passions; and among men they engendered murders, wars, adulteries, all sorts of dissipation, and every species of sin. Thus it was that the poets and writers of legends, unaware that the bad angels and the demons begotten *by* them did those things to men and women, to cities and nations, ascribed them to [their] god himself [Jupiter] and to those whom they thought were sons of his seed and to the children of those whom they called his brothers, Neptune and Pluto, and to the children of their children. For they

---

1 Clemens Alex. (*Stromata*, 4.11.82) stated that this was a favorite pagan retort. Cf. also Arnobius, *Adv. nat.* 2.76; Minucius Felix, *Oct.* 12; Lactantius, *Inst. div.* 5.21.
2 Cf. 1 *Apol.* 5: Tertullian, *Apol.* 22.

called them by the name each of the bad angels had bestowed upon himself and his children.³

Chapter 6

No proper name has been bestowed upon God, the Father of all, since He is unbegotten. For, whoever has a proper name received it from a person older than himself. The words Father, and God, and Creator, and Lord, and Master are not real names, but rather terms of address derived from His beneficent deeds. But His Son, who alone is properly called Son, the Word, who was with Him [God, the Father] and was begotten¹ before all things, when in the beginning He [God, the Father] created and arranged all things through Him [the Son], is called Christ, because He was anointed and because God the Father arranged all the things of creation through Him. This name also has an unknown meaning, just as the term 'God,' which is not a real name, but the expression of man's innate² opinion of a thing that can scarcely be defined. But 'Jesus,'³ which is His name both as Man and Savior, has a meaning. For He also became man, as we stated,⁴ and was born in accordance with the will of God the Father for the benefit of believers, and for the defeat of the demons. Even now, your own eyes will teach you the truth of this last statement. For many demoniacs

---

3 In 1 *Apol.* 5, Justin said the demons chose their own names; here the bad angels, their parents, choose their names. Perhaps in the first Apology Justin uses the word *daimones* for *ággeloi*, but here the *daimones* are the children of the *ággeloi*. Cf. Tertullian, *Apol.* 22; Athenagoras, *Suppl.* 25.

1 Although Justin speaks of the generation of the Son at the creation of the world, this does not detract from the eternity of the Son, for he states that the Son was with the Father before the creation of the world. Cf. Maran (*PG* 6.453).

2 Tertullian expressed the same thought with those famous words: *O testimonium animae naturaliter Christianae* (*Apol.* 17).

3 Justin understood this difference between the names 'Christ' and 'Jesus': the former belonged to the Word before the Incarnation; the latter, after the Incarnation.

4 1 *Apol.* 23 and 33.

throughout the entire world, and even in your own city, were exorcised by many of our Christians in the name of Jesus Christ, who was crucified under Pontius Pilate; and our men cured them, and they still cure others by rendering helpless and dispelling the demons who had taken possession of these men, even when they could not be cured by all the other exorcists, and exploiters of incantations and drugs.

Chapter 7

Therefore God postpones[1] the collapse and dissolution of the universe (through which the bad angels, the demons, and men would cease to exist),[2] because of the Christian seed, which He knows to be the cause in nature [of the world's preservation]. If such were not the case, it would be impossible for you to do the things you do and be influenced by the evil demons; but the fire of judgment would descend and would completely dissolve everything, just as the flood waters once left no one but him, with his family, whom we call Noe and you call Deucalion, from whom in turn so many have been born, some of them bad, others good. In this manner, we claim that the world will finally be destroyed by fire, and not, as the Stoics believe,[3] because all things change into one another according to their disgraceful doctrine of metamorphosis. Nor do we teach [as do the Stoics] that men act and suffer according to the dictates of fate, but that by his own free will each man acts either well or evilly; and that through the influence of evil demons good men, such as Socrates and the like, are persecuted and imprisoned,

---

1 Cf. 1 *Apol.* 28 and 45; *Dialogue* 39; *Letter to Diognetus* 6.
2 Justin would indicate here the annihilation of power rather than of existence.
3 The Stoics considered the final destruction of the world by fire as a natural consumption, not as a punishment for sin.

while Sardanapalus, Epicurus, and the like seem to be endowed with wealth and glory. But the Stoics, ignorant of this demoniacal influence, claimed that everything takes place by the necessity of fate. But, since God from the very beginning created the race of angels and men with free will, they will justly pay the penalty in everlasting fire for the sins they have committed. Indeed, every creature is capable, by nature, of vice and of virtue. Nor would any action of theirs be worthy of praise unless they had the power to incline to either [vice or virtue]. The truth of this is shown everywhere by those legislators and philosophers who, acting according to right reason, have ordered some things to be done and others to be avoided. The Stoic philosophers also, in their moral teaching, always respect the same principles, so it is easily seen how wrong they are in their teaching on principles and incorporeal beings. For, if they state that human acts occur by fate, they will admit either that God is nothing else than those things which continually turn and change and dissolve into the same elements, and will seem to understand only corruptible things, and to affirm that God himself both in part and in whole is in every sin; or else that neither vice nor virtue is anything—which is against every sound idea, reason, and mind.

Chapter 8

We know that the followers of the Stoic teaching, because they were praiseworthy at least in their ethics, as were also the poets in some respects, because of the seed of reason implanted in all mankind, were hated and killed. As examples, we could mention Heraclitus,[1] as we already stated, and

---

[1] It is said that Heraclitus was not killed, but died as a result of his own treatment for dropsy.

Musonius,[1] of our own times, and others. For, as we pointed out, the demons always brought it about that everyone, who strives in any way to live according to right reason and to avoid evil, be an object of hatred. Nor is it surprising that the demons are proved to be the cause why they are much more hated who do not live[2] according to only a part of the seminal word, but by the knowledge and consideration of the whole Word, which is Christ. But these demons shall suffer just punishment and torments, confined to everlasting fire; for the fact that they are overcome even now by men in the name of Jesus Christ is a sign that they and their followers will be punished in eternal fire. All the prophets foretold that it would happen thus, and so taught Jesus, our Teacher.

Chapter 9

Lest any one repeat the mistake of those so-called philosophers who claim that our statements that the sinners are punished in everlasting fire are just boastful words calculated to instill terror, and that we want men to live a virtuous life through fear, and not because such a life is pleasant, I will make this brief reply that, if it is not as we say, then there is no God; or, if there is a God, He is not concerned with men, and virtue and vice are nothing, and, as we already stated, legislators unjustly punish the transgressors of their excellent precepts. But, since these legislators are not unjust, and their Father instructs them through the Word to do as

---

[1] There were many who bore this name in ancient times, and it is not clear which one Justin had in mind.
[2] *Katà spermatikoũ*: the negative particle *ou* must be inserted before this phrase to complete the sense.

He Himself does,[1] they who comply with these legislators are not unjust. If anyone should advance the remonstrance that human laws are different, and say that some men consider one thing good, another bad, while other men deem as good what the former considered bad, and as bad what they thought good, let him listen to this reply. We realize that the bad angels made laws suited to their own iniquity, which are pleasing to their counterparts among men; and the true Word, at His coming, proved that not all opinions and teachings are good, but that some are bad, and others good. Wherefore, I will repeat the same statements and utter similar ones to such men as these, and, if necessary, I shall develop them more at length.[2] But for the present I must return to my subject.

Chapter 10

Beyond doubt, therefore, our teachings are more noble than all human teaching, because Christ, who appeared on earth for our sakes, became the whole Logos, namely, Logos and body and soul.[1] Everything that the philosophers and legislators discovered and expressed well, they accomplished through their discovery and contemplation of some part of the Logos. But, since they did not have a full knowledge of the Logos, which is Christ, they often contradicted themselves. And those who were born before Christ assumed human nature were dragged into law courts as irreligious and med-

---

1 Cf. Tertullian, *Apol.* 45; St. Augustine, *De lib. arbit.* 1.15.
2 The meaning is this: Since legislators order some things to be done and others to be avoided, and since God, as Legislator, has given us a law, then it follows that man has free will either to obey or disobey the law, and the disobedient are unjust.

---

1 St. Augustine, *Sermo* 214.7, thus expressed this thought: *Totus Filius Dei Verbum et homo, atque, ut expressius dicam, Verbum, anima et caro.*

dling persons, when they tried in human narrowness to think out and prove things by reason. Socrates, the most ardent of all in this regard, was accused of the very crimes that are imputed to us. They claimed that he introduced new deities[2] and rejected the state-sponsored gods. But what he did was to ostracize Homer[3] and the other poets, and to instruct men to expel the evil demons and those who perpetrated the deeds narrated by the poets; and to exhort men by meditation to learn more about God who was unknown to them, saying: 'It is not an easy matter to find the Father and Creator of all things, nor, when He is found, is it safe to announce Him to all men.'[4] Yet, our Christ did all this through His own power. There was no one who believed so much in Socrates as to die for his teaching, but not only philosophers and scholars believed in Christ, of whom even Socrates had a vague knowledge (for He was and is the Logos who is in every person, and who predicted things to come first through the prophets and then in person when He assumed our human nature and feelings, and taught us these doctrines), but also workmen and men wholly uneducated, who all scorned glory, and fear, and death. Indeed, this is brought about by the power of the ineffable Father, and not through the instrumentality of human reason.

Chapter 11

Neither should we Christians be put to death, nor would evil men and demons prevail over us, were it not for the fact that absolutely every man who is born must also, by reason of a

---
2 Cf. Plato, *Apol.* Ch. 14.
3 This whole statement was taken from Plato, *Republic* 2.377 ff. and 10. 595 ff.
4 A loose quotation from Plato, *Tim.* 28C. Cf. also Origen, *Contra Celsum* 7.42.

debt, be subject to death. Thus, when we liquidate this debt, we render thanks. Now, for the sake of Crescens and those who rant like him, we deem it proper and fitting to relate here what Xenophon wrote.[1] Hercules, relates Xenophon, once came to a place where three roads met, and there he found Virtue and Vice, who appeared to him in the guise of women. And Vice, in a costly and seductive dress, with an expression made alluring by such adornments, and being instantly fascinating to look at, said to Hercules that, if he would follow her, she would see to it that his whole life would be one of pleasure and that he would be arrayed in the most brilliant finery, such as she herself was then wearing. And Virtue, who was loathsome in appearance and dress, said: 'If you will obey me, you will be adorned, not with passing and perishable ornaments or beauty, but with everlasting and precious adornments.' Indeed, we believe that the one who avoids what only appears to be good and strives for what is considered difficult and unreasonable, will attain happiness. For Vice, to disguise her own actions, appropriated the qualities of Virtue which really are excellent, by imitating what is incorruptible (for Vice neither possesses nor is able to effect incorruptibility) and enslaves low-minded men, attributing her own evil habits to Virtue. But, those who have understood the things that really are good are also unspoiled in virtue. Such persons, every intelligent man should conclude, were the Christians, the athletes, and those who performed the deeds which the poets narrate of the so-called gods;[2] and this conclusion should be drawn from the fact that we Christians scorn escaping from death.

---

1 Xenophon (*Men.* 2.1.21ff.) gives Prodicus credit for this fictitious story.
2 E.g., Hercules, who is said to have scorned death.

Chapter 12

Indeed, when I myself revelled in the teachings of Plato, and heard the Christians misrepresented and watched them stand fearless in the face of death and of every other thing that was considered dreadful, I realized the impossibility of their living in sinful pleasure. For, what sensual or self-indulgent person, who approves of the eating of human flesh,[1] would welcome death that he might be despoiled of his pleasures, and would not rather always try to continue in his present manner of life, and to elude the public officers; and much less would he be apt to denounce himself when the penalty was death? The evil demons have caused these things also to be effected by wicked men. For, after inflicting the death penalty on some because of the false charges lodged against us, they subjected our servants, some of them children and women, to torture, and forced from them by these terrible torments a confession of those fictitious crimes which they themselves publicly commit. But we are not in the least concerned about such crimes, since we do not commit them, having as witness of our thoughts and actions the Unbegotten and Ineffable God. For why did we not acknowledge that we consider these things good, and show how they are divine philosophy, affirming that the mysteries of Saturn[2] have in homicide and in drinking blood the same effect as what you do before the idol[3] you venerate, on which you sprinkle not only the blood of brute animals, but also of men, making a libation of the slain man's blood through the most distinguished and most noble person in your midst? And by imitating

---

[1] An allusion to a favorite pagan accusation against the Christians, which was that of anthropophagy. Cf. 1 *Apol.* 26 n. 6.
[2] The favorite victims of the Phoenician Saturn were boys. Cf. Lactantius, *Inst. div.* 1.21; Tertullian, *Apol.* 9.
[3] The idol of Jupiter Latiaris. Cf. Tertullian, *Apol.* 9.

Jupiter and the other gods in sodomy and sinful relations with women, might they not, in defense of their actions, cite the writings of Epicurus and the poets? But, because we persuade men to avoid such customs and those who practice them, together with their imitators, as we now have striven hard to persuade you with these words, we are assailed in many ways. But we are not in the least worried, for we realize that God is the just supervisor of all. Would that even now some man would ascend a lofty platform and cry out in a loud voice:[4] 'Be ashamed and blush, you who accuse the innocent of the very crimes you yourselves openly commit; and things of which you and your gods are guilty, you charge to those persons who have not the slightest part in them. Change your ways, and come to your senses.'

Chapter 13

When I learned of the evil camouflage which the wicked demons had thrown around the divine doctrines of the Christians to deter others from following them, I had to laugh at the authors of these lies, at the camouflage itself, and at the popular reaction. I am proud to say that I strove with all my might to be known as a Christian, not because the teachings of Plato are different from those of Christ, but because they are not in every way similar; neither are those of other writers, the Stoics, the poets, and the historians. For each one of them, seeing, through his participation of the seminal Divine Word, what was related to it, spoke very well. But, they who contradict themselves in important matters evidently did not acquire the unseen [that is, heavenly] wisdom and the indisputable knowledge. The truths which

---
4 Tragic voice, i.e., the loud voice employed in the recitation, through a mask, of Greek tragedies.

men in all lands have rightly spoken belong to us Christians. For we worship and love, after God the Father, the Word who is from the Unbegotten and Ineffable God, since He even became Man for us, so that by sharing in our sufferings He also might heal us. Indeed, all writers, by means of the engrafted seed of the Word which was implanted in them, had a dim glimpse of the truth. For the seed of something and its imitation, given in proportion to one's capacity, is one thing, but the thing itself, which is shared and imitated according to His grace, is quite another.

Chapter 14

We therefore beseech you to publish this pronouncement, adding your comment to it, so that others may know our customs and be released from the bonds of false beliefs and of ignorance of good; for by their own fault they have become worthy of punishment. Promulgate these words, too, in order that these truths may be made public for all men, because by nature man can know good and evil; and because by denouncing us, of whom they do not know whether they really do such disgraceful things as they pretend, and because they revel in their gods who committed such actions themselves and still permit mankind to commit them, and because by punishing us with death or chains or some such penalty, as if we committed such actions, they so condemn themselves that other judges are not needed.

Chapter 15

[Concerning my countryman[1] Simon Magus, I looked with utter disdain upon his impious and deceitful teachings.]

---

1 Both were from Samaria.

If you will only approve this writing, we will expose him in the eyes of all, so that, if at all possible, they may be converted. For this purpose only have we written these words. After a just deliberation you will find that our teachings are not disgraceful, but are more sublime than all human wisdom. If you do not think them so, at least they bear no resemblance to the teachings of the Sotadists,[2] the Philaenidians,[3] the Archestratians, the Epicureans, and other such doctrines of the poets, with which everyone can familiarize himself, both by hearing them as they are recited and reading them. And now, having done the best we could, we conclude with a prayer that the men of every land be deemed fit to receive the truth. And may you also, as befits your piety and wisdom, judge the case with justice for your own sakes.[4]

---
2 Sotades (from Trace or Crete) gained much fame from his obscene poetry in the third century B.C. Cf. Strabo, *Geogr.* 14.573.
3 The followers of the poetess Philaenis, the composer of a popular textbook on poetry.
4 Cf. Tertullian, *Ad Scap.* 1: *Itaque hunc libellum non nobis timentes misimus, sed vobis et omnibus inimicis nostris.*

THE DIALOGUE
WITH TRYPHO

INTRODUCTION

JUSTIN's *Dialogue with Trypho* has come down to us through the Codex Paris. gr. 450 (of the year 1364), not, however, without some lacunae: one in the introduction, the other in Chapter 74. The missing part of the introduction would have probably told us of the dedication of this work to Marcus Pompeius, who is addressed in Chapter 141, and alluded to in Chapter 8.

The *Dialogue* reports a discussion that took place at Ephesus between Justin and the Jew Trypho, shortly after the end of the war (*ca.* 135) instigated by Bar Kocheba, the Jewish rebel, against the Roman power. While the details of the discussion may be fictitious, the broad outline appears to have been founded in fact. Very little is known about Justin's opponent, Trypho.[1] He was probably a Jewish refugee who fled from Palestine to Ephesus during Bar Kocheba's uprising. Considerable doubt has been cast upon the supposition that he is to be identified with Tarphon, the famous Palestinian Rabbi.

The *Dialogue* which Justin composed at Rome years after[2] the actual debate (i. e., sometime between 155 and 161), is really a defense of Christianity against Judaism. Since the debate lasted two days, an artificial division of the treatise would be into two parts: the first (Chs. 1-74) would correspond to the first day, and the second (Chs. 75-142) to the second day. A more natural and logical division[3] of the 142 chapters would be into five sections: (1) *Introduction* (1-8), in which Justin, after describing his own education

---
1 Cf. p. 12 n. 19.
2 Cf. *Dial. w. Tr.* 80, p. 276
3 Critics disagree about the literary and logical merits of the exposition in Justin's *Dialogue.* Cf. K. Hubik, *loc. cit.* and W. Bousset, "Jüdisch— christlicher Schulbetrieb in Alexandria und Rom.' *Forschungen zur Religion.* N. F. Heft 6 (Göttingen 1915).

and eventual conversion to Christianity, sets the limits of the debate; (2) *Part* I (9-47), which explains why Christians do not observe the Mosaic Law; (3) *Part* II (48-108), which produces arguments to show that Christ is the true Messiah; (4) *Part* III (109-141), which draws the logical conclusion that the Christians are the true heirs of the divine promises; (5) *Conclusion* (142), in which Trypho wishes Justin a happy voyage to Rome and Justin, in turn, expresses the hope that Trypho and his friends will one day believe that Jesus Christ is the true Messiah.

The text used for this translation is that of Migne, *PG* 6.471-800, together with the edition of G.Archambault, *Justin, Dialogue avec Tryphon* (2 vols. Paris 1909).

SELECT BIBLIOGRAPHY

Secondary Works:

F. Cayré, *Patrologie et Histoire de la Théologie* (3rd ed. Paris 1938).
Ph. Haeuser, *Des Hl. Philosophen und Märtyrers Justinus Dialog mit dem Juden Tryphon* (Bibl.d. Kirchenväter Bd. 33, 1917).
A. Harnack, *Judentum und Judenchristentum in Justins Dialog mit Tryphon* (Leipzig 1913).
R. Hirzel, *Der Dialog* (Leipzig 1895).
W. Muenscher, *An Dialogus cum Tryphone Justino Martyri recte adscribatur* (Marburg 1799).
A. Lukeyn Williams, *The Dialogue with Trypho* (London 1930).
Th. Zahn, 'Dichtung und Wahrheit in Justins Dialog mit dem Juden Tryphon, *Zeitschrift für Kirchengeschichte* 8 (1885-1886) 37-66.
O. Zöckler, *Der Dialog im Dienste der Apologetik* (Gütersloh 1893).

CONTENTS

Chapter		Page
1	Justin meets Trypho	147
2	Justin describes his philosophical studies	149
3	The beginning of Justin's conversion	151
4	The soul of its own power unable to see God	153
5	The soul is not in itself immortal	156
6	Plato contradicted	158
7	The knowledge of truth can come only from the Prophets	159
8	This conversation enkindles Justin with love for Christ	160
9	The Christians have not believed foolish reports	161
10	Trypho complains that Christians do not observe the Mosaic Law	162
11	The New Testament abrogated the Old Law	163
12	The Jews break the Eternal Law and misinterpret the Mosaic Law	165
13	Isaias teaches remission of sin through the blood of Christ	166
14	Justifications not by Jewish rites but by repentance and baptism	168
15	True fasting	170
16	Circumcision given to Jews as a mark	171
17	Jews spread calumnies everywhere against Christians	173
18	Why Christians do not observe the Mosaic Law	174

19	Origin of circumcision and of the Mosaic Law	175
20	Origin of the law of meats	177
21	Origin of the Sabbath	178
22	Origin of sacrifices and oblations	179
23	Jewish interpretation of the law dishonors God	182
24	Christian circumcision	183
25	The Jews are not true sons of Abraham	184
26	Salvation open to Jews and Gentiles through Christ	186
27	Trypho's objections	187
28	True justification through Christ	189
29	Christians, not Jews, interpret Scriptures properly	190
30	Christian righteousness the true one	191
31	The power of Christ at His second advent	192
32	The two advents of Christ	194
33	The words of Psalm 109 refer to Jesus Christ, not to Ezechias	196
34	The Seventy-first Psalm not to be applied to Solomon but to Jesus Christ	197
35	Heretics strengthen the faith of true believers	200
36	Christ is the Lord of all	202
37	Further proof from other Psalms	203
38	Justin replies to Trypho's charge of blasphemy	204
39	Hatred of Jews for Christians	206
40	Types of Christ in the Mosaic Law	208
41	The offering of flour was a figure of the Eucharist	209
42	The bells on the priestly robes were a figure of the Apostles	210
43	Christ was the end of the Mosaic Law	212
44	Salvation is to be gained through Jesus Christ alone	213
45	Saints of the Old Testament were saved through Christ	214
46	The Mosaic Law is even now useless for salvation	216

47	The difficulty concerning communion with Judaizers	218
48	Trypho demands proof of the Messiahship of Jesus	220
49	John, not Elias, was the precursor of the first advent of Christ	221
50	John the Baptist was foretold by Isaias	223
51	How the above prophecy of Isaias was fulfilled	225
52	The two advents of Christ foretold by Jacob	226
53	Another prophecy of Jacob	227
54	The blood of the grape	229
55	Trypho asks for clear proof of the Divinity of Christ	230
56	God who appeared to Abraham is distinguished from God the Father	231
57	How could God, the Son, have eaten with Abraham?	237
58	Proof from the visions of Jacob	238
59	God, but not the Father, conversed with Moses	241
60	Jewish interpretation of the divine apparition in the burning bush	242
61	The generation of Wisdom from God, the Father	244
62	The expression, 'Let Us Make Man,' agrees with this testimony	245
63	Proof of the Incarnation of God	247
64	Trypho denies that the Jews need Christ	249
65	Trypho objects that God's glory is not given to another	251
66	The virgin-birth foretold by Isaias	253
67	Trypho compares Jesus with Perseus	254
68	Justin accuses the Jews of bad faith	256
69	Pagan fables imitate truth	259
70	The mysteries of Mithras were imitations of prophecies	261

71	The Jews and the Septuagint	262
72	Passages deleted from Esdras and Jeremias . . .	263
73	Further deletions from the sacred text	264
74	Explanation of the ninety-fifth Psalm	266
75	The Divine Name of Jesus	267
76	The Power and Majesty of Christ	268
77	The Prophecy of Isaias refers to Christ and not to Hezekiah	270
78	Christ alone fulfills the Prophecy	271
79	The revolt of the bad angels	274
80	Justin explains his view of the millennium . . .	275
81	The millennium proved by Isaias and St. John . .	277
82	The gifts of prophecy now transferred to the Christians .	278
83	The Psalm, *'Dixit Dominus,'* does not refer to Hezekiah	280
84	The prophecy of Isaias verified in Christ	281
85	Christ is the Lord of Hosts	282
86	The Cross of Christ was prefigured in the Old Testament	285
87	Justin answers another objection by Trypho . . .	286
88	Christ received the Holy Spirit not because He needed Him	288
89	The Crucifixion a stumbling-block to Trypho . .	290
90	The outstretched hands of Moses foreshadowed the Cross	291
91	Other figures of the Cross	292
92	The grace of God needed to understand Scriptures .	294
93	The same virtues are common to all	295
94	How the curse of the crucifixion is to be understood	297
95	Christ assumed our curse	298

96	The curse of the Cross a prediction of what the Jews would do	299
97	Additional predictions of the Cross of Christ	300
98	Christ depicted in the Twenty-First Psalm	301
99-106	Explanation of the Twenty-first Psalm	302
107	The Resurrection foreshadowed by the history of Jonas	314
108	Jews reject the Resurrection of Christ	315
109	The conversion of the Gentiles foretold by Micheas	316
110	How this prophecy of Micheas has been and will be fulfilled	317
111	Figures of the Blood of Christ	319
112	The inept interpretation of the Jews	320
113	Josue a figure of Christ	322
114	Jewish circumcision different from that of Christians	323
115	The prophecy concerning Christians in Zacharias	325
116	Application of this prophecy to Christians	327
117	The prophecy of Malachias concerning sacrifices of the Christians	328
118	Justin exhorts the Jews to repent before the second coming of Christ	329
119	Christians are the holy people promised to Abraham	331
120	Christians were promised to Isaac, Jacob and Juda	332
121	Belief of the Gentiles a proof that Jesus is the Christ	335
122	The Jews mistakenly refer this prophecy to their proselytes	336
123	Jewish interpretations of Scripture are ridiculous	338
124	Christians are truly children of God	340

125	Explanation of the word 'Israel'	341
126	The various Names of Christ	343
127	These scriptural passages apply to the Word	345
128	The Word is a person distinct from the Father	346
129	Further proof that the word is a distinct Person	348
130	Conversion of the Gentiles prophesied	349
131	The Gentile converts more faithful than the Jews	350
132	The power of the Name of Jesus in the Old Testament	352
133	Christians pray for the obstinate Jews	353
134	The marriages of Jacob a figure of the Church	355
135	Jesus Christ is the King of Israel	356
136	The Jews rejected because they crucified Christ	358
137	Justin pleads with the Jews to repent	359
138	Noe a type of Christ	360
139	Noe's blessings were prophecies	361
140	In Christ all men are free	362
141	Men and angels have free will	364
142	Exchange of farewells	365

DIALOGUE WITH TRYPHO

Chapter 1

ONE MORNING as I was walking along a broad avenue,[1] a man, accompanied by some friends, came up to me and said: 'Good morning, Philosopher.' Whereupon, he and his friends walked along beside me.

After returning his greeting, I asked: 'What is the matter? Is there anything special you wish of me?'

He answered: 'Corinthus the Socratic taught me in Argos never to slight or ignore those who wear your garb,[2] but to show them every consideration and to converse with them, since from such a conversation some good might be derived by them or myself. It would be to the advantage of both if either should benefit from this meeting. Accordingly, whenever I see anyone wearing such a robe, I gladly accost him. So, for this same reason, it has been a pleasure to greet you. These friends of mine share my hope of hearing something profitable from you.'

'Who, indeed, are you, most excellent sir?' I asked with a smile.

He did not hesitate to tell me his name and background. 'Trypho,' he said, 'is my name.[3] I am a Hebrew of the cir-

---
[1] Probably in the city of Ephesus. Cf. Eusebius, *Hist eccl.* 4.18.
[2] Philosophers wore a cloak (*pallium*) that was different from the ordinary layman's robe (*toga*).
[3] Some have identified, perhaps erroneously, this Trypho with Tarphon, a famous fanatical Rabbi of Palestine. Cf. *supra* 12 n. 19.

cumcision, a refugee from the recent war,[4] and at present a resident of Greece, especially of Corinth.'

'How,' I asked, 'can you gain as much from philosophy as from your own lawgiver and prophets?'

'Why not,' he replied, 'for do not the philosophers speak always about God? Do they not constantly propose questions about his unity and providence? Is this not the task of philosophy, to inquire about the Divine?'

'Yes, indeed,' I said, 'we, too, are of the same opinion. But the majority of the philosophers have simply neglected to inquire whether there is one or even several gods, and whether or not a divine providence takes care of us, as if this knowledge were unnecessary to our happiness. Moreover, they try to convince us that God takes care of the universe with its genera and species, but not of me and you and of each individual, for otherwise there would be no need of our praying to Him night and day. It is not difficult to see where such reasoning leads them. It imparts a certain immunity and freedom of speech to those who hold these opinions, permitting them to do and to say whatever they please, without any fear of punishment or hope of reward from God. How could it be otherwise, when they claim that things will always be as they are now, and that you and I shall live in the next life just as we are now, neither better nor worse.[5] But there are others[6] who think that the soul is immortal and incorporeal, and therefore conclude that they will not be punished even if they are guilty of sin; for, if the soul is incorporeal, it cannot suffer; if it is immortal, it needs nothing further from God.'

---

4 The revolutionary war instigated by Bar Kocheba in Palestine. It lasted from A.D. 132 to 135, during which time Hadrian captured Jerusalem and slew thousands of Jews.
5 Probably a reference to the teachings of the Fatalist Stoics.
6 I.e., the Platonists.

Then, smiling politely, he said, 'Explain to us just what is your opinion of these matters, and what is your idea of God, and what is your philosophy.'

Chapter 2

'I will explain to you,' I replied, 'my views on this subject. Philosophy is indeed one's greatest possession, and is most precious in the sight of God, to whom it alone leads us and to whom it unites us, and they in truth are holy men who have applied themselves to philosophy. But, many have failed to discover the nature of philosophy, and the reason why it was sent down to men; otherwise, there would not be Platonists, or Stoics, or Peripatetics, or Theoretics,[1] or Pythagoreans, since this science of philosophy is always one and the same. Now, let me tell you why it has at length become so diversified. They who first turned to philosophy, and, as a result, were deemed illustrious men, were succeeded by men who gave no time to the investigation of truth, but, amazed at the courage and self-control of their teachers as well as with the novelty of their teachings, held that to be the truth which each had learned from his own teacher. And they in turn transmitted to their successors such opinions, and others like them, and so they became known by the name of him who was considered the father of the doctrine. When I first desired to contact one of these philosophers, I placed myself under the tutelage of a certain Stoic. After spending some time with him and learning nothing new about God (for my instructor had no knowledge of God, nor did he consider such knowledge necessary), I left him and

---

[1] Possibly the Skeptics, or the name may be used here to indicate a group of philosophers who devoted themselves primarily to speculation and meditation.

turned to a Peripatetic who considered himself an astute teacher. After a few days with him, he demanded that we settle the matter of my tuition fee in such a way that our association would not be unprofitable to him. Accordingly, I left him, because I did not consider him a real philosopher. Since my spirit still yearned to hear the specific and excellent meaning of philosophy, I approached a very famous Pythagorean, who took great pride in his own wisdom. In my interview with him, when I expressed a desire to become his pupil, he asked me, "What? Do you know music, astronomy, and geometry? How do you expect to comprehend any of those things that are conducive to happiness, if you are not first well acquainted with those studies which draw your mind away from objects of the senses and render it fit for the intellectual, in order that it may contemplate what is good and beautiful?" He continued to speak at great length in praise of those sciences, and of the necessity of knowing them, until I admitted that I knew nothing about them; then he dismissed me. As was to be expected, I was downcast to see my hopes shattered, especially since I respected him as a man of considerable knowledge. But, when I reflected on the length of time that I would have to spend on those sciences, I could not make up my mind to wait such a long time. In this troubled state of mind the thought occurred to me to consult the Platonists, whose reputation was great. Thus it happened that I spent as much time as possible in the company of a wise man who was highly esteemed by the Platonists and who had but recently arrived in our city.[2] Under him I forged ahead in philosophy and day by day I improved. The perception of incorporeal things quite overwhelmed me and the Platonic theory of ideas added wings to

---

2 Probably Ephesus. Others think it might be Flavia Neapolis (Nabloûs), city of his birth, or even the city of Alexandria.

my mind,[3] so that in a short time I imagined myself a wise man. So great was my folly that I fully expected immediately to gaze upon God, for this is the goal of Plato's philosophy.'

Chapter 3

'As I was in this frame of mind and desired absolute solitude devoid of human distractions, I used to take myself to a certain spot not far from the sea. One day, as I approached that place with the intention of being alone, a respectable old man, of meek and venerable mien, followed me at a short distance. I stopped, turned quickly, and stared sharply at him.'

' "Do you know me?" he asked.

'I replied that I did not.'

' "Why, therefore," he continued, "do you stare at me so?" '

' "Because," I answered, "I am surprised to find you here. I didn't expect to see anyone here." '

' "I am worried," he said, "about some missing members of my household, and I am therefore looking around with the hope that they may show up somewhere in the vicinity. But what brings you here?" '

' "I take great delight," I answered, "in such walks, where I can converse with myself without hindrance because there is nothing to distract my attention. Places like this are most suitable for philology."[1] '

' "Are you, then, a philologian,[2]" he asked, "rather than a lover of deeds and of truth? Do you not strive to be a

---

[3] A Platonic expression. Cf. *Phaedrus*, 249D.

[1] Justin used the word 'philology' in the sense of an exercise of the reasoning faculty.
[2] The old man, however, employs the term 'philology' to denote skill in the use of words.

practical man rather than a sophist?"

' "But what greater deed," I replied, "could one perform than to prove that reason[3] rules all, and that one who rules reason and is sustained by it can look down upon the errors and undertakings of others, and see that they do nothing reasonable or pleasing to God. Man cannot have prudence without philosophy and straight thinking. Thus, every man should be devoted to philosophy and should consider it the greatest and most noble pursuit; all other pursuits are only of second or third-rate value, unless they are connected with philosophy. Then they are of some value and should be approved; if they are devoid of philosophy and are not connected with it in any way, they then become base and coarse pursuits to those who practise them."

'Interrupting, he asked, "Does philosophy therefore produce happiness?"

' "Absolutely," I replied, "and it alone."

' "Tell me," he asked, "what is philosophy and what is the happiness it engenders, if there is nothing which prevents your speaking."

' "Philosophy," I answered, "is the knowledge of that which exists, and a clear understanding of the truth; and happiness is the reward of such knowledge and understanding."

' "But how do you define God?" he asked.

' "God is the Being who always has the same nature in the same manner, and is the cause of existence to all else," I replied.

'Pleased with my words, he once again asked, "Is not knowledge a word applied commonly to different matters? For, whoever is skilled in any of the arts, for example, in

---

[3] Reason, i.e., in the philosophical sense.

the art of military strategy or of navigation or of medicine, is called skillful. But this is not true in divine and human matters. Is there a science which furnishes us with an understanding of human and divine things, and, besides, a higher science of the divinity and virtue in them?"

' "Certainly," I replied.

' "Well, now," he asked, "is the knowledge of man and God similar to that of music, arithmetic, astronomy, and the like?"

' "Not at all," I answered.

' "Your answer has not been correct, then," he continued, "for we acquire the knowledge of some things by study or practice, and of other things by sight. Now, if anyone were to say to you that in India there exists an animal different from all others, of such and such a species, assuming many shapes and colors, you would have no definite knowledge of it unless you saw it, nor could you attempt to give any description of it, unless you had heard of it from one who had seen it."

' "Absolutely not," I agreed.

' "Then, how," he reasoned, "can the philosophers speculate correctly or speak truly of God, when they have no knowledge of Him, since they have never seen nor heard Him?"

' "But the Deity, father," I rejoined, "cannot be seen by the same eyes as other living beings are. He is to be perceived by the mind alone, as Plato affirms, and I agree with him."

Chapter 4

' "Does our mind, then," he inquired, "possess such and so great a power? Or does it not perceive that which exists through the senses? Or will the human mind be capable of seeing God, if not aided by the Holy Ghost?"

' "Plato truly states," I retorted, "that the eye of the mind has this special power, which has been given to us in order that we may see with it, when it is pure, the very Being who is the cause of everything the mind perceives, who has neither color, nor form, nor size, nor anything the eye can see, but who is beyond all essence, who is ineffable and indescribable, who alone is beautiful and good, and who comes at once into those souls which are well disposed because of their affinity to and desire of seeing Him."

' "What affinity, then," he asked, "have we with God? Is the soul also divine and immortal and a part of the Supreme Mind itself? And as this Supreme Mind sees God, are we, in like manner, able to perceive the Deity in our mind, and thus be happy even now?"

' "Absolutely," I replied.

' "Do all the souls," he asked, "of all the animals perceive Him? Or is man's soul different from that of a horse or an ass?"

' "No," I answered, "the souls of all creatures are the same."

' "Then," he continued, "shall horses and asses see God, or have they ever seen God at any time?"

' "No," I replied, "for not even most men see Him; only those who are honest in their life, and who have been purified through their justice and every other virtue."

' "Then you would say," he persisted, "that man does not see God because of his affinity with Him, nor because he possesses an intellect, but because he is temperate and just?"

' "Certainly," I answered, "and also because he has the faculty of thinking of God."

' "Would you say," he asked, "that goats or sheep do an injustice to anyone?"

' "They do not in any way do an injustice to anyone," I replied.
' "So, according to your reasoning," he said, "these animals will see God?"
' "No, they won't," I answered, "because they are hindered from doing so by the form of their bodies."
' "If these animals had the power of speech," he retorted, "you can be sure that they would have more right to revile our bodies. But, for the present let us ignore this topic and I'll concede that what you say is true. Tell me this: Does the soul see God while it is in the body, or after it has been released from it?"
' "Even while it is in the human body," I replied, "it can see God by means of the intellect, but especially after it has been released from the body, and exists of itself, does it perceive God whom it always loved."
' "Does it remember," he asked, "this vision of God when it is again united to a human body?"
' "I don't think so," I answered.
' "What, then," he continued, "is the advantage of having seen God? What advantage has he who has seen God over him who has not, unless he at least remembers the fact that he has seen Him?"
' "That I cannot answer," I admitted.
' "And what," asked he, "will be the punishment for those deemed unworthy to see God?"
' "As a punishment," I answered, "they will be imprisoned in the bodies of certain wild beasts."
' "Will they be conscious that for this reason they are imprisoned in such bodies and that they have committed some sin?"
' "I don't think so."
' "Then, it would seem that they benefit in no way from

such punishment; in fact, I would say that they suffer no punishment at all, unless they are conscious that it is a punishment."

' "No, indeed," I conceded.

' "Therefore," he concluded, "souls do not see God, nor do they transmigrate into other bodies, for they would know that they were being thus punished, and they would be afraid thereafter to commit even the slightest sin. But I do concede that souls can perceive that there is a God, and that justice and piety are admirable."

' "You speak the truth," I agreed.

Chapter 5

' "Those philosophers, then, know nothing," he went on, "about such matters, for they can't even explain the nature of the soul."

' "It seems not," I consented.

' "Nor should we call the soul immortal, for, if it were, we would certainly have to call it unbegotten."

' "Some Platonists," I answered, "consider the soul both unbegotten and immortal."

' "Do you affirm," he asked, "that the universe also is unbegotten?"

' "There are some who hold that opinion," I replied, "but I don't agree with them."

' "Right you are," he continued. "Why would one think that a body that is so solid, firm, composite, and mutable, a body that deteriorates and is renewed each day, has not originated from some first cause? Now, if the universe has been begotten, souls, too, of necessity, are begotten. Perhaps there is a time when they do not exist, for they were created for the sake of men and other living creatures, even if you claim that they have been begotten separately by themselves, and not together with their own bodies."

' "I think you are right. The souls, then, are not immortal?"[1]

' "No," he said, "since it appears that the world itself was generated."

' "On the other hand," he continued, "I do not claim that any soul ever perishes, for this would certainly be a benefit to sinners. What happens to them? The souls of the devout dwell in a better place, whereas the souls of the unjust and the evil abide in a worse place, and there they await the judgment day. Those, therefore, who are deemed worthy to see God will never perish, but the others will be subjected to punishment as long as God allows them to exist and as long as He wants them to be punished."[2]

' "Does not your assertion agree with what Plato taught in his *Timaeus*[3] concerning the world, namely, that it can be destroyed since it is a created thing, but that it will not be destroyed or be destined for destruction since such is the will of God? Don't you think that the same thing could be said of the soul and, in short, of all other creatures? For, whatever exists or shall exist after God has a nature subject to corruption, and therefore capable of complete annihilation, for only God is unbegotten and incorruptible. For this reason He is God, and all other things after Him are created and corruptible. This is also the reason why souls die and are punished, for, if they were unbegotten, they would not

---

[1] St. Justin teaches that the soul is not immortal in the sense that it cannot be destroyed, but that it is immortal in the sense that, by the grace of God, it will live forever.
[2] These words of the old man do not suppose that St. Justin denied the eternity of divine punishment, for St. Justin elsewhere clearly states his belief in eternal punishment for sinners. They merely show that God could, if He desired, reduce all souls to nothingness.
[3] Cf. *Timaeus*, 41 AB.

have sinned, nor have become so foolish; they would not have been so timid at one time, and so daring at another; nor would they, of their own account, ever have entered into swine, serpents, and dogs. Furthermore, if they were unbegotten, it would not be right to coerce them, for one who is unbegotten is similar and equal to another unbegotten, nor can he be preferred to the other either in power or in honor. We must conclude, therefore, that there are not many beings that are unbegotten, for, if there were some difference between them, you could not, no matter how you searched, find the cause of such difference; but, after sending your thought always to infinity, you would finally become tired and have to stop before the one Unbegotten and declare that He is the cause of all things. Do you think that these things escaped the notice of Plato and Pythagoras, those wise men who became, so to say, a wall and bulwark of our philosophy?"

Chapter 6

' "I don't care," he answered, "if Plato or Pythagoras or anyone else held such views. What I say is the truth, and here is how you may learn it. The soul itself either is life or it possesses life. If it is life, it would cause something else to exist, not itself, just as motion causes something other than itself to move. Now, no one would deny that the soul lives; and if it lives, it does not live as life itself, but as a partaker of life. But, that which partakes of anything is different from that of which it partakes. Now, the soul partakes of life because God wishes it to live; it will no longer partake of life whenever God doesn't wish it to live. For the power to live is not an attribute of the soul as it is of God. As man does not live forever, and his body is not forever united to his soul, since, whenever this union must be discontinued, the soul leaves the body and man no longer exists, so also, whenever the soul must cease to live, the spirit of life is taken from it and it is no more, but it likewise returns to the place of its origin."

Chapter 7

' "If these philosophers," I asked, "do not know the truth, what teacher or method shall one follow?"

' "A long time ago," he replied, "long before the time of those reputed philosophers, there lived blessed men who were just and loved by God, men who spoke through the inspiration of the Holy Spirit and predicted events that would take place in the future, which events are now taking place. We call these men the Prophets. They alone knew the truth and communicated it to men, whom they neither deferred to nor feared. With no desire for personal glory, they reiterated only what they heard and saw when inspired by the Holy Spirit. Their writings are still extant, and whoever reads them with the proper faith will profit greatly in his knowledge of the origin and end of things, and of any other matter that a philosopher should know. In their writings they gave no proof at that time of their statements, for, as reliable witnesses of the truth, they were beyond proof; but the happenings that have taken place and are now taking place force you to believe their words. They also are worthy of belief because of the miracles which they performed, for they exalted God, the Father and Creator of all things, and made known Christ, His Son, who was sent by Him. This the false prophets, who are filled with an erring and unclean spirit, have never done nor even do now, but they undertake to perform certain wonders to astound men and they glorify the demons and spirits of error. Above all, beseech God to open to you the gates of light, for no one can perceive or understand these truths unless he has been enlightened by God and His Christ."

Chapter 8

'When he had said these and many other things which it is not now the fitting time to tell, he went his way, after admonishing me to meditate on what he had told me, and I never saw him again. But my spirit was immediately set on fire, and an affection for the prophets, and for those who are friends of Christ, took hold of me; while pondering on his words, I discovered that his was the only sure and useful philosophy. Thus it is that I am now a philosopher. Furthermore, it is my wish that everyone would be of the same sentiments as I, and never spurn the Savior's words; for they have in themselves such tremendous majesty that they can instil fear into those who have wandered from the path of righteousness, whereas they ever remain a great solace to those who heed them. Thus, if you have any regard for your own welfare and for the salvation of your soul, and if you believe in God, you may have the chance, since I know you are no stranger to this matter, of attaining a knowledge of the Christ of God, and, after becoming a Christian,[1] of enjoying a happy life.'

At these words, my dearest [Pompey],[2] Trypho's friends began to laugh, and he himself replied, smiling, 'I commend all your other statements, and I admire your burning desire

---
[1] Literally, 'having become perfect.' Some understand this to refer to initiation by baptism; others refer it to the perfection of life. The word 'Christian' would, perhaps, embody both ideas.
[2] The Greek text does not have the name Pompey, but the Latin version has *charissime Pompei*. This person, to whom St. Justin apparently addressed the *Dialogue*, is explicitly mentioned in Ch. 141.

to know divine things, but it would be better for you to concentrate on the philosophy of Plato or some other philosopher, and in this way attain constancy, continency, and moderation, rather than be ensnared by false teachings, and become a partisan of worthless men. For, while you adhered to your former school of philosophy and lived a blameless life, there was hope of a better destiny for you, but, when you have turned away from God and have placed your hope in man, what chance of salvation do you have? If you will listen to me (indeed I already think of you as a friend), first be circumcised, then observe the precepts concerning the Sabbath, the feasts, and God's new moons; in brief, fulfill the whole written law, and then, probably, you will experience the mercy of God. But if the Messiah has been born and exists anywhere, He is not known, nor is He conscious of His own existence, nor has He any power until Elias comes to anoint Him and to make Him manifest to all. But you [Christians] have believed this foolish rumor, and you have invented for yourselves a Christ for whom you blindly give up your lives.'

Chapter 9

'My friend,' I replied, 'I pardon you, and may the Lord forgive you, for you don't know what you say; you have been instructed by teachers who are ignorant of the meaning of the Scriptures, and, like a fortune-teller, you blurt out whatever comes into your mind. If you will consent to hear our account of Him, how we have not been deceived by false teachings, and how we shall not cease to profess our faith in Him (even though men thereby persecute us, and the most cruel tyrant tries to force us to deny Him), I will prove to you, here and now, that we do not believe in groundless myths nor in teachings not based on reason, but in doctrines that are inspired by the Divine Spirit, abundant with power, and teeming with grace.'

Trypho's companions once again broke out in such loud, rude, and raucous laughter that I got up and was ready to walk away. But Trypho seized me by my cloak and said he wouldn't let me go until I had kept my promise [to defend the Christians].

'Then, don't let your friends,' I insisted, 'cause such a commotion, or act so insultingly. If they wish, let them listen in silence, or, if they have something more important to do, let them depart; then we can go somewhere to rest and finish our conversation.

Trypho consented, and we then agreed to retire to the middle of the stadium of the Xystus. Two of his friends, joking and making fun of our earnestness, went their way. When we came to that part of the stadium where there were stone seats on both sides, Trypho's other companions went to sit on the one side and after one of them had made a remark about the war waged in Judaea, they spoke of it.

Chapter 10

When they had finished their conversation, I once again addressed them in this fashion: 'My friends, is there any other accusation you have against us than this, that we do not observe the Law, nor circumcise the flesh as your forefathers did, nor keep the sabbaths as you do? Or do you also condemn our customs and morals? This is what I say, lest you, too, believe that we eat human flesh and that after our banquets we extinguish the lights and indulge in unbridled sensuality.[1] Or do you only condemn us for believing in

---

[1] For further description of these accusations against Christians *see* notes on First Apology, Ch. 26, n. 6.

such doctrines and holding opinions which you consider false?'

'This last charge is what surprises us,' replied Trypho. 'Those other charges which the rabble lodge against you are not worthy of belief, for they are too repulsive to human nature. But the precepts in what you call your Gospel are so marvelous and great that I don't think that anyone could possibly keep them. For I took the trouble to read them. But this is what surprises us most, that you who claim to be pious and believe yourselves to be different from the others do not segregate yourselves from them, nor do you observe a manner of life different from that of the Gentiles, for you do not keep the feasts or sabbaths, nor do you practice the rite of circumcision. You place your hope in a crucified man, and still expect to receive favors from God when you disregard His commandments. Have you not read that the male who is not circumcised on the eighth day shall be cut off from his people?[2] This precept was for stranger and purchased slave alike. But you, forthwith, scorn this covenant, spurn the commands that come afterwards, and then you try to convince us that you know God, when you fail to do those things that every God-fearing person would do. If, therefore, you can give a satisfactory reply to these charges and can show us on what you place your hopes, even though you refuse to observe the Law, we will listen to you most willingly, and then we can go on and examine in the same manner our other differences.'

Chapter 11

'Trypho,' I began, 'there never will be, nor has there ever been from eternity, any other God except Him who created and formed this universe. Furthermore, we do not claim

---
2 Gen. 17.14.

that our God is different from yours, for He is the God who, with a strong hand and outstretched arm, led your forefathers out of the land of Egypt. Nor have we placed our trust in any other (for, indeed, there is no other), but only in Him whom you also have trusted, the God of Abraham and of Isaac and of Jacob. But, our hope is not through Moses or through the Law, otherwise our customs would be the same as yours. Now, indeed,[1] for I have read, Trypho, that there should be a definitive law and a covenant, more binding than all others, which now must be respected by all those who aspire to the heritage of God. The law promulgated at Horeb is already obsolete, and was intended for you Jews only, whereas the law of which I speak is simply for all men. Now, a later law in opposition to an older law abrogates the older; so, too, does a later covenant void an earlier one. An everlasting and final law, Christ Himself, and a trustworthy covenant has been given to us, after which there shall be no law, or commandment, or precept. Have you not read these words of Isaias: "Give ear to me, and listen to me, my people; and ye kings, give ear unto me: for a law shall go forth from me, and my judgment shall be a light to the nations. My Just One approaches swiftly, and my Savior shall go forth, and nations shall trust in my arm"?[2] Concerning this New Covenant, God thus spoke through Jeremias: "Behold the days shall come, saith the Lord, and I will make a new covenant with the house of Israel, and with the house of Juda: not according to the covenant which I made with their fathers, in the day that I took them by the hand to bring them out of the land of Egypt."[3] If, therefore, God predicted that He would make a new covenant, and this for a

---

1 An anacoluthon.
2 Isa. 51.4-5.
3 Jer. 31.31-32.

light to the nations, and we see and are convinced that, through the name of the crucified Jesus Christ, men have turned to God, leaving behind them idolatry and other sinful practices, and have kept the faith and have practiced piety even unto death, then everyone can clearly see from these deeds and the accompanying powerful miracles that He is indeed the New Law, the new covenant, and the expectation of those who, from every nation, have awaited the blessings of God. We have been led to God through this crucified Christ, and we are the true spiritual Israel, and the descendants of Juda, Jacob, Isaac, and Abraham, who, though uncircumcised, was approved and blessed by God because of his faith and was called the father of many nations. All this shall be proved as we proceed with our discussion.'

Chapter 12

I also cited this quotation from Isaias: 'Hear my words, and your soul shall live, and I will make an everlasting covenant with you, the sure mercies of David. Behold, I have given Him for a witness to the people; behold, nations that know thee not shall call upon thee, and peoples that knew thee not shall run to thee, because of the Lord thy God, and for the Holy One of Israel, for He hath glorified thee.'[1]

'You have scorned this very law, and have made light of His new holy covenant, and even now you don't accept it, nor are you repentant of your evil actions. Jeremias has indeed exclaimed: "For your ears are closed, your eyes are blinded, and your heart is hardened";[2] but still you won't listen. The Lawgiver has come, and you do not see Him; "the poor have the Gospel preached to them, the blind see,"[3] yet you do not understand. What you really need is

---
1 Isa. 55.3-5.
2 Not in Jeremias, but in Isa. 6.10.
3 Matt. 11.5; Luke 7.22.

another circumcision, though you boast of that of the flesh. The New Law demands that you observe a perpetual Sabbath, whereas you consider yourselves pious when you refrain from work on one day out of the week, and in doing so you don't understand the real meaning of that precept. You also claim to have done the will of God when you eat unleavened bread, but such practices afford no pleasure to the Lord our God. If there be a perjurer or thief among you, let him mend his ways; if there be an adulterer, let him repent; in this way he will have kept a true and peaceful sabbath of God. If anyone has unclean hands, let him wash them and be pure.'

Chapter 13

'Indeed, Isaias did not send you to the bath to wash away murder and other sins which all the water of the ocean could not cleanse, but, as expected, it was of old that bath of salvation which he mentioned and which was for the repentant, who are no longer made pure by the blood of goats and sheep, or by the ashes of a heifer, or by the offerings of fine flour, but by faith through the blood and the death of Christ who suffered death for this precise purpose. So Isaias himself shows in these words: "The Lord shall bare His holy arm in the sight of all the Gentiles, and all the nations and the ends of the earth shall see the salvation that is from God. Depart, depart, depart,[1] go ye out from hence, and touch no unclean thing; go out from the midst of her, be ye sanctified, you that carry the vessels of the Lord, for you shall not go out in a tumult. For the Lord will go before you, and the God of Israel will gather you together. Behold my servant shall understand, and shall be exalted, and shall be glorified

---

1 Only once in the Septuagint.

greatly. As many shall be astonished at Thee, so Thy form and Thy comeliness shall be despised by men; so shall many nations be astonished at Him and kings shall shut their mouths; for they to whom it was not told of Him, shall see: and they that heard not, shall understand. Lord, who hath believed our report? And to whom is the arm of the Lord revealed? We have announced Him as a child before Him, as a root in dry ground. There is no beauty in Him or comeliness; and we have seen Him and He hath no form or beauty; but His form is dishonored, and more despicable than any of the sons of men. He is a man of sorrows, and acquainted with infirmity; because His face was turned away, He was despised and esteemed not. He hath borne our infirmities and carried our sorrows; and we did esteem Him to be in pain, and under the stroke, and in affliction. But He was wounded for our iniquities, He was bruised for our sins; the chastisement of our peace was upon Him, and by His bruises we are healed. All we like sheep have gone astray. Everyone hath turned aside into his own way; and the Lord hath laid on Him the iniquities of us all; and He, because of his afflictions, does not open His mouth. He was led as a sheep to the slaughter, and as a lamb before his shearer is dumb, so He opens not His mouth. In His humiliation His judgment was taken away. But who shall declare His generation? For He is cut off out of the land of living; for the wickedness of my people He came unto death. And I will give the ungodly for His burial, and the rich for His death, because He hath done no iniquity, neither was there deceit in his mouth. And the Lord wills to purify Him from affliction. If He shall lay down His life for sin, your soul shall see a long-lived seed. And the Lord wills to take His soul away from trouble, to show Him light, and to form Him in understanding, to justify the just one who serves many well. And He shall bear our sins; therefore He shall inherit many, and shall divide the spoils of the strong, because His soul was delivered unto death; and He was reputed with the wicked, and He hath borne the sins of many, and was delivered for their transgressions. Give praise, O thou barren, that bearest not; sing forth praise, and make a joyful noise, thou that didst not travail with child; for many are the children of the desolate, more than of her that hath a husband. For the Lord said: Enlarge the place of thy tent, and of thy curtains; fix them, spare not, lengthen thy cords, and strengthen thy stakes; stretch forth to thy right and thy left; and thy seed shall inherit the Gentiles, and thou shalt inhabit the desolate cities. Fear not because thou hast been ashamed; neither be thou confounded because thou hast been reproached; for thou shalt forget thine everlasting shame, and thou shalt not remember the reproach of thy widowhood, because the Lord has made a name for Himself, and He who has redeemed thee shall be called through the whole earth the God of Israel. For the Lord hath called thee as a woman forsaken and faint in spirit; as a woman hated from her youth." [2]

Chapter 14

'Thus it is that we have believed through the baptism of repentance and knowledge of God, which was instituted for the sins of the people of God, as Isaias testifies, and we know that that same baptism which he announced, and which alone can purify penitents, is the water of life. The wells which you have dug for yourselves are broken and useless. For, of what value is that baptism which cleanses only the flesh and body? Wash your souls free of anger, of avarice, of jealousy, and of hatred; then the whole body will be pure. This is the symbolic

---

2 Isa. 52.10-15; 53.1-12; 54.1-6.

meaning of unleavened bread, that you do not commit the old deeds of the bad leaven. You, however, understand everything in a carnal way, and you deem yourselves pious if you perform such deeds, even when your souls are filled with deceit and every other kind of sin. Therefore, after eating unleavened bread for seven days, you were ordered by God to prepare new leaven for yourselves, that is, to practise other deeds, not to repeat your old sinful ones. To prove to you that this is what the new Lawgiver orders you to do, I will again cite the above-quoted passages, together with others which I omitted. Here is what Isaias says: "Hear and your soul shall live, and I will make an everlasting covenant with you, the sure mercies of David. Behold I have given him for a witness to the people, for a leader and a master to the Gentiles. Nations which know Thee not shall call upon Thee, and the people who know Thee not shall run unto Thee, because of Thy God, the Holy One of Israel, for He hath glorified Thee. Seek ye God, and when ye find Him, call upon Him while He is near. Let the wicked forsake his way, and the unjust man his thoughts, and let him return to the Lord, and he will obtain mercy, for He will abundantly pardon yours sins. For My thoughts are not as your thoughts, nor are My ways as your ways; but as far removed as the heavens are from the earth, so far is My way removed from your way, and your thoughts from My thoughts. For as the snow or the rain comes down from heaven, and does not return until it waters the earth, and makes it bring forth and bud, and gives seed to the sower, and bread to the eater, so shall My word be, which shall go forth from My mouth; it shall not return until it shall have accomplished all that I wished, and I shall make all My precepts turn out well. For you shall go out with joy, and be taught with gladness. The mountains and the hills shall leap with joy as they look for you, and all the trees of the fields shall applaud you with their branches. Instead of the thorny bush shall come up the cypress tree, and instead of the needle, shall come up the myrtle tree. And the Lord shall be for a name and for an everlasting sign, and He shall not fail."[1] Trypho, I exclaimed, 'some of these and similar passages from the Prophets refer to the first coming of Christ, in which He is described as coming in disgrace, obscurity, and mortality; other passages allude to His second coming when He shall appear from the clouds in glory; and your people shall see and recognize Him whom they have crucified, as Osee,[2] one of the twelve Prophets, and Daniel[3] have predicted.'

Chapter 15

'In order to please God you must, therefore, learn to observe God's true fast. Listen to what Isaias has to say in this regard: "Cry, cease not, lift up thy voice like a trumpet, and show My people their wicked doings, and the house of Jacob their sins. For they seek Me from day to day, and desire to know My ways, as a nation that hath done justice, and hath not forsaken the judgment of their God. They ask of Me the judgments of justice, and desire to draw near to God, saying, Why have we fasted, and Thou hast not regarded? and humbled our souls, and Thou hast not taken notice? Because in the days of your fasting you find your own pleasure, and oppress all those who are subject to you. Behold you fast for debates and strifes, and strike the humble with your fists. Why do you fast, as you do today, to make your voice be heard on high? This is not the fast which I have chosen, for a man to afflict his soul for a day. Nor, if you

---

1 Isa. 55.3-13.
2 Osee is a mistake for Zacharias 12.10.
3 Probably a reference to Daniel 9.26 or 7.13.

bend your neck in a circle, and spread sackcloth and ashes beneath you, shall you call this a fast, and a day acceptable to the Lord. This is not the fast which I have chosen, saith the Lord. But loose every band of wickedness, undo the bonds of agreements made by violence, let the oppressed go free, and break asunder every unjust bond. Deal thy bread to the hungry, and bring the needy and harborless into thy house; when thou shalt see one naked, cover him; and despise not those of thine own flesh. Then shall thy light break forth as the morning, and thy garments[1] rise up quickly; and thy justice shall go before thee, and the glory of God shall surround thee. Then shalt thou call and the Lord will hear thee; and whilst thou art yet speaking, He shall say, Behold, here I am. And if thou shalt take away from the midst of thee the yoke, the stretching forth of thy hand, and the words of murmuring; and shalt give heartily thy bread to the hungry, and shalt satisfy the afflicted soul; then shall thy light rise up in darkness, and thy darkness shall be as the noonday; and thy God shall be with thee continually, and thou shalt be satisfied as thy soul desireth, and thy bones shall be made fat, and shall be as a watered garden, and like a fountain of water, or like a land whose water fails not."[2] Therefore, be circumcised rather in your heart, as the above-quoted words of God demand.'

Chapter 16

'God Himself, through Moses, exclaimed: "Circumcise therefore the hardness of your hearts, and stiffen your neck no more. For the Lord is your God, and the Lord of lords,

---
[1] *Himátia*: 'garments,' as in all MSS. Others, with the Septuagint, read *hidmata*, 'healings.'
[2] Isa. 58.1-12.

a great God and mighty and terrible, who regardeth not persons nor taketh bribes."¹ And in Leviticus it is written: "Because they have transgressed against Me and despised Me, and because they have walked contrary to Me, I also will walk contrary to them, and I will destroy them in the land of their enemies. Then shall their uncircumcised heart be ashamed."² Indeed the custom of circumcising the flesh, handed down from Abraham, was given to you as a distinguishing mark, to set you off from other nations and from us Christians. The purpose of this was that you and only you might suffer the afflictions that are now justly yours; that only your land be desolate, and your cities ruined by fire; that the fruits of your land be eaten by strangers before your very eyes; that not one of you be permitted to enter your city of Jerusalem.³ Your circumcision of the flesh is the only mark by which you can certainly be distinguished from other men. Nor do I believe that any of you will attempt to deny that God either had or has foreknowledge of future events, and that He does not prepare beforehand what everyone deserves. Therefore, the above-mentioned tribulations were justly imposed upon you, for you have murdered the Just One, and His prophets before Him; now you spurn those who hope in Him, and in Him who sent Him, namely, Almighty God, the Creator of all things; to the utmost of your power you dishonor and curse in your synagogues all those who believe in Christ.⁴ Now, indeed, you cannot use violence against us

---

1 Deut. 10.16-17:
2 Lev. 26.40-41.
3 St. Justin thus considers Jewish circumcision as a divine punishment. After Hadrian captured Jerusalem in A. D. 135, he issued a decree forbidding every Jew from entering the city. Thus, if a person were circumcised, he was not allowed to visit the Holy City. Tertullian says that Bethlehem was also included in the decree.
4 That it was a Jewish custom solemnly to curse the Christians thrice a day is testified to by St. Epiphanius (*Haer.* 1.9) and St. Jerome (*in Isaiam* 52.5).

Christians, because of those who are in power, but as often as you could, you did employ force against us. For this reason, God cries out to you through Isaias, saying: "Behold how the just perisheth, and no man layeth it to heart. For the just man is taken away from before the face of evil. His burial shall be in peace, he is taken away from among us. But draw near hither, you wicked sons, seed of the adulterers and children of the harlot. Upon whom have you jested, and upon whom have you opened your mouth wide, and put out your tongue?" '[5]

Chapter 17

'The other nations have not treated Christ and us, His followers, as unjustly as have you Jews, who, indeed, are the very instigators of that evil opinion they have of the Just One and of us, His disciples. After you had crucified the only sinless and just Man (through whose sufferings are healed all those who approach the Father through Him), and after you realized that He had risen from the dead and had ascended into Heaven (as had been predicted by the Prophets), you not only failed to feel remorse for your evil deed, but you even dispatched certain picked men from Jerusalem to every land,[1] to report the outbreak of the godless heresy of the Christians and to spread those ugly rumors against us which are repeated by those who do not know us. As a result, you are to blame not only for your own wickedness, but also for that of all others. With good reason, therefore, does Isaias cry out: "Because of you My name is blasphemed among the Gentiles."[2] And: "Woe unto their

---

5 Isa. 57.1-4.

---

1 Cf. Eusebius, *Hist. eccl.* 4.18.
2 Isa. 52.5.

soul, for they have taken evil counsel against themselves, saying, Let us bind the Just One, for he is useless to us. Therefore they eat the fruit of their deeds. Woe unto the wicked: evil shall be rendered to him, in accordance with the works of his hands."³ And again, in another passage: "Woe unto them that draw iniquity as with a long cord, and their injustices as it were with the rope of a cart. That say: Let his speed come near, and let the counsel of the Holy One of Israel come, that we may know it. Woe unto them that call evil good, and good evil; that put light for darkness, and darkness for light; that put bitter for sweet, and sweet for bitter."⁴ Thus have you spared no effort in disseminating in every land bitter, dark, and unjust accusations against the only guiltless and just Light sent to men by God. For He seemed to be inconvenient to you, when He cried out, "It is written. My house shall be called a house of prayer, but you have made it a den of thieves."⁵ Then He even overturned the money-changers' tables in the temple, and exclaimed, "Woe to you, Scribes and Pharisees, hypocrites! because you pay tithes on mint and rue, and never think of the love of God and justice. You are whited sepulchres, which outwardly appear beautiful, but within are full of dead men's bones."⁶ And to the Scribes He said, "Woe unto you, Scribes, for you have the keys, and you do not enter in yourselves, and you hinder them that are entering; you blind guides!" '⁷

Chapter 18

'Since you, Trypho, admit that you have read the teach-

---

3 Isa. 3.9-11.
4 Isa. 5.18-20.
5 Matt. 21.13.
6 Matt. 23.23.27; Luke 11.13.
7 Luke 11.52.

ings of Him who is our Savior, I do not consider it out of place to have added those few short sayings of His to the quotations from the Prophets: "Wash yourselves, be clean, and take away evil from your souls."[1] Thus does God order you to be washed in this laver, and to be circumcised with the true circumcision. We, too, would observe your circumcision of the flesh, your sabbath days, and, in a word, all your festivals, if we were not aware of the reason why they were imposed upon you, namely, because of your sins and your hardness of heart. If we patiently bear all the evils thrust upon us by vicious men and demons, and still, amid indescribable tortures and death, ask mercy even for our persecutors and do not wish that anybody be requited with even a little of them, as our new Lawgiver decreed, why is it, Trypho, that we should not observe those rites which cannot harm us, such as the circumcision of the flesh, the sabbaths, and the festivals?'

Chapter 19

'That,' interposed Trypho, 'is precisely what we *are* puzzled about—why you endure all sorts of tortures, yet refuse to follow the [Jewish] customs now under discussion.'

'As I already explained,' I answered, 'it is because circumcision is not essential for all men, but only for you Jews, to mark you off for the suffering you now so deservedly endure. Nor do we approve of your useless baptism of the wells, which has no connection at all with our baptism of life. Thus has God protested that you have forsaken Him, "the fountain of living water, and have digged for yourselves broken cisterns which can hold no water."[1] You Jews, who

---
1 Isa. 1.16.

---
1 Jer. 2.13.

have the circumcision of the flesh, are in great need of our circumcision, whereas we, since we have our circumcision, do not need yours. For if, as you claim, circumcision had been necessary for salvation, God would not have created Adam uncircumcised; nor would He have looked with favor upon the sacrifice of the uncircumcised Abel, nor would He have been pleased with the uncircumcised Henoch, who "was seen no more, because God took him."[2] The Lord and His angels led Lot out of Sodom; thus was he saved without circumcision. Noe, the uncircumcised father of our race, was safe with his children in the ark. Melchisedech, the priest of the Most High, was not circumcised, yet Abraham, the first to accept circumcision of the flesh, paid tithes to him and was blessed by him; indeed, God, through David, announced that He would make him a priest forever according to the order of Melchisedech. Circumcision, therefore, is necessary only for you Jews, in order that, as Osee, one of the twelve Prophets, says, "thy people should not be a people, and thy nation not a nation."[3] Furthermore, all these men were just and pleasing in the sight of God, yet they kept no sabbaths. The same can be said of Abraham and his descendants down to the time of Moses, when your people showed itself wicked and ungrateful to God by molding a golden calf as an idol in the desert. Wherefore, God, adapting His laws to that weak people, ordered you to offer sacrifices to His name, in order to save you from idolatry, but you did not obey even then, for you did not hesitate to sacrifice your children to the demons. Moreover, the observance of the sabbaths was imposed upon you by God so that you would be forced to remember Him, as He Himself

---

2 Gen. 5.24.
3 Osee 1.9.

said, "That you may know that I am God your Savior."[4]

Chapter 20

'You were likewise forbidden to eat certain kinds of meat, so that when you ate and drank you would keep God before your eyes, for you have always been disposed to forget Him, as Moses himself testifies: "The people ate and drank, and rose up to play."[1] And in another passage: "Jacob ate and was filled, and grew fat; my beloved kicked, he grew fat and thick and broad, and forsook God who made him."[2] Indeed, Moses makes known to you in the book of Genesis how God allowed the righteous Noe to eat every kind of meat, except the meat with the blood of strangled animals.'[3]

As Trypho was just ready to add, "as the green herbs," I forestalled him by asking, 'Why do you not interpret those words "as the green herbs"[4] in the sense in which God spoke them, namely, that as God gave herbs to man for his sustenance, so did He give him animals for his food? But you object that Noe was ordered to make a distinction between the herbs, because we do not now eat every kind of herb. Such a conclusion is inadmissible. I could easily prove, but we will not spend the time now in doing so, that every vegetable is a herb and may be eaten. Now, if we make a distinction between them and refuse to eat some of them, we do so not because they are common and unclean, but because they are bitter, or poisonous, or thorny; but the

---
4 Ezech. 20.20.

---
1 Exod. 32.6.
2 Deut. 32.15.
3 H. Stephanus suggested the reading *nekrimaion* (which dies of itself), instead of the common reading *ekrimaion* (which is to be cast out). Cf. Gen. 9.3-4.
4 Gen. 9.3.

sweet, nourishing, and good herbs we eat and enjoy, whether they come from the soil or the sea. Then, God, through Moses, ordered you to abstain from all unclean, harmful, and violent animals, for, after you had eaten the manna in the desert and had seen all the miracles God wrought for your sake, you did not hesitate to make and adore the golden calf. With good reason, therefore, does God repeatedly say of you, "Foolish children, in whom there is no faith." [5]

Chapter 21

'As I stated before, it was by reason of your sins and the sins of your fathers that, among other precepts, God imposed upon you the observance of the Sabbath as a mark. He also states that the only reason He allows any of you to remain alive today is for the sake of the Gentiles, that His name might not be profaned among them. If you wish clear proof of this, listen to what He says through Ezechiel: "I am the Lord your God; walk in My statutes, and keep My judgments, and take no part in the customs of Egypt, and sanctify My sabbaths; and they will be a sign between Me and you, that you may know that I am the Lord your God. And you provoked Me, and your children walked not in My statutes, nor observed My judgments to do them; which if a man do, he shall live in them. But they violated My sabbaths. And I threatened to pour out My indignation upon them, and to accomplish My wrath in them in the desert. But I did it not, that My name might not be entirely violated in the sight of the Gentiles. I led them out before their eyes, and I lifted up My hand upon them in the wilderness, to disperse them among the Gentiles, and scatter them through the countries, because they had not done My

---

5 Deut. 32.20.

judgments, and had cast off my statutes, and had violated My sabbaths, and their eyes were after the inventions of their fathers. Therefore I gave them statutes that were not good, and judgments whereby they shall not live. And I will pollute them in their own gifts, when I shall pass over to destroy all that openeth the womb." [1]

Chapter 22

'Not because He needed such sacrifices did God command you to sacrifice to Him, but because of the sins of your people, especially their sins of idolatry. You will admit the truth of my statement if you listen to Amos, one of the twelve Prophets, who said: "Woe to them that desire the day of the Lord: to what end is this day of the Lord to you? It is darkness, and not light. As if a man should flee from the face of a lion, and a bear should meet him: and if he should enter into his house, and lean his hand upon the wall, and a serpent should bite him. Shall not the day of the Lord be darkness, and not light, and obscurity, and no brightness in it? I hate, and have rejected your festivities, and I will not accept the odor of your assemblies. And if you offer me holocausts and sacrifices, I will not accept them; neither will I regard the show of your peace-offerings. Take away from Me the multitude of thy songs and psalms, for I will not hear thy instruments. And judgment shall run down as water, and justice as a mighty torrent. Did you offer victims and sacrifices to Me in the desert, O house of Israel, saith the Lord? And have you not carried the tabernacle of Moloch, and the star of your god Raphan, figures which you made for yourselves? And I will carry you away beyond Damascus, saith the Lord, whose name is God Almighty. Woe to them

---
[1] Ezech. 20.19-26.

that are wealthy in Sion, and that have confidence in the mountain of Samaria. Those who are named among the chiefs have made harvest of the first-fruits of the nations; the house of Israel came in unto themselves. Pass ye over to Chalene, and see, and go from thence unto Amath the great; and then go down to Geth of the strangers, the best of all these kingdoms, if their borders be greater than your borders. They that come to the evil day, they that come near, and hold to false sabbaths; that sleep upon beds of ivory, and fare sumptuously upon their couches; that eat the lambs out of the flock, and the sucking calves out of the midst of the herd; who applaud at the sound of the musical instruments. They thought these things were permanent, and would not pass away, who drink wine in bowls, and anoint themselves with the best ointments, and they are not grieved for the affliction of Joseph. Wherefore now they shall go captive among the first of the nobles who are carried away, and the dwelling place of the wicked shall be removed, and the neighing of horses shall be taken away from Ephraim."[1] And in Jeremias we read: "Gather together your flesh and your sacrifices, and eat. For I commanded not your fathers, in the day that I brought them out of the land of Egypt, concerning the matter of burnt offerings and sacrifices."[2] And David says in his forty-ninth Psalm: "The God of gods, the Lord hath spoken, and hath called the earth from the rising of the sun to the going down thereof. Out of Sion is the perfection of His beauty. God shall come manifestly; our God shall come, and shall not keep silence. A fire shall burn before Him, and a mighty tempest shall be round about Him. He shall call heaven from above, and the earth, to judge His people. Gather ye together His saints to Him,

---

[1] Amos 5.18-27; 6.1-8.
[2] Jer. 7.21-22.

who set His covenant before sacrifices. And the heavens shall declare His justice, for God is judge. Hear, O My people, and I will speak; O Israel, and I will testify to thee: I am God, thy God. I will not reprove thee for thy sacrifices; but thy burnt offerings are always in My sight. I will not take calves out of thy house, nor the goats out of thy flocks. For all the beasts of the field are Mine, the cattle on the hills, and oxen. I know all the fowls of the air, and with Me is the beauty of the field. If I should be hungry, I would not tell thee, for the world is Mine, and the fullness thereof. Shall I eat the flesh of bullocks, or drink the blood of goats? Offer to God the sacrifice of praise, and pay thy vows to the Most High. And call upon Me in the day of trouble; I will deliver thee, and thou shalt glorify Me. But to the sinner God hath said: Why dost thou declare My statutes, and take My Covenant in thy mouth? Seeing thou hast hated discipline, and hast cast My words behind thee. If thou didst see a thief thou didst run with him, and with adulterers thou hast been a partaker. Thy mouth hath abounded with evil, and thy tongue framed deceits. Sitting thou didst speak against thy brother, and didst lay a scandal against thy mother's son. These things hast thou done, and I was silent. Thou thoughtest in thy wickedness that I should be like to you. I will reprove thee, and will set thy sins in order before thine eyes. Understand these things, you that forget God; lest He snatch you away, and there be none to deliver you. The sacrifice of praise shall glorify Me, and there is the way by which I will show him My salvation."[3] Thus, your sacrifices are not acceptable to God, nor were you first commanded to offer them because of God's need of them, but because of your sins. The same can be said of the temple, which you refer

---

[3] Ps. 49.1-23.

to as the Temple in Jerusalem. God called it His house or court, not as if He needed a house or a court, but because, by uniting yourselves to Him in that place, you might abstain from the worship of idols. This can be proved by the words of Isaias: "What is this house you built for Me? saith the Lord. Heaven is My throne, and the earth is My footstool." [4]

Chapter 23

'If we do not accept this conclusion, then we shall fall into absurd ideas, as the nonsense either that our God is not the same God who existed in the days of Henoch and all the others, who were not circumcised in the flesh, and did not observe the sabbaths and the other rites, since Moses only imposed them later; or that God does not wish each succeeding generation of mankind always to perform the same acts of righteousness. Either supposition is ridiculous and preposterous. Therefore, we must conclude that God, who is immutable, ordered these and similar things to be done only because of sinful men, and at the same time we confess Him to be sympathetic toward all men, prescient, needful of nothing, just, and good. If I am wrong, my friends, let me hear your opinions on this subject.' When I received no reply, I continued, 'Permit me, therefore, to repeat to you, Trypho, and to those who wish to become converts, the heavenly doctrine I received from that old man.[1] Is it not evident to you that the elements are not idle, and that they do not observe the sabbaths? Stay as you were at birth. For if circumcision was not required before the time of Abraham,

---
4 Isa. 66.1.

---
1 I.e., the old man who conversed with Justin by the seashore. Cf. Chs. 3-8.

and before Moses there was no need of sabbaths, festivals, and sacrifices, they are not needed now, when in accordance with the will of God, Jesus Christ, His Son, has been born of the Virgin Mary, a descendant of Abraham. Indeed, when Abraham himself was still uncircumcised, he was justified and blessed by God because of his faith in Him, as the Scriptures tell us. Furthermore, the Scriptures and the facts of the case force us to admit that Abraham received circumcision for a sign, not for justification itself. Thus was it justly said of your people: "That soul which shall not be circumcised on the eighth day shall be destroyed out of his people."[2] Moreover, the fact that females cannot receive circumcision of the flesh shows that circumcision was given as a sign, not as an act of justification. For God also bestowed upon women the capability of performing every good and virtuous act. We see that the physical formation of male and female is different, but it is equally evident that the bodily form is not what makes either of them good or evil. Their righteousness is determined by their acts of piety and justice.'

Chapter 24

'Now, friends,' I continued, 'I could prove how the eighth day has some mysterious meaning (made known to us by God through these rites), rather than the seventh, but, lest you think I am wandering from the subject, understand what I now state, that the blood of circumcision is now abolished, and we now trust in the blood of salvation. Another testament, a new Law, has now come out of Sion. As was

---

2 Gen. 17.14.

taught of old, Jesus Christ circumcises with knives of stone[1] all those who want it, that they may become a righteous nation, a faithful, truthful, and peace-loving people. Come with me, all you who are Godfearing and desirous of seeing the prosperity of Jerusalem. "Come let us walk in the light of the Lord, for He hath liberated His people, the house of Jacob."[2] Come all nations, let us assemble at Jerusalem, no longer disturbed by war because of the peoples' sins. As the Lord cries out through the mouth of Isaias, "I was made manifest to them that seek Me not; I was found of them that asked not for Me. I said, Behold Me, to a nation that did not call upon My name. I have spread forth My hands all the day to an unbelieving and contradicting people, who walk in a way that is not good, but after their own sins. It is a people that provoketh Me to My face." '[3]

Chapter 25

'They who attempt to justify themselves, and claim that they are sons of Abraham, hope to receive along with us[1] even a small part of the divine legacy. This is evident from what the Holy Spirit said when He spoke through Isaias in their name: "Look down from Heaven, and behold from Thy holy habitation and the place of Thy glory. Where is Thy zeal and Thy strength? Where is the multitude of Thy mercy, for Thou hast sustained us, O Lord? For thou art our

---

1 Later (Chs. 113-114), St. Justin distinguishes between the first circumcision (of Moses), which was administered by iron knives, and the second circumcision (of Josue), which was done with stone knives. Josue's circumcision was a figure of Christian circumcision, which also is done with knives of stone, i. e., with the precepts of Christ (whom Scripture calls a Stone).
2 Isa. 2.5-6.
3 Isa. 65.1-3.

---

1 Mss. have 'with you,' but most editors, with Langus, prefer 'with us.'

Father, and Abraham hath not known us, and Israel hath been ignorant of us. But Thou, O Lord, our Father, deliver us; from the beginning Thy name is upon us. O Lord, why hast Thou made us to err from Thy way; and hardened our heart, that we should not fear Thee? Return for the sake of Thy servants, the tribes of Thine inheritance, that we may inherit for a little Thy holy mountain. We are become as in the beginning, when Thou didst not rule over us, and when Thy name was not called upon us. If Thou wilt open the heavens, trembling shall seize the mountains before Thee; and they shall be melted, as wax melts before the fire; and fire shall consume Thine enemies, and Thy name shall be made known to Thine adversaries; the nations shall tremble at Thy presence. When Thou shalt do glorious things, trembling shall seize the mountains in Thy presence. From the beginning of the world we have not heard nor have our eyes seen a God besides Thee, and Thy works, the mercy which Thou shalt show to those who repent. He will meet them that work righteousness, and they shall remember Thy ways. Behold, Thou art angry, and we have sinned. Wherefore we have erred and are all become as one unclean, and all our justice as the rag of a menstruous woman. And we have all fallen as leaves, because of our iniquities; thus the wind will carry us away. There is none that calleth upon Thy name, none that remembereth to take hold of Thee; for Thou hast hid Thy face from us, and hast delivered us up because of our sins. And now return, O Lord, for we are all Thy people. The city of Thy sanctuary is become a desert; Sion is as a desert, Jerusalem is a curse. The house, our sanctuary, and the glory which our fathers blessed, is burnt with fire, and all our glorious customs are turned into ruins. And in addition to these things Thou hast refrained Thyself, O Lord, and hast held Thy peace, and hast humbled us very much." '²

'Do I understand you to say,' interposed Trypho, 'that none of us Jews will inherit anything on the holy mountain of God?'

Chapter 26

'I didn't say that,' I replied, 'but I do say that those who have persecuted Christ in the past and still do, and do not repent, shall not inherit anything on the holy mountain, unless they repent. Whereas the Gentiles, who believe in Christ and are sorry for their sins, shall receive the inheritance, along with the Patriarchs, the Prophets, and every just descendant of Jacob, even though they neither practise circumcision nor observe the sabbaths and feasts. They shall undoubtedly share in the holy inheritance of God, for thus speaks God through Isaias: "I, the Lord God, have called thee in justice, and I will take thee by the hand, and will strengthen thee. And I have given thee for a covenant of the people, for a light of the Gentiles, that thou mightest open the eyes of the blind, and bring forth the prisoner out of prison, and them that sit in darkness out of the prison-house."¹ And again, in another passage: "Lift up the standard for the Gentiles. For behold, the Lord hath made it to be heard in the ends of the earth. Say to the daughters of Sion, Behold, thy Savior cometh; behold His reward is with Him, and His work before Him. And He shall call this the holy people, the redeemed of the Lord. And thou shalt be called a city sought after, and not forsaken. Who is this that cometh from Edom, in red garments. from Bosor? This beautiful one in His robe, walking in the greatness of His strength. I speak justice, and the judg-

---

2 Isa. 63.15-19; 64.1-12.

1 Isa. 42.6-7.

ment of salvation. Why then is Thy apparel red, and Thy garments as from the trodden wine-press? Full of the trodden grape, I have trodden the wine-press alone, and of the Gentiles there was not a man with Me. I have trampled on them in My indignation, and I have trodden on them as the earth, and have spilled their blood upon the earth. For the day of vengeance is come upon them, and the year of My redemption is come. I looked about, and there was none to help; I sought, and there was none to give aid; and My arm saved for Me, and My fury came upon them, and I have trodden them in My wrath, and I have spilled their blood upon the earth." [2]

Chapter 27

'Why,' objected Trypho, 'do you quote only those passages from the Prophets which prove your point, and omit those quotations which clearly command the observance of the Sabbath? Isaias, for example, speaks thus: "If thou turn away thy foot from the sabbath, from doing thine own will in My holy day, and shalt call the sabbaths the holy delights of thy God; if thou shalt not lift thy foot to work, and shalt not speak a word from thine own mouth, and shalt trust in the Lord; then He shall lift thee up to the good things of the earth, and feed thee with the inheritance of Jacob, thy father; for the mouth of the Lord hath spoken it." ' [1]

'My friends,' I replied, 'I have not purposely omitted such passages from the Prophets because they do not coincide with my teaching, but because (as you well understand), although God through His Prophets gives you identical commands

---
2 Isa. 62.10-12; 63.1-7.

---
1 Isa. 58.13-14.

as He did through Moses, this was done only on account of your hardness of heart and ingratitude toward Him. He repeated those precepts in the hope that even so you might possibly repent some time and thus please Him, and no longer sacrifice your children to the demons, nor remain the "companions of thieves, nor lovers of gifts, nor seekers of rewards; judging not for the fatherless, nor suffering the cause of the widow to come unto you, nor having your hands full of blood. For the daughters of Sion have walked with stretched-out necks, flirting with their twinkling eyes, and swishing their dresses as they passed."[2] And He exclaims: "All have turned out of the way, they are become unprofitable together. There is none that understandeth, no not one. With their tongues they have dealt deceitfully, their throat is an open sepulchre, the venom of asps is under their lips; destruction and misery are in their paths, and the way of peace they have not known."[3] Thus, as your sinfulness was the reason why God first issued those precepts, so now because of your enslavement to sin, or rather your greater inclination to it, by means of the same precepts, He calls you to remember and know Him. But you Jews are a ruthless, stupid, blind, and lame people, children in whom there is no faith. As God Himself says: "Honoring Him only with your lips, but your hearts are far from Him, teaching your own doctrines and not His."[4] Now, tell me, was it God's desire that your high priests commit sin when they offer oblations on the sabbaths? Or did He wish that they who received or performed circumcision on that day be guilty of sin, since it is His command that circumcision be given on the eighth day after birth, even though that day may

---
2 Isa. 1.23; 3.16.
3 This quotation seems to have been made up of various verses from Rom. 3.11-17.
4 Isa. 29.13.

fall on a Sabbath? If He knew it would be sinful to perform that act on a Sabbath, could He not have decreed that infants be circumcised either a day before or a day after the Sabbath? And why did He not instruct those persons who lived before the time of Moses and Abraham to observe these same precepts; men, who are called just and were pleasing to God, even though they were not circumcised in the flesh, and did not keep the sabbaths?'

Chapter 28

Trypho then observed, 'We listened attentively before when you put this question, and, to tell you the truth, you deserved our attention, but it does not seem good to me, as it does to most, only to say that it was God's will. For that is always the sly stock reply of those who cannot answer the question.'

Then I replied, 'Since I base my arguments and suggestions on the Scriptures and facts, you should not hesitate to believe me, notwithstanding the fact that I am uncircumcised, for there is only a short time left for conversion. If Christ should come again before your conversion, you will weep and repent in vain, for then He will not heed you. "Break up anew your fallow ground, and sow not upon thorns," cried out Jeremias to the people. "Be circumcised to the Lord, and circumcise the foreskin of your heart."[1] Do not sow, therefore, amid thorns and upon unploughed soil, from which you can reap no fruit. Acknowledge Christ, and then fallow ground, rich and fertile, will certainly be in your hearts. "For behold, the days come, saith the Lord, and I will visit upon every one that hath the foreskin circumcised; upon Egypt, and Juda, and Edom, and upon the children of Moab. For all the Gentiles are uncircumcised in the flesh,

---
1 Jer. 4.3-4.

but all the house of Israel are uncircumcised in the heart."[2] Do you not see that God does not desire that circumcision which is given as a sign? For such circumcision is of no use to the Egyptians, the Moabites, or the Edomites.[3] Even though a man be a Scythian or a Persian, and yet knows God and His Son, and observes His lasting precepts of justice, he is circumcised with the only good and useful circumcision, and both he and his offerings are pleasing to God. In this regard, permit me, my friends, to quote the words which God spoke to His people through Malachias, one of His twelve Prophets: "I have no pleasure in you, saith the Lord; and I will not receive your sacrifices from your hands; for from the rising of the sun even to the going down, My name has been glorified among the Gentiles; and in every place there is sacrifice, and there is offered to My name a clean oblation; for My name is honored among the Gentiles, saith the Lord, but you profane it."[4] And through the mouth of David God said: "A people which I knew not, hath served Me; at the hearing of the ear they have obeyed me."[5]

Chapter 29

'Let us come together, O Gentiles, and glorify God, for He has deigned to look down upon us also. Let us glorify Him through the King of glory and the Lord of hosts. For He has shown His benevolence toward us Gentiles, too, and He accepts our sacrifices more willingly than He does yours. If I have been approved by God, what need have I of circumcision? If I have already been baptized with the grace of the Holy Spirit, what use have I of your baptism?

---

2 Jer. 9.25-26.
3 Cf. *Pseudo-Barnabas* 9.6; Origen, *Contra Celsum* 5.47.
4 Mal. 1.10-11.
5 Ps. 19.45.

I am positive that I can persuade by these words even those of weak intellectual faculties, for the words which I use are not my own, nor are they embellished by human rhetoric, but they are the words as David sang them, as Isaias announced them as good news, as Zacharias proclaimed them, and as Moses wrote them. Aren't you acquainted with them, Trypho? You should be, for they are contained in your Scriptures, or rather not yours, but ours. For we believe and obey them, whereas you, though you read them, do not grasp their spirit. You should not be angry with us, therefore, nor blame us for the uncircumcision of our body; indeed, God created us that way. Nor should you consider it dreadful if we drink hot water[1] on the Sabbath, for God doesn't stop controlling the movement of the universe on that day, but He continues directing it then as He does on all other days. Besides, your chief priests were commanded by God to offer sacrifices on the Sabbath, as well as on other days. Then, too, there are so many just men who are approved by God Himself, yet they never performed any of your legal ceremonies.'

Chapter 30

'The fact that God can be falsely accused by the foolish of not having always taught the same truthful doctrines to all, you can blame on your own sinfulness. Indeed, many deemed such doctrines senseless and unworthy of God, for they were not illumined by grace to understand that these same doctrines have called your people, mired in sin and sick of

---

[1] It was not permitted to a Jew to light a fire (Cf. Exod. 35.3), or to cook food on the Sabbath (Cf. Exod. 16.23). However, from ancient times it was customary to have a Gentile to light the fire on the Sabbath.

a spiritual disease, to conversion and spiritual repentance;[1] nor did they understand that prophecy, which was given to mankind after the death of Moses, is eternal. This, my friends, is indeed mentioned in the Psalm. That we, who have been enlightened by these doctrines, consider them to be "sweeter than honey and the honey-comb,"[2] is evident from the fact that even under the threat of death we do not deny His name. Furthermore, it is equally clear (as the word of the prophecy, speaking in the name of one of His followers, metaphorically affirms) that we believers beseech Him to safeguard us from strange, that is, evil and deceitful, spirits. We constantly ask God through Jesus Christ to keep us safe from those demons who, while they are strangers to the worship of God, were once adored by us; we pray, too, that, after our conversion to God through Christ, we may be without blame. We call Him our Helper and Redeemer, by the power of whose name even the demons shudder; even to this day they are overcome by us when we exorcise them in the name of Jesus Christ, who was crucified under Pontius Pilate, the Governor of Judaea. Thus, it is clear to all that His Father bestowed upon Him such a great power that even the demons are subject both to His name and to His pre-ordained manner[3] of suffering.'

Chapter 31

'If such power is shown to have accompanied and still now accompanies His Passion, just think how great shall be His power at His glorious Advent! For, as Daniel foretold,

---

1 Or, 'repentance of the Father.' The *patrós* of the Greek text is probably a mistake for *pneúmatos*. The copyist could have confused the two abbreviations, *prs* and *pns*.
2 Ps. 18.11.
3 I. e., the sign of the cross.

He shall come on the clouds as the Son of Man, accompanied by His angels. Here are the exact words of Daniel: "I beheld till the thrones were set, and the Ancient of days sat, whose garment was white as snow, and the hair of His head like clean wool. His throne was like the flames of fire, His wheels like a burning fire. A swift stream of fire issued forth from before Him. Thousands of thousands ministered to Him, and ten thousand times ten thousand stood before Him. The books were opened and the judgment was set. I beheld then the voice of the great words which the horn speaks; and the beast was tortured, and the body thereof was destroyed, and given to the fire to be burnt. And the power of the other beasts was taken away, and times of life were appointed them for a time and a time. I beheld therefore in the vision of the night, and lo, one like the Son of Man came with the clouds of heaven, and He came even to the Ancient of days, and stood before Him. And they who stood by brought Him near, and He gave Him power and a glorious kingdom, and all the peoples of the earth by their families, and glory, serve Him. His power is an everlasting power that shall not be taken away; and His kingdom shall not be destroyed. And my spirit trembled within me, and the visions of my head troubled me. I went near to one of them that stood by, and asked the truth of him concerning all these things, and he told me the interpretation of the words, and instructed me. These four great beasts are four kingdoms, which shall perish from the earth, and shall not receive the kingdom forever, even forever and ever. After this I would diligently learn concerning the fourth beast, which destroyed all the others, and was exceedingly terrible; his teeth were of iron, and his claws of brass; he devoured and broke in pieces, and the rest he stamped upon with his feet. And [I was instructed] concerning the ten horns that he had on his head; and concerning the other that came up, before which three horns fell; and that horn had eyes, and a mouth speaking great things, and its countenance excelled the rest. I beheld that horn waging war against the saints, and prevailing over them, until the Ancient of days came and gave judgment to the saints of the Most High, and the time came and the saints of the Most High obtained the kingdom. And it was told me concerning the fourth beast, that it should be the fourth kingdom upon earth, which shall be greater than all the kingdoms, and shall devour the whole earth, and shall tread it down and break it in pieces. And the ten horns are ten kings that shall arise; and one shall arise after them, and he shall surpass the first kings in wickedness, and he shall bring down three kings, and he shall speak words against the Most High, and shall crush the saints of the Most High, and he shall think himself able to change times and seasons, and they shall be delivered into his hand until a time, and times, and half a time. And the judgment sat, and they shall take away his power, to break into pieces and destroy it unto the end. And the kingdom, and the power, and the greatness of the kingdom under the whole heaven, were given to the holy people of the Most High, that they may reign in an everlasting kingdom; and all powers shall serve and obey Him. Hitherto is the end of the word. I, Daniel, was very much astonished at the vision, and my speech was changed in me, but I kept the word in my heart." [1]

Chapter 32

When I paused, Trypho objected, 'Your quotations from Scripture prove that we must look forward to that glorious and great Messiah who, as the Son of Man, receives the everlasting kingdom from the Ancient of days. But, the one

---

[1] Dan. 7.9-28.

whom you call Christ was without glory and honor to such an extent that he incurred the last curse of God's law, namely, he was crucified.'

I immediately replied, 'My friends, if I had not explained from the above-quoted Scriptural passages that the appearance of Christ should be without glory and His generation beyond description, that for His death the rich should incur death, that through His suffering we should be healed, that He should be led as a sheep to the slaughter, and if I had not made clear that there should be two advents of Christ (the first in which He was pierced by you, the second in which you shall look up and recognize Him as the one whom you pierced, and then your tribes shall mourn tribe by tribe, the women apart and the men apart),[1] then my words must have been ambiguous and obscure. Now, I shall derive all my proofs from all the words I adduce from your sacred and prophetic Scriptures, in the hope that some one may be found among you to be of that seed which, by the grace of the Lord of Sabaoth, is reserved for everlasting salvation. To clarify this matter further for you, I shall cite other passages from the blessed David, from which you can see that Christ is also called Lord by the Holy Prophetic Spirit, and that God, the Father of all, raised Him up from the earth, and placed Him at His right hand, until He makes His enemies His footstool; which, indeed, actually happened when our Lord Jesus Christ ascended into Heaven, after His resurrection from the dead. Thus were the times being fulfilled, and he whom Daniel foretold[2] would reign for a time, times, and a half, is now at the doors, ready to utter bold and blasphemous words against the Most High. In ignorance of how long he will reign, you hold a different opinion, based

---
1 Zach. 12.12-13.
2 Dan. 7.25.

on your misinterpretation of the word "time" as meaning one hundred years. If this is so, the man of sin must reign at least three hundred and fifty years, computing the holy Daniel's expression of "times" to mean two times only. I have digressed at length for the sole purpose of convincing you of the truth of what God said against you, namely, that you are foolish children, and "Therefore behold, I will proceed to take away this people, and I will remove them, and I will take away the wisdom of their wise men, and I will hide the understanding of their prudent men."³ Knowing this, why don't you stop deceiving yourselves and those around you? Why don't you learn from us who have been taught wisdom by the grace of Christ? But, to get back to the point in question, here are the convincing words of David: 'The Lord said to my Lord: Sit Thou at My right hand, until I make Thy enemies Thy footstool. The Lord will send forth the sceptre of Thy power out of Sion: and rule Thou in the midst of Thy enemies. With Thee is the principality in the day of Thy strength, in the brightness of Thy saints, from the womb before the day star I begot Thee. The Lord hath sworn, and He will not repent: Thou art a priest forever according to the order of Melchisedech. The Lord at thy right hand hath broken kings in the day of His wrath. He shall judge among nations. He shall fill ruins.⁴ He shall drink of the torrent in the way; therefore shall He lift up the head." ⁵

Chapter 33

'Now I know,' I continued, 'that you dare to refer the

---
3 Isa. 29.14.
4 Or, 'He shall fill the places with dead bodies.' There seems to be an omission of words in the Greek text, due possibly to a copyist's negligence.
5 Ps. 109.1-7.

words of the above-quoted Psalm to king Ezechias, but I am going to show you from the very words of the Psalm that you are wrong. Among the words of the Psalm are the following two statements: "The Lord hath sworn, and He will not repent," and "Thou art a priest forever according to the order of Melchisedech."¹ Now, you must admit that Ezechias neither was nor is an everlasting priest of God. If your ears were not so dull, or your hearts so hardened, you would see that the words refer to our Jesus. For, by the words, "The Lord hath sworn, and He will not repent; Thou art a priest forever according to the order of Melchisedech," God, because of your lack of faith, swore that Jesus is the High Priest according to the order of Melchisedech. For, as Melchisedech was the priest of the Most High (as Moses tells us), and as he was the priest of the uncircumcised, and blessed the circumcised Abraham who offered him tithes, so has God announced that His eternal Priest, called Lord by the Holy Spirit, should be the priest of the uncircumcised. Those circumcised persons who approach Him with faith in their hearts and a prayer on their lips for His blessings will be welcomed and blessed by Him. The concluding words of the Psalm, "He shall drink of the torrent in the way," and, "Therefore shall He lift up the head,"² prove that Christ was to be first humble man, and later He was to be exalted.'

Chapter 34

'As a further proof of your ignorance of the Scriptures, I am going to quote another Psalm, dictated to David by the Holy Spirit, which you erroneously think refers to your king Solomon, but which in reality refers to our Christ. One

---
1 Ps. 109.4.
2 Ps. 109.7.

cause of your error is that you are misled by the false interpretation of equivocal terms. For, when the law of God is called a "blameless law,"[1] you do not understand it as applying to the law that was to come after Moses, but to the Mosaic Law itself, even though God Himself had promised to establish a new law and a new testament. And when the Psalm says, "Give to the king Thy judgment, O God,"[2] you claim that the words were spoken of Solomon because he was a king, whereas the words clearly proclaim that they were spoken of the eternal King, that is, Christ. I prove from all the Scriptures that Christ is spoken of as a King, and a Priest, and God, and Lord, and an Angel, and a Man, and a Leader, and a Stone, and a Begotten Son, and as One who at first endured suffering, then ascended into Heaven, and as returning to earth with glory and having the eternal kingdom. In support of what I have said, I cite the following words of the Psalm: "Give to the king Thy judgment, O God, and to the king's son Thy justice, to judge Thy people with justice, and Thy poor with judgment. Let the mountains receive peace for the people, and the hills justice. He shall judge the poor of the people, and shall save the children of the poor, and shall humble the slanderer. And He shall continue with the sun, and before the moon throughout all generations. He shall come down like rain upon the fleece, and as showers falling gently upon the earth. In His days shall justice spring up, and abundance of peace, till the moon be taken away. And He shall rule from sea to sea, and from the rivers unto the ends of the earth. Before Him the Ethiopians shall fall down, and His enemies shall lick the ground. The kings of Tharsis and the islands shall offer presents; the kings of the Arabians and of Saba shall bring gifts. And all

---
1 Ps. 18.7.
2 Ps. 71.1.

kings of the earth shall adore Him, all nations shall serve Him. For He shall deliver the poor from the mighty, and the needy that had no helper. He shall spare the poor and needy, and He shall save the souls of the poor. He shall redeem their souls from usuries and iniquity, and His name shall be honorable in their sight. And He shall live, and to Him shall be given of the gold of Arabia, and they shall pray continually for Him, and they shall bless Him all the day. And there shall be a firmament on the earth on the tops of mountains; His fruit shall be on Libanus, and they of the city shall flourish like the grass of the earth. His name shall be blessed for evermore, His name continued before the sun. And in Him shall all the tribes of the earth be blessed, all nations shall call Him blessed. Blessed be the Lord, the God of Israel, who alone doth wonderful things. And blessed be the name of His majesty forever, and the whole earth shall be filled with His majesty. So be it. So be it."[3] And this Psalm ends with these words: "The praises of David, the son of Jesse, are ended." '

'Now, we all know that Solomon was the great and famous king, who constructed the renowned Temple at Jerusalem. But it is equally evident to all that none of the things foretold in the above-mentioned Psalm happened to him, for not all the kings adored him, nor did his power extend to the ends of the earth, nor did his enemies fall down prostrate before him and lick the ground. Furthermore, I do not hesitate to quote the Book of Kings where it is written that Solomon committed idolatry at Sidon[4] for the sake of a woman. On the contrary, the Gentiles who know God, the

---
3 Ps. 71.1-20.
4 The Books of Kings do not expressly state such a fact, although it could have happened. Some think that the words 'at Sidon' were originally a marginal note, later incorporated into the text by some transcriber.

Creator of the world, through the crucified Jesus, would rather endure every torture and pain, even death itself, than worship idols, or eat meat sacrificed to idols.'

Chapter 35

At this point, Trypho interrupted me by saying, 'I know that there are many who profess their faith in Jesus and are considered to be Christians, yet they claim there is no harm in their eating meats sacrificed to idols.'

'The fact that there are such men,' I replied, 'who pretend to be Christians and admit the crucified Jesus as their Lord and Christ, yet profess not His doctrines, but those of the spirits of error, only tends to make us adherents of the true and pure Christian doctrine more ardent in our faith and more firm in the hope He announced to us. As we look about us, we see events actually taking place which He predicted would happen in His name. Indeed, He foretold: "Many shall come in My name, clothed outwardly in sheep's clothing, but inwardly they are ravening wolves."[1] And: "There shall be schisms and heresies."[2] And: "Beware of false prophets, who come to you in clothing of sheep, but inwardly they are ravening wolves."[3] And: "There shall arise many false Christs and false Apostles, and they shall deceive many of the faithful."[4]

'My friends, there were, and still are, many men who, in the name of Jesus, come and teach others atheistic and blasphemous doctrines and actions; we call them by the name of the originator of each false doctrine. (For each has his own peculiar method of teaching how to blaspheme the

---
1 Matt. 7.15.
2 1 Cor. 11.18.
3 Matt. 7.15.
4 Matt. 24.11.24.

Creator of the universe, and Christ, whose Advent was foretold by Him, and the God of Abraham, and of Isaac, and of Jacob.[5] They are all outside of our communion, for we know them for what they are, impious atheists and wicked sinners, men who profess Jesus with their lips, but do not worship Him in their hearts. These men call themselves Christians in much the same way as some Gentiles engrave the name of God upon their statues, and then indulge in every kind of wicked and atheistic rite.) Some of these heretics are called Marcionites,[6] some Valentinians, some Basilidians, and some Saturnilians, and others by still other names, each designated by the name of the founder of the system, just as each person who deems himself a philosopher, as I stated at the beginning of this discussion, claims that he must bear the name of the philosophy he favors from the founder of that particular school of philosophy. Not only from these events do we conclude, as I said, that Jesus possessed foreknowledge of what would happen to Him, but also from the many other happenings which He predicted would befall those who believe and profess that He is the Messiah. He even foretold all the suffering we would have to bear when those of our own household put us to death. Consequently, we can find no fault with either His words or actions. For this reason, too, we pray for you and for everyone else who hates us, that you may repent with us, and refrain from blaspheming Jesus Christ, who is proved to be totally without blame and reproach by His own deeds and

---

5 Although St. Justin elsewhere refers to Christ as the God of Abraham, of Isaac, and of Jacob, it would seem that in this passage he applies it to God, the Father. Thus, the heretics here mentioned would not be the Ebionites, who attacked the divinity of Christ, but some sect of the Gnostics.
6 *Markianoí*: not the disciples of Mark, the Valentinian Gnostic, but of Marcion.

by the miracles which even now are wrought in His name by the words of His teaching and the prophecies concerning Him. We pray, also, that you may believe in Jesus Christ, and thus at His second triumphant coming you will be saved and not be condemned by Him to the fire of hell.'

Chapter 36

Trypho then said, 'It may also be admitted that this is exactly as you say, and that the Prophets predicted that Christ was to suffer, that He was to be called a Stone, that His first advent in which He was proclaimed to appear in suffering would be followed by another in glory, and that He would thenceforth be the Judge of all men, and the Eternal King and Priest. But prove to us that Jesus Christ is the one about whom these prophecies were spoken.'

'At the proper time,' I replied, 'I will supply the proofs you wish, but for the present permit me to quote the following prophecies to show that the Holy Spirit by parable called Christ God, and Lord of hosts and of Jacob. God Himself calls your interpreters stupid[1] because they claim that these prophecies were not spoken of Christ, but of Solomon, when he transported the ark of testimony into the temple built by himself. Listen to these words of David's Psalm: "The earth is the Lord's and the fulness thereof; the world, and all they that dwell therein. For He hath founded it upon the seas, and hath prepared it upon the rivers. Who shall ascend into the mountain of the Lord; or who shall stand in His holy place? The innocent in hands, and clean of heart, who hath not taken his soul in vain, nor sworn deceitfully to his neighbor. He shall receive a blessing from the Lord, and mercy from God his Savior. This is the generation of them

---
1 Jer. 4.22.

that seek Him, of them that seek the face of the God of Jacob. Lift up your gates, O ye princes, and be ye lifted up, O eternal gates, and the King of Glory shall enter in. Who is this King of Glory? The Lord who is strong and mighty in battle. Lift up your gates, O ye princes, and be ye lifted up, O eternal gates, and the King of Glory shall enter in. Who is this King of Glory? The Lord of hosts, He is the king of Glory."[2] This proves that Solomon was not the Lord of hosts. But, when our Christ arose from the dead and ascended into Heaven, the heavenly princes chosen by God were ordered to open the gates of Heaven that the King of Glory might enter and sit at the right hand of the Father until He makes His enemies His footstool (as it is stated in another[3] psalm). Now, when these heavenly princes saw that He was in appearance without beauty, honor, or glory, and not recognizing Him, they asked: "Who is this King of Glory?" And the Holy Spirit, either in His own name or in the Father's, answered: "The Lord of Hosts. He is the King of Glory." But I am sure that everyone will admit that none of the gate-keepers of the Temple at Jerusalem ever said of Solomon (though he was ever so glorious a king), or of the ark of testimony, "Who is this King of Glory?" '

Chapter 37

'Christ is thus further described,' I continued, 'in the diapsalm of the forty-sixth Psalm, "God is ascended with jubilee, and the Lord with the sound of a trumpet. Sing praises to our God, sing ye; sing praises to our king, sing ye. For God is the king of all the earth, sing ye wisely. God hath reigned over the Gentiles; God sitteth on His holy throne. The

---
2 Ps. 23.1-10.
3 Ps. 109.1.

princes of the people are gathered together with the God of Abraham, for the strong ones of the earth are of God, and have been exceedingly exalted."¹ And in Psalm ninety-eight the Holy Spirit reprimands you, and announces that He whom you refuse to recognize as your king is the King and Lord of Samuel, Aaron, Moses, and of every other man. Here are the words of that Psalm: "The Lord hath reigned, let the people be angry. He that sitteth on the cherubim; let the earth be moved. The Lord is great in Sion, and high above all people. Let them give praise to Thy great name, for it is terrible, and holy; and the King's honor loveth judgment. Thou hast prepared directions; Thou hast done judgment and justice in Jacob. Exalt ye the Lord our God, and adore His footstool, for He is holy. Moses and Aaron among His priests, and Samuel among them that call upon His name. They called upon the Lord (say the Scriptures), and He heard them. He spoke to them in the pillar of the cloud. They kept His testimonies, and the commandment which He gave them. Thou didst hear them, O Lord our God. Thou wast merciful to them, O God, and [yet] taking vengeance on all their inventions. Exalt ye the Lord our God, and adore at His holy mountain; for the Lord our God is holy." '²

Chapter 38

'It would be better for us,' Trypho concluded, 'to have obeyed our teachers who warned us not to listen to you Christians, nor to converse with you on these subjects, for you have blasphemed many times in your attempt to convince us that this crucified man was with Moses and Aaron, and

1 Ps. 46.6-10.
2 Ps. 98.1-9.

spoke with them in the pillar of the cloud; that He became man, was crucified, and ascended into Heaven, and will return again to this earth; and that He should be worshipped.'

'I am aware,' I replied, 'that, as the Word of God testifies, this great wisdom of Almighty God, the Creator of all, is concealed from you. It is, therefore, with feelings of pity that I exert every possible effort to help you understand our teachings, which to you seem paradoxical. If I fail, then I shall not be held accountable on judgment day. I shall recount to you other doctrines which may seem even more paradoxical to you, but don't be disturbed; instead of leaving me, become more zealous and inquisitive listeners. At the same time, forsake the tradition of your teachers, for they are convicted by the Prophetic Spirit of being incapable of understanding the truths spoken by God, and of preferring to spread their own opinions. The forty-fourth Psalm speaks thus of Christ: "My heart hath uttered a good word; I speak my works to the King. My tongue is the pen of a scrivener that writeth swiftly. Thou art beautiful above the sons of men; grace is poured abroad in Thy lips; therefore hath God blessed thee forever. Gird Thy sword upon Thy thigh, O Thou most mighty. With Thy comeliness and Thy beauty set out, proceed prosperously, and reign, because of truth and meekness and justice; and Thy right hand shall conduct Thee wonderfully. Thy arrows are sharp, O Mighty One; under Thee shall people fall; in the heart of the King's enemies. Thy throne, O God, is forever and ever; the sceptre of Thy kingdom is a sceptre of uprightness. Thou hast loved justice, and hated iniquity; therefore God, Thy God, hath anointed Thee with the oil of gladness above Thy fellows. Myrrh and stacte and cassia perfume Thy garments, from the ivory houses, whereby they have made Thee glad. King's daughters are in Thy honor. The queen stood at Thy right hand, in gilded clothing, surrounded with variety. Hearken, O daughter, and see, and incline thy ear, and forget thy people and thy father's house. And the king shall greatly desire thy beauty, for He is the Lord thy God, and Him they shall adore. And the daughter of Tyre shall be there with gifts; the rich among the people shall entreat Thy countenance. All the glory of the king's daughter is within in golden borders, clothed round about with varieties. After her shall virgins be brought to the King; her neighbors shall be brought to Thee. They shall be brought with gladness and rejoicing; they shall be brought into the temple of the King. Instead of Thy fathers, sons are born to Thee. Thou shalt make them princes over all the earth. I will remember Thy name throughout all generations. Therefore shall people praise Thee forever, and forever and ever." [1]

Chapter 39

'It is small wonder,' I continued, 'that you Jews hate us Christians who have grasped the meaning of these truths, and take you to task for your stubborn prejudice. Indeed, Elias, when interceding for you before God, spoke thus: "Lord, they have slain Thy prophets, and have destroyed Thy altars; and I am left alone, and they seek my life." And God answered: "I still have seven thousand men, whose knees have not been bowed before Baal."[1] Therefore, just as God did not show His anger on account of those seven thousand men, so now He has not yet exacted judgment of you, because He knows that every day some of you are forsaking your erroneous ways to become disciples in the

---
1 Ps. 44.1-18.
---
1 3 Kings 19.18.

name of Christ, and this same name of Christ enlightens you to receive all the graces and gifts according to your merits. One receives the spirit of wisdom, another of counsel, another of fortitude, another of healing, another of foreknowledge, another of teaching, and another of the fear of God.'

'Don't you realize,' interposed Trypho, 'that you are out of your mind to say such things?'

'Listen to me, my friend,' I retorted, 'and I'll prove that I'm not out of my mind when I mention these special gifts. For it was predicted that, after His Ascension into Heaven, Christ would free us from the captivity of error and endow us with gifts. Here are the words of the prophecy: "He ascended on high; He led captivity captive; He gave gifts to men."[2] Thus, having received gifts from Christ, who ascended into Heaven, we can show from the prophecies that you "who are wise in your own eyes and prudent in your own sight,"[3] are in reality stupid, for you honor God and His Christ only with your lips. We, on the other hand, who have been well instructed in His whole truth,[4] honor Them with our actions, our knowledege, and our hearts, even unto death. The reason why you hesitate to acknowledge that Jesus is the Christ (which is proved by the Scriptures, the events which you yourselves witnessed, and the miracles wrought in His name) is, perhaps, to avoid the harsh persecution of the officials, who, influenced by the serpent (that evil and treacherous spirit), will not cease to persecute and slaughter those who acknowledge the name of Christ until He shall come again to destroy them all and to distribute rewards according to merit.'

'Prove to us,' interrupted Trypho, 'that this man who you

---
2 Ps. 67.19.
3 Isa. 5.21.
4 Here it indicated a contrast between orthodox Christians and heretics, or between Christians and Jews.

claim was crucified, and ascended into Heaven, is the Christ of God. It has indeed been proved sufficiently by your Scriptural quotations that it was predicted in the Scriptures that Christ should suffer, and that He should come again in glory to accept the eternal kingdom over all nations, and that every kingdom should be made subject to Him. But what we want you to prove is that this Jesus is the Christ spoken of in the Scriptures.'

'My dear friends,' I replied, 'anyone with ears would know that I have already proved that very point, and it can be shown also from the facts which you yourselves have admitted. But, lest you think that I am not able to furnish further proof that Jesus is the Messiah, I renew my promise to produce additional arguments in their proper place. For the present, however, I would like to continue on the same subject we were discussing.'

Chapter 40

'The mystery of the lamb which God ordered you to sacrifice as the Passover was truly a type of Christ, with whose Blood the believers, in proportion to the strength of their faith, anoint their homes, that is, themselves. You are all aware that Adam, the result of God's creative act, was the abode of His inspiration. In the following fashion I can show that God's precept concerning the paschal lamb was only temporary. God does not allow the paschal lamb to be sacrificed in any other place than where His name is invoked (that is, in the Temple at Jerusalem), for He knew that there would come a time, after Christ's Passion, when the place in Jerusalem (where you sacrificed the paschal lamb) would be taken from you by your enemies, and then all sacrifices would be stopped. Moreover, that lamb which you were ordered to roast whole was a symbol of Christ's Passion on the Cross. Indeed, the lamb, while being roasted, resembles the figure of the cross, for one spit transfixes it horizontally from the lower parts up to the head, and another pierces it across the back, and holds up its forelegs. Likewise, the two identical[1] goats which had to be offered during the fast (one of which was to be the scapegoat and the other the sacrificial goat) were an announcement of the two advents of Christ: of the first Advent, in which your priests and elders sent Him away as a scapegoat, seizing Him and putting Him to death; of the second Advent, because in that same place of Jerusalem you shall recognize Him whom you had subjected to shame, and who was a sacrificial offering for all sinners who are willing to repent and to comply with that fast which Isaias prescribed when he said "loosing the knot of violent contracts,"[2] and to observe likewise all the other precepts laid down by him (precepts which I have already mentioned[3] and which all Christian believers fulfill). You also know very well that the offering of the two goats, which had to take place during the fast, could not take place anywhere else outside of Jerusalem.'

Chapter 41

'Likewise,' I continued, 'the offering of flour,[1] my friends, which was ordered to be presented for those cleansed from leprosy, was a prototype of the Eucharistic Bread, which our Lord Jesus Christ commanded us to offer in remembrance[2]

---

1 Scripture did not require that the goats be alike, but this was a common Jewish practice.
2 Isa. 58.6.
3 Cf. Chapter 15.

---

1 Cf. Lev. 14.10.
2 Luke 22.19.

of the Passion He endured for all those souls who are cleansed
from sin, and that at the same time we should thank God
for having created the world, and everything in it, for the
sake of mankind, and for having saved us from the sin in
which we were born, and for the total destruction of the
powers and principalities of evil through Him who suffered
in accordance with His will. Thus, as I already stated, God
speaks through Malachias, one of the twelve Prophets, concerning the sacrifices you then offered up to Him: "I have
no pleasure in you, saith the Lord, and I will not receive
your sacrifices at your hands. For from the rising of the
sun even to the going down, My name is great among the
Gentiles, and in every place incense is offered to My name,
and a clean oblation; for My name is great among the
Gentiles, saith the Lord, but you profane it."[3] By making
reference to the sacrifices which we Gentiles offer to Him
everywhere, the Eucharistic Bread and the Eucharistic Chalice, He predicted that we should glorify His name, but that
you should profane it. Furthermore, the precept of circumcision, obliging you without fail to circumcise your sons on
the eighth day, was a type of the true circumcision by which
we are circumcised from error and wickedness through our
Lord Jesus Christ who arose from the dead on the first day
of the week. For the first day of the week, while it remains
the first of all the days, yet is called the eighth, according to
the number of all the days of the cycle, and still it remains
the first.'

Chapter 42

'The twelve bells[1] which had to be attached to the long

---

[3] Mal. 1.10-12.

[1] Exod. 28.33-34 does not mention the exact number of bells. Justin
could have been thinking of the twelve gems in the high-priest's
breastplate. (Cf. Exod. 28.17-21).

robe of the high priest, were representative of the twelve
Apostles, who relied upon the power of Christ, the Eternal
Priest. Through their voices the whole world is filled with
the glory and grace of God and His Christ. David testified
to this truth when he said: "Their sound hath gone forth
into all the earth, and their words unto the ends of the
world."[2] And Isaias speaks as though in the person of the
Apostles (when they relate to Christ that the people were
convinced, not by their words, but by the power of Him who
sent them), and says: "Lord, who hath believed our report,
and to whom is the arm of the Lord revealed? We have
preached before Him as a little child, as if a root in a
thirsty ground."[3] (And the rest of the prophecy as quoted
above.) When the passage, spoken in the name of many,
states: "We have preached before Him," and adds, "as a
little child," it proves that sinners shall obey Him as servants,
and shall all become as one child in His sight. An example
of this is had in a human body: although it is made up
of many members, it is called, and is, one body. So also in
the case of the people and the Church: although they are
many individuals, they form one body and are called by one
common name. Therefore, (I concluded), if I were to enumerate all the other Mosaic precepts, my friends, I could
show that they are types, symbols, and prophecies of what
would happen to Christ and those who were foreknown as
those who would believe in Him, and similarly of the deeds
of Christ Himself. But, since I believe that I have already
mentioned a sufficient number of examples, I shall now return to the next point in the order of our discussion.'

---

2 Ps. 18.5.
3 Isa. 53.1-2.

Chapter 43

'As circumcision originated with Abraham, and the Sabbath, sacrifices, oblations, and festivals with Moses (and it has already been shown that your people were commanded to observe these things because of their hardness of heart), so it was expedient that, in accordance with the will of the Father, these things should have their end in Him who was born of the Virgin, of the race of Abraham, of the tribe of Juda, and of the family of David: namely, in Christ, the Son of God, who was proclaimed as the future Eternal Law and New Testament for the whole world (as the above-quoted prophecies clearly show). We, indeed, who have come to God through Jesus Christ, have received not a carnal, but a spiritual, circumcision, as did Henoch and those like him. Through God's mercy we received this by means of baptism, since we had become sinners, and all men should likewise receive it. But the topic to which we must now direct our attention is the mystery of the Birth of Christ. Isaias already stated that man cannot describe it, when he exclaimed: "Who shall declare His generation? Because He is cut off out of the land of the living; for the wickedness of My people He was led to death."[1] The Prophetic Spirit thus declared that the Birth of Him who was to die in order to save us sinners by His stripes was inexpressible. Furthermore, the same Prophetic Spirit, through the same Isaias, informed the faithful how Christ was to be born and how He was to come into this world. The words of the prophecy are: "And the Lord spoke again to Achaz saying: Ask thee a sign of the Lord thy God, in the depth, or in the height above. And Achaz said: I will not ask, and I will not tempt the Lord. And Isaias said: Hear ye therefore, O house of David; Is it a small thing for you to

---
1 Isa. 53.8.

contend with men, that you are to contend with God also? Therefore the Lord Himself shall give you a sign. Behold a Virgin shall conceive, and bear a Son, and His name shall be called Emmanuel. He shall eat butter and honey before He knows to refuse the evil, and to choose the good. For before the Child shall know good or evil, He refuses evil to choose the good. For before the Child knows how to call father or mother, He shall receive the power of Damascus and the spoil of Samaria in the presence of the king of Assyria. And the land shall be forsaken, which thou shalt hardly endure on account of the presence of the two kings. But God shall bring upon thee, and upon thy people, and upon the house of thy father, days that have not yet come upon thee, since the day that He took away Ephraim from Juda the king of the Assyrians."[2] Now, it is clear to all that no one of the race of Abraham was ever born, or even said to be born, of a virgin, except of our Christ. But, since you and your teachers venture to assert that the real words of Isaias are not "Behold, a virgin shall conceive," but "Behold a young woman shall conceive, and bear a son;" and since you refer this prophecy to your king Hezekiah, I will attempt to answer you and show that this prophecy applies to Him whom we profess as our Christ.'

Chapter 44

'I will be absolutely without blame in my obligations to you, if I endeavor to convince you with every possible proof. But, if you persist in your obstinacy of heart and feebleness of mind, or if you refuse to agree to the truth through fear of the death[1] which awaits every Christian, you will have only

---

2 Isa. 7.10-16.

---

1 This refers to the death penalty to which every Christian was then liable, solely because he was a Christian.

yourselves to blame. And you are sadly mistaken if you think that, just because you are descendants of Abraham according to the flesh, you will share in the legacy of benefits which God promised would be distributed by Christ. No one can by any means participate in any of these gifts, except those who have the same ardent faith as Abraham, and who approve of all the mysteries. For I say that some precepts were given for the worship of God and the practice of virtue, whereas other commandments and customs were arranged either in respect to the mystery of Christ [or] the hardness of your people's hearts. To prove this, God thus says through the mouth of Ezechiel: "If Noe and Jacob[2] and Daniel should ask for either sons or daughters, it will not be given unto them."[3] And the same is stated in Isaias: "The Lord God said: And they shall go out and see the carcasses of the men that have transgressed against Me: for their worm shall not die, and their fire shall not be quenched, and they shall be a loathsome sight to all flesh."[4] As men who have cut your souls off from this hope, it is necessary that you know how to obtain pardon of your sins and a hope of sharing in the promised blessings. There is no other way than this, that you come to know our Christ, be baptized with the baptism which cleanses you of sin (as Isaias testified), and thus live a life free of sin.'

Chapter 45

Trypho then interposed, 'Although you insist that your arguments must be lined up in the order predetermined by yourself, permit me to interrupt you at this point to ask a very urgent question.'

---

2 The Septuagint has 'Job.'
3 Ezech. 14.20.
4 Isa. 66.24.

'Ask me,' I replied, 'whatever you please. Then, after such questions and answers have been disposed of, I'll resume my discussion and try to complete it.'

'Then tell me,' he went on, 'whether or not those who have regulated their lives according to the Mosaic Law shall live again together with Jacob, Henoch, and Noe in the resurrection of the dead?'

'My friend,' I answered, 'when I quoted Ezechiel to the effect that "Although Noe, Daniel, and Jacob should ask for sons and daughters, it will not be granted them,"[1] but each one should be saved by his own virtue, I also stated that those who obeyed the Mosaic Law would likewise be saved. They who are obliged to obey the Law of Moses will find in it not only precepts which were occasioned by the hardness of your people's hearts, but also those which in themselves are good, holy, and just. Since they who did those things which are universally, naturally, and eternally good are pleasing to God, they shall be saved in the resurrection, together with their righteous forefathers, Noe, Henoch, Jacob, and others, together with those who believe in Christ, the Son of God, who existed before the morning star and the moon, yet deigned to become Incarnate, and be born of this virgin of the family of David, in order that by this dispensation He might conquer the serpent, that first sinner, and the angels who followed his example, and that He might thwart death and bring it to an end, so that, at the second Advent of Christ, it would no longer have any power over those who believe in Him and live according to His principles. At this second Advent of Christ, some will be condemned to suffer eternally in the fires of Hell, while others will be eternally free from suffering, corruption, and sorrow.'

---

1 Ezech. 14.20.

Chapter 46

'But,' inquired Trypho, 'if some even now desire to live in accordance with the precepts of the Mosaic Law, and yet believe that the crucified Jesus is the Christ of God and that to Him it has been given to judge without exception all men, and that His kingdom is eternal, could they also be saved?'

'Let us examine this together,' I replied, 'and see whether anyone is able now to observe all of the Mosaic precepts.'

'No,' he answered, 'for we recognize, as you said, that it is impossible to sacrifice the paschal lamb anywhere else, or to offer the goats required for the fast, or to present all the other oblations.'

'Then tell me yourself,' I begged, 'some of the commandments which can be observed. Then you could be convinced that, though a man has not practiced or observed your so-called eternal precepts, he can quite certainly be saved.'

'We can keep the Sabbath,' answered Trypho, 'be circumcised, observe the months, and wash ourselves after touching something forbidden by Moses or after sexual relations.'

'Then,' I asked, 'do you think that Abraham, Isaac, Jacob, Noe, Job, and all the others before or after them who also were good people—like Sarah the wife of Abraham, Rebecca the wife of Isaac, Rachel the wife of Jacob, Lia, and the other women like them, down to the time of the mother of Moses the faithful servant—all of whom did not observe these laws, will be saved?'

Trypho replied, 'Were not Abraham and his posterity circumcised?'

'I know,' I retorted, 'that Abraham and his posterity were circumcised. But I have already stated at great length why circumcision was enjoined upon them. If what I have said has not embarrassed you, let us take up the matter again. You know well that not one of those just men who lived before the time of Moses observed, or was ordered to observe, any of the precepts now under discussion, with the exception of circumcision which began with Abraham.'

'That we know,' he answered, 'and we admit that they were saved.'

'You also know,' I continued, 'that, because of the hardness of your hearts, God imposed such commandments upon you through Moses, in order that, by observing these many precepts, you might have Him constantly before your eyes and refrain from every unjust or impious act. Thus, He commanded you to wear a red ribbon[1] as a constant reminder of Him; and for the same purpose He ordered you to wear the phylactery,[2] made up of very thin pieces of parchment upon which were inscribed what we consider truly sacred letters. By these very ordinances He urges you to have God always in mind and, at the same time, His reproach. Notwithstanding this reminder, you still continued to practice idolatry. In the times of Elias, when God was enumerating those who had not bowed the knee to Baal, He could count only seven thousand. And in Isaias He scolds you for having sacrificed your children to idols. But we Christians, because we refuse to offer sacrifice to those whom we formerly worshipped, suffer the most severe punishments, and even rejoice in enduring the death penalty, because we believe that one day God will raise us up again through Christ and will make us free forever from corruption, pain, and death. And we are positive

---

1 Cf. Num. 15.38-41.
2 A small box containing parchments on which were written in Hebrew the following texts: Exod. 13.1-16; Deut. 6.4-9; 11.13-21. During prayers, this box was attached to the left arm or forehead by means of leather straps.

that the precepts, imposed upon you on account of your people's hardness of heart, are in no way conducive to acts of justice and piety.'

Chapter 47

'But,' Trypho again objected, 'if a man knows that what you say is true, and, professing Jesus to be the Christ, believes in and obeys Him, yet desires also to observe the commandments of the Mosaic Law, shall he be saved?'

'In my opinion,' I replied, 'I say such a man will be saved, unless he exerts every effort to influence other men (I have in mind the Gentiles whom Christ circumcised from all error) to practice the same rites as himself, informing them that they cannot be saved unless they do so. You yourself did this at the opening of our discussion, when you said that I would not be saved unless I kept the Mosaic precepts.'

'But why,' pressed Trypho, 'did you say, "In my opinion such a man will be saved?" There must, therefore, be other Christians who hold a different opinion.'

'Yes, Trypho,' I conceded, 'there are some Christians who boldly refuse to have conversation or meals with such persons. I don't agree with such Christians. But if some [Jewish converts], due to their instability of will, desire to observe as many of the Mosaic precepts as possible—precepts which we think were instituted because of your hardness of heart—while at the same time they place their hope in Christ, and if they desire to perform the eternal and natural acts of justice and piety, yet wish to live with us Christians and believers, as I already stated, not persuading them to be circumcised like themselves, or to keep the Sabbath, or to perform any other similar acts, then it is my opinion that we Christians should receive them and associate with them in every way as kinsmen and brethren. But if any of your people, Trypho, profess their belief in Christ, and at the same time force the Christian Gentiles to follow the Law instituted through Moses, or refuse to share in communion with them this same common life, I certainly will also not approve of them. But I think that those Gentiles who have been induced to follow the practices of the Jewish Law, and at the same time profess their faith in the Christ of God, will probably be saved. Those persons, however, who had once believed and publicly acknowledged Jesus to be the Christ, and then later, for one reason or another, turned to the observance of the Mosaic Law, and denied that Jesus is the Christ, cannot be saved unless they repent before their death. The same can be said of those descendants of Abraham, who follow the Law and refuse to believe in Christ to their very last breath. Especially excluded from eternal salvation are they who in their synagogues have cursed and still do curse those who believe in that very Christ in order that they may attain salvation and escape the avenging fires of Hell. God in His goodness, kindness, and infinite richness considers the repentant sinner to be just and innocent, as He declared through the Prophet Ezechiel,[1] and the one who turns from the path of piety and justice to follow that of injustice and impiety God judges to be an impious and unjust sinner. Thus has our Lord Jesus Christ warned us: "In whatsoever things I shall apprehend you, in them also shall I judge you."[2]

---
1 Cf. Ezech. 33.11-20.
2 These words are not found either in the Old or in the New Testament. The author of the *Quis dives salvetur* also cites this saying. Some think it may have been in one of the Apocryphal Gospels, e. g., the Gospel to the Hebrews. Justin may also have had in mind Ezech. 33.16-20, and he could have quoted the words as spoken by Christ, since he was so conscious of the feeling that Christ spoke to men in the Old Testament.

Chapter 48

'We have now heard your opinion on these matters,' interrupted Trypho. 'Resume your discourse where you left off, and bring it to an end, for it seems to be entirely absurd and utterly impossible of proof. Your statement that this Christ existed as God before all ages, and then that He consented to be born and become man, yet that He is not of human origin, appears to be not only paradoxical, but preposterous.'

'I am aware,' I replied, 'that my assertion must seem paradoxical, especially to you Jews, who were never in the least interested in knowing or doing the things of God, but only the things of your teachers, as God Himself testifies.[1] However, Trypho, the fact that this Man is the Christ of God is not to be denied, even if I were unable to prove that He, being God, pre-existed as the Son of the Creator of the universe and became Man through a virgin. Since it has been proved beyond all doubt that He is the Christ of God, whatever that Christ eventually is to be, even if I fail to show that He pre-existed, and consented to become man with a body and feelings like our own, according to the will of the Father; only in this last regard could you rightly claim that I have been wrong. But you cannot deny that He is the Christ, even though He apparently is of human origin, and evidently became the Christ by the Father's choice. For, my friends, there are some of our race,[2] who acknowledge that Jesus is the Christ, but claim that He has a merely human

---
1 Cf. Isa. 29.3.
2 Some read, 'of your race,' and then apply the passage to the Ebionites (Christian heretics of Jewish origin); but most critics retain the reading, 'of our race,' arguing that St. Justin would have considered the Ebionites first as Christians (even though they were heretical), and then as Jews.

origin. I naturally disagree with such persons, nor would I agree with them even if the majority of those who share my opinions were to say so. For we have been told by Christ Himself not to follow the teachings of men, but only those which have been announced by the holy Prophets and taught by Himself.'

Chapter 49

'It appears to me,' said Trypho, 'that they who assert that He was of human origin, and was anointed as the Christ only by choice, propose a doctrine much more credible than yours. We Jews all expect that Christ will be a man of merely human origin, and that Elias will come to anoint Him. If this man appears to be the Christ, He must be considered to be a man of solely human birth, yet, from the fact that Elias has not yet come, I must declare that this man is not the Christ.'

Then I asked him, 'Does not the holy book of Zacharias[1] state that Elias shall come before the great and terrible day of the Lord?'

'Most assuredly,' he replied.

'If, therefore, Scripture forces you to admit that it was predicted that there would be two Advents of Christ—one in which He will appear in suffering and without honor or beauty, and the second in which He will return in glory to judge all men, as has been proved by the many previously quoted passages from Scripture—must we not conclude that the word of God has foretold that Elias will be the forerunner of the great and terrible day, namely, of His second Advent?'

'Certainly,' was his answer.

'We have been taught,' I continued, 'by our Lord Himself

---

1 Not Zacharias, but Mal. 4.5.

that this would be so, namely, that Elias also would come; and we know that this will take place when our Lord Jesus Christ will be about to come from Heaven in glory, just as the spirit of God that was in Elias, in the person of John, who was a prophet of your race, after whom no other prophet has appeared among you, came forth as the precursor of His first Advent. For John cried out as he sat by the River Jordan: "I indeed baptize you with water, for repentance; but He who is coming after me is mightier than I, and His sandals I am not worthy to bear. He will baptize you with the Holy Spirit and with fire. His winnowing fan is in His hand, and He will thoroughly clean out His threshing floor, and will gather His wheat into the barn; but the chaff He will burn up with unquenchable fire."[2] Your King Herod imprisoned this Prophet John, and, during Herod's birthday party, his niece's[3] dancing pleased him so much that he promised to give her whatever she desired. At her mother's instigation, the young girl asked for the head of the imprisoned John. Thereupon, Herod ordered the head of John to be brought in on a platter. Wherefore did our Christ, who was on earth at this time, reply to those who were saying that Elias must come before the appearance of Christ: "Elias indeed is to come and will restore all things. But I say to you that Elias has come already, and they did not know him, but did to him whatever they wished."[4] And it is added: "Then the disciples understood that He had spoken to them of John the Baptist."[5]

'You seem to me,' replied Trypho, 'to be talking paradoxically again when you say that God's Prophetic Spirit

---
[2] Matt. 3.11-12; Luke 3.16-17.
[3] Literally, 'cousin.'
[4] Matt. 17.11-12.
[5] Matt. 17.13.

which was in Elias was also in John.'

'Must you not admit,' I retorted, 'that the same thing happened in the case of Josue, son of Nun, who succeeded Moses as leader of your people, when Moses was ordered to lay his hands on him, while God Himself said: "I will transfer some of the spirit that is in you to him?"'[6]

'That I admit,' he replied.

'Therefore,' I concluded, 'as God took the spirit that was in Moses, while he was on earth, and communicated it to Josue, so was He able to transfer the spirit from Elias to John, in order that, as Christ appeared without glory at His first Advent, so likewise the first Advent of the spirit, which ever remained in the same state of purity[7] in Elias, might be perceived to be without glory, as was Christ's first Advent. The Lord is said to fight against Amalec with hidden hand, and you will have to admit that Amalec has fallen. But, if it is affirmed that war will be waged against Amalec only at the glorious Advent of Christ, how would that fulfill the Scriptural quotation, "God will fight Amalec with hidden hand?"[8] You can see, therefore, that the hidden power of God was in the crucified Christ, before whom the demons and shortly all the powers and authorities of the earth tremble.'

Chapter 50

'You seem,' said Trypho, 'to have debated with many persons on every possible topic, and consequently are ready to answer any of my questions. Tell me then, first of all, how can you prove that there is another God besides the Creator

---
6 Justin may have confused the story of the selection of the seventy elders (Num. 11.17 ff.) with the election of Josue (Num. 27.18 and Deut. 34.9).
7 I. e., Elias lost nothing by the transmission of his spirit to John.
8 Exod. 17.16.

of the world, and then show that He condescended to be born of a virgin.'

'Allow me first,' I requested, 'to quote some passages from the Prophet Isaias concerning John the Baptist, who was also a Prophet and the herald of our Lord Jesus Christ.'

'Go ahead,' said he.

'Here are the predictions of Isaias,' I went on, 'concerning John as forerunner: "And Ezechias said to Isaias: The word of the Lord, which He hath spoken, is good: only let peace and truth be in my days." And: "Comfort ye the people; speak, ye priests, to the heart of Jerusalem and comfort her, because her humiliation is completed. Her iniquity is forgiven, for she hath received of the hand of the Lord double for all her sins. A voice of one crying in the desert: Prepare ye the way of the Lord, make straight the paths of our God. Every valley shall be exalted, and every mountain and hill shall be made low, and the crooked shall become straight, and the rough ways plain. And the glory of the Lord shall be revealed, and all flesh shall see the salvation of God, for so hath the Lord spoken. The voice of one saying: Cry. And I said: What shall I cry? All flesh is grass, and all the glory of man as the flower of grass. The grass is withered, and the flower is fallen; but the word of the Lord remaineth forever. Get thee up upon a high mountain, thou that bringest good tidings to Sion; lift up thy voice with strength, thou that bringest good tidings to Jerusalem; lift it up, fear not. Say to the cities of Juda: Behold your God. Behold the Lord comes with strength and His arm rules. Behold His reward is with Him, and His work before Him. He shall feed His flock like a shepherd, and He shall gather together the lambs with His arm, and He shall comfort her that is with young. Who hath measured the waters in the hollow of his hands, and weighed the heavens with his palm, and all the earth with his fist? Who hath weighed the mountains in scales, and the hills in a balance? Who hath known the mind of the Lord? And who hath been His counsellor, and hath taught Him? Or with whom hath He consulted, and who hath instructed Him? Or who showed Him the path of justice, or the way of understanding? All nations are as a drop of a bucket, and are counted as the smallest grain of a balance, and shall be reckoned as spittle. And Libanus shall not be enough to burn, nor the beasts thereof sufficient for a burnt offering; and all nations are considered as nothing, and have been counted as nothing." [1]

Chapter 51

When I had finished, Trypho remarked, 'My friend, the words of the prophecy which you just quoted are ambiguous, and they certainly do not prove what you want them to prove.'

'If,' I replied, 'prophets had not ceased in your race, Trypho, but still now appeared after this John, you might undoubtedly consider ambiguous what I say about Jesus Christ. But, if John came as forerunner, exhorting men to repent, and then Christ came and brought to a close his prophesying and baptizing at the River Jordan, and preached the Gospel in person, affirming that the Kingdom of Heaven is imminent, and that He had to suffer much at the hands of the Scribes and Pharisees, and be crucified, and rise again on the third day, and appear again at Jerusalem to eat and drink with His disciples; and predicted that in the meantime before His second Advent there would arise, as I already stated, heresies and false prophets in His name (which has been verified), how can there be a question of

---
1 Isa. 39.8; 40.1-17.

ambiguity, when the facts speak for themselves? He also mentioned that there would no longer be any prophets among your people, and that men would acknowledge that the New Testament, which God long since had promised to establish, was then an actuality, namely, that He Himself was the Christ. Here are His words: "The Law and the Prophets were until John the Baptist, from which time the Kingdom of Heaven suffereth violence, and the violent take it away by force. And if you are willing to receive it, he is Elias who was to come. He who has ears to hear, let him hear." [1]

Chapter 52

'It also was foretold by the Patriarch Jacob,' I continued, 'that there would be two Advents of Christ, and that in the first He would be subject to suffering, and that after this Advent your people would have neither prophet nor king, and that the Gentiles who believe in the suffering Christ would look forward to His second coming. For this reason the Holy Spirit spoke these things obscurely in parables, when He said: "Juda, thee hath thy brethren praised; thy hands shall be on the necks of thine enemies; the sons of thy father shall bow down to thee. Juda is a lion's whelp; from the germ, my son, thou art sprung up. Resting thou hast couched as a lion, and as a lion's whelp; who shall rouse him? There shall not fail a leader out of Juda, nor a ruler from his thigh, until those things that are reserved for him shall have come; and he shall be the expectation of nations. Tying His foal to the vine, and the foal's ass to the tendril of the vine, He shall wash His robe in wine, and His garment in the blood of the grape. His eyes are more sparkling than

---

[1] Matt. 11.12-15; Luke 16.16.

the wine, and His teeth are as white as milk."[1] You will not have the nerve to assert, nor could you prove it if you did, that your race did not always have a prophet or king from the beginning until the time when Jesus Christ was born and suffered. Although you claim that Herod, after whose reign Christ suffered, was from Ascalon,[2] you still must admit that you then had a high priest of your own race, so that even then you had one who offered sacrifices and observed the other legal ceremonies of the Mosaic Law. And since you also had a continuous succession of prophets down to John (even when your people were led captive into Babylon, your lands ravaged by war, and your sacred vessels carried away), there never ceased to be a prophet in your midst who was lord and leader and ruler of your people. Indeed, even your kings were appointed and anointed by the spirit in these prophets. But, since the advent and death of our Jesus Christ in your midst, you have not had a prophet, nor do you now possess one. Furthermore, you no longer live under your own king, and, in addition, your land has been laid waste, and abandoned as "a lodge in a garden."[3] And those words spoken by Jacob, "And He shall be the expectation of nations,"[4] signified figuratively His two Advents, and also that the Gentiles would believe in Him, which you can now certainly verify as a fact. For we Christians, made up of all nationalities, have become pious and just through our faith in Christ, and we look forward to His second Advent.'

Chapter 53

'And the passage, "Tying His foal to the vine, and the

---
1 Gen. 49.8-12.
2 And, therefore, not a Jew.
3 Isa. 1.8.
4 Gen. 49.10.

foal's ass to the tendril of the vine,"¹ was a prophecy both of the deeds He would perform at His first coming and of the Gentiles' belief in Him. For the Gentiles, like a foal, had never been harnessed or felt a yoke upon their necks, until our Christ arrived and sent His disciples to convert them. They have borne the yoke of His word, and have bent their backs to endure all things, because they look forward to the many priceless rewards which He promised them. Indeed, our Lord Jesus Christ, when He was about to enter Jerusalem, ordered His disciples to get Him the ass with its foal, which was tied at a gate of the village of Bethphage, and He rode upon it as He entered Jerusalem. Since it had been explicitly foretold that the Christ would do precisely this, when He had done it in the sight of all He furnished clear proof that He was the Christ. And yet, even after these things have happened and are proved from the Scriptures, you persist in refusing to believe. Zacharias, one of the twelve Prophets, predicted this very event when he said: "Rejoice greatly, O daughter of Sion; shout for joy, O daughter of Jerusalem. Behold thy King will come to thee, the just and savior; meek and lowly, riding upon an ass, and upon the foal of an ass."² Now that the Prophetic Spirit, as well as the Patriarch Jacob, mentioned the ass, an animal accustomed to the yoke, and its foal, which were in His possession, and that He bade his disciples, as I have said before, to lead the beasts to Him, constituted a prediction that both you coming from the synagogue and those who would come from the Gentiles would believe in Him. As the unharnessed foal was a figure of the former Gentiles, so the ass, accustomed to the yoke, was a symbol of those coming from among your people.

---

1 Gen. 49.11.
2 Zach. 9.9.

For you have the Law laid upon you by the Prophets as a yoke. The same Zacharias foretold that Christ would be struck, and His disciples scattered, which actually happened. For, after He was crucified, His disciples were dispersed until He arose again from the dead, and proved to them that it had been predicted that He would have to suffer. When they were convinced of this, they went out to all the world teaching these things.³ Thus we are firm in our faith in Him and in His doctrine, because our faith is grounded upon both the Prophets and those who, openly throughout the world, are worshippers of God in the name of the Crucified One. Indeed, Zacharias said: "Awake, O sword, against My shepherd, and against the man of My people, saith the Lord of hosts. Strike the shepherd, and His sheep shall be scattered." ⁴

Chapter 54

'And those prophetical words of Jacob, as recorded by Moses, namely, "He shall wash His robe in wine, and His garment in the blood of the grape,"¹ signified that He would wash in His own blood those who believed in Him. For the Holy Spirit called those whose sins were forgiven by Christ, His robe; among whom He is always present in power, but among whom will be manifestly present in person at His second coming. The expression, "the blood of the grape," indictates allegorically that Christ has blood not from human seed, but from the power of God. For, as God, not man, has made the blood of the grape, so it has been foretold that the blood of Christ would not be from human seed, but from divine power. Therefore, my friends, this prophecy which

---

3 Apparently an allusion to Mark 16.20.
4 Zach. 13.7.

---

1 Gen. 49.11.

I have quoted shows that Christ is not a man of mere human origin, begotten in the ordinary human manner.'

Chapter 55

'We will keep in mind this interpretation of yours,' replied Trypho, 'if you can vindicate your point with other arguments as well. But now, return to the original topic and prove to us that the Prophetic Spirit ever admits the existence of another God, besides the Creator of all things; and do be careful not to mention the sun and moon, which, Scripture tells us, God permitted the Gentiles to worship as gods.[1] Even prophets often misuse the word in this sense, when they say: "Thy God is God of gods and Lord of lords," often adding: "the great and mighty and terrible."[2] Such words are used, not as if they were really gods, but because the word is instructing us that the true God, the Creator of all, is the sole Lord of all those who are falsely regarded as gods and lords. To convince us of this the Holy Spirit said through David: "The gods of the Gentiles (although reputed as gods) are idols of demons, and not gods."[3] And He places a curse upon those who make or worship such idols.'

'Trypho,' I answered, 'these are not the proofs I was about to offer, for from your quotations I know that they who worship these and similar objects are justly condemned, but I am ready to adduce arguments that no one can contradict, arguments which may seem unusual to you, although you read them every day. Hence, we readily understand why, on account of your iniquity, God has hidden from you the power of discerning the wisdom of His words, with

---
1 Deut. 4.19 might be interpreted that way by Jews, but Justin proves, by the words of the Prophets, that only God is to be worshipped.
2 Deut. 10.17.
3 Cf. Ps. 95.5.

the exception of those few to whom, in His infinite mercy, He has left a seed for salvation (to use the words of Isaias), lest your race perish completely from this earth, as did the people of Sodom and Gomorrah. Listen, therefore, to these Scriptural quotations which need no explanation, but only to be heard.'

Chapter 56

'Moses, that faithful and blessed servant of God, tells us that He who appeared to Abraham under the oak tree of Mamre was God, sent with two accompanying angels to judge Sodom by Another who ever abides in the super-celestial sphere, who has never been seen by any man, and with whom no man has ever conversed, and whom we call Creator of all and Father. Here are the words of Moses: "And God appeared to him under the oak in Mamre, as he was sitting at the door of his tent, in the very heat of the day. And when he had lifted up his eyes, he saw and beheld three men standing near him. And as soon as he saw them he ran to meet them from the door of his tent, and he bowed himself toward the ground, and said,"[1] and so on, to the words: "And Abraham got up early in the morning to the place where he stood before the Lord; and he looked toward Sodom and Gomorrah, and the whole land of that country, and behold, he saw a flame go up from the earth as the smoke of a furnace." '[2]

At this point I asked them if they understood this quotation. They answered that they knew the meaning of the cited passages, but failed to see how they proved that, besides the Creator of the world, any other God or Lord exists or is mentioned by the Holy Spirit.

---
1 Gen. 18.1-2.
2 Gen. 19.27-28.

'Then,' I replied, 'since you understand these quotations from Scripture, I shall attempt to prove my assertion, namely, that there exists and is mentioned in Scripture another God and Lord under the Creator of all things, who is also called an Angel, because He proclaims to man whatever the Creator of the world—above whom there is no other God—wishes to reveal to them.'

Then, repeating the previously-quoted Scriptural passages, I asked Trypho if he really believed that God appeared to Abraham under the oak in Mamre, as the Scriptures stated.

'I certainly do,' he replied.

'Was He one of those three,' I asked, 'who, the Prophetic Spirit says, were seen as men by Abraham?'

'No,' Trypho answered, 'but God appeared to him before he saw the three men. Furthermore, those three whom the Scripture calls men were angels. Two of them were commissioned to destroy Sodom, while the third was sent to impart to Sara the good news that she was to have a son (and having fulfilled his mission, he departed.)'

'How do you explain,' I went on, 'that one of the three who was in the tent, and who promised, "I will return to thee in due season, and Sara shall have a son,"[3] did return after Sara gave birth to her son, and the prophecy then asserts that He is God? For a clearer insight into the truth of my words, listen to these quite explicit words of Moses: "And when Sara had seen the son of Agar, the Egyptian bondwoman, whom she bore to Abraham, playing with her son Isaac, she said to Abraham: Cast out this bondwoman and her son, for the son of the bondwoman shall not be heir with my son Isaac. Abraham took this grievously because of his son. And God said to Abraham: Let it not seem grievous

---

3 Gen. 18.10.

to thee for the boy and for thy bondwoman; in all that Sara hath said to thee, hearken to her voice; for in Isaac shall thy seed be called."[4] Do you not see, therefore, that He who promised under the oak that He would return, since He knew He would be needed to counsel Abraham to do what Sara wished, did return according to the Scriptures, and is God, as these following words indicate: "And God said to Abraham: Let it not seem grievous to thee for the boy and for thy bondwoman" '?[5]

'That's right,' said Trypho, 'but you have not thereby proved that this is another God besides Him who appeared to Abraham, and who appeared also to the other Patriarchs and Prophets. All you have shown is that we were mistaken in our assumption that the three who were in the tent with Abraham were all angels.'

'Then,' I said, 'if I could not prove to you from the Scriptures that one of these three is God, and yet is termed an Angel or "messenger" (because, as stated above, He delivered the messages of God, the Creator of all to whomsoever God desires), and that He who appeared to Abraham on earth in human form (as did the two angels who accompanied Him) was in fact the God who existed before the creation of the universe, it would be logical for you to adhere to the common doctrine of your people.'

'Without a doubt,' he replied, 'for this has been our belief up to now.'

'Then,' I said, 'let us return to the Scriptures and I shall try to convince you that He who is said to have appeared to Abraham, Jacob, and Moses, and is called God, is distinct from God, the Creator; distinct, that is, in number, but not

---
4 Gen. 21.9-12.
5 Gen. 21.12.

in mind. For I state that He never did or said anything else than what the Creator—above whom there is no other God—desired that He do or say.'

'Prove now,' said Trypho, 'that He exists, so that we can agree also upon this. For we understand that you deny that He affirmed, did, or said anything contrary to the will of the Creator.'

'The previously quoted Scriptural passages will make this evident to you,' I replied. 'Here are the words: "The sun was risen upon the earth, and Lot entered into Segor. And the Lord rained upon Sodom brimstone and fire from the Lord out of Heaven. And He destroyed these cities, and all the country round about." '[6]

Then the fourth of the companions who remained with Trypho spoke up: 'It must therefore be admitted that one of the two angels who went down to Sodom, and whom Moses in the Scriptures calls Lord, is different from Him who is also God, and appeared to Abraham.'

'Not only because of that quotation,' I said, 'must we certainly admit that, besides the Creator of the universe, another was called Lord by the Holy Spirit. For this was attested to not only by Moses, but also by David, when he said: "The Lord said to my Lord: Sit Thou at My right hand, until I make Thy enemies Thy footstool."[7] And in other words: "Thy throne, O God, is forever and ever; the sceptre of Thy kingdom is a sceptre of uprightness. Thou hast loved justice, and hated iniquity; therefore God, Thy God, hath anointed Thee with the oil of gladness above Thy fellow."[8] Tell me if it is your opinion that the Holy Spirit calls another God and Lord, besides the Father of all things

---

6 Gen. 19.23-25.
7 Ps. 109.1.
8 Ps. 44.7-8.

and His Christ. For, I am now going to prove to you from the Scriptures themselves that He, who was termed Lord in the Scriptures, is not one of the two angels who went down to Sodom, but He who accompanied them, and is called God, who appeared to Abraham.'

'Hurry on with your proof, then,' said Trypho, 'for, as you see, it is getting late in the day, and we are not ready to make any unguarded replies, for we have never before heard anyone who made such inquiries, examinations, or proofs. In fact, we would not have listened to you thus far, had you not constantly cited the Scriptures in your attempts to prove your point, and had you not stated that there is no God superior to the Creator of the world.'

'You must surely know,' I went on, 'the following quotation from Scripture: "And the Lord said to Abraham: Why did Sara laugh, saying: Shall I who am an old woman bear a child indeed? Is there anything impossible to God? According to appointment I will return to thee in due season, and Sara shall have a son."[9] And a little later: "And the men rose up from thence, and turned their eyes towards Sodom and Gomorrah; and Abraham walked with them, bringing them on the way. And the Lord said: I will not hide from Abraham My servant what I am doing."[10] And again, soon after, it is written: "And the Lord said: The cry of Sodom and Gomorrah is multiplied, and their sin is become exceedingly grievous. I will go down and see whether they have done according to the cry that is come to Me; or whether it be not so, that I may know. And they turned themselves from thence, and went their way to Sodom; but Abraham as yet stood before the Lord. And Abraham drew

---

9 Gen. 18.13-14.
10 Gen. 18.16-17.

near and said: Wilt Thou destroy the just with the wicked?"[11] (And so forth, for I don't deem it necessary to repeat the words I have already written, but only those which really clinched my argument with Trypho and his friends.) Thus, I passed over to the following words of Scripture: "And the Lord departed, after He had left speaking to Abraham; and Abraham returned to his place. And two angels came to Sodom in the evening; and Lot was sitting at the gate of Sodom."[12] And so on, until: "But the men put forth their hands, and drew Lot into the house unto them, and shut the door."[13] And then the following words occur: "And the angels took his hand, and the hand of his wife, and of his daughters, because the Lord spared him. And it came to pass, when they had brought them forth out of the city, they said, Save, save thy life. Look not back, neither stay thou in all the country about; but save thyself in the mountain, lest thou also be consumed. But Lot said to them: I beseech Thee my Lord, because Thy servant hath found grace before Thee, and Thou hast magnified Thy mercy, which Thou hast shown to me in saving my life; but I cannot escape to the mountain, lest some evil seize me, and I die. Behold, there is this city here at hand, to which I may flee, and it is little; there I shall be safe, since it is little, and my soul shall live. And He said to him: Behold also in this I have heard thy prayers, not to destroy the city for which thou hast spoken. Make haste and be saved there, because I cannot do anything till thou go in thither. Therefore he called that city Segor. The sun was risen upon the earth, and Lot entered into Segor. And the Lord rained upon Sodom and Gomorrah brimstone and fire from the

---

11 Gen. 18.20-23.
12 Gen. 18.33-19.1.
13 Gen 19.10.

Lord out of heaven. And He destroyed those cities, and all the country about." [14] At this point I asked, 'Do you not see, my friends, that one of the three, who is both God and Lord, and ministers to Him who is in Heaven, is Lord of the two angels? When they went on to Sodom, He stayed behind and talked with Abraham, as Moses testified. Then He went His way after His conversation, and Abraham returned to his place. And when He came to Sodom, it was no longer the two angels, but He Himself, who talked with Lot, as is evident from the Scriptures. He, indeed, is the Lord who was commissioned by the Lord in Heaven, that is, the Creator of all things, to inflict those dreadful punishments upon Sodom and Gomorrah, which are described in the Scriptures in this fashion: "The Lord rained upon Sodom and Gomorrah brimstone and fire from the Lord out of Heaven." [15]

Chapter 57

When I had finished, Trypho admitted, 'The Scriptures evidently compel us to agree with you. But you must admit that our perplexity is justified at those words which describe how the Lord ate the food which was prepared and presented to Him by Abraham.'

'It is indeed written,' I replied, 'that they ate. But, if we heard it said that the three did eat, and not the two only, who were in reality angels and were evidently fed in Heaven, though not with the same kind of food that humans consume (for, in speaking of the manna which your forefathers ate in the desert, the Scriptures say[1] that they ate the food of angels), then I would say that when the Scripture asserts

---
14 Gen. 19.16-26.
15 Gen. 19.24.

---
1 Ps. 77.25.

they ate, it is to be understood in the same way as when we say that fire devours everything, but not in the sense that they ate by chewing the food with their teeth and jaws. Thus, if we are in any way familiar with the use of figurative modes of expression, even in this Scriptural passage there should be nothing puzzling to us.'

'It is possible,' conceded Trypho, 'that your explanation of the different ways of eating would solve the difficulty arising from the statement that Abraham's guests, in consuming the food set before them, are said to have eaten it. So go on, now, to prove how this God who appeared to Abraham, and ministered to the Creator of the universe, was born of a virgin, and became a man, as you claim, suffering like all others.'

'Before I produce the proof that you ask, Trypho,' I said, 'permit me to offer you some additional arguments on the topic under discussion, that you also may be persuaded about it.'

'Go ahead,' he replied, 'for that will be agreeable to me.'

Chapter 58

'I wish to quote Scripture to you,' I said, 'without any merely artistic arrangement of arguments. Indeed, I have no such skill, but this grace alone was given me from God to understand His Scriptures, in which grace I invite everyone to share freely and abundantly, lest I should be held accountable at the judgment which God, the Creator of the universe, shall hold through my Lord Jesus Christ.'

'In doing so,' said Trypho, 'you surely show true piety toward God, but when you state that you have no talent in the art of discussion, I suspect that you are just pretending ignorance in this matter.'

'If you think so,' I replied, 'we will not argue the point, but I still feel that I spoke the truth. Be that as it may, if you will give me your undivided attention, I'll present the rest of my proof.'

'Proceed,' he said.

'My brethren,' I went on, 'it has been stated by Moses that He who is termed God, and who appeared to the Patriarchs, is also called Angel and Lord, in order that by these expressions you may recognize Him as the minister of the Father of all things (which you have already admitted, but which through additional arguments you shall believe more firmly). The word of God, as recorded by Moses, speaks of Jacob, grandson of Abraham, in the following manner: "And it came to pass at that time that the sheep conceived; I saw them with my eyes in my sleep. And behold the he-goats and rams which leaped upon the sheep and she-goats were white-streaked, and spotted, and speckled. And the angel of God said unto me in my sleep, Jacob, Jacob. And I answered: What is it, Lord? And He said: Lift up thy eyes, and see the he-goats and rams which leap upon the sheep and she-goats are white-streaked, and spotted, and speckled. For I have seen all that Laban hath done to thee. I am the God who appeared to thee in Bethel, where thou didst anoint the stone, and make a vow to Me. Now therefore arise, and go out of this land, and return into thy native country, and I will be with thee."[1] And another passage speaks thus of Jacob: "And rising early he took his two wives, and his two handmaids, with his eleven sons, and passed over the ford of Jaboc. And he took them, and sent them over the brook, and sent over all his belongings. And Jacob was left alone; and an Angel wrestled with him till morning. And when He saw

---
1 Gen. 31.10-14.

that He could not overcome him, He touched the sinew of his thigh while they wrestled, and forthwith it became numb. And He said to him: Let Me go, for it is break of day. He answered: I will not let Thee go except Thou bless me. And He said: What is thy name? He answered: Jacob. But He said: Thy name shall not be called Jacob, but Israel, for thou hast prevailed with God, and shalt be powerful with men. Jacob asked: Tell me by what name art Thou called? And He answered: Why dost thou ask My name? And He blessed him in the same place. And Jacob called the name of the place, The Vision of God, saying: I have seen God face to face, and my soul rejoiced."[2] And again in another place it is written of the same Jacob: "And Jacob came to Luza, which is in the land of Chanaan, surnamed Bethel; he and all the people that were with him. And he built there an altar, and called the name of that place Bethel, for there God appeared to him when he fled from his brother Esau. At the same time Debora, the nurse of Rebecca, died and was buried at the foot of Bethel under an oak; and Jacob called the name of that place, The Oak of Mourning. And God appeared again to Jacob, after he returned from Mesopotamia of Syria, and He blessed him; saying: Thou shalt not be called any more Jacob, but Israel shall be thy name."[3]

'He is called God, He is God, and shall always be God.' At these words they all nodded their heads in agreement. Then I said, 'I consider it most appropriate that I repeat here the Scriptural passage which tells how He who is Angel and God and Lord, and who appeared as a man to Abraham, and who wrestled in human form with Jacob, was seen by the same Jacob as he fled from his brother Esau. Here are the sacred words: "And Jacob went out from the Well of

---
2 Gen. 32.22-31.
3 Gen. 35.6-10.

the Oath, and went towards Charran. And he came to a certain place, and slept there, because the sun was set. And he took of the stones that lay there, and putting them under his head, he slept in that place. And he saw in his sleep a ladder standing upon the earth, and the top thereof touching heaven; and the angels of God ascended and descended upon it. And the Lord leaning upon the ladder, said: I am the Lord God of Abraham thy father, and of Isaac; fear not. The land wherein thou sleepest, I will give to thee and to thy seed. And thy seed shall be as the dust of the earth, and shall be spread abroad to the sea, and to the south, and to the north, and to the east; and in thee and thy seed all the tribes of the earth shall be blessed. And I will be thy keeper withersoever thou goest, and will bring thee back into this land; neither will I leave thee, till I shall have accomplished all that I have said. And when Jacob awaked out of his sleep, he said: indeed the Lord is in this place, and I knew it not. And trembling he said: How terrible is this place! This is no other but the house of God, and the gate of Heaven. And Jacob, arising in the morning, took the stone, which he had laid under his head and set it up for a monument, pouring oil upon the top of it. And Jacob called the name of the city Bethel, which before was called Ulmmaus." '[4]

Chapter 59

Then I continued, 'Allow me now to show you from the words of the book of Exodus how this very Person who was at the same time Angel and God and Lord and Man, and who was seen by Abraham and Jacob,[1] also appeared and talked to Moses from the flame of the fiery bush.' And when

---
4 Gen. 28.10-19.

1 The MSS. have 'Isaac,' which may have been a transcriber's error.

I was assured by my audience that they would listen gladly, patiently, and eagerly, I went on, 'In the Book of Exodus it is written: "Now after a long time the king of Egypt died, and the children of Israel groaned by reason of the works."[2] And so on, until it is written: "Go, gather together the ancients of Israel, and thou shall say to them: The Lord God of your fathers, the God of Abraham, the God of Isaac, and the God of Jacob, hath appeared to me, saying: Visiting I have visited you, and I have seen all that hath befallen you in Egypt."[3] Then I asked, 'My friends, do you not see that He whom Moses speaks of as an Angel who conversed with him from the fiery bush is the same who, being God, signifies to Moses that He is the God of Abraham, of Isaac, and of Jacob?'

Chapter 60

'From the words you quoted,' replied Trypho, 'the only conclusion we can draw is that it was an Angel who was seen in the fiery bush, but God who talked with Moses; so that in the apparition there were really two Persons together: Angel and God.'

'Even if it were so,' I answered, 'that both an Angel and God appeared together in the apparition to Moses, yet, as my previously quoted passages prove, it will not be the Creator of the world who is the God who said to Moses that He was the God of Abraham, of Isaac, and of Jacob, but it will be He who was proved to you to have been seen by Abraham and Jacob, doing the will of the Creator of the universe, and putting into execution His will in the judgment of Sodom. Thus, even if there were two persons, as you claim, an Angel and God, yet no one with even the slightest in-

---
[2] Exod. 2.23.
[3] Exod. 3.16.

telligence would dare to assert that the Creator and Father of all things left His super-celestial realms to make Himself visible in a little spot on earth.'

'It has already been shown,' agreed Trypho, 'that He who appeared to Abraham, and was called God and Lord, executed the commission (which He received from the Lord in Heaven) to punish the Sodomites. Even if the God who appeared to Moses was accompanied by an Angel, we cannot identify the God who spoke to Moses from the bush with God, the Creator of all, but with Him who certainly appeared to Abraham, Isaac, and Jacob, and who was also called and perceived to be the Angel of the Creator, because He made known to men the will of the Father and Creator.'

'Trypho,' I said, 'I now wish to prove to you that in the apparition under discussion, He who is termed an Angel and is God was the only One who talked to and was seen by Moses. Here is the Scriptural proof: "The Angel of the Lord appeared to him in a flame of fire out of the midst of a bush; and he saw that the bush was on fire and was not burnt. And Moses said: I will go and see this great sight, why the bush is not burnt. And when the Lord saw that He went forward to see, He called to him out of the midst of the bush."[1] Now, as the Scripture refers to Him who appeared to Jacob in a dream as an Angel, and then states that the same Angel said to Jacob in his sleep, "I am the God who appeared to thee when thou didst flee from the face of thy brother Esau";[2] and as Scripture also affirms that, in the judgment of Sodom in the days of Abraham, the Lord executed the will of the Lord who is in Heaven; so when the Scripture here states that an Angel of the Lord appeared to Moses, and then announces that He is Lord and God, it

---
1 Exod. 3.2-4.
2 Gen. 35.7.

refers to the same Person who is identified in many of our earlier quotations as the minister to God, who is above the world, and above whom there is no other God.'

Chapter 61

'So, my friends,' I said, 'I shall now show from the Scriptures that God has begotten of Himself a certain rational Power as a Beginning[1] before all other creatures. The Holy Spirit indicates this Power by various titles, sometimes the Glory of the Lord, at other times Son, or Wisdom, or Angel, or God, or Lord, or Word. He even called Himself Commander-in-chief when He appeared in human guise to Josue, the son of Nun. Indeed, He can justly lay claim to all these titles from the fact both that He performs the Father's will and that He was begotten by an act of the Father's will. But, does not something similar happen also with us humans? When we utter a word, it can be said that we beget the word, but not by cutting it off, in the sense that our power of uttering words would thereby be diminished. We can observe a similar example in nature when one fire kindles another,[2] without losing anything, but remaining the same; yet the enkindled fire seems to exist of itself and to shine without lessening the brilliancy of the first fire. My statements will now be confirmed by none other than the Word of Wisdom, who is this God begotten from the Universal Father, and who is the Word and Wisdom and Power and Glory of Him who begot Him. Here are His words as spoken by Solomon: "If I shall declare to you what happens daily, I shall call to

---

[1] *Archèn*: 'beginning,' not 'in the beginning.' Maran notes that Justin does not allude to the eternal generation of the Son, but to that by which the Father is said to have generated Him as the beginning of all creatures. Cf. Migne, *PG* 6.613, n.77.
[2] The *lumen de lumine*, incorporated, through Tertullian, into the Nicene Creed.

mind events from eternity, and recount them. The Lord begot Me in the beginning of His ways for His works. I was set up from eternity, before He made the earth, and before He made the depths, before the fountains of waters had sprung out, before the mountains had been established. Before all the hills He begets Me. God made the earth, and the desert, and the highest inhabited places under the sky. When He prepared the heavens, I was present. When He set up His throne on the winds, when He established the clouds above, and strengthened the fountains of the deep, when He balanced the foundations of the earth, I was with Him arranging all things. I was that in which He delighted; daily and at all times I delighted in His presence, because He rejoiced for having finished the habitable world, and delighted in the sons of men. Now therefore, My son, hear Me. Blessed is the man that heareth Me, and the man that shall keep My ways, watching daily at My gates, and waiting at the posts of My doors, for My ways are the ways of life; and My will has been prepared by the Lord. But they that sin against Me, hurt their own souls, and they that hate Me love death." '[3]

Chapter 62

'My friends,' I continued, 'the word of God, through Moses, stated exactly the same thing, when it revealed to us that at the creation of man God spoke of Him (who was pointed out by Moses) in the same sense. Here is the Scriptural passage: "Let us make man to Our image and likeness; and let them have dominion over the fishes of the sea, and the fowls of the air, and over the cattle, and the whole earth, and every creeping creature that moveth upon the earth.

---
[3] Prov. 8.1-36.

And God created man; to the image of God did He create him; male and female He created them. And God blessed them, saying: Increase and multiply, and fill the earth, and subdue it."'[1]

'Lest you distort the meaning of these words by repeating what your teachers say—either that God said to Himself, "Let us make," just as we, when on the verge of doing something, say to ourselves, "Let us make"; or that God said "Let us make" to the elements, that is, to the earth or other similar substances of which we think man was composed—I wish again to quote Moses to prove beyond all doubt that He spoke with One endowed with reason, and different in number from Himself. These are the words of Moses: "And God said: Behold Adam is become as one of Us, knowing good and evil."[2] Now, the words "as one of Us" clearly show that there were a number of persons together, and they were at least two. I do not consider that teaching true which is asserted by what you call a heretical sect of your religion, nor can the proponents of that heresy prove that He spoke those words to angels, or that the human body was the result of the angel's work. But this Offspring, who was truly begotten of the Father, was with the Father and the Father talked with Him before all creation, as the Scripture through Solomon clearly showed us, saying that this Son, who is called Wisdom by Solomon, was begotten both as a beginning before all His works, and as His Offspring. God has testified to this same truth in the revelation to Josue, the son of Nun. To be fully convinced, listen to these words of the book of Josue: "And it came to pass, when Josue was near Jericho, he lifted up his eyes, and saw a man standing over against him. And Josue went to Him and said: Art

---
1 Gen. 1.26-28.
2 Gen. 3.22.

Thou one of ours, or of our adversaries? And He answered: I am the Prince of the host of the Lord, and now I am come. Josue fell on his face to the ground, and said to Him: Lord, what commandest Thou Thy servant? And the Lord's Prince said to Josue: Loose thy shoes from off thy feet; for the place whereon thou standest is holy. Now Jericho was shut up and fortified, and no one went out of it. And the Lord said to Josue: Behold, I have given into thy hands Jericho, and the king thereof, and all the valiant men." [3]

Chapter 63

'My friend,' said Trypho, 'you have proved your point with much force and copious arguments. Now prove to us that He condescended to become man by a virgin, in accordance with His Father's will, and to be crucified, and to die; show us, too, that He arose from the dead and ascended into Heaven.'

'Gentlemen,' I replied, 'I have already proved this by previously quoted prophecies, but, in order to convince you on this point also, I will repeat and explain those passages for you. Do not these words of Isaias, "Who shall declare His generation? For His life is taken from earth,"[1] seem to indicate that He, who is said to have been consigned to death by God [the Father] because of the sins of the people, did not have mere human origin? Moses, too, in speaking of His blood in a formerly quoted parable, said: "He shall wash His robe in the blood of the grape,"[2] since His blood did not originate from human seed but from the will of God. And then, there are the words of David: "In the brightness of Thy saints,

---

3 Jos. 5.13-16; 6.1-2.

---

1 Isa. 53.8.
2 Gen. 49.11.

from the womb before the day star I begot Thee. The Lord hath sworn, and He will not repent: Thou art a Priest forever according to the order of Melchisedech."³ Do not these words signify that from ancient times God, the Father of all things, intended Him to be begotten again and of a human womb? In another passage previously cited, He says: "Thy throne, O God, is forever and ever; the sceptre of Thy kingdom is a sceptre of uprightness. Thou hast loved justice, and hated iniquity; therefore God, Thy God, hath anointed Thee with the oil of gladness above Thy fellows. Myrrh and stacte and cassia perfume Thy garments, from the ivory houses, whereby they have made Thee glad. King's daughters are in Thy honor. The queen stood at Thy right hand, in gilded clothing, surrounded with variety. Hearken, O daughter, and see, and incline thy ear, and forget thy people and thy father's house. And the king shall greatly desire thy beauty, for He is thy Lord, and Him thou shalt adore."⁴ These words also show clearly that He who did all things [God the Father] testified that He [Jesus] is to be worshipped both as God and Christ. They further show that the Word of God speaks to His faithful (who are of one soul and one synagogue and one church) as to a daughter, namely, the Church which was established by and partakes in His name (for we all are called Christians). That this is so, and that we are instructed to forget the ancient customs of our ancestors, the following words imply: "Hearken, O daughter, and see, and incline thy ear, and forget thy people and thy father's house; and the king shall greatly desire thy beauty, for He is thy Lord, and Him thou shalt adore." ⁵

---

3 Ps. 109.3-4.
4 Ps. 44.7-12. Cf. Chapter 38.
5 Ps. 44.11-12.

Chapter 64

'You who come from the Gentiles,' said Trypho, 'who are all called Christians from His name, may profess Him to be Lord and Christ and God, as the Scriptures signify, but we Jews, who adore the God who made Him, are not obliged to confess or worship Him.'

'Trypho,' I replied, 'if I were as contentious and shallow-brained as you, I would have discontinued this discussion long ago, for you make no effort to understand my arguments, but only rack your brain to make any kind of reply. But now, in fear of God's judgment, I shall not be bold enough to state whether or not any one of your race, by the grace of the Lord of Sabaoth, may be saved. Even though you continue to quibble, I shall continue to answer whatever difficulty or objection you advance as I do for persons of any nationality who seek my opinion or advice. Had you given your full attention to the passages of Scripture which I have quoted, you would have already understood that those Jews who attain salvation are saved through Him and are His partisans. Had you understood this, you certainly would not have questioned me in this regard. For your benefit I am going to repeat those quotations from David, and I ask you to be attentive in order to understand them, instead of making a point only of maliciously contradicting them. Here are the words of David: "The Lord hath reigned, let the people be angry; He who sitteth above the cherubim; let the earth be moved. The Lord is great in Sion, and high above all people. Let them give praise to Thy great name, for it is terrible and holy; and the King's honor loveth judgment. Thou hast prepared directions; Thou hast done judgment and justice in Jacob. Exalt ye the Lord our God, and adore His footstool of His feet, for He is holy. Moses and Aaron among His priests; and

Samuel among them that call upon His name. They called upon the Lord, and He heard them. He spoke to them in the pillar of the cloud. They kept His testimonies, and the commandment which He gave them."¹ And from the other previously quoted passages from David, which, because they were inscribed "to Solomon," you ignorantly claim to have been referred to him, it can be proved that they were not spoken of Solomon, that Christ existed before the sun, and that they who are saved from among your people shall be saved by Him. These are the words: "Give to the king Thy judgment, O God, and to the king's son Thy justice, to judge Thy people with justice, and Thy poor with judgment. Let the mountains receive peace for the people, and the hills justice. He shall judge the poor of the people, and shall save the children of the poor, and shall humble the slanderer. And He shall continue with the sun, and before the moon throughout all generations."² And so forth, until the words: "His name continued before the sun. And in Him shall all the tribes of the earth be blessed, all nations shall call Him blessed. Blessed be the Lord, the God of Israel, who alone doth wonderful things. And blessed be the name of His majesty forever, and the whole earth shall be filled with His majesty. Amen. Amen."³ Keep in mind, too, that from other words of David which I cited above it can be proved that He would come forth from the highest heavens and was to ascend again to the same place, in order that you may know that He came forth as God from above, and became man in the midst of men, and will one day return to earth, when they who pierced Him will look upon Him and weep. The words are as follows: "The heavens show forth the glory of God, and the

---

1 Ps. 98.1-7.
2 Ps. 71.1-5.
3 Ps. 71.17-19.

firmament declareth the work of His hands. Day to day uttereth speech, and night to night showeth knowledge. There are no tongues nor words, whose voices are not heard. Their sound hath gone forth into all the earth and their words unto the ends of the world. He hath set His tabernacle in the sun, and He, as a bridegroom coming out of His chamber, hath rejoiced as a giant to run his course. His going out is from the end of heaven, and His circuit even to the end thereof, and there is none who shall be hidden from His heat." '4

Chapter 65

'I am puzzled,' said Trypho, 'by so many quotations from Scripture, and I am at a loss how to explain that passage from Isaias in which God states that He shares His glory with no other, when He says: "I am the Lord, God; this is My name; My glory and My powers I will not give to another." '1

I answered, 'If you quoted that passage honestly and without malice, Trypho, and stopped without adding the words which both precede and follow it, then you may be excused. But you are sadly mistaken if you did so in the hope of embarrassing me into admitting that some passages of Scripture contradict others, for I would not be so bold as to assert, or even imagine, such a thing. If such a passage were quoted, and apparently contradicted another (since I am positive that no passage contradicts another), I would rather openly confess that I do not know the meaning of the passage, and I shall do my utmost to have my opinion shared by those who imagine that the Scriptures are sometimes contradictory. Only God knows why you proposed this last difficulty, but

---

4 Ps. 18.1-6.

1 Isa. 42.8.

I will repeat the passage for you in its exact wording, so that you may see that God gives His glory to His Christ alone. And, gentlemen, I will add a few words of the context of the passage quoted by Trypho, and also those which immediately follow them. The words which I cite will not be taken from another chapter, but only from the context. I ask you, then, to reflect on the following words: "Thus saith the Lord God that created the heavens, and stretched them out; that established the earth, and the things that spring out of it; that giveth bread to the people upon it, and spirit to them that tread thereon. I the Lord Thy God have called Thee to justice, and will hold Thy hand, and will make Thee strong. And I have given Thee for a covenant of the people, for a light to the Gentiles, to open the eyes of the blind, to free the prisoners of their chains, and to bring forth them that sit in darkness out of the prison. I am the Lord God; this is My name; I will not give My glory to another, nor My powers to graven images. Things which were from the beginning, behold they are come to pass; they are new things which I declare, and before they are announced they are made manifest to you. Sing ye to the Lord a new song: His Beginning is from the ends of the earth. You that go down to the sea, and sail on it; ye islands and ye inhabitants of them. Rejoice, O desert, and the villages and houses thereof; and the inhabitants of Cedar shall rejoice, and the inhabitants of the rock shall shout from the top of the mountains; they shall give glory to God; they shall declare His powers in the islands. The Lord God Almighty shall go forth; He shall destroy all war; He shall stir up zeal, and He shall shout vigorously against His enemies."[2]

'Do you not see,' I asked on concluding the quotation, 'that

---
2 Isa. 42.5-13.

God affirms that He will give His glory to Him alone whom He has appointed to be the light of the Gentiles, and not, as Trypho claims, that He will reserve His glory for Himself only?'

'We can see that,' conceded Trypho. 'Now, finish the rest of the argument.'

Chapter 66

Then I resumed my argument where I had left off. I was proving that Christ was born of a virgin, and that Isaias had foretold that He was to be so born. I repeated the words of the prophecy, as follows: "And the Lord spoke again to Achaz saying: Ask thee a sign of the Lord thy God, in the depth, or in the height above. And Achaz said: I will not ask, and I will not tempt the Lord. And Isaias said: Hear ye therefore, O house of David: Is it a small thing for you to contend with men, that you are to contend with God also? Therefore the Lord Himself shall give you a sign. Behold a virgin shall conceive, and bear a Son, and His name shall be called Emmanuel. He shall eat butter and honey before He knows to refuse the evil, and to choose the good. For before the Child shall know good or evil, He refuses evil to choose the good. For before the Child knows how to call father or mother, He shall receive the power of Damascus and the spoils of Samaria in the presence of the king of Assyria. And the land shall be forsaken, which thou shalt hardly endure on account of the presence of the two kings. But God shall bring upon thee, and upon thy people, and upon the house of thy father, days that have not come upon thee, since the day that He took away Ephraim from Juda the king of the Assyrians." [1]

---
1 Isa. 7.10-17.

'Everyone knows,' I added, 'that of all the carnal descendants of Abraham, no one was ever born of a virgin, or even claimed to be so born, except our Christ.'

Chapter 67

Then Trypho objected, 'The quotation is not "Behold a virgin shall conceive and bear a Son," but "Behold a young woman shall conceive and bear a son," and so forth, as you quoted it. Furthermore, the prophecy as a whole refers to Hezekias, and it can be shown that the events described in the prophecy were fulfilled in him. Besides, in Greek mythology there is a story of how Perseus was born of Danae, while she was a virgin, when the one whom they call Zeus descended upon her in the form of a golden shower. You Christians should be ashamed of yourselves, therefore, to repeat the same kind of stories as these men, and you should, on the contrary, acknowledge this Jesus to be a man of mere human origin. If you can prove from the Scriptures that He is the Christ, confess that He was considered worthy to be chosen as such because of His perfect observance of the Law, but do not dare to speak of miracles, lest you be accused of talking nonsense, like the Greeks.'

'Trypho,' I replied, 'I want you and everyone else to be certain of this, that even if you resort to worse taunts in your ridicule and mockery of me, you will not be able to turn me from my set purpose, for I will continue to employ those very words and examples (which you produced to confuse me), together with the Scriptures, to show the truth of my assertions. But you are neither fair nor truthful when you endeavor to eliminate those points on which we have mutually agreed, for example, that some precepts of the Law were instituted by Moses because of your people's hardness of heart. For you stated that if Jesus can indeed be proved to be Christ, it is so only because of His strict adherence to the Mosaic Law.'

'Yet you admitted,' rejoined Trypho, 'that He was circumcised and observed the other precepts of the Mosaic Law.'

'Yes I did,'[1] I replied, 'and I still do, but I do not admit that He submitted to this, as though justification could be acquired by it, but simply to complete the plan of our redemption in accordance with the will of His Father, Lord and God and Creator of all things. I also admit that He condescended to become man, that He was crucified and died after enduring all the suffering inflicted upon Him by your own people. Now, Trypho, since you deny the points which you had previously admitted, tell me if those just men and patriarchs who lived before Moses, and therefore did not observe those precepts which Scripture shows were first commanded by Moses, have attained salvation in the inheritance of the blessed?'

'The Scriptures,' said Trypho, 'force me to admit that they have.'

'Answer this question, too,' I persisted. 'Did God order your ancestors to offer up oblations and sacrifices because He needed them, or because of their hardness of heart and tendency to idolatry?'

'The Scriptures,' he answered, 'also compel me to admit the second reason.'

'And have those same Scriptures also predicted that God had announced a new Covenant, other than that which He made at Mount Horeb?'

'They have,' he admitted.

---

[1] But thus far, nothing has been said about the circumcision of Jesus and of His observance of the Law.

'And was not that old Covenant,' I continued, 'delivered to your ancestors amid such fear and trembling that they could not listen to God?'

'That also is true,' he conceded.

'Then why do you argue?' I went on to ask. 'God promised another covenant, different from the old one, which would be delivered to them without fear and trembling and flashes of lightning, and which would indicate what precepts and actions God knows to be eternal and fit for every nationality, and what precepts He issued as suited only to the hardness of your people's hearts (as He proclaimed through His Prophets).'

'They who love the truth and not strife,' replied Trypho, 'must agree with you completely.'

'I don't know,' I said, 'how you can accuse others of admiring strife, when you yourself so often seem to do just that, for you frequently contradict what you had previously conceded.'

Chapter 68

'Because,' replied Trypho, 'you are attempting to prove what is incredible and practically impossible, namely, that God deigned to be born and to become man.'

'If I had tried to prove this only by the teachings and arguments of men,' I said in reply, 'you should not listen to me. But if I constantly appeal to various passages of Scripture to prove my point and beg you to understand them, then it is only your obstinacy that prevents you from knowing the mind and will of God. If you refuse to change, I surely will suffer no harm, but, holding fast to my former convictions, I will go my way.'

'My friend,' protested Trypho, 'remember that it was given to you to master these truths after much trouble and toil, and it is only that, before we can assent to what the Scriptures indicate, we also must first examine closely all that meets us.'

'I do not ask you,' I answered, 'to abstain from scrutinizing carefully every point of our discussion, but, please, when you are at a loss what to say, do not deny what you have already admitted.'

'We will try to do as you wish,' said Trypho.

'Now,' said I, 'in order to bring this debate to a speedy conclusion, I would like to ask a few more questions.'

'Go ahead and ask them,' granted Trypho.

'Is it your opinion that there is any other to be worshipped and called Lord and God in the Scriptures, except the Creator of the world and Christ, who has been proved to you by so many Scriptural passages to have become man?'

'How could we admit such a statement,' asked Trypho, 'when in our lengthy discussion it has not been determined whether there is any God other than the Father?"

'I must ask this question,' I responded, 'in order to know whether you hold a different opinion from that which you already admitted.'

'I do not,' he said.

'Since you admit these things in truth,' I went on, 'and since Scripture states, "Who shall declare His generation,"[1] should you not also immediately agree that He is not of human generation?'

'How, then,' asked Trypho, 'does the Scripture say to David that of his loins God would take to Himself a Son, would establish His kingdom, and would install Him upon the throne of His glory?'

'Trypho,' I replied, 'if this prophecy of Isaias, "Behold, a

---

1 Isa. 53.8.

virgin shall conceive," did not refer to the house of David, but to some other house of the twelve tribes, then the problem would, perhaps, be difficult; but, since the prophecy itself refers to the house of David, Isaias explained exactly how that which was spoken in mystery to David by God would happen. Perhaps, my friends, you do not realize that many of the sayings which were expressed mysteriously in metaphorical or obscure language or were hinted at by symbolic actions were later expounded by the Prophets who lived after those who had uttered or done them.'

'Undoubtedly,' agreed Trypho.

'If, then,' I continued, 'I establish the fact that this prophecy of Isaias speaks of our Christ and not Hezekiah, as you claim, will you not be obliged to doubt your teachers who dare to assert that the translation [of the Scriptures] made by your seventy elders at the court of the Egyptian King Ptolemy is inaccurate in some places? For, whenever there arises in the Scriptures an evident contradiction of their silly and conceited doctrine, your teachers boldly affirm that it was not so written in the original text. And they conspire to distort other statements, harmonizing them with human actions and claiming that they have been spoken not of this our Jesus Christ, but of him of whom they attempt to interpret them. For instance, they taught you that the quotation under discussion is to be interpreted as referring to Hezekiah, a statement which, as I promised, I will prove to be a lie. Under pressure, they are forced to agree that some of the passages we cited—passages already quoted to you which clearly prove that Christ was to suffer, to be worshipped, and to be called God—were indeed spoken of Christ. They boldly deny that He whom we worship is the Christ, yet they admit that a Messiah will come to suffer and rule and be worshipped. This opinion, too, I will prove to be absurd and senseless. But, as you have compelled me to first answer what you have said in ridicule, I will do so, and then I will pass on to the proofs of the other subjects.'

Chapter 69

'You may rest assured, Trypho,' I went on, 'that my knowledge of the Scriptures and my faith in them have been well confirmed by the things which he who is called the Devil counterfeited in the fictions circulated among the Greeks (just as he accomplished them through the Egyptian magicians and the false prophets in the days of Elias). For, when they say that Bacchus was born of Jupiter's union with Semele, and narrate that he was the discoverer of the vine, and that, after he was torn to pieces and died, he arose again and ascended into heaven, and when they use wine[1] in his mysteries, is it not evident that the Devil has imitated the previously quoted prophecy of the patriarch Jacob, as recorded by Moses? And when it is asserted that Hercules,[2] the son of Jupiter and Alcmene, was strong and traversed the whole earth, and that, after death, he, too, ascended into heaven, ought I not conclude that the Scriptural passage about Christ, "strong as a giant to run His course,"[3] was similarly imitated? And when the Devil presents Aesculapius as raising the dead to life and curing all diseases, has he not, in this regard, also, emulated the prophecies about Christ? But, as I have not yet quoted a passage from Scripture to prove to you that Christ would do these things, I must now call one to your attention, from

---
1 Some MSS. have '*ónon*' (ass) as a marginal note. Although the ass was sacred to Bacchus, it need not be accepted as the proper reading here, for the word 'wine' (*oînon*) agrees better with the context. Cf. I *Apol.* 54, n. 4.
2 Here, Justin attacks the fable concerning Hercules; more directly does he answer Trypho in the next chapter, when he treats of the myth of Perseus.
3 Ps. 18.6.

which you can easily perceive how the Scriptures foretold that they who were destitute of the knowledge of God (I allude to the Gentiles who had eyes and saw not, hearts and understood not, but worshipped material idols) should abandon their idols and place their hope in Christ. Here is the quotation: "Be glad, O thirsty wilderness, let the desert rejoice, and flourish as the lily; and the deserts of the Jordan shall blossom abundantly and rejoice; and the glory of Libanus was given to it, and the honor of Carmel. And my people shall see the exaltation of the Lord and the glory of God. Be strong, ye feeble hands and weak knees. Be comforted, ye fearful in heart; be strong, fear not. Behold our God brings, and will bring, the revenge of recompense. He shall come and save us. Then shall the eyes of the blind be opened, and the ears of the deaf shall hear. Then shall the lame man leap as a hare, and the tongue of the stammerers shall be free; for water is broken out in the desert, and a stream in a thirsty land, and the dry land shall become swamps, and in the thirsty land there shall be a spring of water."[4]

'The fountain of living water which gushed forth from God upon a land devoid of the knowledge of God (that is, the land of the Gentiles) was our Christ, who made His appearance on earth in the midst of your people, and healed those who from birth were blind and deaf and lame. He cured them by His word, causing them to walk, to hear, and to see. By restoring the dead to life, He compelled the men of that day to recognize Him. Yet, though they witnessed these miraculous deeds with their own eyes, they attributed them to magical art; indeed, they dared to call Him a magician[5] who misled the people. But He performed these deeds

---
4 Isa. 35.1-7.
5 This passage is the earliest record we have that the Jews attributed the miracles of Christ to magic.

to convince His future followers, that if any one, even though his body were in any way maimed, should be faithful to His teaching, He would raise him up at His second coming entirely sound, and make him free forever from death, corruption and pain.'

Chapter 70

'Now, when those who hand down the mysteries of Mithras[1] claim that he was born of a rock, and call the place where they initiate his believers a cave, am I not right in concluding that they have imitated that dictum of Daniel, "a stone was cut without hands out of a great mountain"?[2] In similar fashion, have they not attempted to imitate all the sayings of Isaias? For the demons urged the priests of Mithras to exhort their followers to perform righteous acts. Here are the words of Isaias which I must quote that you may know from them that this is so: "Hear, you that are far off, what I have done; and they that are near shall know My strength. The sinners in Sion have departed; trembling shall seize the impious. Who shall announce to you the everlasting place? He that walketh righteously, and speaketh truth, that hateth iniquity and injustice, and keepeth his hands clean from bribes; that stoppeth his ears from hearing the unjust judgment of blood, that shutteth his eyes from seeing evil; he shall dwell in the lofty cave of the strong rock. Bread shall be given to him, and his water shall be sure. You shall see the King in his glory, and your eyes shall look far off. Your soul shall meditate on the fear of the Lord. Where is the scribe? Where are the counsellors? Where is he that counteth those

---

1 Mithras was a Persian god, whose adherents closely linked his worship with that of the sun. At Justin's time, Mithraism had many followers and was Christianity's strongest rival at Rome.
2 Dan. 2.34.

who are nourished, the small and the great people? With whom they did not take counsel, nor knew the depth of the voices, so that they did not hear. A shameless people, and there is no understanding in him who hears." '³

'It is quite evident that this prophecy also alludes to the bread which our Christ gave us to offer in remembrance of the Body which He assumed for the sake of those who believe in Him, for whom He also suffered, and also to the cup which He taught us to offer in the Eucharist, in commemoration of His Blood. The prophecy also states that we shall see this same King in the splendor of His glory; that the foreknown future believers in Him would have in mind the fear of the Lord; and that they who think they know the very letter of the Scriptures, and who listen to the prophecies, have no understanding of them. And, Trypho (I said), when I hear it asserted that Perseus was born of a virgin, I know that this is another forgery of that treacherous serpent.'

Chapter 71

'I certainly do not trust your teachers when they refuse to admit that the translation of the Scriptures made by the seventy elders at the court of King Ptolemy of Egypt is a correct one, and attempt to make their own translation.¹ You should also know that they have deleted entire passages from the version composed by those elders at the court of Ptolemy, in which it is clearly indicated that the Crucified One was foretold as God and man, and as about to suffer death on the cross. But, since I know that all you Jews deny the authenticity of these passages, I will not start a discussion

---

3 Isa. 33.13-19.

1 Perhaps of certain passages only, not their own translation of the whole Old Testament.

about them, but I will limit the controversy to those passages which you admit as genuine. Thus far, you have admitted the authenticity of all my quotations, except this, "Behold, a virgin shall conceive," which you claim reads, "Behold, a young woman shall conceive." And I promised to show that this prophecy was not spoken of Hezekiah, as you were taught, but of my Christ. This I now intend to prove.'

'Before you do,' interrupted Trypho, 'we would like you to quote some of the passages you claim were entirely omitted [from the elders' translation].'

Chapter 72

'Since you asked,' I replied, 'here is an example. They have deleted the following passage in which Esdras expounded the law of the Passover: "And Esdras said to the people: This Passover is our Savior and refuge. And if you have understood, and it has entered into your hearts, that we are about to humiliate Him on a cross, and afterwards hope in Him, then this place will never be forsaken, saith the Lord of hosts. But if you will not believe Him, nor listen to His teaching, you shall be the laughing-stock of the Gentiles."[1] They have also expunged these words from Jeremias: "I was as a meek lamb that is carried to be a sacrificial victim; they devised counsels against Me, saying: Come, let us put wood on His bread, and cut Him off from the land of the living, and let His name be remembered no more."[2] Since this passage from the words of Jeremias is still found in some copies of Scripture in the Jewish synagogues (for it was deleted only a short time ago), and since it is also proved from these words that the Jews planned to crucify Christ Himself and to slay

---

1 The origin of this passage is unknown. Lactantius cites it in Latin in his *Inst. div.* 4.18.
2 Jer. 11.19.

Him, and since He is shown, as was likewise prophesied by Isaias, as led like a lamb to slaughter, and in accordance with this passage He is marked as "an innocent lamb," they are so confused by such words that they resort to blasphemy. Similarly have they removed the following words from the writings of the same Jeremias: "The Lord God, the Holy One of Israel, remembered His dead that slept in their graves, and He descended to preach to them His salvation."[3]

Chapter 73

'Furthermore, from a verse of the ninety-fifth Psalm of David they have left out the short phrase, "from the tree." For they have changed the verse, "Say ye to the Gentiles: The Lord hath reigned from the tree,"[1] to "Say ye to the Gentiles: The Lord hath reigned." Now, no one of your people was ever said to have reigned as God and King over the Gentiles, except the Crucified One, who (as the Holy Spirit testifies in the same Psalm) was freed from death by His resurrection, and thus showed that He is not like gods of the Gentiles, for they are but the idols of demons. To clarify this point, I will repeat the whole Psalm for you. It is as follows: "Sing ye to the Lord a new canticle; sing to the Lord, all the earth. Sing ye to the Lord and bless His name; show forth His salvation from day to day. Declare His glory among the Gentiles; His wonders among all people.

---

3 This passage is not found in the Sacred Text. However, Irenaeus quotes it (*Adv. haereses* 3, 20) and attributes it to Isaias, but in *Adv. haereses* 4, 22 and in his *Preaching* 78, he ascribes the words to Jeremias.

1 Ps. 95.10. The words, 'from the tree,' (i.e., the cross), are commonly quoted by the Latin Fathers. They are not found in the Septuagint (except in one Greek MS.), nor in the Hebrew. Cf. 1 *Apol.* 41.4, and the Latin hymn, *Vexilla Regis*, written by Fortunatus at close of sixth century.

For the Lord is great, and exceedingly to be praised; He is to be feared above all gods. For all the gods of the Gentiles are devils; but the Lord made the heavens. Praise and beauty are before Him; holiness and majesty in His sanctuary. Bring ye to the Lord, O ye kindreds of the Gentiles, bring ye to the Lord glory and honor, bring to the Lord glory unto His name. Bring up sacrifices, and come unto His courts. Adore ye the Lord in His holy court. Let all the earth be moved at His presence. Say ye among the Gentiles, the Lord hath reigned [from the tree].[2] For he hath established the world, which shall not be moved; He will judge the people with justice. Let the heavens rejoice, and let the earth be glad. Let the sea be moved, and the fullness thereof. The fields and all things that are in them shall be joyful. Then all the trees of the woods rejoice before the face of the Lord, because He cometh; because He cometh to judge the earth. He shall judge the world with justice, and the people with His truth." [3]

'Only God knows,' remarked Trypho, 'whether or not our leaders have deleted portions of the Scriptures as you say. But such an assertion seems incredible.'

'Yes,' I agreed, 'it does seem incredible. For it is more dreadful than the erecting of the golden calf (which they made while still satiated with the manna that fell to earth), and more revolting than the sacrifice of their children to demons, or the slaughter of the Prophets. You, indeed, appear not to have even heard of the Scriptures which I said they had mutilated. But the many passages which I have already cited, together with those which you have preserved, and which are still to be quoted are more than enough to prove the points at issue.'

---
2 To prove his point, St. Justin must have inserted the words from the tree, but the copyists probably omitted them.
3 Ps. 95.1-13.

Chapter 74

'We are aware,' said Trypho, 'that you have quoted those passages for us at our request. But the Psalm of David which you just cited seems to have been spoken of nobody else than the Father, who created the heavens and earth. You, however, claim that it refers to Him who suffered, and who you are anxious to prove is the Christ.'

'Please meditate,' I pleaded, 'as I repeat the words uttered by the Holy Spirit in this Psalm, and you shall understand that I have not spoken maliciously, nor have you in truth been deceived. Besides, you will thus, when you are by yourselves, be able to grasp many other statements of the Holy Spirit. "Sing ye to the Lord a new canticle; sing to the Lord, all the earth. Sing ye to the Lord and bless His name; show forth His salvation from day to day, His wonders among all people."[1] With these words He commands all those inhabitants of this globe who know this mystery of salvation (the Passion of Christ), through which He saved them, to sing out and constantly praise the Father of all, since they realize that He is both to be feared and to be praised, and is the Creator of heaven and earth, who redeemed mankind, who, after He died on the cross, was deemed worthy by Him to reign over the whole world. As also by[2] ... of the "land into which it enters; and they will forsake Me, and will make void the

---

1 Ps. 95.1-3.
2 The text is here mutilated, and it is not clear just how much is lost. Some think that only a few words are missing, because the same topic is discussed in the words which follow. Others, however, point out that the lacuna must be lengthy, because Justin makes no mention of the end of the first day's debate and the beginning of the second day's discussion. It could be that the first day's debate finished at this point, which the missing part (perhaps no more than a chapter) would have described, together with the resumption of the debate at the point where it had been interrupted the day before.

covenant which I have made with them in that day. And I will forsake them, and will hide My face from them; and there shall be a devouring, and many evils and afflictions shall overtake them, so that they shall say in that day: In truth it is because the Lord my God is not with us, that these evils have come upon us. But I will hide My face from them in that day, for all the evils which they have done, because they have followed strange gods."'[3]

[End of the first day's discussion.][4]

Chapter 75

'Now, from the book of Exodus we know that Moses cryptically indicated that the name of God Himself (which He says was not revealed to Abraham or to Jacob) was also Jesus. For it is written: "And the Lord said to Moses, say to this people: Behold, I send My angel before thy face, to keep thee in thy journey, and bring thee into the place that I have prepared for thee. Take notice of him, and obey his voice; do not disobey him, for he will not pardon thee, because My name is in him."[1] Consider well who it was that led your fathers into the promised land, namely, he who was at first named Auses [Osee], but later renamed Jesus [Josue].[2] If you keep this in mind, you will also realize that the name of him who said to Moses, "My name is in him,"[3] was Jesus. Indeed, He was also called Israel, and he similarly bestowed this name upon Jacob. From Isaias

---
3 Deut. 31.16-18.
4 Not in text. *See* note 2 above.

---
1 Exod. 23.20-21.
2 Moses changed Osee's name to Josue when he sent him out to spy in the Promised Land. The Greek form of the name is Jesus. Cf. Num. 13.16.
3 Exod. 3.21.

we know that the Prophets who were sent to carry His messages to man are called angels and apostles of God, for Isaias uses the expression, "Send me."[4] Equally evident to all is the fact that he who was called by the name Jesus [Josue] became a mighty and great prophet. If, then, we are convinced that that God has appeared in so many forms to Abraham, Jacob, and Moses, how can we doubt and refuse to believe that, in conformity with the will of the Universal Father, He could also be born man of a virgin, particularly when we have so many Scriptural passages which clearly show that even this has taken place according to the will of the Father?'

Chapter 76

'Does not Daniel allude to this very truth when he says that He who received the eternal kingdom is "as a Son of Man"?[1] The words, "as a Son of Man," indicate that He would become man and appear as such, but that He would not be born of a human seed. Daniel states the same truth figuratively when he calls Christ "a Stone cut out without hands";[2] for, to affirm that He was cut out without hands signifies that He was not the product of human activity, but of the will of God, the Father of all, who brought Him forth. And the words of Isaias, "Who shall declare His generation?"[3] show that His origin is indescribable, and no mere man has such an origin. When Moses affirmed that "He shall wash His robe in the blood of the grape,"[4] did he not mystically foretell what I have frequently mentioned to you,

---
4 Isa. 6.8.

---
1 Dan. 7.13.
2 Dan. 2.34.
3 Isa. 53.8.
4 Gen. 49.11.

namely, that Christ would have blood, but not from men, just as it is not man, but God, who gave blood to the grape? And, in calling Him "the Angel of great counsel,"[5] did not Isaias predict that Christ would be a teacher of those truths which He expounded when He came upon this earth? For He alone openly taught the great counsels that the Father intended for those who either were or shall be pleasing to Him, as well as for those men or angels who withdrew from His will. Here are His words of instruction: "They shall come from the east and the west, and shall sit down with Abraham and Isaac and Jacob in the kingdom of heaven; but the children of the kingdom shall be cast out into exterior darkness."[6] And: "Many will say to Me in that day, Lord, Lord, did we not eat and drink and prophesy and cast out devils in Thy name? And then I will say to them: Depart from Me."[7] Again, in other words, with which He will condemn them who are not worthy to be saved, He said: "Depart into exterior darkness, which the Father has prepared for the devil and his angels."[8] And He also said: "I give you power to tread upon serpents and scorpions and poisonous insects, and over all the power of the enemy."[9] Indeed, we believers in Jesus our Lord, who was crucified under Pontius Pilate, cast out all devils and other evil spirits and thus have them in our power. Now, if the Prophets foretold cryptically that Christ would suffer first and then be Lord of all, it was still well nigh impossible for anyone to grasp the full meaning of such prophecies, until Christ Himself convinced His Apostles that such things were explicitly proclaimed in the Scriptures. For, before His crucifixion He

---

5 Isa. 9.6.
6 Matt. 8.11-12.
7 Matt. 7.22-23.
8 Matt. 25.41.
9 Luke 10.19.

said: "The Son of Man must suffer many things, and be rejected by the Scribes and Pharisees, and be crucified, and rise again on the third day."[10] And David predicted that He would be born from the womb before the sun and the moon, in accordance with the Father's will, and he announced that He, being Christ, was the mighty God, and was thus to be adored.'

Chapter 77

'I admit,' said Trypho, 'that your arguments are so numerous and forceful that they suffice to make me confused, but I again call to your attention that I want the proof of that Scriptural passage which you have so often promised. Please go on now and show us how that passage refers to your Christ, and not to Hezekiah, as we Jews believe.'

'I will do as you wish,' I replied, 'but, first, prove to me that Hezekiah was the one spoken of in the following words: "Before he had known how to call father or mother, he received the power of Damascus and the spoils of Samaria in the presence of the king of Assyria."[1] Indeed, I will not accept your explanation that Hezekiah waged war with the people of Damascus and Samaria in the presence of the king of Assyria. For the prophecy reads thus: "Before the child knows how to call father or mother, He shall take the power of Damascus and the spoils of Samaria in the presence of the king of Assyria." Now, if the prophecy had not said this by way of addition, "Before the Child knows how to call father or mother, He shall take the power of Damascus and the spoils of Samaria," but had only said, "And she shall bring forth a son and he shall take the power of

---
10 Mark 8.31.
---
1 Isa. 8.4.

Damascus and the spoils of Samaria," you could reply that because God foreknew that he would take them, He had foretold it. But the prophecy actually has the addition, "Before the Child knows how to call father or mother, He shall take the power of Damascus and the spoils of Samaria." Now, you cannot prove that this ever happened to any of you Jews, but we Christians can show that it did happen to our Christ. For, at the time of His birth, the Magi came from Arabia and worshipped Him, after they had met Herod, then king of your country, whom Scripture calls king of Assyria because of His wicked ungodliness. For you well know that the Holy Spirit often speaks in parables and similitudes, just as He did to all the people of Jerusalem when He frequently said to them: "Thy father was an Amorite and thy mother a Hittite." [2]

Chapter 78

'At the time when the Magi from Arabia came to King Herod and said, "From the star which has appeared in the heavens we know that a King has been born in your country, and we have come to worship Him,"[1] he asked the elders of your people and learned from them that Christ was to be born in Bethlehem; for they replied that it was written in the Prophet, "And thou, Bethlehem, in the land of Juda, art by no means least among the princes of Juda; for out of thee shall come forth a Ruler who shall shepherd My people."[2] Now, these Magi from Arabia came to Bethlehem, worshipped the Child, and presented to Him gifts of gold, frankincense and myrrh. After they had worshipped Him in

---
2 Ezech. 16.3.

---
1 Matt. 2.2.
2 Mich. 5.2; Matt. 2.5-6.

Bethlehem, they were admonished [in a vision] not to return to Herod. And Joseph, the spouse of Mary (who at first had decided to put her away because he thought she was pregnant through human intercourse, namely, fornication), was likewise commanded in a vision not to do so, when the angel appeared to him and told him that what she had conceived was of the Holy Spirit. Consequently, overwhelmed with awe, he did not put her away. But when Quirinius was taking his first census in Judea, Joseph traveled from Nazareth, where he lived, to Bethlehem (to which he belonged), to be enrolled, for he was by birth of the tribe of Juda which inhabited that region. Then he was ordered [in a vision] to go with Mary into Egypt and to remain there with the Child until another revelation should advise them to return into Judea. Now, concerning the birth of the Child in Bethlehem, [you should know that] when Joseph could find no lodging place in the village, he went to a cave nearby, and there Mary gave birth to the Child and laid Him in a manger, and there the Arabian Magi found Him. I have already quoted the words of Isaias in which he foretold the symbol of the cave, but, for the benefit of those who have joined you today I will repeat the passage.'

Then I repeated the words of Isaias which I have written above, and added that by these words the priests who performed the mysteries of Mithras were urged by the Devil to declare that they were initiated by Mithras himself in a place they call a cave.

'Now, when the Arabian Magi failed to return to Herod, as he had requested, but had gone to their own country by another route, as they had been ordered, and when Joseph, Mary and the Child had already retired into Egypt, as they were divinely directed, Herod, since he did not know who the Child was whom the Magi had come to worship, ordered every boy in Bethlehem without exception to be slain. This, too, had been foretold by Jeremias, when the Holy Spirit spoke through him in this fashion: "A voice was heard in Rama, weeping and great lamentation; Rachel weeping for her children, and refusing to be comforted for them, because they are not."[3] Therefore, because of the voice which was to be heard as far as Rama, that is, as far as Arabia (for even today there is a place in Arabia called Rama), lamentation was to fill the place where Rachel (the wife of the holy Patriarch Jacob, whose name was later changed to Israel) lies buried, that is, Bethlehem, for the women were weeping for their massacred children and had no consolation for that which had occurred. And the words of Isaias, "He shall take the power of Damascus and the spoils of Samaria,"[4] meant that the power of the wicked demon that dwelt in Damascus should be crushed by Christ at His birth. This is shown to have taken place. For the Magi, held in servitude (as spoils) for the commission of every wicked deed through the power of that demon, by coming and worshipping Christ, openly revolted against the power that had held them as spoils, which power the Scripture indicated by parable to be located in Damascus. And in the parables that sinful and wicked power is fittingly called Samaria. Now, even among you none can deny that Damascus was and is a part of the land of Arabia, although it now belongs to Syro-Phoenicia. So it would be to your advantage, my friends, to learn what you do not understand from us Christians, who have received the grace of God, and not to exert every effort to defend your peculiar teachings and scorn those of God. Isaias shows why this grace was given to us, when he says: "This people draws near Me, with

---
3 Jer. 31.15.
4 Isa. 8.4.

their lips they glorify Me, but their heart is far from Me. But in vain they worship Me, teaching the precepts and doctrines of men. Therefore, behold, I will proceed to remove this people, and I will transplant them. And I will take away the wisdom of their wise men, and will bring to nought the understanding of their prudent men." [5]

Chapter 79

Then Trypho, showing by his countenance that he was rather angry, yet retaining a great reverence for the Scriptures, said to me, 'The words of God are indeed holy, but your interpretations are not only artificial, as is evident from those you have given, but evidently even blasphemous, for you affirm that the angels have sinned and have fallen away from God.'

Desiring to retain his attention, I answered in much milder language, 'Sir, I respect your piety, and I pray that you may feel the same way toward Him whom the angels are said to serve, as Daniel says, "One as the Son of Man is led to the Ancient of days, and all dominion is given to Him forever and ever."[1] But, in order to show you, friend,' said I, 'that it was not presumption that induced us to formulate the interpretation which you blame, I would like to cite as evidence the words of Isaias himself, who stated that the bad angels have dwelt and still dwell in the Egyptian city of Tanis. These are the words of Isaias: "Woe to you apostate children! Thus saith the Lord: You have taken counsel, but not by Me; and have made agreements, but not by My spirit, that you might add sin upon sin; who walk to go down into Egypt, and have not asked at My mouth, hoping

---
5 Isa. 29.13-14.

---
1 Dan. 7.13-14.

for help in the strength of Pharao, and trusting in the shadow of Egypt. For the shadow of Pharao shall be a disgrace to you, and a reproach to those who trust in the Egyptians, for the rulers in Tanis are bad angels. In vain shall they toil with a people which will not help nor profit them, but will be their shame and reproach."[2] Even Zacharias affirms, as you yourself mentioned, that "Satan stood at the right hand of Jesus [Josue], the priest, to be his adversary. And the Lord said: the Lord who has chosen Jerusalem rebuke thee."[3] Here is the testimony of Job (whom you also quoted): "The angels came to stand before the Lord, and the devil came with them."[4] And in the beginning of the Book of Genesis, Moses writes that the serpent deceived Eve, and was thereupon cursed. Furthermore, we know that in Egypt there were magicians who tried to imitate the miraculous deeds performed by God through His faithful servant Moses. And as you well know, David said: "The gods of the Gentiles are devils." '[5]

Chapter 80

'Sir,' said Trypho, 'as I already remarked, you are very careful to keep close to the Scriptures in all your statements. But, tell me truthfully, do you really believe that this place Jerusalem shall be rebuilt, and do you actually expect that you Christians will one day congregate there to live joyfully with Christ, together with the patriarchs, the prophets, the saints of our people and those who became proselytes before your Christ arrived? Or did you admit this only to win the argument?'

'Trypho,' I replied, 'I am not such a wretch as to say one

2 Isa. 30.1-5.
3 Zach. 3.1-2.
4 Job 1.6; 2.1.
5 Ps. 95.5.

thing and to think another. I have declared to you earlier[1] that I, with many others, feel that such an event will take place. However, I did point out that there are many pure and pious Christians who do not share our opinion. Moreover, I also informed you that there are some who are Christians in name, but in reality are godless and impious heretics[2] whose doctrines are entirely blasphemous, atheistic, and foolish. However, that you may be assured that I am not making this admission in your presence only, I promise to write up our whole debate in book form as well as I can, and in it I will insert the admission I just made to you, for I do not desire to be a follower of men and their teachings, but of God and His doctrines. If you have ever encountered any so-called Christians who do not admit this doctrine [of the millennium], but dare to blaspheme the God of Abraham and the God of Isaac and the God of Jacob by asserting that there is no resurrection of the dead, but that their souls are taken up to Heaven at the very moment of their death, do not consider them to be real Christians; just as one, after careful examination, would not acknowledge as Jews the Sadducees[3] or the similar sects of the Genistae, Meristae, Galileans, Hellenians, and the Baptist Pharisees[4] (please take no offense if I speak my mind), but would realize that they are

---

1 Perhaps in the missing portion of the *Dialogue?*
2 The Ebionites, Gnostics, etc.
3 The Sadducees denied the resurrection of the body from the dead.
4 Little is known about these sects. The *Genistae* might have been so called because of their purity of race, due to the fact that they had never intermarried with Gentiles, especially during the Babylonian Captivity. The *Meristae* probably were those fatalistic Jews who mutilated the Holy Writ. The *Galilaeans* are said to have been the followers of Judas the Galilaean who started a Jewish war of insurrection against the Romans in A.D. 6. The *Hellenians* may have been the same as the better known *Herodians*, the supporters of the Roman power in Palestine. The *Baptist Pharisees* probably were the Hemero-Baptists, who bathed themselves every morning in order to recite their daily prayers with a clean body.

Jews and children of Abraham in name only, paying lip service to God, while their hearts (as God Himself declared) are far from Him. But I and every other completely orthodox Christian[5] feel certain that there will be a resurrection of the flesh, followed by a thousand years in the rebuilt, embellished, and enlarged city of Jerusalem, as was announced by the Prophets Ezechiel, Isaias and the others.'

Chapter 81

'These are the words of Isaias concerning the millennium: "For there shall be a new heaven and a new earth, and the former shall not be remembered nor come into their heart, but they shall be glad and rejoice in these things, which I create. For, behold, I make Jerusalem a rejoicing, and My people a joy; and I shall rejoice over Jerusalem, and be glad over My people. And the voice of weeping shall no more be heard in her, nor the voice of crying. There shall no more be an infant of days there, nor an old man that shall not fill up his days; for the child shall die a hundred years old, and the sinner being a hundred years old shall be accursed. And they shall build houses and inhabit them; and they shall plant vineyards, and eat the fruits of them, and drink the wine. They shall not build, and others inhabit; they shall not plant, and others eat. For as the days of the tree of life, so shall be the days of My people, and the works of their hands shall be multiplied. My elect shall not labor in vain, nor bring forth children for a curse; for they shall be a righteous seed blessed

---

5 The belief in the millennium was not as general as Justin's words imply. The only other early supporters of this doctrine were Papias of Hierapolis and Irenaeus. Many other Christian writers then opposed this belief of a thousand year's *earthly* happiness with Christ at Jerusalem after the resurrection from the dead. Justin, however, did point out at the beginning of this chapter that his opinion is not shared by all.

by the Lord, and their posterity with them. And it shall come to pass that before they call, I will hear; as they are yet speaking, I will say, What is it? Then shall the wolves and lambs feed together, and the lion shall eat straw like the ox, and the serpent shall eat earth like bread. They shall not hurt nor destroy on My holy mountain, saith the Lord."[1] Now, by the words, "For as the days of the tree of life, so shall be the days of My people, and the works of their hands shall be multiplied," we understand that a period of one thousand years is indicated in symbolic language. When it was said of Adam that "in the day that he eateth of the tree, in that he shall die,"[2] we knew he was not a thousand years old. We also believe that the words, "The day of the Lord is as a thousand years,"[3] also led to the same conclusion. Moreover, a man among us named John, one of Christ's Apostles, received a revelation and foretold that the followers of Christ would dwell in Jerusalem for a thousand years, and that afterwards the universal and, in short, everlasting resurrection and judgment would take place.[4] To this our Lord Himself testified when He said: "They shall neither marry, nor be given in marriage, but shall be equal to the angels, being sons of God, [that is] of the resurrection." '[5]

Chapter 82

'From the fact that even to this day the gifts of prophecy exist among us Christians, you should realize that the gifts which had resided among your people have now been transferred to us. And, just as there were false prophets among

---
1 Isa. 65.17-25.
2 Gen. 2.17.
3 Ps. 89.4.
4 Apoc. 20.4-6.
5 Luke 20.35-36.

you at the time your holy Prophets lived, so now there also are in our midst many false teachers, against whom we had been warned by our Lord Himself, so that we should be prepared for anything, since we are aware that He foreknew what would befall us after His resurrection from the dead and ascension into heaven. He predicted that we would be martyred and hated because of His name, and that many false prophets and false Christs would start preaching in His name, and would mislead many; and this has actually happened. Many have disseminated atheistic, blasphemous, and wicked doctrines, falsely stamping them with His name, and they have taught, and still do, whatever that unclean spirit of the Devil has suggested to their minds. And we do our very best to warn them, as we do you, not to be deluded, for we know full well that whoever can speak out the truth and fails to do so shall be condemned by God, who said through Ezechiel: "I have made thee a watchman to the house of Juda. If the wicked man shall sin, and thou hast not warned him, he indeed shall die in his iniquity, but I will require his blood at thy hand; but if thou hast warned him, thou shalt be innocent."[1] It is not from a love of wealth, or of glory, or of pleasure, therefore, but because of fear of a future judgment, that we strive to speak in accordance with the Scriptures. For no person can justly accuse us of such vices. Nor do we wish to emulate the lives of your rulers, whom God thus censures: "Your princes are companions of thieves; they all love bribes and run after rewards."[2] Now if, unfortunately, you should encounter such men even among us Christians, do not for that reason blaspheme Christ and attempt to misinterpret the Scriptures.'

---

1 Ezech. 3.17-19.
2 Isa. 1.23.

Chapter 83

'For instance, your teachers have presumed to refer the words, "The Lord said to my Lord: Sit Thou at My right hand, till I make Thy enemies Thy footstool,"[1] to Hezekiah as if he were ordered to sit on the right side of the Temple, when the Assyrian king sent men to him with menacing messages and he was warned by Isaias not to be afraid. Now, we all know and acknowledge that what Isaias predicted did actually happen, and that in the days of Hezekiah the Assyrian king was checked from waging war on Jerusalem, and that an angel of the Lord put to death about one hundred and eighty-five thousand in the Assyrian camp. But, it is evident that the quoted Psalm does not refer to Hezekiah, for thus is it worded: "The Lord said to my Lord: Sit Thou at My right hand, till I make Thy enemies Thy footstool. He shall send forth the sceptre of power upon Jerusalem, and He shall rule in the midst of Thy enemies. In the brightness of the saints, before the morning star I begot Thee. The Lord hath sworn and He will not repent: Thou art a priest forever according to the order of Melchisedech."[2] Now, who will not concede that Hezekiah was not a priest forever according to the order of Melchisedech? And who is not aware that he was not the redeemer of Jerusalem? And who does not know that he did not send the sceptre of power upon Jerusalem, and did not rule in the midst of his enemies? (For was it not God who turned his enemies away while he wept and moaned?) But, although our Jesus has not yet returned in glory, He has sent forth into Jerusalem the sceptre of power, namely, the call to repentance to all the nations over which the demons used to rule, as David test-

---

1 Ps. 109.1.
2 Ps. 109.1-4.

ifies: "The gods of the Gentiles are demons."³ And the power of His word compelled many to abandon the demons whom they used to obey, and through Him to believe in Almighty God, because the gods of the Gentiles are demons. Furthermore, we have proved earlier that the words, "In the brightness of the saints, from the womb before the morning star I begot Thee,"⁴ were addressed to Christ.'

Chapter 84

'So also was the prophecy beginning with the words, "Behold a virgin shall conceive and bear a Son,"¹ spoken of Him. For, if the one of whom Isaias spoke was not to be born of a virgin, to whom did the Holy Spirit allude when He said: "Behold, the Lord Himself shall give you a sign: Behold, a virgin shall conceive and bear a Son"? If He was to be born of human intercourse like any other first-born son, why did God solemnly announce that He would give a sign which is not common to all first-born? What is truly a sign, and what was to be an irrefutable proof to all men, namely, that by means of a virgin's womb the First-born of all creatures took flesh and truly became man, was foreknown by the Prophetic Spirit before it took place and foretold by Him in different ways, as I have explained to you. Indeed, He foretold this in order that, when it did take place, everyone would understand that it all happened by the power and purpose of the Creator of the world; just as Eve was made from one of Adam's ribs, and as all living beings were created by the Word of God in the beginning. But here, too, you dare to distort the translation of this passage made by

---
3 Ps. 95.5.
4 Ps. 109.3.

---
1 Isa. 7.14.

your elders at the court of Ptolemy, the Egyptian king, asserting that the real meaning of the Scriptures is not as they translated it, but should read, "Behold a young woman shall conceive," as though something of extraordinary importance was signified by a woman conceiving after sexual intercourse, as all young women, except the barren, can do. And even the barren can become fertile by the power of God. Samuel's mother, who had been sterile, gave birth to her child by the will of God. The same thing can be said of the wife of the holy Patriarch Abraham, and of Elizabeth, who bore John the Baptist, and of many other women You must realize, therefore, that nothing is impossible for God to do, if He wills it. And, especially when it was prophesied that this would happen, you should not venture to mutilate or misinterpret the prophecies, for in doing so you do no harm to God, but only to yourselves.'

Chapter 85

'Then, too, some of you dare to explain the following words, "Lift up your gates, O ye princes, and be ye lifted up, O eternal gates, that the King of Glory may enter,"[1] as if they referred to Hezekiah, while others of you apply them to Solomon. On the contrary, we can prove that they were spoken neither of one nor of the other, nor of any of your kings, but only of our Christ, who appeared without beauty or honor (as Isaias, David, and all the Scriptures testify); who is Lord of hosts by the will of the Father who bestowed that honor upon Him; who arose again from the dead and ascended into Heaven (as is stated in the Psalm and other Scriptural passages which also declared Him to be Lord of hosts). You can easily see the truth of this, if you will

---

1 Ps. 23.7.

but open your eyes and look at the things that are happening around you. Every demon is vanquished and subdued when exorcised in the name of this true Son of God, who was the First-born of all creatures, who was born of a virgin, who suffered and was crucified by your people under Pontius Pilate, who died and then, after His resurrection from the dead, ascended into Heaven. But, when you attempt to exorcise them in the name of any man born among you (whether kings, just men, prophets or patriarchs), not one of the demons will be subject to you. If any man among you should exorcise them in the name of the God of Abraham, and the God of Isaac, and the God of Jacob, they will, perhaps, become subject to you. But some of your exorcists, as I have already noted, adjure the demons by employing the magical art of the Gentiles, using fumigations and amulets. The words of David also show that there are angels and powers whom the word of the prophecy, through David, ordered to lift up the gates in order that He who arose from the dead, Jesus Christ, the Lord of hosts, should enter in accordance with the Father's will. For the sake of those who were not with us yesterday, I will repeat the prophecy of David and summarize much of what was said at that time. I do not think it useless to do so, even though it means frequently repeating myself. It would be foolish to observe the sun and moon and other stars as they revolve in their same courses and effect the same change of seasons; and to consider a mathematician as he constantly gives the answer "four" when asked how many two times two are; and to speak always in the same way in acknowledging all other things that are firmly established as true—and yet, when discoursing about the meaning of the prophecies contained in the Scriptures, to prefer not to quote always the same Scripture, but to think oneself capable of inventing and uttering words superior to the Scriptures.

Here is the passage from which I showed that God revealed to us that there are angels and powers in Heaven: "Praise ye the Lord from the heavens; praise ye Him in the high places. Praise ye Him, all His angels; praise ye Him, all His hosts."[2]

At this point, one of the men who had joined them on the second day, Mnaseas by name, remarked, 'We greatly appreciate your kindness in taking the trouble to repeat those passages for our sake.'

'My friends,' I replied, 'listen to the Scripture which prompts me to do this. Jesus commanded us to love even our enemies, as Isaias also had announced at some length, in whose words is included the mystery of the new birth, both of us and of all who look forward to the glorious coming of Christ in Jerusalem and strive in their every action to please Him. Here are the words of Isaias: "Hear the word of the Lord, you that tremble at His word. Say, our brethren, to them that hate and detest you, that the name of the Lord is glorified. He hath appeared in their joy, and they shall be confounded. A voice of clamor from the city, a voice from the temple, the voice of the Lord that rendereth recompense to the proud. Before she was in labor she brought forth; before her time came to be delivered she brought forth a male child. Who hath ever heard such a thing, or who hath seen the like to this? Has the earth brought forth in one day? And has she brought forth a nation at once? Because Sion hath been in labor and hath brought forth her children. But I gave this expectation even to her who does not bring forth, saith the Lord. Behold I have made her that begetteth and her that is barren, saith the Lord. Rejoice, O Jerusalem, and hold a joyous gathering, all you that love her. Be glad,

---

2 Ps. 148.1-2.

all you that mourn for her, that you may suck and be filled with the breasts of her consolations; that having sucked out, you may be delighted with the entrance of His glory." '³

Chapter 86

After I had quoted this passage, I continued, 'Now, gentlemen, I want you to understand how He whom the Scriptures announce as about to return in glory after the crucifixion was symbolized both by the tree of life (which is said to have been planted in Paradise) and by the events¹ which were to happen to all the just. When Moses was sent with a rod to deliver the people, he held it in his hands at their head, and he divided the sea. With this rod he touched the rock and saw water gush forth. And, by throwing a tree into the bitter waters of Marah, he made them sweet. Jacob, by placing rods in their drinking-places, caused the sheep of his mother's brother to conceive, so that he might gain possession of their young. The same Jacob boasts that he crossed the river with his rod. He also claimed that he saw a ladder, and the Scriptures state that God rested on it (and we have shown by the Scriptures that this was not the Father). And when Jacob had poured oil over a stone at the same place, God appeared to him and told him that he had anointed a pillar in honor of the God whom he had seen. We also have proved that in many Scriptural passages Christ is symbolically called a Stone. We have likewise shown that every chrism, whether of oil, or of myrrh, or of any other balsam compound, was a figure of Christ; for the Scriptures say: "Therefore God, Thy God, hath anointed Thee with

---

3 Isa. 66.5-13.
1 These events were described in Exod. 4.7; 14.16-21; 15-23-25; 17.5-6; Gen. 28.12-18; 30.31-42; 31.13.

the oil of gladness above Thy fellows."[2] All kings and other anointed persons trace to Him their titles of Kings and Anointed, just as He Himself received from the Father the titles of King and Christ and Priest and Angel and all other titles of this kind which He has or had. By the blossoming of his rod, Aaron was proved to be the high priest. Isaias, indeed, foretold that Christ would come forth as a rod from the root of Jesse. And David declared that the just man is "like a tree which is planted near the running waters, which shall bring forth its fruit in due season, and his leaf shall not fall off." And, again, it is said that the righteous man shall "flourish like a palm tree."[3] God appeared to Abraham from a tree, as it is written, "by the oak of Mamre."[4] After crossing over the Jordan, the people found seventy willow trees and twelve springs. David declares that God comforted him with a rod and staff. Eliseus, by throwing a piece of wood into the River Jordan, brought up to the surface the iron head of the axe with which the sons of the Prophets had begun to cut wood for the construction of a building[5] in which they proposed to read and study the precepts of God; just as our Christ, by being crucified on the wood of the cross and by sanctifying us by water raised up us who had been immersed in the mire of our mortal sins, and made us a house of prayer and worship. Finally, it was a rod which signified that Juda was the father of the twins who were born of Thamar by a great mystery.'

Chapter 87

When I had finished, Trypho said, 'Now, when I ask the following question I want you to know that I do so, not for

---

[2] Ps. 44.8.
[3] Ps. 91.13.
[4] Gen. 18.1.
[5] Cf. 4 Kings 6.1-8.

the purpose of contradicting you, but only for the sake of gaining information on the subject. Explain to me the following words of Isaias: "There shall come forth a rod out of the root of Jesse, and a flower shall rise up out of his root. And the spirit of God shall rest upon him, the spirit of wisdom and understanding, the spirit of counsel and fortitude, the spirit of knowledge and piety; and he shall be filled with the spirit of the fear of the Lord."[1] Now you have admitted (he said) that these words were spoken of Christ, who, you claim, already existed as God, and, becoming incarnate by the will of God, was born of a virgin. This, then, is my question: How can you prove that Christ already existed, since He is endowed with those gifts of the Holy Spirit which the above-quoted passages of Isaias attribute to Him as though He had lacked them?'

'You proposed a very sensible and intelligent question,' I remarked, 'which appears to raise a real difficulty. But, if you really wish a solution to this difficulty, please listen to to me. The Scriptures state that these gifts of the Holy Spirit were bestowed upon Him, not as though He were in need of them, but as though they were about to rest upon Him, that is, to come to an end with Him, so that there would be no more Prophets among your people as of old (as is plainly evident to you, for after Him there has not been a prophet among you). Furthermore, please give my words your careful attention, so you may understand that each of your Prophets, by receiving one or two powers from God, did and said those things which we have learned from the Scriptures. Solomon had the spirit of wisdom, Daniel that of understanding and counsel, Moses that of strength and piety, Elias that of fear, Isaias that of knowledge, and the others likewise had one or two gifts, as had Jeremias, and

---
1 Isa. 11.1-3.

the twelve Prophets, and David, and, in short, all your other Prophets. The Spirit therefore rested, that is, ceased, when Christ came. For, after man's redemption was accomplished by Him, these gifts were to cease among you, and, having come to an end in Him, should again be given, as was foretold, by Him, from the grace of His Spirit's powers, to all His believers according to their merits. I have already affirmed, and I repeat, that it had been predicted that He would do this after His Ascension into Heaven. It was said, therefore: "He ascended on high; He led captivity captive; He gave gifts to the sons of men."[2] And in another prophecy it is said: "And it shall come to pass after this, that I will pour out My Spirit upon all flesh, and upon My servants, and upon My handmaids, and they shall prophesy."[3]

Chapter 88

'Now, if you look around, you can see among us Christians both men and women endowed with gifts from the Spirit of God. Thus, it was not because He needed the powers enumerated by Isaias that it was foretold that they would come on Him, but only because they would not exist any more afterwards. As additional proof, remember what I said about the Magi of Arabia; how they came as soon as the Child was born, and worshipped Him. For, as soon as He was born, He possessed His powers, and, growing up like any other man, He exercised appropriate powers at each stage of growth, being nourished by every sort of food, and waiting for about thirty years until John went on before Him as the herald of His arrival and precursor of His baptism, as I have pointed out previously. And when Jesus came to the River Jordan, where John was baptizing, He stepped

---
2 Ps. 67.19.
3 Joel 2.28-29.

down into the water and a fire ignited[1] the waters of the Jordan; and when He came up out of the water the Holy Spirit alighted upon Him in form of a dove, as the Apostles of this our Christ Himself testify. We indeed know that He did not approach the river because He needed either the baptism or the Spirit who came down upon Him in the shape of a dove. So, too, He did not condescend to be born and to be crucified because He was in need of birth or crucifixion; He did it solely for the sake of man, who from the time of Adam had become subject to death and the deceit of the serpent, each man having sinned by his own fault. For God, in His desire to have the angels and men (who were endowed with the personal power of free will) do whatever He had enabled them to do, created them such that, if they chose to do things pleasing to Him, He would preserve them immortal and free from punishment, but, if they preferred to do evil, He would punish each one as He pleased. It was not His entry into Jerusalem upon an ass (which we have shown was predicted) that gave Him the power to be the Christ, but it did prove to men that He is the Christ; just as in the days of John the Baptist men needed proof, that they might discern who was the Christ. For, when John, wearing only a cincture of skins and a cloak of camel's hair, and eating only locusts and wild honey, sat by the River Jordan and preached the baptism of repentance, men supposed that he was the Christ, but he cried out to his listeners: "I am not the Christ, but the voice of one crying; for there will come He that is stronger than I, whose shoes I am not worthy to carry."[2] When Jesus came to the Jordan, therefore, being considered the son of Joseph the

---

1 Justin learned this either from tradition or from some apocryphal works, e.g., the Ebionite Gospel or the *Praedicatio Pauli*, which both mention this phenomenon.
2 John 1.23. Cf. Isa. 40.3.

carpenter,[3] and having no comeliness, as the Scriptures affirmed, He was thought to be a carpenter (for, when He was on earth He used to work as a carpenter, making ploughs and yokes, and thereby giving us symbolic lessons of the necessity of leading a just and active life); but then, as I already stated, the Holy Spirit for the sake of mankind descended upon Him in the form of a dove, and at the same instant a voice out of the heavens spoke the words which had also been uttered by David, when he, in the person of Christ, spoke what was later to be said to Christ by the Father: "Thou art My Son; this day have I begotten Thee,"[4] meaning that His birth really began for men when they first realized who He was.'

Chapter 89

'You know very well,' said Trypho, 'that we Jews all look forward to the coming of the Christ, and we admit that all your Scriptural quotations refer to Him. I also admit that the name Jesus [Josue], which was given to the son of Nave [Nun], has prompted me to incline to this opinion. But we doubt whether the Christ should be so shamefully crucified, for the Law declares that he who is crucified is to be accursed.[1] Consequently, you will find me very difficult to convince on this point. It is indeed evident that the Scriptures state that Christ was to suffer, but you will have to show us, if you can, whether it was to be the form of suffering cursed by the Law.'

'If, indeed, Christ was not to suffer,' I replied, 'and if the Prophets did not predict that because of the sins of the

---
3 Luke 3.16.
4 Ps. 2.7.

---
1 Deut. 21.23.

people He would be put to death, and be dishonored and scourged, and be numbered among sinners, and be led as a sheep to the slaughter, whose birth (the Prophet declares) no one can describe, your feelings of astonishment would be justified. But, if these things are marks which reveal Him to all, how can we do otherwise than confidently believe in Him? And all who have grasped the meaning of the Prophets' words, as soon as they hear that He was crucified, will affirm that He is the Christ and no other.'

Chapter 90

'Show us this from the Scriptures, therefore,' said Trypho, 'that we, too, may believe you. We are indeed aware that He was to endure suffering, and to be led as a sheep to the slaughter. But what we want you to prove to us is that He was to be crucified and be subjected to so disgraceful and shameful a death (which even in the Law is cursed). We find it impossible to think that this could be so.'

'You know,' I said, 'in fact, you already admitted, that what the Prophets said or did they often expressed in parables and types, thus hiding the truth they held. Consequently, it is not easy for the multitude to understand most of what they taught, but only those who take the trouble to find out and learn.'

'We never doubted it,' they replied.

'Then, please listen,' I said, 'to what I am going to say. Moses was the first to make known this apparent curse of Christ by the symbolic acts which He performed.'

'What acts do you mean?' asked Trypho.

'When your people,' I answered, 'waged war with Amalec,[1] and Jesus [Josue], the son of Nun, was the leader of the

---
1 Cf. Exod. 17.9-12.

battle, Moses himself, stretching out both hands, prayed to God for help. Now, Hur and Aaron held up his hands all day long, lest he should become tired and let them drop to his sides. For, if Moses relaxed from that figure [of outstretched hands], which was a figure of the cross, the people were defeated (as Moses himself testifies), but as long as he remained in that position Amalec was defeated, and the strong derived their strength from the cross. In truth, it was not because Moses prayed that his people were victorious, but because, while the name of Jesus was at the battle front, Moses formed the sign of the cross. Who among you does not know that that prayer is the most pleasing to God which is uttered with lamentation and tears, with prostrate body or bended knees? But on this occasion Moses (or any after him) did not pray in such a manner; he was seated on a stone. And I have shown that even the stone is symbolical of Christ.'

Chapter 91

'Furthermore, God indicated in yet another way the power of the mystery of the cross when He said through Moses, in the blessing pronounced over Joseph: "From the blessing of the Lord in his land; for the seasons of heaven, and for the dews, and for the deep springs from beneath, and for the fruits brought forth by the course of the sun, and for the conjuctions of the months, and for the tops of the ancient mountains, and for the top of the hills, and for the ever-flowing rivers, and for the abundance of the fruits of the earth. And let those things which are pleasing to Him who appeared in the bush come upon the head and crown of Joseph, who was glorified among his brethren. His beauty is as of a firstling of a bullock, and his horns are the horns of a rhinoceros; with them shall he push the nations even to the ends of the earth."¹ Now, no one can assert or prove that the horns of a rhinoceros represent any other matter or figure than that of the cross. The one beam of the cross stands upright, from which the upper part is lifted up like a horn when the crossbeam is fitted on, and the ends of the crosspiece resemble horns joined to that one horn. And the part which is fixed in the middle of the cross, on which the bodies of the crucified are supported, also projects like a horn, and it, too, looks like a horn when it is shaped and joined to the other horns. And the words, "With them shall he push the nations even to the ends of the earth,"² clearly describe what is now taking place in all the nations. For, men of all nations have been pushed by the horns, that is, goaded to compunction, by means of this mystery [of the cross], and have abandoned their vain idols and demons to turn to the worship of God. But to unbelievers, the same sign of the cross is shown to be the cause of their destruction and condemnation, as when the people had come out of Egypt, and Israel was victorious over conquered Amalec by the sign of Moses' outstretched hands and by the imposition of the name Jesus [Josue] upon the son of Nun. Likewise, the figure and sign, erected to counteract the effects of the serpents that bit Israel, was clearly intended for the salvation of those who believe that this sign was to show that through the Crucified One death was to come to the serpent, but salvation to those who had been bitten by the serpent and had sought protection of Him who sent His Son into the world to be crucified. Actually, the Prophetic Spirit, through Moses, did not instruct us to believe in a serpent, since He announces that the serpent was cursed by God from the beginning, and through Isaias

---

1 Deut. 33.13-17.
2 Deut. 33.17.

He informs us that it will be slain as an enemy by the great sword, which is Christ.'

Chapter 92

'If, therefore, one were not endowed with God's great grace to understand the words and deeds of the Prophets, it would be quite useless for him to relate their words and actions, when he can give no explanation of them. Moreover, will not those words and deeds seem despicable to most people if they are told by those who do not understand them? For, if anyone were to ask you why, when Henoch, and Noe with his children, and all others like them, were pleasing to God without being circumcised or without observing the Sabbath, God required by new leaders and another law, after the lapse of so many generations, that those who lived between the times of Abraham and Moses should be justified by circumcision, and that those who lived after Moses be justified by both circumcision and the other precepts (that is, the Sabbaths, sacrifices, ashes, and oblations), [God would be unjustly criticized] unless you point out, as I have already said, that God in His foreknowledge was aware that your people would deserve to be expelled from Jerusalem and never be allowed to enter there. I have previously shown that you are distinguishable by no other means than by the circumcision of the flesh. Abraham, indeed, was considered just, not by reason of his circumcision, but because of his faith. For, before his circumcision it was said of him: "Abraham believed God, and it was reputed to him unto justice."[1] We also, therefore, because of our belief in God through Christ, even though we are uncircumcised in the flesh, have the salutary circumcision, namely, that of the

---
1 Gen. 15.6.

heart, and we thereby hope to be just and pleasing to God, since we have already obtained this testimony from Him through the words of the Prophets. But you Jews were ordered to observe the Sabbaths and make offerings, and you were allowed by God to erect a place in which He could be invoked, so that you might not worship idols and forget God, and thus become impious and godless, as, indeed, you always seem to have been. (Now it was precisely for this reason that God issued His ordinances about the sabbaths and oblations, as I have already proved by my previous words, but for the sake of the new arrivals today I had better repeat most of my proofs.) If this had not been the reason [that is, to save you from idolatry], God could be accused of not having foreknowledge and of not teaching all men to know and to observe the same just precepts (for there surely were many generations of men before the time of Moses), and the Scripture would be judged false which says: "God is true and just, and all His ways are judgments, and there is no iniquity in Him."[2] But, since the Scripture is evidently true, God does not desire that you always remain foolish and conceited as you now are, but that you may be saved with Christ, who pleased God and was approved by Him, as I have already shown from the writings of the holy Prophets.'

Chapter 93

'God shows every race of man that which is always and in all places just, and every type of man knows that adultery, fornication, murder, and so on are evil. Though they all commit such acts, they cannot escape the knowledge that they sin whenever they do so, except those who, possessed by an unclean spirit, and corrupted by bad education and

---

2 Deut. 32.4; Ps. 24.10; 91.16.

evil habits and wicked laws, have lost (or rather have stifled and stamped out) their natural feelings of guilt. For one may observe how such persons are unwilling to endure what they inflict upon others, and with sinister conscience they criticize others for the very things that they themselves do. Hence, I am of the opinion that our Lord and Savior Jesus Christ very aptly explained that all justice and piety are summed up in these two commandments: "Thou shalt love the Lord thy God with thy whole heart, and with thy whole strength, and thy neighbor as thyself."[1] For, he who loves God with all his heart and all his strength has a mind that is devoted to God, and he will worship no other as God, but he will, since God desires it, revere the Angel who is loved by the same Lord and God. And the man who loves his neighbor as himself will wish for him the very same blessings that he wishes for himself (and no man wishes evil for himself). Consequently, he who loves his neighbor will both pray and work that his neighbor may attain the same blessings as himself. Now, a man's neighbor is none other than that creature endowed with reason and passions like his own —man. Therefore, since all justice is directed toward two ends, namely, God and man, whoever loves the Lord God with all his heart, says the Scripture, and with all his strength, and his neighbor as himself, will surely be a just man. But, as for you Jews, you have never evidenced any friendship or love either toward God, or toward the Prophets, or toward one another, but you have shown yourselves always to be idolaters and murderers of the just; in fact, you even did violence to Christ Himself. Indeed, you continue along your wicked way even to this day, cursing even those who prove to you that He whom you crucified was the Christ. Why, you even go so far as to maintain (and this shows how irra-

---

1 Matt. 22.37-39.

tional are your mental functions) that He has been crucified as an accursed enemy of God. Though you have a starting point to understand, from the signs wrought by Moses, that this man is the Christ, you will not; further, imagining that you can baffle us, you ask whatever questions come to your mind, and you yourselves lack sound arguments whenever you encounter a well-instructed Christian.'

Chapter 94

'Tell me, did not God, through Moses, forbid the making of an image or likeness of anything in the heavens or on earth, yet He Himself had Moses construct the brazen serpent in the desert and set it up as a sign by which those who had been bitten by the serpents were healed, and in doing so was He not free of any sin? By this, as I stated above, He announced a mystery by which He proclaimed that He would break the power of the serpent, which prompted the sin of Adam, and that He would deliver from the bites of the serpent (that is, evil actions, idolatries, and other sins) all those who believe in Him who was to be put to death by this sign, namely, the cross. If this is not the interpretation of the passage, give me one reason why Moses set up the brazen serpent on the sign [cross],[1] and commanded all who had been bitten to look upon it; and they were healed, and this, in spite of the fact that he himself had forbidden them to make an image of anything whatsoever.'

Another of those who had come on the second day interrupted me by saying, 'You are right. We cannot give a reason. I have personally asked our teachers about this question on numerous occasions, but none of them could ever give me a reasonable answer. Therefore, please continue on this topic,

---

1 Justin supposes that the image of the serpent was hung on a cruciform piece of wood.

for we are most attentive as you reveal a mystery [of contradictions] through which the teachings of the Prophets are exposed to calumny.'

'As God ordered the sign to be made by the brazen serpent,' I went on, 'and yet is not guilty [of the crime of making graven images], so in the Law a curse is placed upon men who are crucified, but not upon the Christ of God, by whom are saved all who have committed deeds deserving a curse.'

Chapter 95

'Indeed, the whole human race could be said to be under a curse. For it is written in the Law laid down by Moses: "Cursed be he that abideth not in the words of the book of the Law, and fulfilleth them not in work."[1] Not even you will dare to assert that anyone ever fulfilled all the precepts of the Law exactly; some have kept them more, some less, than others. But, if those who are subject to the Law are certainly under a curse, because they have not kept the whole Law, how much more so will all the Gentiles evidently be cursed, since they commit idolatry, seduce youths, and perform other wicked deeds? If, therefore, the Father of the Universe willed that His Christ should shoulder the curses of the whole human race, fully realizing that He would raise Him up again after His crucifixion and death, why do you accuse Him, who endured such suffering in accordance with the Father's will, of being a cursed person, instead of bewailing your own iniquity? For, although He suffered for mankind according to the will of the Father Himself, it was not in obedience to the will of God that you made Him suffer. Nor did you practise piety when you put the Prophets to death. Nor can any of you say in self-defense: "If the

---

1 Deut. 27.26. Cf. Gal. 3.10.

Father willed Him to suffer these things, in order that by His wounds mankind might be healed, we did no wrong [in putting Him to death]." If you would say this while you repent for your wicked actions, and acknowledge Jesus to be the Christ, and observe His precepts, then, as I said above, you will receive remission of your sins. But, if you curse Him and those who believe in Him, and, whenever it is in your power, put them to death, how will you prevent retribution from being demanded of you for having laid hands on Him, as of unjust and sinful men who are completely devoid of feeling and wisdom?'

Chapter 96

'The words of the Law, "Cursed is every one who hangeth on a tree,"[1] strengthen our hope which is sustained by the Crucified Christ, not because the Crucified One is cursed by God, but because God predicted what would be done by all of you Jews, and others like you, who are not aware that this is He who was before all things, the Eternal Priest of God, the King, and Christ. Now, you can clearly see that this has actually happened. For, in your synagogues you curse all those who through Him have become Christians, and the Gentiles put into effect your curse by killing all those who merely admit that they are Christians. To all our persecutors we say: "You are our brothers; apprehend, rather, the truth of God." But when neither they nor you will listen to us, but you do all in your power to force us to deny Christ, we resist you and prefer to endure death, confident that God will give us all the blessings which He promised us through Christ. Furthermore, we pray for you that you might experience the mercy of Christ; for He in-

---
1 Deut. 21.23.

structed us to pray even for our enemies, when He said: "Be kind and merciful, even as your Heavenly Father is merciful."[2] We can observe that Almighty God is kind and merciful, causing His sun to shine on the ungrateful and on the just, and sending rain to both the holy and the evil; but all of them, He has told us, He will judge.'[3]

Chapter 97

'Besides, the fact that the Prophet Moses remained until evening in the form of the cross, when his hands were held up by Aaron and Hur, happened in the likeness of this sign. For the Lord also remained upon the cross almost until evening, when He was buried. Then He arose from the dead on the third day, as David foretold when he said: "I have cried to the Lord with My voice, and He hath heard Me from His holy hill. I have slept and have taken My rest; and I have risen up, because the Lord hath sustained Me."[1] Isaias likewise foretold the manner of His death in these words: "I have spread forth My hands to an unbelieving and contradicting people, who walk in a way that is not good."[2] And the same Isaias also predicted His resurrection: "His burial has been taken out of the midst,"[3] and: "I will give the rich for His death."[4] And again, David, in his twenty-first Psalm, refers to His passion on the cross in mystical parable: "They have pierced My hands and feet. They have numbered all My bones. And they have looked and stared upon Me. They parted My garments amongst them, and upon My vesture

---

2 Luke 6.36.
3 Cf. Matt. 5.45.

1 Ps. 3.5-6.
2 Isa. 65.2.
3 Isa. 57.2.
4 Isa. 53.9.

they cast lots."[5] For, when they nailed Him to the cross they did indeed pierce His hands and feet, and they who crucified Him divided His garments among themselves, each casting lots for the garment he chose. You are indeed blind when you deny that the above-quoted Psalm was spoken of Christ, for you fail to see that no one among your people who was ever called King ever had his hands and feet pierced while alive, and died by this mystery (that is, of the cross), except this Jesus only.'

Chapter 98

'Permit me to quote that whole Psalm, that you may perceive how He reveres His Father and how He refers all things to Him, as when He prays to be freed by Him from this death; at the same time pointing out in the Psalm what sort of men His enemies were, and proving that He indeed became a man who was capable of suffering. The Psalm is as follows: "O God, my God, look upon me, why hast Thou forsaken me? Far from my salvation are the words of my sins. O my God, I shall cry by day, and Thou wilt not hear, and by night, and it is not for want of understanding in me. But Thou dwellest in the holy place, Thou praise of Israel. In Thee have our fathers hoped; they have hoped and Thou hast delivered them. They cried to Thee, and they were saved; they trusted in Thee and were not confounded. But I am a worm, and no man; the reproach of men, and and the outcast of the people. All they that saw me have laughed me to scorn; they have spoken with the lips, and wagged the head; He hoped in the Lord, let Him deliver him; let Him save him, seeing He desires him. For Thou art He that hast drawn me out of the womb; my hope from

---

5 Ps. 21.18-19.

the breasts of my mother. I was cast upon Thee from the womb. From my mother's womb Thou art my God. Depart not from me, for tribulation is very near; for there is none to help me. Many calves have surrounded me; fat bulls have besieged me. They have opened their mouths against me as a lion ravening and roaring. All my bones are poured out and scattered like water. My heart is become like wax melting in the midst of my belly. My strength is dried up like a potsherd, and my tongue hath cleaved to my jaws; and Thou hast brought me down into the dust of death. For many dogs encompassed me; the council of the malignant hath besieged me. They have pierced my hands and feet. They have numbered all my bones. And they have looked and stared upon me. They parted my garments amongst them; and upon my vesture they cast lots. But Thou, O Lord, remove not Thy help to a distance from me; look towards my defense. Deliver my soul from the sword, and my only-begotten from the power of the dog. Save me from the lion's mouth; and my lowness from the horns of the unicorns. I will declare Thy name to my brethren; in the midst of the church will I praise Thee. Ye that fear the Lord, praise Him; all ye the seed of Jacob, glorify Him. Let all the seed of Israel fear Him.' [1]

Chapter 99

Then I continued, 'I will now show you that the whole Psalm referred to Christ, by repeating and expounding it. The opening words of the Psalm, "O God, my God, look upon me, why hast Thou forsaken me," foretold in old times what would be said in Christ's time. For, while hanging on the cross, He exclaimed, "My God, My God, why hast Thou

---
1 Ps. 21.1-25.

forsaken Me"?¹ And the words, "Far from my salvation are the words of my sins. O my God, I shall cry by day, and Thou wilt not hear, and by night, and it is not for want of understanding in me," depicted the very things that He was about to do. For, on the day of His crucifixion He took three of His disciples to the Mount of Olives, opposite the Temple in Jerusalem, and prayed thus: "Father, if it be possible, let this cup pass away from Me;' but He ended His prayer by saying, 'Not My will, but Thine be done,'² thus making it clear that He had really become a man capable of suffering. To offset the calumny that He did not know then that He was to suffer, He immediately adds in the Psalm, "And it is not want of understanding in Me." Just as it was not from lack of understanding that God asked Adam where he was, and Cain where Abel was, but to convince each what sort of man he was, and to provide us with knowledge of all things through the Holy Writ; so Christ signified that there was no lack of understanding on His part, but on the part of those who, refusing to believe that He was the Christ, thought that they put Him to death and that He would remain in Hades as any ordinary person.'

Chapter 100

'And the words, "But Thou dwellest in the holy place, Thou praise of Israel," signified that He would do something worthy of praise and admiration, which He did when through the Father He arose again from the dead on the third day after the crucifixion. I have indeed pointed out earlier that Christ is called both Jacob and Israel, and that not only in the blessing of Joseph and Juda have things been predicted mysteriously of Him, but also in the Gospel it is written

---

1 Matt. 27.46.
2 Matt. 26.39.

that He said: "All things have been deliverd to Me by My Father; and no one knows the Father except the Son; nor does anyone know the Son except the Father, and those to whom the Son will reveal Him."[1] He thus revealed to us all that we have learned from the Scriptures by His grace, so that we know Him as the First-begotten of God before all creatures, and as the Son of the patriarchs, since He became incarnate by a virgin of their race, and condescended to become a man without comeliness or honor, and subject to suffering. Hence, He alluded to His imminent passion in this way, "The Son of Man must suffer many things, and be rejected by the Pharisees and Scribes, and be crucified, and rise again on the third day."[2] He called Himself Son of Man, either because of His birth by the virgin who was, as I said, of the family of David and Jacob and Isaac and Abraham, or because Adam himself was the father of those above-mentioned Patriarchs from whom Mary traces her descent. It is clear that the fathers of girls are also considered the fathers of the children born to their daughters. And Christ changed the name of one of His disciples from Simon to Peter,[3] when he, enlightened by the Father, recognized Him to be Christ, the Son of God. And since we find it written in the Memoirs of the Apostles that He is the Son of God, and since we call Him by that same title, we have understood that this is really He and that He proceeded before all creatures from the Father by His power and will (for in the prophetic writings He is called Wisdom, the Day, the East, Sword, Stone, Rod, Jacob, and Israel, always in a different way); and that He is born of the Virgin, in order that the disobedience caused by the serpent might be destroyed in the same manner in

---

1 Matt. 11.27.
2 Cf. Matt. 16.21; Mark 8.31-39; Luke 9.22-27.
3 Cf. Matt. 16.15-18.

which it had originated. For Eve, an undefiled virgin, conceived the word of the serpent, and brought forth disobedience and death. But the Virgin Mary, filled with faith and joy, when the angel Gabriel announced to her the good tidings that the Spirit of the Lord would come upon her, and the power of the Highest would overshadow her, and therefore the Holy One born of her would be the Son of God, answered: "Be it done unto me according to Thy word."[4] And, indeed, she gave birth to Him, concerning whom we have shown so many passages of Scripture were written, and by whom God destroys both the serpent and those angels and men who have become like the serpent, but frees from death those who repent of their sins and believe in Christ.'

Chapter 101

'Now, the next words of the Psalm are these: "In Thee have our fathers hoped; they have hoped and Thou hast delivered them. They cried to Thee, and they were saved; they trusted in Thee and were not confounded. But I am a worm, and no man; the reproach of men, and the outcast of the people." This passage proves that He acknowledges as His fathers those who trusted in God and were saved by Him, who were also the fathers of the virgin by whom He was born and became man, while He states that He will be saved by the same God, and in His humility does not claim to do anything of His own will or power. He did the same when He was on earth. For, when one of His followers said to Him, "Good Master," He asked, "Why callest thou Me good? One is good; that is, My Father who is in Heaven."[1] And when He said, "I am a worm, and no man; the re-

---

4 Luke 1.35.

---

1 Matt. 19.16-17.

proach of men, and the outcast of the people," He foretold what would clearly take place and happen to Him. For He is everywhere a reproach to us who believe in Him, and He is the outcast of the people, for He was cast out in disgrace by your people, and He endured all the indignities which you directed toward Him. And by the words which follow, "All they that saw me have laughed me to scorn; they have spoken with their lips, and wagged the head: He hoped in the Lord, let Him deliver him, seeing He desires Him," He again predicted what would happen to Himself. For they that beheld Him on the cross wagged their heads, curled their lips in scorn, turned up their noses, and sarcastically uttered the words which are recorded in the Memoirs of the Apostles: "He called Himself the Son of God, let Him come down from the cross and walk! Let God save Him!" [2]

Chapter 102

'The next words of the Psalm are: "My hope from the breasts of my mother. I was cast upon Thee from the womb. From my mother's womb Thou art my God. Depart not from me, for tribulation is very near; for there is none to help me. Many calves have surrounded me; fat bulls have besieged me. They have opened their mouths against me as a lion ravening and roaring. All my bones are poured out and scattered like water. My heart is become like wax melting in the midst of my belly. My strength is dried up like a potsherd, and my tongue hath cleaved to my jaws." This passage, too, was a prophecy of events to come. For the words, "My hope from my mother's breasts," may be explained in the following manner. As soon as Christ was born in Bethlehem, as I stated above, King Herod learned all

---

2 Matt. 27.39-43; Luke 23.35-37. Justin added the words 'and walk.'

about Him from the Arabian Magi, and plotted to kill Him. But Joseph, at God's command, took Him with Mary and left for Egypt.[1] For it was the Father's design that His Only-begotten be put to death only after He had reached maturity and had preached His message. But if anyone should ask us if God were not able instead to kill Herod, I reply, in anticipating this question, by asking if God were not able in the beginning to destroy the serpent, instead of declaring: "I will place enmity between it and the woman, and between its seed and her seed?"[2] And could He not have created at once a great throng of men? Yet, because He knew that it was good, He created both angels and men free to perform acts of justice, and He set the limits of time during which He knew it would be good for them to enjoy such freedom of will. So, too, because He knew it was good, He established general and particular judgments, safeguarding, however, each person's free will. Hence, at the time that the foundation of the tower [of Babel] was laid, when the diversity and confusion of languages originated, the Scriptures say: "And the Lord said: Behold, it is one people, and all have one tongue; and they have begun to do this, neither will they leave off from their designs."[3] And the expression, "My strength is dried up like a potsherd, and my tongue hath cleaved to my jaws," was also a prediction of what He would do in conformity with His Father's will. For the power of His mighty word with which He always refuted the Pharisees and Scribes, and indeed all the teachers of your race who disputed with Him, was stopped like a full and mighty fountain whose waters have been suddenly shut off, when He remained silent and would no longer answer His accusers before Pilate, as was

---

1 Cf. Matt. 2.
2 Gen. 3.15.
3 Gen. 11.6.

recorded in the writings of the Apostles, in order that those words of Isaias might bear fruit in action: "The Lord gives me a tongue, that I may know when I ought to speak."[4] And His words, "Thou art my God, depart not from me," teach us to put all our trust in God, the Creator of all things, and to seek aid and salvation from Him alone; and not to imagine, as other men do, that we can attain salvation by means of birth, or wealth, or power, or wisdom. This is precisely your practice, for you once made a golden calf, and always appeared ungrateful, and murderers of the just, and inflated with pride because of your birth. For, if the Son of God clearly states that it is not because He is the Son, nor because He is powerful or wise, but that, even though He be sinless (for Isaias said that He did not sin even by word, "He hath done no iniquity, neither was there deceit in His mouth"[5]), He cannot be saved without God [the Father], how can you or others who expect to be saved without this hope, fail to realize that you are deceiving yourselves?'

Chapter 103

'And the following words of the Psalm, "For tribulation is very near; for there is none to help. Many calves have surrounded me; fat bulls have besieged me. They have opened their mouths against me as a lion ravening and roaring. All my bones are poured out and scattered like water," were also a prophecy of the things that would happen to Him. For, on that night when your kinsmen, sent by the Pharisees, Scribes, and teachers, met Him from the Mount of Olives,[1]

---

4 Isa. 50.4.
5 Isa. 53.9.

1 *Apò toû órous*: 'from the mountain,' would indicate that Justin thought that the Jews came down from some part of the mounatin to seize Jesus in a valley below. But the Gospel story does not coincide with Justin's description of the event. There is a possibility that the original text was altered.

they surrounded Him, and were thus called by the Scripture "calves" with horns and predestined for perdition. By the words, "fat bulls have besieged me," He foretold the deeds of those who acted like calves, when He was led before your teachers. Holy Scripture described these persons as bulls, for, as we know, bulls are the fathers of calves. Now, as bulls are the fathers of calves, so your teachers were the cause of their children going out to Mount Olivet to capture and lead Him to them. So also the words, "For there is none to help," were indicative of what would take place; for there was not even one single person to help Him, sinless as He was. And the expression, "They have opened their mouths against me as a roaring lion," means Herod, the king of the Jews at that time, a successor of that other, who slaughtered all the boys that were born in Bethlehem at the time of Christ's birth, thinking that He, concerning whom the Arabian Magi had spoken, would surely be among them. But he was not aware of the designs of Almighty God, who ordered Joseph and Mary to take the Child and go into Egypt and remain there until it should be revealed to them again that they should return into their own country. And after their departure they stayed there until the death of Herod, the assassin of the babes of Bethlehem. Archelaus, who succeeded him, also died before Christ fulfilled by His crucifixion the Father's plan of our redemption. And when Herod succeeded Archelaus and received the authority that had fallen to his share, Pilate favored him by sending Jesus bound to him,[2] which God in His foreknowledge foretold in these words, "And they brought Him to the Assyrian, a present to the king."[3] Or, it could be that by the lion that roared against Him He meant the Devil himself, that is, the one whom Moses called the

---
2 Cf. John 18.24.
3 Osee 10.6.

serpent, Job and Zacharias the Devil, and Jesus addressed as Satanas, indicating that he had a compound name made up of the actions which he performed; for the word "Sata" in the Jewish and Syrian tongue means "apostate," while "nas" is the word which means in translation "serpent"; thus, from both parts is formed the one word "Satanas." It is narrated in the Memoirs of the Apostles that as soon as Jesus came out of the River Jordan and a voice said to Him: "Thou art My Son, this day I have begotten Thee,"[4] this devil came and tempted Him, even so far as to exclaim: "Worship me"; but Christ replied: "Get thee behind Me, Satan; the Lord thy God shalt thou worship, and Him only shalt thou serve."[5] For, since the devil had deceived Adam, he fancied that he could in some way harm Him also. Now the passage, "All my bones are poured out and scattered like water; my heart is become like wax melting in the midst of my belly," foretold what would happen on that night when they came to Mount Olivet to capture Him. For in the Memoirs of the Apostles and their successors, it is written that His perspiration poured out like drops of blood as He prayed and said: "If it be possible, let this cup pass from Me."[6] His heart and bones were evidently quaking, and His heart was like wax melting in His belly, so that we may understand that the Father wished His Son to endure in reality these severe sufferings for us, and may not declare that, since He was the Son of God, He did not feel[7] what was done and inflicted upon Him. And the words, "My strength is dried up like a potsherd, and my tongue hath cleaved to my jaws," predicted that He would remain silent; for, indeed, He who

---

4 Ps. 2.7. Cf. Chapter 88
5 Matt. 4.10.
6 Luke 22.44.
7 As the Docetists declared.

proved that all your teachers are without wisdom replied not a word in His own defense.'

Chapter 104

'The next words of the Psalm are: "Thou hast brought me down into the dust of death. For many dogs have encompassed me; the council of the malignant hath besieged me. They have pierced my hands and feet. They have numbered all my bones. And they have looked and stared upon me. They parted my garments amongst them; and upon my vesture they cast lots."[1] This passage, I have already shown, was a prophecy of the kind of death to which He would be condemned by the assembly of the wicked, whom He calls both dogs and hunters, affirming that they who hunted Him united to use every possible means to condemn Him. This event, too, is recorded in the Memoirs of the Apostles. And I have pointed out that after His crucifixion they who crucified Him divided His garments among themselves.'

Chapter 105

'Now, here are the next words of the Psalm: "But Thou, O Lord, remove not Thy help to a distance from me; look towards my defense. Deliver my soul from the sword, and my only-begotten from the power of the dog. Save me from the lion's mouth; and my lowness from the horns of the unicorns." These words, too, point out what He would be and what would happen to Him. I have proved that He is the Only-begotten of the Father of the universe, having been properly begotten from Him as His Word and Power, and afterwards becoming man by a virgin, as we have learned from the

---
1 Ps. 21.15-18.

Memoirs of the Apostles.[1] That He would die by crucifixion, He also predicted, for the words, "Deliver my soul from the sword, and my only-begotten from the power of the dog. Save me from the lion's mouth; and my lowness from the horns of the unicorns," were spoken by One who foretold by what manner of torment He would die, namely, by crucifixion. I explained above that the "horns of the unicorn" have the shape of a cross only. And His plea that His soul might be saved from the sword, from the lion's mouth, and from the dog's paw, was a prayer that no one should have power over His soul, so that, when we approach the end of life, we may beg the same favor of God, who can prevent every bad and brazen angel from stealing our souls. Now, I have proved that souls survive [after death] from the fact that Samuel's soul was invoked by the witch, as Saul demanded. And it seems that the souls of other just men and Prophets were subjected to such powers, as is evident from the facts in the case of this witch. Thus, God through His Son also teaches us (for whom these things seem to have happened) always to do our utmost to become righteous and at our death to pray that we may not fall into any such power. For, the Memoirs of the Apostles said that, as He was giving up His spirit on the cross, He said: "Father, into Thy hands I commend My spirit."[2] Further, He urged His disciples to excel the Pharisees' way of living, warning them that otherwise they should know that they would not be saved; His words on this occasion are thus recorded in the Memoirs of the Apostles: "Unless your justice exceeds that of the Scribes and Pharisees, you shall not enter the kingdom of Heaven."[3]

---

1 Cf. John 1.18.
2 Luke 23.46.
3 Matt. 5.20.

Chapter 106

'The rest of the Psalm shows that He knew that His Father would grant all His requests, and would raise Him from the dead. It also shows that He encouraged all who fear God to praise Him, because through the mystery of the Crucified One He had mercy on the faithful of every race; and that He stood in the midst of His brethren, the Apostles (who, after He arose from the dead and convinced them that He had warned them before the Passion that He had to suffer, and that this was foretold by the Prophets, were most sorry that they had abandoned Him at the crucifixion). The Psalm finally shows that He sang hymns to God while He was with them, which actually happened, according to the Memoirs of the Apostles. Here are the words of the Psalm: "I will declare Thy name to my brethren; in the midst of the church will I praise Thee. Ye that fear the Lord, praise Him; all ye the seed of Jacob, glorify Him. Let all the seed of Israel fear Him." Now, when we learn from the Memoirs of the Apostles that He changed the name of one of the Apostles to Peter (besides having changed the names of the two brothers, the sons of Zebedee, to that of Boanerges, which means "sons of thunder"), we have an indication that it was also He who gave Jacob the surname of Israel, and Osee [Auses] the added name of Jesus [Josue], under whose name the survivors of those who escaped from Egypt were led into the land promised to the Patriarchs. And Moses predicted that He would arise like a star from the seed of Abraham, when he said: "A star shall rise out of Jacob, and a leader from Israel."[1] And another passage reads: "Behold the Man; the Orient is His name."[2] Therefore, when a star

---

[1] Num. 24.17.
[2] Zach. 6.12.

arose in the heavens at the time of His Nativity, as the Apostolic Memoirs attest,[3] the Magi from Arabia knew the fact from this sign, and came to worship Him.'

Chapter 107

'And these Memoirs also testify to the fact of His resurrection from the dead on the third day after the crucifixion, for it is therein recorded that in answer to the contentious Jews who said to Him, "Show us a sign," He replied, "An evil and adulterous generation demands a sign, and no sign shall be given it but the sign of Jonas."[1] Though these words were mysterious, His listeners could understand that He would arise from the dead on the third day after His crucifixion. And He showed that your generation was more evil and adulterous than that of the Ninevites, who, when Jonas (after being cast up on shore from the belly of the whale on the third day) warned them that they would all perish within three (in other versions, forty)[2] days, announced a fast for all living creatures, men and beasts, accompanied by the wearing of sackcloth, unrestrained mourning, truly sincere repentance, and a resolution to shun sin, believing that God is merciful and benevolent toward all those who avoid sin. Thus, even the king of that city and his nobles, too, wore sackcloth, and fasted and prayed constantly, and so through their prayers the city was spared. Then, when Jonas was vexed because the city had not been destroyed on the third (fortieth) day, as he had announced, a gourd[3] sprang

---

3 Matt. 2.10-11.

1 Matt. 12.38-39.
2 This parenthesis is part of the text. The Septuagint has the number *three,* but the Hebrew text has *forty.* Justin, who usually follows the Septuagint text here combines both, unless the parenthesis is the work of a copyist.
3 *Sikuóna*: here translated as 'gourd' instead of 'ivy,' as some render it.

up out of the earth at God's design, and Jonas sat under it and was shaded from the heat of the sun (now this was a round gourd which had sprung up spontaneously to provide Jonas with shade, and he had neither planted nor watered it), and when at the other design of God, this withered away and Jonas was grieved, God pointed out to him how unjust was his displeasure over the sparing of the city of Nineve, and He said: "Thou art grieved for the gourd, for which thou hast not labored, nor made it grow; which in one night came up and in one night perished. And shall not I spare Nineve, that great city, in which there are more than a hundred and twenty thousand persons that know not how to distinguish between their right hand and their left, and also many beasts?" [4]

Chapter 108

'Now, you Jews were well acquainted with these facts in the life of Jonas, and though Christ proclaimed to you that He would give you the sign of Jonas, and He pleaded with you to repent of your sins at least after His resurrection from the dead, and to lament before God as did the Ninevites that your nation and city might not be seized and destroyed, as it has been; yet you not only refused to repent after you learned that He arose from the dead, but, as I stated, you chose certain men and commissioned them to travel throughout the whole civilized world and announce: "A godless and lawless sect has been started by an impostor, a certain Jesus of Galilee, whom we nailed to the cross, but whose body, after it was taken from the cross, was stolen at night from the tomb by His disciples, who now try to deceive men by affirming that He has arisen from the dead and has as-

---

[4] Jonas 4.10-11.

cended into Heaven." And you accuse Him of having taught those irreverent, riotous, and wicked things, of which you everywhere accuse all those who look up to and acknowledge Him as their Christ, their Teacher, and the Son of God. And, to top your folly, even now, after your city has been seized and your whole country ravaged, you not only refuse to repent, but you defiantly curse Him and His followers. But, as far as we Christians are concerned, we do not hate you, nor those who believed the wicked rumors you have spread against us; on the contrary, we pray that even now you may mend your ways and find mercy from God the Father of all, who is most benign and compassionate.'

Chapter 109

'Permit me now to quote a few passages from Micheas, one of the twelve Prophets, to prove that the Gentiles would repent of their sinful manner of life, after they heard and learned the doctrine preached by the Apostles from Jerusalem. Here are his words: "And it shall come to pass in the last days, that the mountain of the Lord shall be prepared in the top of the mountains, and high above the hills; and people shall flow to it. And many nations shall come and say: Come, let us go up to the mountain of the Lord, and to the house of the God of Jacob; and they will teach us His way, and we will walk in His paths. For the law shall go forth out of Sion, and the word of the Lord out of Jerusalem. And He shall judge among many people, and rebuke strong nations afar off; and they shall beat their swords into ploughshares, and their spears into spades. Nation shall not take sword against nation, neither shall they learn war any more. And every man shall sit under his vine, and under his fig-tree, and there shall be none to make him afraid; for the mouth of the Lord of Hosts hath spoken. For all people will walk every one in the name of his god; but we will walk in the name of the Lord our God forever. And it shall happen in that day, that I will gather her that is afflicted; and her that I had cast out, I will gather up, and her whom I had oppressed. And I will make her that is afflicted a remnant, and her that is oppressed a strong nation. And the Lord will reign over them in Mount Sion from this time now and forever." [1]

Chapter 110

When I had concluded this quotation, I remarked, 'Gentlemen, I am aware that your teachers admit that this whole passage refers to Christ; I also know that they affirm that Christ has not yet come. But they say that even if He has come, it is not known who He is, until He shall become manifest and glorious; then, they say, He shall be known. Then, they state, everything foretold in the above-quoted prophecy will be verified, as if not a word of the prophecy had yet been fulfilled. What brainless beings! For they have missed the point of all the cited passages, namely, that two advents of Christ have been proclaimed: the first, in which He is shown to be subject to suffering and the crucifixion, without glory or honor; and the second, in which He will come from the heavens in glory, when the *man of apostasy*,[1] who utters extraordinary things[2] against the Most High, will boldly attempt to perpetrate unlawful deeds on earth against us Christians. For, we Christians, who have gained a knowledge of the true worship of God from the Law and from the word which went forth from Jerusalem by way of the Apostles of

---
1 Mich. 4.1-7.

---
1 Cf. 2 Thess. 2.3, and Chapter 33 above.
2 Cf. Dan. 11.36.

Jesus, have run for protection to the God of Jacob and the God of Israel. And we who delighted in war, in the slaughter of one another, and in every other kind of iniquity have in every part of the world converted our weapons of war into implements of peace—our swords into ploughshares, our spears into farmers' tools—and we cultivate piety, justice, brotherly charity, faith, and hope, which we derive from the Father through the Crucified Savior; each one of us sitting under his vine, that is, each one living with only his own wife. For, as you know, a prophetic writing says, "His wife shall be as a fruitful vine."[3] Now it is obvious that no one can frighten or subdue us who believe in Jesus throughout the whole world. Although we are beheaded and crucified, and exposed to wild beasts and chains and flames, and every other means of torture, it is evident that we will not retract our profession of faith; the more we are persecuted, the more do others in ever-increasing numbers embrace the faith and become worshippers of God through the name of Jesus. Just as when one cuts off the fruit-bearing branches of the vine, it grows again and other blossoming and fruitful branches spring forth, so it is with us Christians. For the vine planted by God and Christ the Redeemer is His people. But the rest of the prophecy will be fulfilled at His second coming. For the words, "her that is afflicted and cast out"[4] (that is, from the world), indicate that, whenever you and all other men have the power, you cast out every Christian not only from his own property but even from the whole world, for you allow no Christian to live. You object that this same fate has befallen your people. But, since you have been cast out after defeat in battle, such sufferings are your just deserts, as Holy Writ testifies. We, on the contrary, who are

---

3 Ps. 127.3.
4 Mich. 4.6.

guilty of no such crime after we knew the divine truth, are assured by God that we are to be taken from the earth together with the most just and immaculate and sinless Christ. Indeed, Isaias exclaims: "Behold how the just perisheth, and no man layeth it to heart; and the just men are taken away, and no man considereth." '[5]

Chapter 111

'I pointed out earlier[1] that it was mystically predicted at the time of Moses by means of the symbol of the goats offered up at the fast, that there would be two advents of this Christ. The same was figuratively announced and foretold by the actions of Moses and Josue: for Moses sat upon the hill until evening with his hands stretched out and supported (which was a type of nothing but the cross); while Josue, whose name had been changed [from Osee] to Jesus [Josue], was the general in the battle in which the Israelites were victorious. And one could understand that these actions were done by both these holy men and Prophets of God, because one of himself could not have borne both these mysteries, that is, the type of the cross and the type of the name. For this power is and was and shall be the attribute of One only, at whose name every power shudders and suffers agonizing pain because it is to be destroyed by Him. Our suffering and crucified Christ was not cursed by the Law, but showed that He alone would save those who hold firm to His faith. And the blood of the Passover, which was smeared on the side posts and transoms of the doors, saved those fortunate ones in Egypt who escaped the death inflicted upon the first-born of the Egyptians. The Passover, indeed, was Christ, who was

---

5 Isa. 57.1.

---

1 Cf. Chapter 40.

later sacrificed, as Isaias foretold when he said: "He was led as a sheep to the slaughter."[2] It is also written that on the day of the Passover you seized Him, and that during the Passover you crucified Him. Now, just as the blood of the Passover saved those who were in Egypt, so also shall the blood of Christ rescue from death all those who have believed in Him. Would God have been mistaken, then, if this sign had not been made over the doors? That is not what I say, but I do say that He thus foretold that salvation was to come to mankind through the blood of Christ. So, too, the red rope, which the spies sent by Josue, son of Nun, gave to Rahab the harlot in Jericho, instructing her to tie it to the same window through which she lowered them down to escape their enemies, was a symbol of the blood of Christ, by which those of every nationality who were once fornicators and sinful are redeemed, receiving pardon of their past sin and avoiding all sin in the future.'

Chapter 112

'But you explain these passages in a repulsive manner, imputing to God every sort of weakness, when you interpret them baldly, without analyzing the spirit of the words. According to you, even Moses would be judged a violator of the Law, for he, after ordering that no image of any of the things in heaven or on earth or in the sea should be made, personally constructed a brazen serpent and set it up as a sign, commanding those who had been bitten by the serpents to gaze upon it. And they who looked up to it were healed thereby. Shall it be thought, then, that the serpent saved the people at that time; the serpent which, as I pointed out, God cursed at the beginning and slew with the great sword,

---

2 Isa. 53.7.

as Isaias testifies?¹ Shall we, therefore, accept such stupid interpretations of these things as given by your teachers, instead of regarding them as symbols? And should we not see in this sign a reference to the image of the Crucified Jesus, when Moses, by his outstretched hands, and he who was surnamed Jesus achieved victory for your people? For, in this way, we shall no longer be in doubt concerning the deeds of the lawgiver, since he did not forsake God when inducing the people to place their hope in a beast which was the cause of man's sin of disobedience. Indeed, all these things were said and done by the blessed Prophet with much reflection and hidden meaning. Nor can anyone rightly condemn any of the words or actions of the Prophets in general, if he has the knowledge that was in them. But, if your teachers, as many as you have, only explain to you why [male] camels are not mentioned in a certain passage, or what the so-called female camels are,² or why so many measures of fine flour and so many of oil are used in the offerings, and even explain this in a low and trivial manner, while they never dare to mention or explain the really important matters that deserve to be investigated, will they not merit to hear these words of our Lord Jesus Christ spoken against them: "You whited sepulchres, which outwardly appear beautiful, but within are full of dead men's bones; you pay tithe on mint; you swallow the camel, you blind guides"?³ Unless, therefore, you detest the doctrines of those proud teachers who aspire to be called Rabbi, and apply yourself with such persistence and intelligence to the words of the Prophets that you suffer

---

1 Isa. 27.1.
2 A question arose among the Jewish rabbis why in Gen. 32.15 only female camels are mentioned, while of the other animals both sexes are specified. The better reading might be: 'why male camels are not mentioned in this or that passage.'
3 Matt. 23.27.

the same indignities from the hands of your people as the Prophets did, you cannot derive any benefit from the prophetic writings.'

Chapter 113

'Here is an example of what I am trying to say. Jesus [Josue], as I said before, whose name had been Osee, was called Jesus [Josue] by Moses, when he was sent out as a spy with Caleb into the land of Chanaan. Now, you are not curious to know why he did this, nor do you ask or investigate the reason. Hence, you have never discovered Christ, and when you read, you fail to understand; when you hear us now telling you that Jesus is our Christ, you do not study the question to discover that He was given this name by design, and not by accident. Instead, you conduct a theological debate of the question why one *"a"* was added to Abraham's original name, and you seriously dispute why one *"r"* was added to Sara's name.[1] But you never inquire why the name of Osee the son of Nun, which his father gave him, was changed to Jesus [Josue]; especially since not only was his name changed, but also, after becoming Moses' successor, he alone of all his contemporaries who fled Egypt led the rest of the people into the Holy Land. And just as he, not Moses, conducted the people into the Holy Land and distributed it by lot among those who entered, so also will Jesus the Christ gather together the dispersed people and distribute the good land to each, though not in the same manner. For, Josue gave them an inheritance for a time only, since he was not Christ our God, nor the Son of God; but Jesus, after the holy resurrection, will give us an inheritance for eternity. Josue indeed made the sun stand still because he

---

1 According to the Septuagint, the Greek word *Abram* was changed to *Abraam*, and *Sara* to *Sarra*.

had been surnamed by the name of Jesus and had received the power from His Spirit. For I have proved that it was Jesus who appeared to and talked with Moses, Abraham, and, in short, with all the Patriarchs, doing the will of the Father. He also became man by the Virgin Mary and lives forever. After His coming the Father will, through Him, renew heaven and earth. This is He who is to shine in Jerusalem as an eternal light. This is He who is King of Salem and Priest of the Most High forever according to the order of Melchisedech. Josue is reputed to have circumcised the people a second time by means of stone knives[2] (which was a sign of that circumcision by which Jesus Christ Himself has cut us off from idols made of stone and other materials), and to have gathered together those who everywhere from the uncircumcision (that is, from worldly error) were circumcised with stone knives, namely, the words of our Lord Jesus. For I have already pointed out that the Prophets used to call Him figuratively a Stone and Rock. By the stone knives, therefore, we understand His words, by which so many who were in error have been circumcised from their uncircumcision with the circumcision of the heart. From that time God commanded through Jesus that they who had the circumcision which began with Abraham should be circumcised again with the circumcision of the heart, for He said that Josue performed a second circumcision with stone knives upon those who entered into the Holy Land.'

Chapter 114

'The Holy Spirit sometimes caused something that was to be a type of the future to be done openly, and on other occasions He spoke of things of the future as though they

---
2 Cf. Jos. 5.2, and Chapters 24 and 94.

were actually taking place, or had already taken place. Unless readers are familiar with this manner of speaking, they will not be able to grasp the full meaning of the Prophet's words. To illustrate this point, I shall quote some words of prophecy. When the Holy Spirit says through Isaias, "He was led as a sheep to the slaughter, and as a lamb before the shearer,"[1] He speaks as though the Passion had already taken place. And when He says, "I have stretched out My hands to a disobedient and contradicting people,"[2] and, "Lord, who hath believed our report,"[3] He likewise speaks of events as though they had already happened. I have shown above how He often calls Christ a Stone in parable, and uses the names Jacob and Israel in figurative speech. And when He says, "I shall see the heavens, the work of Thy fingers,"[4] unless I comprehend the operation of His Word, I shall not understand the passage. Then I would be like your teachers, who imagine that the Father of the universe, the unbegotten God, has hands and feet and fingers and a soul like a compound creature. As a result of this belief, they claim that the Father Himself appeared to Abraham and Jacob. We who have received the second circumcision with stone knives are indeed happy. For your first circumcision was and still is administered by iron instruments, in keeping with your hardness of heart. But our circumcision, which is the second, for it was instituted after yours, circumcises us from idolatry and every other sin by means of sharp stones, namely, by the words uttered by the Apostles of Him who was the Cornerstone and the Stone not cut with human hands. Indeed, our hearts have been so circumcised from sin that we even rejoice as we

---

1 Isa. 53.7.
2 Isa. 65.2.
3 Isa. 53.1.
4 Ps. 7.4.

die for the name of that noble Rock, whence gushes forth living water for the hearts of those who through Him love the Universal Father, and who proffers the water of life to those desiring it. But you fail to grasp the meaning of my words, because you do not know the things which, it was foretold, Christ would do, nor do you believe us when we refer you to the Scriptures. For, Jeremias thus exclaims: "Woe to you, because you have forsaken the Living Fountain, and have dug for yourselves broken cisterns that can hold no water.⁵ Shall there be a wilderness where Mount Sion is, because I gave Jerusalem a bill of divorce in your sight?" '⁶

Chapter 115

'But you should believe Zacharias when he thus describes by hidden parable the mystery of Christ: "Rejoice and be glad, O daughter of Sion; for behold I come, and I will dwell in the midst of thee, saith the Lord. And many nations shall be joined to the Lord in that day, and they shall be My people; and I will dwell in the midst of thee, and they shall know that the Lord of Hosts hath sent me unto thee. And the Lord shall possess Juda His portion in the sanctified land, and shall again choose Jerusalem. Let all flesh fear at the presence of the Lord, for He is raised up out of His holy clouds. And He showed me Jesus [Josue] the high priest standing before the angel [of the Lord]; and the devil stood at his right hand to oppose him; and the Lord said to the devil: The Lord who has chosen Jerusalem rebuke thee! Behold, is not this a brand plucked out of the fire?" '¹

As Trypho was about to answer and contradict me, I

---
5 Jer. 2.13.
6 Jer. 3.8.

---
1 Zach. 2.10-13; 3.1-2.

said, 'Just a moment! Please hear me out, for I am not going to interpret this passage, as you think, as if there never was a priest named Jesus in Babylon, the land of your people's captivity. Even if I did, I should have proved that, if there was a priest named Jesus among your people, the Prophet did not see him in his revelation, just as he did not see the Devil or the Angel of the Lord with his own eyes, since in his revelation he was not in a normal state, but in an ecstasy. I claim that just as the Holy Spirit asserted that by the name of Jesus [Josue], which was bestowed upon the son of Nun, he wrought miracles and other deeds which foreshadowed what our Lord would do, so will I prove that the revelation made among your people in Babylon in the days of Jesus [Josue] the priest was a prediction of what was to be done by our Priest and God and Christ, the Son of the Universal Father.'

'I was indeed surprised a while ago,' I continued, 'that you remained silent and did not contradict me when I stated that the son of Nun was the only one of his contemporaries who fled from Egypt to enter the Holy Land together with those described as the youth of that generation. For you swarm together and light like flies upon sores. Even if one utters ten thousand words accurately, and one little word should offend you, because it is not sufficiently intelligible or exact, you completely overlook the many accurate words, and pounce on one little word, doing your utmost to make it appear blasphemous and evil. Consequently, when you are judged by God with the same kind of judgment, you will have to render stricter account for your bold crimes, whether they be sinful actions or false and perverse interpretations of Scripture; "For with what judgment you judge, it is right that you be judged." '[2]

---

[2] Matt. 7.2.

Chapter 116

'To explain more fully the revelation of our holy Jesus Christ, I will continue my discourse by stating that the above-quoted revelation [of Zacharias] was given to us who believe in Christ, the High Priest and Crucified One. For we, who once practised fornication and every other kind of filthy action, have, through the grace conferred upon us by our Jesus according to the will of His Father, cast off all those foul garments[1] of sin in which we were dressed. Although the Devil stands nearby ready to oppose us and anxious to ensnare all of us for himself, the Angel of God (namely, the power of God which was sent to us through Jesus Christ) rebukes him, and he departs from us. And we have been, so to speak, snatched from the fire, when we were purified from our former sins, and [delivered] from the fiery torment with which the Devil and his assistants try us. From such dangers does Jesus, the Son of God, again snatch us. He has also promised, if we obey His commands, to dress us in garments which He has set aside for us, and to reward us with an eternal kingdom. For, just as that Jesus [Josue], who is called a priest by the Prophet, was seen wearing filthy clothes (because he was said to have married a harlot), and is called a brand snatched out of the fire[2] (because he was forgiven his sins when the devil that opposed him was rebuked), so we, who through the name of Jesus have as one man believed in God the Creator of all, have taken off our dirty clothes, that is, our sins, through the name of His first-begotten Son. Having been set on fire by the word of His calling, we are now of the true priestly family of God, as He Himself testifies when He says that in every place among

1 Cf. Zach. 3.3-4.
2 Cf. Zach. 3.2.

the Gentiles pure and pleasing sacrifices are offered up to Him. But God receives sacrifices from no one, except through His priests.'

Chapter 117

'God has therefore announced in advance that all the sacrifices offered in His name, which Jesus Christ commanded to be offered, that is, in the Eucharist of the Bread and of the Chalice, which are offered by us Christians in every part of the world, are pleasing to Him. But He refuses to accept your sacrifices and those offered through your priests, saying, "And I will not receive your sacrifices at your hands. For from the rising of the sun even to the going down, My name is glorified among the Gentiles; but you profane it."[1] Even now, for the sake of an argument, you maintain that God did not accept the sacrifices of the Israelites who then dwelt at Jerusalem, but that He has declared that the prayers of the Jews who were then in the Dispersion were pleasing to Him and that He calls their prayers sacrifices. Now, I also admit that prayers and thanksgivings, offered by worthy persons, are the only perfect and acceptable sacrifices to God. For Christians were instructed to offer only such prayers, even at their thanksgiving for their food, both liquid and solid, whereby the Passion which the Son of God[2] endured for us is commemorated. But your high priests and teachers have caused His name to be profaned and blasphemed throughout the whole world. But those filthy garments, (that is, falsehoods), which you place upon all those who by the name of Jesus embrace Christianity, will be thrown off us when He raises all of us up, and makes some incorruptible, immortal, and free from pain in an everlasting and indissolu-

---

[1] Mal. 1.10-12.
[2] The Greek text has 'God of God,' probably a copyist's error.

ble kingdom, and banishes others into the eternal torment of fire. But you and your teachers fool yourselves when you explain this passage of Scripture as referring to the Jews of the Dispersion, and affirm that it says their prayers and sacrifices were pure and acceptable in every place. You should realize that you are uttering lies and are striving in every way to deceive yourselves. In the first place, your nation does not even now extend from the rising of the sun to the going down thereof, for there are nations among which none of your race has ever yet lived. But there is not one single race of men—whether barbarians, or Greeks, or persons called by any other name, nomads, or vagabonds, or herdsmen dwelling in tents—among whom prayers and thanksgivings are not offered to the Father and Creator of the universe in the name of the Crucified Jesus. Furthermore, Scripture clearly shows us that at the time the Prophet Malachias uttered these words, the Dispersion of your people over the face of the earth, as it now exists, had not yet taken place.'

Chapter 118

'It would be much better for you, therefore, if, instead of being so contentious, you should repent before the great day of judgment comes, for then, as I showed from Scripture, all those of your tribes who crucified Christ shall lament. Now, I have explained[1] the meaning of the words, "The Lord swore, [Thou art a Priest forever] according to the order of Melchisedech."[2] I have also shown that the prophecy of Isaias, "His burial has been taken away from the midst,"[3] referred to Christ who was to be buried and to rise again.

---
1 Cf. Chapter 33.
2 Ps. 109.4.
3 Isa. 53.8.

I have stated at length that this same Christ will be the Judge of both the living and the dead. Further, Nathan spoke thus of Him to David: "I will be His Father, and He shall be My Son, and I will not take My mercy away from Him, as I did from them that were before Him; and I will establish Him in My house, and in His kingdom forever."[4] And Ezechiel states[5] that He shall be the only Prince in this house, for He is the chosen Priest and Eternal King and the Christ, since He is the Son of God. And do not suppose that Isaias or the other Prophets speak of sacrifices of blood or libations being offered on the altar at His second coming, but only of true and spiritual praises and thanksgivings. We, indeed, have not believed in Him in vain, nor have we been led astray by our teachers, but by wonderful divine providence it has been brought about that we, through the calling of the new and eternal testament (namely, Christ), should be found more understanding and more religious than you, who are reputed to be, but in reality are not, intelligent men and lovers of God. Isaias, in wonderment at this, said: "And kings shall shut their mouth; for they to whom it was not told of Him, shall see; and they that heard not, shall understand. Lord, who hath heard our report? And to whom is the arm of the Lord revealed?" '[6]

'Trypho,' I went on, 'as far as is possible I am trying to repeat in a brief and concise form what I have already said, for the benefit of those who have come here with you today.'

'That is fine,' rejoined Trypho. 'But, even if you were to repeat the same thing at greater length, rest assured that all of us here present will gladly listen to you.'

---

4 2 Kings 7.14-15.
5 Ezech. 44.3.
6 Isa. 52.15; 53.1.

Chapter 119

'Do you gentlemen suppose,' I went on, 'that we could have grasped the meaning of these Scriptural passages without a special grace from Him who willed them, so that the words spoken by Moses might be fulfilled? Here are the words: "They provoked Me with strange gods; they stirred Me up to anger with their abominations. They sacrificed to devils whom they knew not; new gods that came recently, whom their fathers knew not. Thou hast forsaken the God that begot thee, and hast forgotten the God that nourisheth thee. And the Lord saw, and was jealous, and was moved to wrath by reason of the anger of His sons and daughters, and He said: I will hide My face from them, and I will show what their last end shall be; for they are a perverse generation, and unfaithful children. They have provoked Me to jealousy with that which is no god, and have angered Me with their idols; and I will move them to jealousy with that which is no people, and will vex them with a foolish nation. For a fire is kindled in My wrath, and shall burn even to the lowest hell. It shall devour the earth with her increase, and shall burn the foundations of the mountains. I will heap evils upon them."[1] And after the Just One was put to death, we blossomed forth as another people, and sprang up like new and thriving corn,[2] as the Prophet exclaimed: "And many nations shall flee unto the Lord in that day for a people; and they shall dwell in the midst of the whole earth."[3] But we Christians are not only a people, but a holy people, as we have already shown: "And they shall call it a holy people, redeemed by the Lord."[4] Wherefore, we are not a

---

1 Deut. 32.16-23.
2 Cf. Osee 2.23; Ezech. 17.24.
3 Zach. 2.11.
4 Isa. 62.12.

contemptible people, nor a tribe of barbarians, nor just any nation as the Carians or the Phrygians, but the chosen people of God who appeared to those who did not seek Him. "Behold," He said, "I am God to a nation which has not called upon My name."[5] For, this is really the nation promised to Abraham by God, when He told him that He would make him a father of many nations, not saying in particular that he would be father of the Arabs or the Egyptians or the Idumaeans, since Ismael became the father of a mighty nation and so did Esau; and there is now a great throng of Ammonites. Noe was the father of Abraham, and indeed, of all men. And other nations had other ancestors. What greater favor, then, did Christ bestow on Abraham? This: that He likewise called with His voice, and commanded him to leave the land wherein he dwelt. And with that same voice He has also called of us, and we have abandoned our former way of life in which we used to practice evils common to the rest of the world. And we shall inherit the Holy Land together with Abraham, receiving our inheritance for all eternity, because by our similar faith we have become children of Abraham. For, just as he believed the voice of God, and was justified thereby, so have we believed the voice of God (which was spoken again to us by the Prophets and the Apostles of Christ), and have renounced even to death all worldly things. Thus, God promised Abraham a religious and righteous nation of like faith, and a delight to the Father; but it is not you, "in whom there is no faith." '[6]

Chapter 120

'Notice how He makes the same promises to Isaac and

---
[5] Isa. 65.1.
[6] Deut. 32.20.

Jacob. Here are His words to Isaac: "In thy seed shall all the nations be blessed."¹ And to Jacob: "In thee and in thy seed all the tribes of the earth shall be blessed."² But He does not address this blessing to Esau, nor to Ruben, nor to any other, but only to them from whom Christ was to come through the Virgin Mary in accordance with the divine plan of our redemption. If you were to think over the blessing of Juda, you would see what I mean. For the seed is divided after Jacob, and comes down through Juda and Phares and Jesse and David. Now, this was a sign that some of you Jews would be certainly children of Abraham, and at the same time would share in the lot of Christ; but that others, also children of Abraham, would be like the sand on the beach, which, though vast and extensive, is barren and fruitless, not bearing any fruit at all, but only drinking up the water of the sea. Of this is a great part of your people guilty, for you all drink in bitter and godless doctrines, while you spurn the word of God. For in the passage relating to Juda, He says: "A Prince shall not fall from Juda, nor a Ruler from his thighs, until what is laid up for Him shall come; and He shall be the expectation of the Gentiles."³ It is evident that the expected one was not Juda, but Christ. For all of us who are of the Gentiles are not expecting Juda, but Jesus, who also delivered your forefathers from Egypt. For the prophecy referred to the coming of Christ: "Until He comes for whom it is laid up; and He shall be the expectation of the Gentiles." Jesus came, therefore, as I have proved minutely, and He is expected to come again upon the clouds. You yourselves have defiled His name, and you strive to have His name profaned throughout the world.'

---

1 Gen. 26.4.
2 Gen. 28.14.
3 Gen. 49.10.

'Now, gentlemen,' I continued, 'I could argue with you about the passage which you claim should be written, "Until the things laid up for Him come." For, the Seventy did not translate as you do, but, "Until He come for whom it is laid up." But, since the rest of the passage ("And he shall be the expectation of the Gentiles") clearly refers to Christ, I will not dispute with you the exact wording of the passage, just as I refrained from basing my arguments about Christ upon the Scriptures which you do not admit as genuine, (namely, upon the words [attributed to] Jeremias, Esdras, and David, which I indeed quoted), but only upon those passages recognized by you until now as authentic. For, if your teachers had understood them, they would most assuredly have expunged them from the text, as they did the words describing the death of Isaias, whom you Jews sawed in half with a wooden saw.[4] This incident, too, was a symbol of Christ, who is going to cut your nation in two, and to admit the worthy half into His eternal kingdom with the holy Patriarchs and Prophets. But the rest, He has said, He will condemn to the undying flames of Hell, together with all those of all nations who are likewise disobedient and unrepentant. Indeed, He said: "For they will come from the east and from the west, and will sit down with Abraham and Isaac and Jacob in the kingdom of Heaven; but the children of the kingdom will be put forth into the darkness outside."[5] In speaking, I have only one thought in mind, namely, to tell the truth, and in doing so I have not the slightest fear, even if you were to tear me at once to pieces. For I was not afraid either of any one of my people (the Samaritans), when I wrote an address[6] to Caesar, and affirmed that they were

---

4 Cf. Heb. 11.37; the *Martyrdom of Isaias;* and the *Ascension of Isaias.*
5 Matt. 8.11-12.
6 Cf. 1 *Apol.* 26; 2 *Apol.* 15.

mistaken in trusting Simon Magus in their nation, and in placing him above every principality, authority and power.'

Chapter 121

While they remained silent, I continued, 'My friends, when Scripture through David speaks of Christ, it says that not "in His seed" shall the Gentiles be blessed, but "in Him." Here are the words: "His name shall endure forever; it shall rise above the sun; and all nations shall be blessed in Him."[1] But, if all nations are blessed in Christ, and we who are from all nations believe in Him, then He is the Christ, and we are they who are blessed through Him. It is written[2] that God once allowed the sun to be worshipped, and yet you cannot discover anyone who ever suffered death because of his faith in the sun. But you can find men of every nationality who for the name of Jesus, have suffered, and still suffer, all kinds of torments rather than deny their faith in Him. For His word of truth and wisdom is more blazing and bright than the might of the sun, and it penetrates the very depths of the heart and mind. Thus Scripture says: "His name shall arise above the sun."[3] And Zacharias affirms: "The East is His name."[4] And again: "They shall mourn tribe by tribe."[5] But, if He was so brilliant and powerful at His first Advent (when, without honor or comeliness, He was scorned) that He is known in every nation, and some men of every nationality have repented of their former wicked manner of life; and even the devils were subject to His name, and all the powers and kingdoms fear His name more than

---
1 Ps. 71.17.
2 Deut. 4.19.
3 Ps. 71.17.
4 Zach. 6.12.
5 Zach. 12.12.

they fear all the dead, shall He not at His coming in glory completely destroy all who hated Him and maliciously turned their backs on Him, while bestowing upon His faithful followers rest and every other blessing they expected? We, therefore, were endowed with the special grace of hearing and understanding, of being saved by Christ, and of knowing all truths revealed by the Father. Thus, He says to Him: "It is a great thing for Thee that Thou shouldst be My servant to raise up the tribes of Jacob, and to bring the dispersions of Israel back. I have given Thee to be the light of the Gentiles, that Thou mayest be their salvation even to the farthest part of the earth." '[6]

Chapter 122

'You really suppose that the above-cited passage refers to the stranger[1] and the proselyte, but in reality it refers to us Christians who have been enlightened by Jesus. Certainly, Christ could have mentioned them, too, but, as He Himself affirmed, "You now become double sons of hell."[2] Therefore the Prophet also does not speak of them, but of us, of whom the Holy Scripture testifies: "I will lead the blind into the way which they know not. And in the paths which they were ignorant of I will make them walk.[3] And I am witness, saith the Lord God, and my servant whom I have chosen."[4] To whom, then, does Christ give this testimony? Evidently, to those who have believed. But, the proselytes

---

6 Isa. 49.6.

1 *Geóras*: 'stranger.' Justin seems to use this word as synonymous with *proselýtos*, 'proselyte.' The words *kaì toùs proselýtous* could have been incorporated into the text from a marginal note.
2 Matt. 23.15.
3 Isa. 42.16.
4 Isa. 43.10.

not only do not believe, but they blaspheme His name twice as much as you do and they, too, strive to torture and kill us who believe in Him, for they endeavor to follow your example in everything. And in another place He exclaims: "I the Lord have called Thee in justice, and will take Thee by the hand, and strengthen Thee, and I will give Thee for a covenant of the people, for a light of the Gentiles, to open the eyes of the blind, and to bring forth the prisoner out of prison."[5] These words, also, gentlemen, have been spoken of Christ and concern the enlightened Gentiles. Or do you again assert that He speaks of the Law and the proselytes?'

Then some of those who had come on the second day started to shout as though they were in a theatre: 'Why not? Does He not mean the Law and those who were enlightened by it? These are, of course, the proselytes.'

'No,' I replied, looking straight at Trypho, 'for, if the Law had the power to enlighten the Gentiles and all those who possess it, what need would there be for a new testament? But, since God foretold that He would send a new testament, and an eternal law and commandment, we should not apply the above-quoted passage to the Old Law and its proselytes, but to Christ and His proselytes, that is, us Gentiles whom He has enlightened, as He says somewhere: "Thus saith the Lord: In an acceptable time I have heard Thee, and in the day of salvation I have helped Thee; and I gave Thee to be a covenant of the people, to establish the earth, and to inherit the deserted."[6] What, then, is the inheritance of Christ? Is it not the Gentiles? What is the covenant of God? Is it not Christ? So He states in another place in Scripture: "Thou art My Son, this day have I begotten Thee.

---

5 Isa. 42.6-7.
6 Isa. 49.8.

Ask of Me, and I will give Thee the Gentiles for Thy inheritance, and the utmost parts of the earth for Thy possession."⁷

Chapter 123

'Now, since all these passages refer to Christ and the Gentiles, you should concede that those others do, also. For your proselytes have no need of a new covenant, since, as one and the same Law binds all who are circumcised, Scripture speaks of them as follows: "And the stranger also shall be joined to them, and shall adhere to the house of Jacob."¹ [Secondly, proselytes have no need of a new covenant] because a proselyte who is circumcised in order to be incorporated into the body of the Jewish people is thereby considered as a native-born among you, but we who are deemed worthy of being called a people are likewise a proper nation because we are uncircumcised. Besides, it is even absurd for you to believe that the eyes of your proselytes are opened, but that your own are not; and that you should be called blind and deaf, but they, enlightened. And it will be still more absurd if you assert that the Law was given to the Gentiles, but that you yourselves do not know that Law. For, you would have feared the wrath of God, and would not have been lawless and wandering children, but frightened to hear Him say repeatedly: "Faithless children,"² and: "Who is blind, but my servants? And deaf, but they who rule over them? And the servants of God are blind. You see often, but have not observed; your ears were open, and you have not heard."³ Is God's praise of you good? And is God's testimony fitting for His servants? Even though you hear these words often,

---
7 Ps. 2.7-8.

---
1 Isa. 14.1.
2 Deut. 32.20.
3 Isa. 42.19-20.

you are not ashamed, nor do you tremble when God threatens, for you are a stupidly stubborn people. "Therefore, behold, saith the Lord, I will proceed to remove this people, and I will remove them, and I will destroy the wisdom of the wise, and will hide the understanding of the prudent."[4] And justly so. For you are neither wise nor understanding, but sly and treacherous; wise only for evil actions, but utterly unfitted to know the hidden will of God, or the trustworthy covenant of the Lord, or to find the everlasting paths. For this reason He says: "I will raise up to Israel and Juda a seed of men and a seed of beasts."[5] And through Isaias He speaks thus of another Israel: "In that day shall Israel be third among the Assyrians and the Egyptians, blessed in the land which the Lord of Hosts blessed, saying: Blessed shall My people be which is in Egypt, and which are among the Assyrians, and My inheritance is Israel."[6] Since God blesses and calls this people Israel, and announces aloud that it is His inheritance, why do you not feel compunction both for fooling yourselves by imagining that you alone are the people of Israel, and for cursing those whom God has blessed? Indeed, when He spoke to Jerusalem and the surrounding communities, He said: "And I will beget men upon you, My people Israel, and they shall inherit you, and you shall be their inheritance, and you shall no more be bereaved by them of children."[7]

'Do you mean to say,' asked Trypho, 'that you are Israel, and that God says all this about you?'

'If we had not already discussed this question from every angle,' I answered, 'I might think that your question was

---
4 Isa. 29.14.
5 Jer. 31.27.
6 Isa. 19.24-25.
7 Ezech. 36.12.

prompted by your ignorance, but since, to prove this point, I offered arguments to which you agreed, I cannot believe that your question was the result of ignorance of what was said, or another example of your desire to quibble, but a challenge to repeat my arguments for the sake of the newcomers here present.'

As he nodded in agreement, I continued, 'If you have ears to hear it, in Isaias, God, speaking of Christ in parable, calls Him Jacob and Israel. Thus does He speak: "Jacob is My servant, I will uphold Him; Israel is my elect. I will put my spirit upon Him and He shall bring forth judgment to the Gentiles. He shall not strive nor cry, neither shall any man hear His voice in the streets. The bruised reed He shall not break, and smoking flax He shall not quench, but He shall bring forth judgment unto truth. He shall shine, and shall not be broken, till He set judgment in the earth; and in His name shall the Gentiles trust."[8] Therefore, as your whole people was called after that one Jacob, surnamed Israel, so we who obey the precepts of Christ, are, through Christ who begot us to God, both called and in reality are, Jacob and Israel and Juda and Joseph and David and true children of God.'

Chapter 124

When I noticed that my listeners were perturbed because I had stated that we Christians are also children of God, I forestalled their objection by saying, 'Gentlemen, hear how the Holy Spirit says that this people are all sons of the Most High, and that Christ Himself shall be present in their assembly to pass judgment on every race. Here are His words as spoken through David, and as translated by you yourselves:

---
8 Isa. 42.1-4.

"God standeth in the congregation of gods; and in the midst He judgeth gods. How long do you judge unjustly, and accept the persons of the wicked? Judge for the needy and fatherless, and do justice to the humble and the poor. Rescue the poor, and deliver the needy out of the hand of the sinner. They have not known nor understood; they walk on in darkness; all the foundations of the earth shall be moved. I have said: You are gods, and all of you the sons of the Most High. But you die like men, and fall like one of the princes. Arise, O God, judge Thou the earth, for Thou shalt inherit among all the nations."[1] In the Septuagint it is written, "Behold, you die like men, and fall like one of the princes," to point out the disobedience of men, that is, of Adam and Eve, and the fall of one of the princes, namely, the serpent who fell with a great fall because he deceived Eve. But, since it is not my purpose to develop this point, but to prove to you that the Holy Spirit reprimands men, who were created like God, free from pain and death, provided they obeyed His precepts, and were deemed worthy by Him to be called His sons, and yet, like Adam and Eve, brought death upon themselves, hold whatever interpretation of the Psalm you please. It has been shown that they were considered worthy to become gods, and to have the capability of becoming sons of the Most High, yet each is to be judged and convicted, as were Adam and Eve. I have also proved at length that the Holy Spirit calls Christ God.'

Chapter 125

'Gentlemen,' I said, 'I would like you to tell me the significance of the name of *Israel*.' When no one replied, I continued, 'Well, I shall give you what I think is the ex-

---
1 Ps. 81.1-8.

planation, for, when I know a thing, I do not believe it is right not to share it with others, nor do I believe it is right to be always anxious, suspecting that you know the answer to my question and yet deceive yourselves through envy or through inexperience in the faculty of volition. I do not hesitate for a moment to speak out simply and frankly, as my Lord said, "A sower went out to sow his seed, and some fell by the wayside, some among thorns, some upon rocky ground, and some upon good ground."[1] One must therefore speak in the hope that his words will, somehow, fall upon good ground. For, at His coming, my mighty and powerful Lord will demand His property from all, and will not denounce His steward when He realizes that, because the steward knows that His Lord is mighty and will come again to require the return of His possession, he has intrusted it to every bank, and has not, for any cause whatsoever, dug up the earth and hidden it therein.'[2]

'The name Israel, then, means a man who overcomes power, for *Isra* is "a man who overcomes" and *El* is "power." That Christ would do this when He became man was thus foretold by the mystery of Jacob's wrestling with Him who appeared to him, in that Christ ministered to the will of God, yet He is God, because He is the First-begotten of all creatures. For, after His Incarnation, as I have already said, He was approached by the Devil (that power which is also called Serpent and Satan), who tempted Him and tried to overcome Him by demanding that He worship him. But he was utterly crushed and overcome by Christ, who convicted him of his wickedness when, in violation of the Scriptures, he asked to be adored as God, thus becoming an apostate from the will of God. This was His reply: "It is written: The Lord

---
1 Matt. 13.3-8.
2 Cf. Matt. 25.18-27.

thy God shalt thou worship and Him only shalt thou serve."[3] The Devil, defeated and rebuked, then departed. By touching Jacob's thigh and making it numb, Christ showed that He, too, would grow numb (that is, in physical and mental suffering), at His crucifixion. But His name from old times was Israel—a name which He conferred upon the blessed Jacob when He blessed him with His own name, announcing thereby that all who come to the Father through Him are part of the blessed Israel. You, however, have comprehended nothing of this, nor do you make any effort to understand, but, expecting with assurance to be saved only because you are descendants of Jacob according to the flesh, you again deceive yourselves, as I have repeatedly shown.'

Chapter 126

'But, Trypho,' I continued, 'if you had known who He is who is sometimes called Angel of Great Counsel and Man by Ezechiel, and the Son of Man by Daniel, and a Child by Isaias, and Christ and God who is to be adored by David, and Christ and Stone by many Prophets, and Wisdom by Solomon, and Joseph and Juda and a Star by Moses, and the East by Zacharias, and the Suffering One and Jacob and Israel by Isaias again, and a Rod and Flower and Cornerstone and Son of God, you would not have blasphemed Him who has come, and assumed human nature, and suffered, and ascended into heaven. And He shall return again, and then your twelve tribes will weep and mourn. Indeed, if you had understood the words of the Prophets, you would not deny that He is God, Son of the One, Unbegotten, Ineffable God. For, somewhere in the Book of Exodus, Moses said: "And the Lord spoke to Moses, saying: I am the

---
[3] Matt. 4.10.

Lord, and I appeared to Abraham, to Isaac, and to Jacob, being their God, and My Name I did not make known to them, and I made My covenant with them."[1] And again when he says, "A man wrestled with Jacob," he asserts that the Man was God, for he declares that Jacob said: "I have seen God face to face, and my life is saved."[2] And Moses also testifies that Jacob called the place where God appeared to him, wrestled with him, and blessed him, "the Face of God."[3] Moses also declares that God appeared to Abraham near the oak of Mamre, as he sat at the entrance of his tent at noon. Then he continues: "And when he had lifted up his eyes, there appeared to him three men standing near him; and as soon as he saw them he ran to meet them."[4] And shortly afterwards, one of the three promises a son to Abraham: 'Why did Sara laugh, saying: Shall I who am an old woman bear a child indeed? Is there any thing impossible with God? At the appointed time I shall return and Sara shall have a son. And they left Abraham."[5] And, again, he speaks thus of these men: "And the men rose up from thence and turned their eyes towards Sodom."[6] Then He who was and is spoke to Abraham these words: "I will not hide from Abraham what I am about to do." '[7] (Then I repeated the words of Moses which followed and which I had previously expounded.) 'From these passages,' I went on, 'it has been conclusively proved that He who appeared to Abraham, Isaac, Jacob, and the other Patriarchs was appointed by the Father and Lord, and administers to His will, and is called

---

1 Exod. 6.2-4.
2 Gen. 32.24-30.
3 Gen. 32.30.
4 Gen. 18.1-2.
5 Gen. 18.13-14.
6 Gen. 18.16.
7 Gen. 18.17.

God.' Then, I added what I had not said before: 'So, too, when the people desired to eat meat, and Moses had no faith in Him, who is there called an Angel, when He promised that God would give them all the meat they could eat, He Himself, being God and Angel sent by the Father, is shown to have said and done all this. For, thus says the Sacred Scripture: "And the Lord said to Moses: Shall the hand of the Lord be unable? Thou shalt presently see whether My word shall come to pass unto thee or not."[8] Elsewhere, he says: "The Lord also hath said to me: Thou shalt not pass over this Jordan. The Lord thy God who goeth before thee will destroy the nations."[9]

Chapter 127

The other passages from the Lawgiver and the Prophets are very similar to the above-quoted words. And I presume that I have shown sufficiently that when God says, "God went up from Abraham,"[1] or, "The Lord spoke to Moses,"[2] and, "The Lord came down to see the tower which the children of men built,"[3] or, "God closed the ark of Noe from without,"[4] you should not imagine that the Unbegotten God Himself descended or ascended from any place. For, the Ineffable Father and Lord of all neither comes to any place, nor walks, nor sleeps, nor arises, but always remains in His place, wherever it may be, acutely seeing and hearing, not with eyes or ears, but with a power beyond description. Yet He surveys all things, knows all things, and none of us can

---

8 Num. 11.23.
9 Deut. 31.2-3.

1 Gen. 17.22.
2 Exod. 6.29.
3 Gen. 11.5.
4 Gen. 7.16.

escape His notice. Nor is He moved who cannot be contained in any place, not even in the whole universe, for He existed even before the universe was created. How, then, could He converse with anyone, be seen by anyone, or appear in the smallest place of the world, when the people were not able to behold the glory of God's messenger at Sinai; and when Moses had not the power to enter the tabernacle he had built, when it was resplendent with the glory of God; and when the priest could not remain standing before the shrine when Solomon brought the ark into the building he had erected for it in Jerusalem? Thus, neither Abraham, nor Isaac, nor Jacob, nor any other man saw the Father and Ineffable Lord of all creatures and of Christ Himself, but [they saw] Him who, according to God's will, is God the Son, and His Angel because He served the Father's will; Him who, by His will, became man through a virgin; who also became fire when He talked to Moses from the bush. Unless we interpret the Scriptures in this manner, we would be forced to conclude that the Father and Lord of all was not in Heaven when what Moses thus described took place: "And the Lord rained upon Sodom fire and brimstone from the Lord out of heaven."[5] And, again, when it was said through David: "Lift up your gates, O ye princes, and be ye lifted up, O eternal gates, and the King of Glory shall enter in."[6] And yet again, when he says: "The Lord said to My Lord: Sit Thou at My right hand, until I make Thy enemies Thy footstool." [7]

Chapter 128

'I have taken great care to prove at length that Christ is the Lord and God the Son, that in times gone by He appeared

---
[5] Gen. 19.24.
[6] Ps. 23.7.
[7] Ps. 109.1.

by His power[1] as man and angel, and in the glory of fire as in the bush, and that He was present to execute the judgment against Sodom.' Then I repeated all that I had already quoted from the Book of Exodus concerning the vision in the bush, and the imposition of the name Jesus [Josue], and continued, 'Gentlemen, please do not accuse me of being verbose or repetitious in my explanations. My remarks are rather lengthy because I know that some of you are about to anticipate them, and to declare that the power which was sent from the Universal Father and appeared to Moses, Abraham, or Jacob, was called Angel because He came to men (since by that power the Father's messages are communicated to men); is called Glory, because He sometimes appears in visions that cannot be contained; is called a man and human being, because He appears arrayed in such forms as please the Father; and they call Him the Word, because He reveals to men the discourses of the Father. But some[2] teach that this power is indivisible and inseparable from the Father, just as the light of the sun on earth is indivisible and inseparable from the sun in the skies; for, when the sun sets, its light disappears from the earth. So, they claim, the Father by His will can cause His power to go forth and, whenever He wishes, to return again. In this manner, they declare, God also made the angels. But it has been proved that the angels always exist and are not reduced again into that from which they were created. It has also been shown at length that this power which the prophetic word also calls God and Angel not only is numbered as different by its name (as is the light of the sun), but is something distinct in real number, I have already briefly discussed. For I stated

---

[1] Later, He will appear in His real presence at the Incarnation.
[2] I. e., some Jews, like Philo, or some Christians, like the Monarchians (e.g., Noetus, Praxeas, Paul of Samosata, etc.).

that this power was generated from the Father, by His power and will, but not by abscission, as if the substance of the Father were divided; as all other things, once they are divided and severed, are not the same as they were before the division. To illustrate this point, I cited the example of fires kindled from a fire; the enkindled fires are indeed distinct from the original fire which, though it ignites many other fires, still remains the same undiminished fire.'

Chapter 129

'To prove this point, I will now repeat some of the Scriptural passages I already quoted. When the word of the prophecy says, "The Lord rained fire from the Lord out of heaven,"[1] it indicates that they are two in number: One on earth, who came down to witness the cry of Sodom, and One in Heaven, who is the Lord of that Lord on earth, and as His Father and God was the cause of His being the Mighty One and Lord and God. And when the Scripture states that in the beginning God said, "Behold Adam has become as one of Us,"[2] the phrase, "as one of Us," is in itself an evidence of number, and cannot be interpreted in a metaphorical sense, as the sophists attempt to do, who neither can know nor speak the truth. And the Book of Wisdom says: "If I should tell you the daily events, I would have to enumerate them from the beginning. The Lord made Me as the beginning of His ways for His works. From eternity He set Me up, in the beginning, before He made the earth, and before the fountains of water came forth, before the mountains were established; and before all the hills He begets Me."[3]

At this point I said, 'Gentlemen, if you have followed me

---
[1] Gen. 19.24.
[2] Gen. 3.22.
[3] I.e., Prov. 8.21-25.

closely, you can see that Scripture declares that the Son was begotten of the Father before all creatures, and everybody will admit that the son is numerically distinct from the Father.'

Chapter 130

When they all agreed, I continued, 'Permit me, now, to quote some passages of Scripture which I have not yet mentioned. They were spoken in parable by that faithful servant Moses, and begin thus: "Rejoice, O Heaven, with Him, and let all the angels of God adore Him."[1] Then I quoted the rest of the passage which follows: "Rejoice, O ye Gentiles, with His people; and let all the angels of God be strengthened in Him; for He avenges, and will avenge, the blood of His sons; and will render vengeance to His enemies, and will recompense them that hate Him; and the Lord will purge the land of His people."[2] By these words he indicates that we Gentiles rejoice with His people, that is, Abraham, Isaac, Jacob, the Prophets, and in fact every Jew who is pleasing to God, as we have already agreed. But we know that these words do not apply to all members of your race, for Isaias[3] tells us that the limbs of sinners shall be consumed by the worm and unquenchable fire, but with it all remaining immortal as a spectacle to all men. Now, gentlemen, I wish to call to your attention other passages from Moses, from which you will perceive that in the beginning God dispersed all men according to nationality and language, and from all these nations He chose for Himself yours—a useless, disobedient, and faithless nation. And He showed that those of every nationality who were chosen have obeyed His will through

---

[1] Deut. 32.43 (LXX).
[2] Ibid.
[3] Cf. Isa. 66.24.

Christ, whom He calls Jacob, and surnames Israel, so those [Christians] should also be Jacob and Israel, as I have proved at great length. For, when He exclaims, "Rejoice, ye Gentiles, with His people," He gives them a share in a similar legacy and attributes to them a similar name; but by calling them "Gentiles," and stating that they rejoice with His people, He does so as a reproach to your nation. For, just as you angered Him by your acts of idolatry, so has He deemed them, though they are likewise idolaters, worthy to know His will and to share in His inheritance.'

Chapter 131

'Here are the words which show that God divided all the nations: "Ask thy father, and he will declare to thee; thy elders and they will tell thee. When the Most High divided the nations; when He separated the sons of Adam, He appointed the bounds of the nations according to the number of the *children* of Israel. And the Lord's portion was Jacob His people, and Israel was the lot of His inheritance."[1] And I observed that in the Septuagint it was translated thus: "He set the bounds of the nations according to the number of the *angels* of God." But, since here again my argument is in no wise weakened by this difference, I have given your interpretation. Now, if you will confess the truth, you must admit that we Christians are more faithful to God than you are. For we, who have been called to God by the mystery of the despised and dishonorable cross (for such faith, obedience, and piety we have been punished, even with the death penalty, by the demons and by the host of the Devil, through the service rendered them by you), endure all things rather than deny, even with a word, Christ who calls us to the

---
1 Deut. 32.7-9.

salvation prepared for us by the Father. Yet, you were delivered from Egypt by a mighty arm and a visitation of great glory, when the sea was divided and a dry road was made for you to walk across, while your enemies, pursuing you in mighty numbers and magnificent chariots, were slain by Him when the sea which had been made passable for you came together again. A pillar of light also shone for you, so that, more than any other people in the world, you might have a peculiar, constant, and unfailing light. For you He rained down food that was the bread of the heavenly angels, that is, manna, lest you should be forced to procure your own food. For you, also, He sweetened the water at Marah. And a sign of Him who was to be crucified was given to you, as I have already said, both in the case of the serpents that bit you (thus before all these mysteries were fulfilled they were given to you by a benevolent God, toward whom you are convicted of being always ungrateful), and in the case of Moses, by the sign of his outstretched arms, and of Osee, by his being named Jesus [Josue] when they were waging war against Amalec, which fact God commanded to be recorded, having admonished you not to forget the name of Jesus, who was to erase the memory of Amalec from the face of the earth. However, it is obvious that the memory of Amalec still remains after the time of the son of Nun. God makes it clear that by the Crucified Jesus (of whom even those signs were predictions of what would happen to Him) the demons were to be destroyed, and to shudder at His name; and that all the authorities and kingdoms were to tremble before Him; and that out of every nationality those who believe in Him would be shown to be pious and peaceful. And the facts, Trypho, have borne out this prediction. And when you had a craving for meat, so many landrails were sent to you that they could not be counted. And for your benefit water gushed forth from a rock, and a cloud followed you as a shade from the heat and a defense against the cold, indicating the fashion and promise of another new heaven; your shoelaces were not broken, nor did your shoes or clothes wear out, and your children's apparel became larger as they grew.'

Chapter 132

'Notwithstanding all this, you still constructed the golden calf, and you are eager to fornicate with the daughters of aliens and to worship idols. And you did the same things even after the [promised] land was handed over to you with so miraculous a display of power that you witnessed the sun stand in the heaven and not set for thirty-six hours[1] at the command of him who was surnamed Jesus [Josue], and you beheld all the other miraculous events that took place each in its time for your benefit. One of these, I think, I must now mention, because it will help to give you a better understanding of Jesus, whom we acknowledge as Christ the Son of God, who was crucified, arose from the dead, ascended into Heaven, and will come to judge every man who ever lived, even back to Adam himself. You certainly know that when the Tabernacle of Testimony was carried off by the enemies who inhabited the region of Azotus, and a dreadfully incurable plague had broken out among them, they decided to place the Tabernacle upon a cart to which they yoked cows that had recently borne calves, in order to determine whether they had been plagued by God's power because of

---

[1] It would seem that Justin supposed that Josue started to pray at daybreak, and that the sun did not set until the following evening. Eccli. 46.5 says simply that one day became as two.

the Tabernacle, and whether it were God's will that it be returned to the place from which they had taken it. In the execution of this plan, the cows, without any human guidance, proceeded not to the place whence the Tabernacle had been taken, but to the farm of a man named Osee (the same name as his whose name was changed to Jesus [Josue], as was said above, and who led your people into the promised land and distributed it among them by lot). When the cows came to this farm they halted.[2] Thus it was shown to you that they were guided by the powerful name [of Jesus], just as the survivors among your people who fled Egypt were guided into the promised land by him whose name was changed from Osee to Jesus [Josue].'

Chapter 133

'And although these and other marvelous miracles were wrought for you, and were witnessed by you as they happened, still you are censured by the Prophets for having even sacrificed your own children to the demons, and for having, besides all this, dared to do such things against Christ (and you still dare); for all of which may God forgive you and grant you mercy and salvation from Himself and Christ. Knowing beforehand that you would be guilty of such excesses, God pronounced this curse against you through Isaias: "Woe to their soul! They have taken evil counsel against themselves, saying: Let us bind the Just One, because He is distasteful to us. Therefore they shall eat the fruit of their own doings. Woe to the wicked! Evil shall befall him according to the work of his hands. O my people, your oppressors plunder you, and your exactors shall rule over you. O my people, they that call you blessed cause you to err, and disturb the

---

2 Cf. 1 Kings 6.10-14.

way of your steps. But now the Lord will stand up to
judge, and will bring His people to judgment. The Lord
Himself will enter into judgment with the ancients of the
people and its princes. But why have you burnt up my
vineyard? And why is the spoil of the poor in your houses?
Why do you afflict my people, and make the faces of the
poor to blush?"[1] And, in other words, the same Prophet
spoke in similar fashion: "Woe to them that draw their
sins as it were with a long rope, and iniquities as it were
with a cart-rope; who say: Let him make haste, and let
the counsel of the Holy One of Israel come, that we may
know it. Woe to them that call evil good, and good evil;
that put light for darkness, and darkness for light; that put
bitter for sweet, and sweet for bitter. Woe to them that are
wise in their own eyes, and prudent in their own sight. Woe
to them that are mighty among you, who drink wine, and
men of strength, who mingle strong drink; that justify the
wicked for rewards, and take away the justice of the just.
Therefore, as rubble shall be burnt with coals of fire, and
shall be consumed with a burning flame; their root shall be
as down, and their blossom shall go up as dust; for they
have cast away the law of the Lord of Hosts, and have despised the word of the Lord, the Holy One of Israel. And
the Lord of Hosts was very angry, and laid His hands upon
them, and struck them; and He was provoked to anger against
the mountains, and their carcasses became as dung in the
middle of the street. And for all this they have not repented,
but their hand is lifted up still."[2] Indeed, your hand is still
lifted to do evil, because, although you have slain Christ, you
do not repent; on the contrary, you hate and (whenever you
have the power) kill us who through Him believe in God, the

---
[1] Isa. 3.9-15.
[2] Isa. 5.18-25.

Father of All, and you cease not to curse Him and those who belong to Him, though we pray for you and for all men, as we were instructed by Christ, our Lord. For He taught us to pray even for our enemies, and to love those that hate us, and to bless those that curse us.'[3]

Chapter 134

'If, therefore, the precepts of God and His Prophets trouble you, then you should obey God rather than your blind and stupid teachers, who even now permit each of you to have four or five wives;[1] and, if any of you see a beautiful woman and desire to have her, they cite the example of Jacob, who was Israel, and the other Patriarchs to prove that there is no evil in such practices. How wretched and ignorant they are even in this respect! For, as I have said, in each such action certain divine plans were mysteriously fulfilled. I will explain what divine design and prophecy were accomplished in the marriages of Jacob, that you may finally come to know that even in this your teachers never considered the more divine in the purpose for which each thing was done, but rather what concerned base and corruptible passions. Give me your kind attention, therefore, and heed my words. The marriages of Jacob were types of what Christ would do. It was not lawful[2] for Jacob to marry two sisters at the same time. So he worked in the service of Laban for [one of] his daughters, and, when he was deceived about the younger, he worked another seven years.[3] Now, Lia represented your

---

3 Cf. Matt. 5.44; Luke 6.27.
1 Comparing this statement with that made in Chapter 141, it may be inferred that monogamy was the normal and usual Jewish practice, even though certain Jewish rabbis saw no harm in polygamy.
2 I.e., by custom and unwritten law. It was explicitly forbidden in the Law afterwards during the time of Moses. Cf. Lev. 18.18.
3 Cf. Gen. 29.

people and the Synagogue, while Rachel was a figure of our Church. And Christ still serves for these and for His servants that are in both. For, while Noe gave to his two sons the seed of the third as servants, Christ has now come to redeem both the free sons and their servants, conferring the same blessings upon all who keep His commandments, just as all those who were born to Jacob of the free women and of the bond women became his sons, and were given equal honor. And it was foretold what éach would be in rank and in foreknowledge. Jacob served Laban for the spotted and speckled sheep,[4] and Christ served, even to the servitude of the cross, for men of different colors and features from every nationality, redeeming them by His blood and the mystery of the cross. As the eyes of Lia were weak,[5] so, too, are the eyes of your souls exceedingly weak. As Rachel stole the gods of Laban[6] and hid them to this day, so, too, have we been stripped of our ancestral and material gods. Jacob was always hated by his brother,[7] just as we and our Lord Himself are hated by you and, in general, all other men who are all brothers by nature. Jacob was surnamed Israel;[8] and it has been shown that Israel is also Christ, who is, and is called, Jesus.'

Chapter 135

'Now, when Scripture says, "I am the Lord God, the Holy One of Israel, who showed Israel your King,"[1] will you not concede that Christ the eternal King is meant? You know that Jacob, the son of Isaac, was never king. Thus, in explain-

---

4 Cf. Gen. 30.
5 Cf. Gen. 29.17.
6 Cf. Gen. 31.19.
7 Cf. Gen. 27.
8 Gen. 32.28.

---

1 Isa. 43.15.

ing what king is meant by the name of Jacob and Israel, Scripture says: "Jacob is My servant, I will uphold Him; and Israel is My elect, My soul shall embrace Him. I have given My spirit upon Him, and He shall bring forth judgment to the Gentiles. He shall not cry, nor shall His voice be heard abroad. The bruised reed He shall not break, and smoking flax He shall not quench, till He shall bring forth judgment to victory. He shall take up judgment, and He shall not be broken, till He set judgment on the earth; and in His name shall the Gentiles trust."[2] Is it, therefore, in the Patriarch Jacob, and not in Christ, that you and the former Gentiles trust? As Christ is called Israel and Jacob, so we, hewn out of the side of Christ,[3] are the true people of Israel. But let us listen to the words of Scripture: "And I will bring forth the seed of Jacob and of Juda, and it shall inherit My holy mountain. My elect and My servants shall inherit it, and shall dwell there. And there shall be in the forest folds of sheep, and the valley of Achor shall be to My people who sought Me a resting place for their herds. But as for you, who forsake and forget My holy mountain, and prepare a table for the demons, and fill mixed wine for the demons, I will deliver you up to the sword. You shall all fall by slaughter, because I called you and you did not obey; I spoke and you did not heed; and you did evil in My eyes, and you have chosen the things that displease Me."[4] There you have the very words of Scripture. You can readily see that the seed of Jacob mentioned here is of another kind, for you cannot understand it as referring to your people. It is absurd to think that those who are of the seed of Jacob should leave a right of entrance to them who are born of Jacob, or that He

---
2 Isa. 42.1-4.
3 This mixed metaphor is probably an explanation of Isa. 51.1.
4 Isa. 65.9-12.

who repudiated His people as being unworthy of His inheritance should again promise it to them as though He received them. But the Prophet says: "And now, O house of Jacob, come ye, and let us walk in the light of the Lord. For He has dismissed His people, the house of Jacob; because their land was filled, as from the beginning, with oracles and divinations."[5] So, we must here conclude that there were two seeds of Juda, and two races, as there are two houses of Jacob: the one born of flesh and blood, the other of faith and the Spirit.'

Chapter 136

'Now, you see how He speaks to the people, after He had stated above: "As a grain shall be found in the cluster, and they shall say: Harm it not, for a blessing is in it, so will I do for My servants' sake. For His sake I will destroy them all";[1] and then He adds: "And I shall bring forth the seed of Jacob and of Juda."[2] It is, therefore, quite evident that, if He is angry with them and threatens to save only a very few of them, He swears to lead forth others to dwell in His mountain; and they are the persons He said He would sow and beget. For you ignore Him when He calls, and you do not listen when He speaks, but you have sinned in His presence. And the height of your iniquity is this, that you hate the Just One whom you put to death, as well as those who through His grace are pious, just, and charitable. For this reason, the Lord said: "Woe to their soul, because they have taken evil counsel against themselves, saying: Let us take away the Just One, for He is distasteful to us."[13] Though

---

5 Isa. 2.5-6.

1 Isa. 65.8.
2 Isa. 65.9.
3 Isa. 3.9.

you did not offer sacrifice to Baal, as your forefathers did, nor offer cakes in groves and on hills to the heavenly army, yet [you were warned because] you did not accept His Christ. For he who is ignorant of Him is likewise ignorant of God's will; and he who scorns and hates Him clearly hates and scorns Him also who sent Him; and he who has no faith in Him does not believe the words of the Prophets, who preached His Gospel and proclaimed Him to all men.'

Chapter 137

'Speak not harshly, my brothers, against the Crucified One, nor scoff at His wounds, by which every one may be healed, just as we have been. For it would be wonderful if you would obey the Scriptures and be circumcised from the hardness of your heart, not with the circumcision which you have according to your deep-rooted idea, for the Scriptures convince us that such a circumcision was given as a sign and not as a work of righteousness. Agree with us, therefore, and do not insult the Son of God; ignoring your Pharisaic teachers, do not scorn the King of Israel (as the chiefs of your synagogues instruct you to do after prayers). For, if he who touches those who are not pleasing to God is as he who touches the apple of God's eye,[1] how much more so is he who touches His Beloved. And it has been sufficiently proved that this is He.'

When they made no reply, I went on, 'My friends, I will now quote Scripture according to the Septuagint version. For, when I cited those passages as you read them,[2] I was trying to ascertain your frame of mind. In quoting the passage, "Woe to them, because they have taken evil counsel

---
1 Cf. Zach. 2.8.
2 I.e., according to the Hebrew text.

against themselves, saying,"³ I. added the words of the Septuagint: "Let us *take away* the Just One, for He is distasteful to us." Yet, at the beginning of our discussion I cited it according to your version: "Let us *bind* the Just One, for He is distasteful to us." At the time you seemed to have been preoccupied, and to have heard my words without due attention. But, since the day is now almost at an end—for the sun is ready to set—I will add one more observation and then conclude. Although I have already mentioned this point before, I think it ought to be explained once more.'

Chapter 138

'You are aware, then, gentlemen,' I said, that through Isaias God has said to Jerusalem: "In the deluge of Noe I saved thee."¹ By this, God meant that the mystery of redeemed mankind was implicit in the deluge. At the time of the flood, the just Noe, with his wife and three sons and their wives, making eight persons in all, were a figure of that eighth day (which is, however, always first in power) on which our Lord appeared as risen from the dead. Now, since Christ was the First-born of every creature, He founded a new race which is regenerated by Him through water and faith and wood, which held the mystery of the cross (just as the wood saved Noe and His family, when it held them safely on the waters). Therefore, when the Prophet declares, "In the time of Noe I saved thee," as I said before, he addresses those people who were likewise faithful to God, and possess the same signs. Moses led your people safely through the sea when he held the staff in his hand. But you are mistaken when you think that He spoke these words only to your people

---

3 Isa. 3.9.

1 Isaias does not say this. It may be a reconstruction of Isa. 54.8-9.

or your land. Yet, when the Sacred Text states that the entire earth was inundated, as the water reached a height of twenty-three feet above the highest mountains,[2] it is evident that God did not address your land, but those who are faithful to Him, for whom He has arranged a restful haven in Jerusalem.[3] All the signs that accompanied the flood prove my assertion. For, by the expression, "by water and faith and wood,"[4] it is indicated that they who prepare themselves and repent of their sins shall escape the future judgment of God.'

Chapter 139

'You are unaware of yet another mystery which was foretold by the things accomplished in the days of Noe. It is this. In the blessings with which Noe blesses his two sons, he also curses his son's son.[1] For the Prophetic Spirit would not curse that son himself, since he had already been blessed by God, together with the other sons of Noe. But, since the punishment of the sin was to be transmitted down to all the posterity of the son who laughed at his father's nudity, he made the curse begin with the son's son. Now, by Noe's words it was foretold that the descendants of Sem would possess the possessions and dwellings of Chanaan, and that these possessions in turn would pass from the Semites to the descendants of Japheth, who would rob the Semites just as they had robbed the Chanaanites. Listen, while I explain how this prophecy has been fulfilled. You indeed, who are Semites, entered the land of the Chanaanites, in accordance with God's will, and held it in possession. It is

---

2 Cf. Gen. 7.19-20.
3 During the Millennium.
4 Cf. Wisd. 10.4.

---

1 Cf. Gen. 9.25-27.

also clear that the descendants of Japheth[2] have in turn, by God's judgment, taken your land away from you and now possess it. This is how it was foretold in Scripture: "And when Noe awoke from his wine, and learned what his younger son had done to him, he said: Cursed be Chanaan the servant; a servant shall he be unto his brethren. And he said: Blessed be the Lord God of Sem, and Chanaan shall be his servant. May the Lord enlarge Japheth, and may he dwell in the houses of Sem, and let Chanaan be his servant."[3] Thus, as two peoples were blessed, namely, the Semites and Japhethites, and it was declared that the Semites would first possess the houses of Chanaan, which would later be seized by the descendants of Japheth, and as the one people (the Chanaanites) was forced into the servitude of the other two; so Christ has come in His power from the Almighty Father, and, calling all men to friendship, benediction, repentance, and community life, which should take place in the same land of all the saints, of which He has pledged that there shall be an allotted portion for all the faithful, as has been shown before. Wherefore, men from every land, whether slaves or free men, who believe in Christ and recognize the truths of His words and those of the Prophets, fully realize that they will one day be united with Him in that land, to inherit imperishable blessings for all eternity.'

Chapter 140

'Wherefore, Jacob, as he was also a type of Christ, married also the two slave girls of his two free wives and had sons by them, to indicate in advance that Christ would welcome into His company as children and co-heirs, together with the

---

2 I.e., the Romans.
3 Gen. 9.24-27.

free sons, even the Chanaanites who are among the race of Japheth. Now, we are the children and co-heirs of Christ, though you cannot understand it, because you are unable to drink from the living fountain of God, but only from the broken wells which can retain no water, as the Scriptures tell us.[1] They really are broken wells that hold no water which your teachers have dug for you, as the Scriptures express it, "teaching for doctrines, the commandments of men."[2] Besides this, those teachers deceive both themselves and you when they suppose that those who are descendants of Abraham according to the flesh will most certainly share in the eternal kingdom, even though they be faithless sinners and disobedient to God, suppositions which the Scriptures show have no foundation in fact. Otherwise, Isaias would not have said: "And except the Lord of Hosts had left us seed, we had become as Sodom and Gomorrah."[3] And Ezechiel: "And though Noe and Jacob and Daniel should pray for sons or daughters, their request shall not be granted. But neither shall the father perish for the son, nor the son for the father; but every one shall perish for his own sin, and every one shall be saved by his own good acts."[4] And, again, Isaias: "They shall look upon the carcasses of the men that have transgressed against me. Their worm shall not cease, and their fire shall not be quenched; and they shall be a loathsome sight to all flesh."[5] And our Lord would not have affirmed, in conformity with the will of the Father and Lord of the universe, who sent Him: "They will come from the east and from the west, and will feast with Abraham and Isaac and Jacob in the kingdom of heaven; but the children of the kingdom will be put

---

1 Cf. Jer. 2.13.
2 Isa. 29.13.
3 Isa. 1.9.
4 Ezech. 14.20; 18.4-20; Deut. 24.16.
5 Isa. 66.24.

into the darkness outside."⁶ Besides, I have already shown that they who were foreknown as future sinners, whether men or angels, do become so, not through God's fault, but each through his own fault.'

Chapter 141

'Now, to forestall any excuse you may offer by saying it was necessary for Christ to be crucified, and that it was necessary that the transgressors belong to your race, and that it could not have been otherwise, I wish to observe that, although God wanted men and angels to follow His will, He nevertheless was pleased to create them with free will to practice virtue, with the faculty of reasoning in order to know Him who created them (that is, through whom they passed from the state of non-existence to that of existence), and with a law that they should be judged by Him, if they do anything contrary to sound reason. Thus, unless we quickly repent, we, both men and angels, shall be found guilty of our sins. And, if the word of God predicts that some men and angels will assuredly be punished, it is because God foreknew that they would be incorrigibly sinful, not, however, because God created them so. Wherefore, everyone who repents can, if he desires, obtain the mercy of God, and he is called blessed by the Scripture which says: "Blessed is the man to whom the Lord will not impute sin."¹ In other words, when one repents of his sins, he receives the pardon of them from God. And not, as you and others like you,² declare, that, even though they commit sin and yet know God, the Lord will not impute sin to them. For an example,

---

6 Matt. 8.11-12.

1 Ps. 31.2.
2 E. g., antinomian Gnostics.

Scripture tells us of David's one sin, committed through his self-conceit, but forgiven through his tearful repentance. Now, if pardon were not granted to such a person before repentance, but only when the great King and Anointed One and Prophet wept and lamented as he did, how can impure wretches ever hope that the Lord will not charge them with their sins, unless they repent with tears and lamentations? Indeed, gentlemen, this one transgression of David with the wife of Urias shows that the Patriarchs took many wives, not to commit adultery, but that certain mysteries might thus be indicated by them. For, had it been permissible to take any wife whomever, or as many as one desired (as women are taken under the name of marriage by your countrymen all over the world, wherever they live or are sent), David certainly would have been permitted this by much greater right.'

At this point, my dearest Marcus Pompeius, I concluded my discourse.

Chapter 142

After a brief pause, Trypho said, 'You know that it was quite by accident that we began the discussion of these matters, but I must admit that I have been exceedingly fascinated as a result of our meeting, and I believe these friends of mine share my feelings. We have heard things beyond our very expectation. If we could meet more frequently and continue our study of the Scriptures, we certainly would profit even more by it. But, since you are about to leave the city, and expect to set sail any day now, do not hesitate to remember us as friends when you depart.'

'As regards myself,' I replied, 'if I had stayed here, I would have liked to continue this discussion every day. But, since I expect to embark at once, with God's will and help, I beg of you to put your every effort into this great struggle for your own salvation, and to embrace the Christ of Almighty God in preference to your teachers.'

After this, they left me, wishing me a safe voyage and deliverance from every disaster.

And I in turn prayed for them, saying, 'I can wish you no greater blessing than this, gentlemen, that, realizing that wisdom is given to every man through this Way [of Life],[1] you also may one day come to believe entirely as we do that Jesus is the Christ of God.'

---

[1] I.e., the Christian way of life.

EXHORTATION TO THE GREEKS

INTRODUCTION

THE TEXT of the *Exhortation to the Greeks* is preserved in four Greek manuscripts, the earliest of which is the *Arethas-Codex* (cod. Paris. 451) of the year 914. These manuscripts as well as the original Greek edition and the first Latin translation list it among the genuine works of Justin.[1] However, not only because of its literary style, but also by reason of its doctrinal content (for example, its criticism of pagan philosophers), this work does not appear to have issued from the pen of St. Justin Martyr. However, since it was ascribed to him by Stephen Gobarus as far back as the sixth century,[2] it is listed among the doubtful writings. Those who deny its genuineness assign to the work various dates, ranging from 180 to 360.[3]

The *Exhortation* points out to the pagans that they have no reliable teachers of religion, for their wise men, poets and philosophers, had no sound knowledge of religious matters. What rays of truth may have appeared here and there in their writings were borrowed from the Jewish Prophets, who were older and wiser than they. In order to gain a full knowledge of true religion, the Greeks therefore should study the writings of the Prophets and of the Christians who depend upon them.

The texts used for this translation are the Greek text of Migne, PG 6.241-312, and that of J.C.T. von Otto, *Corpus apologetarum Christianorum saeculi secundi* (Jena 1879) II 18-126.

---

[1] So does Eusebius (*Hist. eccl.* 4.18.1); cf. above p. 16 notes 44 and 45.
[2] Cf. Photius, cod. 232; *P.G.* 103.1100 D.
[3] Ph. Haeuser, *Pseudo-Justinus Mahnrede an die Hellenen* (Bibl. d. Kirchenväter Bd. 33, 1917) 238f. thinks the complete absence of Neoplatonic ideas suggests its composition before 250 A.D.

SELECT BIBLIOGRAPHY

Secondary Works:

J. R. Asmus, 'Ist die pseudojustinische Cohortatio ad Graecos eine Streitschrift gegen Julian,' *Zeitschrift für wissenschaftl. Theol.* 38 (1895) 115-155.

J. Dräseke, 'Zu Apollinarios' von Laodicea Ermunterungschrift an die Hellenen' *Zeitschrift für wissenschaftl. Theol.* 43 (1900) 227-236.

W. Gaul, *Die Abfassungsverhältnisse der pseudojustinischen Cohortatio ad Graecos* (Giessen 1902).

Ph. Haeuser, *Pseudo-Justinus Mahnrede an die Hellenen* (Bibl. d. Kirchenväter, Bd. 33, 1917).

W. Widmann, 'Die Echtheit der Mahnrede Justins des Märtyrers an die Heiden' *Forschungen zur christl. Literatur-und Dogmengeschichte* 3, 1 (1902).

CONTENTS

Chapter		Page
1	Introduction	373
2	Greek poets are not reliable religious teachers	374
3	The teachings of Thales and his followers	377
4	The teachings of Pythagoras, Epicurus, and Empedocles	378
5	The doctrines of Plato and Aristotle	379
6	Plato and Aristotle disagreed on some points	381
7	Plato contradicts himself	382
8	The Christian's teachers	383
9	The testimony of Greek writers concerning the antiquity of Moses	384
10	The early life of Moses	386
11	Even pagan oracles give testimony of Moses	387
12	Moses more ancient than the pagan Philosophers	388
13	The Septuagint	389
14	Warning to shun the error of their forefathers	391
15	Monotheism in the writings of Orpheus	391
16	Monotheism in the oracles of the Sibyl	393
17	Monotheism in the *Iliad* of Homer	394
18	Monotheism of Sophocles	395
19	Monotheism of Pythagoras	396
20	Monotheism of Plato	397
21	God has no Name	398
22	Plato, through fear, was ambiguous	399

23	Discrepancy in Plato	401
24	Homer and Plato both taught Monotheism	401
25	Plato feared to mention the name of Moses	403
26	Plato read the prophetic writings	405
27	Plato and the judgment	406
28	Homer's debt to the Prophets	408
29	Plato's doctrine of form borrowed from Moses . . .	411
30	Plato and Homer followed Moses' doctrine of man's origin	412
31	Another example of Plato's dependence upon the Prophets	413
32	Plato knew of the Holy Spirit	414
33	Plato's conception of time borrowed from Moses . .	415
34	Even the idol-makers were influenced by the Scriptures .	416
35	Plea to the Greeks	417
36	The philosophers did not have true knowledge . . .	418
37	The Sibylline oracles	419
38	Plea to heed the Sibyl and the Prophets	422

EXHORTATION TO THE GREEKS

Chapter 1

I BESEECH GOD, at the beginning of this my plea to you Greeks, that I may know the words which I ought to address to you, and that, after you have restrained your usual fondness for polemics and have been freed of your fathers' error, you may prefer to accept what is for your own good. And if what at first seemed useless to you now appears to be useful, do not think that you thereby offend your ancestors. A thorough examination often shows that things which had appeared to be of great value proved to be otherwise when subjected to close scrutiny. Now, since we intend to discuss the true religion (and it is my studied opinion that they who wish to pass their lives in safety consider nothing more important than true religion, because of the judgment which awaits us at the end of this life, and which is proclaimed not only by our ancestors in God, namely, the prophets and lawgivers, but also by those men from your midst whom you consider wise, not only poets, but also philosophers, who proclaimed among you that they had reached the true knowledge of God), I deem it advisable that we first examine the teachers of religion, both our teachers and yours, in order to determine who they were, when they lived, and how great a reputation they enjoy. Thus, they who inherited a false religion from their ancestors may, on perceiving the truths, be freed from their old error. While we, by this means, may make manifest that we practice the religion of our forefathers in God.

Chapter 2

Whom, therefore, my dear friends from Greece, do you consider your religious teachers? The poets? You surely would not admit that to men who know the poets, for such men know what silly ideas the poets have concerning the origin of the gods. Take, for example, that prince of poets, your most illustrious Homer. First of all, he states that the gods originated from water, for he wrote:

'[To visit there] *the parent of the Gods
Oceanus, and Tethys* [his espoused],
Mother of all.'[1]

Remember, too what he wrote of the one whom you deem the first of the gods, and whom he often calls the father of gods and men, for he said: '*Jupiter, who is the dispenser of war to men.*'[2]

In truth, he claims that Jupiter was not only the dispenser of war to the army, but also, through his daughter [Venus], caused the Trojans to take a false oath. Homer further portrays him in love, and in a fit of anger, and bemoaning his lot, and as the object of a plot on the part of the other gods, and as once saying about his own son:

'*Alas, he falls, my most beloved of men!
Sarpedon, vanquished by Patroclus, falls!
So will the fates.*'[3]

And on another occasion Jupiter said of Hector:

'*Ah, I behold a warrior dear to me
Around the walls of Ilium driven, and grieve
For Hector.*'[4]

---

1 Cf. William Cowper's translation of *Iliad* 14.360. The words enclosed in brackets are not in Justin's quotation.
2 Cf. Cowper, *Iliad* 19.266.
3 *Ibid.* 16.526.
4 *Ibid.* 22.195.

What he has to say of the plot of the other gods against Jupiter is evident from his following verses:

> 'When the other Olympians—Juno, Neptune and Minerva wished to bind him.'[5]

And Jupiter would most certainly have been bound by these blessed gods had they not feared the one they call Briareus. By using Homer's own words, we must recall for your benefit what he said of Jupiter's love affairs. Indeed, he said that Jupiter thus addressed Juno:

> 'For never Goddess pour'd, nor woman yet
> So full a tide of love into my breast;
> I never loved Ixion's consort thus
> [Who bore Pirithoüs, wise as we in heaven;]
> Nor sweet Acrisian Danäe, [from whom
> Sprang Perseus, noblest of the race of man;]
> Nor Phoenix' daughter fair, [of whom were born
> Minos unmatch'd but by the powers above,
> And Rhadamanthus;] nor yet Semele,
> Nor yet Alcmena, who in Thebes [produced
> The valiant Hercules; and though my son
> By Semele were Bacchus, joy of man;]
> Nor Ceres golden-hair'd, nor high-enthroned
> Latona in the skies, no—nor thyself
> [As now I love thee, and my soul perceive
> O'erwhelm'd with sweetness of intense desire.]'[6]

We should also recall what can be learned from the Homeric poems of the other gods, especially what sufferings they endured at the hands of mortal men. For example, he relates how Mars and Venus were wounded by Diomede. Another example of the sufferings of many other gods is had in the

---
5 *Ibid.* 1.491.
6 *Ibid.* 14.378. The bracketed words are not in Justin's quotation.

case of Dione, who said, to console her daughter:

> 'My child! how hard soe'er thy sufferings seem
> Endure them patiently. Full many a wrong
> From human hands profane the Gods endure,
> And many a painful stroke, mankind from ours.
> Mars once endured much wrong, when on a time
> Him Otus bound and Ephialtes fast,
> Sons of Alöeus, and full thirteen moons
> In brazen thraldom held him. [There, at length,
> The fierce blood-nourished Mars had pined away,
> But that Eëriboea, loveliest nymph,
> His step-mother, in happy hour disclosed
> To Mercury the story of his wrongs;
> He stole the prisoner forth, but with his woes
> Already worn, languid and fetter-gall'd.]
> Nor Juno less endured, when erst the bold
> Son of Amphytrion with tridental shaft
> Her bosom pierced; she then the misery felt
> Of irremediable pain severe.
> Nor suffer'd Pluto less, of all the Gods
> Gigantic most, by the same son of Jove
> Alcides, at the portals of the dead
> Transfix'd and fill'd with anguish; he the house
> Of Jove and the Olympian summit sought
> Dejected, torture-stung, for sore the shaft
> Oppress'd him, into his huge shoulder driven.'[7]

Nor would it be amiss to recall the spectacle of your gods, arrayed against one another in battle formation, for your own poet tells that tale when he writes:

> 'A dreaded spectacle; with such a sound
> The Powers eternal into battle rush'd.

---

[7] *Ibid.* 5.443.

> *Opposed to Neptune, King of the vast Deep,*
> *Apollo stood with his wing'd arrows arm'd;*
> *Pallas to Mars; Diana shaft-expert,*
> *Sister of Phoebus, in her golden bow*
> *Rejoicing, with whose shouts the forests ring*
> *To Juno; Mercury, for useful arts*
> *Famed, to Latona.*[8]

Such things have you been taught, not only by Homer, but also by Hesiod. If, therefore, you believe your most famous poets, when they describe the genealogies of your gods, you must come to the conclusion that your gods exist actually as portrayed by the poets, or that they did not exist at all.

Chapter 3

Now, if you refrain from quoting the poets, because you claim that poetic license permits them to fabricate myths and, under the guise of mythology, to attribute many false things to the gods, what other teachers of religion would you have, and where would you say they acquired such knowledge of your religion? (For it is impossible to gain a knowledge of such great and divine matters, unless from those who were already acquainted with these matters.) Undoubtedly, you will reply: the sages and philosophers. For it is your custom to run to them, as to a fortified wall, whenever your poets' opinions of the gods are quoted. Therefore, since we should proceed in chronological order, I shall cite the opinions of your wise men in that order, and you will see that their theology is much more ridiculous than that of your poets. First of all, Thales of Miletus, that pioneer student of natural philosophy, claimed that the first principle of all things was

---
8 *Ibid.* 20.85.

water, for he taught that all things came from water and that eventually all things returned to water. Another native of Miletus, Anaximander, later held that the first principle of all things was the infinite, from which everything sprang and into which all things fell back. A third Miletan, Anaximenes, thought that air was the first principle from which all things originated and into which they all resolved. Heraclitus and Hippasus, both from Metapontus, claim that fire is the first cause from which all things proceed, and in which they will all terminate. Anaxagoras of Clazomenae asserts that the homogeneous particles are the first principles of all things. The Athenian Archelaus, son of Apollodorus, says that the infinite air, with its density and rarity, is the first principle of all things. All these men, forming a succession from Thales on, followed what they called a natural philosophy.

Chapter 4

Tracing another school of thought, we see that Pythagoras of Samos, son of Mnesarchus, considers numbers, with their proportion and harmony, and their resultant elements, as the basis of things. In his system he also includes the unity and infinite duality of numbers.[1] Epicurus, the Athenian, son of Neocles, teaches the first cause of beings to be bodies which are perceived by the mind, but which have no emptiness, are not begotten, cannot deteriorate or be broken; which cannot be formed or changed by their parts, and, therefore, can be perceived by the mind. Empedocles of Agrigentum, son of Meton, asserted that there were four elements, (namely, fire, air, water and earth), and two principal powers, love

---

1 Pythagoras taught that the number one (unity) was equal to God, while the number two (the indefinite duality) was equal to evil; a strange dualism based on numbers.

(the power of union) and hate (the power of separation). You can readily perceive the confusion that exists among those who you say are your wise men—whom you call your teachers of religion. Some of them affirm that water is the first principle of all things; others say that air is; still others, fire; and others claim that some other of the above-mentioned elements were the first causes. These men actually said these things; furthermore, all of them used specious arguments to prove their unsound teachings, and each one endeavored to show that his own doctrine was more acceptable than the next. Can you tell me, therefore, my dear Greek friends, how they who look for salvation could safely approach these philosophers to learn from them the true religion, when the philosophers themselves cannot agree among themselves, but in their philosophical disputes contradict one another's opinions?

Chapter 5

Perhaps they who refuse to abandon their ancient and antiquated error will insist that they did not receive their religious instruction from the above-mentioned persons, but from those two whom they consider the most noted and accomplished philosophers, namely, Plato and Aristotle. Indeed, they think that these two have assimilated a knowledge of the true and perfect religion. But I would first like to inquire of those who make such a claim: From whom have Plato and Aristotle acquired such knowledge? It would not be possible for them to either have such knowledge or be able to transmit it accurately to others, unless they learned such great and divine matters from someone who knew them. Secondly, it is my opinion that the teachings of these two philosophers should be submitted to a close examination, in order to determine whether they openly contradict each other.

If we discover that they do not agree with each other, we should easily conclude that they also are ignorant. For Plato, acting as though he had just descended from Heaven and had accurately learned and witnessed all celestial matters, states that the Most High God exists in a fiery substance. Yet Aristotle, in explaining at length his own system of philosophy in a book addressed to Alexander the Macedonian, openly and expertly refutes Plato's opinion, claiming that God does not exist in a fiery substance. Instead, he said that God exists in a mysterious sort of ethereal and immutable body, a kind of fifth substance which he himself invented. Here are his words: 'It is not true, as some have erroneously stated of the Divinity, that God exists in a fiery substance.' Furthermore, as if not satisfied with this defamation of Plato, he quotes as a witness to the truth of this theory of an ethereal body, one whom Plato had expelled from his republic, after branding him a liar and a third imitator of the images of truth[1] (for that is what Plato calls Homer). Aristotle wrote: 'Thus states Homer: "Jupiter obtained the broad heaven in the air and the clouds." '[2] In this way, he hoped to give further weight to his opinion by the authority of Homer's testimony, not realizing that, if he used Homer to prove the truth of his statements, many of his doctrines would, on the contrary, be proved false. Thales of Miletus, one of their first philosophers, using Homer as his authority, will refute Aristotle's first opinions of the causes of things. Indeed, while Aristotle affirmed that God and matter are the first causes

---

[1] Cf. *De Republica* 10.2. Ideas, according to Plato, could be acted upon in three ways. First of all, God is the cause of an idea. Then, a workman may give that idea a concrete form, for example, a carpenter who constructs a table. Finally, another may reproduce or imitate this concrete object, for example, an artist on canvas or a poet in verse. Thus, the poet, an imitator, would be the third to act on the same idea. Cf. Migne, *PG* 6.252.
[2] *Iliad* 15.192.

of things, Thales, their oldest sage, claimed that water is the first principle of all things, since they not only come from water, but eventually will all be resolved into water. He first bases his opinion upon the fact that the seed of all living creatures, which is really their first cause, is moist. His second reason is that all plants grow and bear fruit when they have moisture, but wither away and die when deprived of it. Apparently not satisfied with these reasons, he finally quoted as his most authoritative testimony the words of Homer: *'Ocean, the origin of all things.'*[3] Might not Thales, with good reason, object: 'Why, O Aristotle, do you regard Homer as a paragon of truth when you use him to refute the tenets of Plato, but think him untruthful when you hold an opinion contrary to ours?'

Chapter 6

It is also quite evident that these great sages of yours even disagree on other points of teaching. While Plato teaches three first causes of all things, namely, God, matter, and form (God, the creator of all things; matter, the subject of the first formation of creatures, and the object upon which God exercises His almighty power; and form, the type of each creature), Aristotle names only God and matter as first principles, not mentioning form at all. They even disagree in their conception of heavenly matters. Plato claims that the First God and the ideas occupy the first place in the immovable sphere of the highest heaven, whereas Aristole teaches that next to the First God are, not ideas, but certain gods, discernible only to the mind. Thus, therefore, do they disagree about heavenly matters. Thus, it is clear that they not only cannot grasp earthly matters, but also, since they are unable to agree on such

---
3 Cf. Cowper, *Iliad* 14.360.

topics, they cannot command our respect of their teachings on heavenly matters. From their own statements it is also evident that their teachings on the present nature of the human soul do not coincide. According to Plato, the human soul is made up of three parts, each part having a special faculty: the first, of reasoning, the second, of feeling, and the third, of desiring. Aristotle, on the contrary, declares that the human soul has only the reasoning faculty, and he denies that it is composed of those other corruptible parts. Furthermore, Plato emphatically affirms that 'the entire soul is immortal.' While Aristotle, calling the soul the culmination [of each thing's potentialities], declares that it is not immortal, but mortal. Plato claims that it is always in motion, whereas Aristotle states that it is immovable, since it precedes all motion.

Chapter 7

The above statements prove that these two philosophers held contradictory views. From a close study of their writings, one can see that they even contradicted their own utterances. Plato, to cite at least one example, in one passage states that there are three first causes of all things, God, matter, and form; but in another passage he adds a fourth cause, the universal soul. In another place he teaches that matter is uncreated; but in a later passage, that it is created. At one time he asserts that form is a specific first principle which exists of itself; at another, he states that it belongs to the realm of perceptions. After asserting that every created thing is subject to destruction, he contradicts himself by saying that some created things are indestructible and immortal. Why do your supposedly wise men contradict each other and themselves? Because they will not learn from those who know; instead, they think that they can arrive at a full knowledge of heavenly things by the subtlety of their human reasoning, when they cannot understand even earthly matters. Indeed, some of your philosophers affirm that the human soul is in us, while others are sure that it is around us. Thus, even on the subject of the soul they failed to come to an agreement, but, split into factions, they argued and, as it were, apportioned ignorance among themselves. For some of them state that the soul is fire, or the air; others claim that it is the mind, or motion, or an exhalation; others affirm that it is a power emanating from the stars; others, that it is a number endowed with the power of motion; and others, a fertilizing water. As a result, a state of confusion prevails, due to their discordant teachings, and the one redeeming feature of this, in the minds of prudent men, is that they have succeeded in pointing out one another's faulty and erroneous doctrines.

Chapter 8

It is logical, then, since you cannot learn any religious truths from your own teachers, whose ignorance is evident to you from their contradictions, to turn to our [Christian] forefathers. Indeed, they lived long before your teachers, and what they taught was not of their own invention. Neither did they contradict or argue with one another. Instead, without strife or quarrel, they passed on to us the knowledge they had received from God. Men cannot naturally perceive such great divine truths through their human faculties, but only by means of the special gift which came from Heaven upon these holy men. These men were not obliged to rely upon rhetorical expressions, nor did they have to indulge in a war of words, but only to submit their purified persons to the direction of the Holy Spirit, so that this divine plectrum from Heaven, as it were, by using them as a harp or lyre, might reveal to us divine and celestial truths. Therefore, as if by one mouth and one tongue, without contradicting themselves or one another, they have instructed us concerning God, the origin of the world, the creation of man, the immortality of his soul, the future judgment, and all other things which we should know. Thus, in various places and at different times they have handed down to us the divine doctrine.

Chapter 9

I will begin with Moses, our first Prophet and lawmaker. First of all, I will describe at what time in history he appeared, and this I will do by citing the testimony of writers whom you consider most trustworthy. For it is not my purpose to prove my statements only from our own divine historical documents, which you as yet refuse to recognize because of the deep-rooted error you inherited from your forefathers, but also by your own historical writings, which, you will notice, make no reference to our religion. Thus, I will prove to you (and I have also the Greek histories to back me up), that Moses, our first religious instructor, was much older than any of your teachers, whether he be sage, poet, historian, philosopher, or lawgiver. Indeed, Moses is mentioned as the chief ruler of the Jewish people even in the days of Ogyges and Inachus, who are regarded by some of your poets as having their origin from the soil itself. As references, you may consult the first book of Polemon's *History of the Greeks,* the book against the Jews written by Appion, son of Posidonius, and the fourth book of Appion's *History,* where he states that, while Inachus was king of Argos, Moses led the Jews in a revolt against Amasis, king of the Egyptians. Ptolemy the Mendesian makes the same statements in his *History of Egypt.* Moses also is depicted as a very ancient and venerable leader of the Jews by such writers of Athenian history as Hellanicus, Philochorus (author of the *History of Attica*), Castor, Thallus, and Alexander Polyhistor, as well as by those very learned Jewish historians, Philo and Josephus. This last-named historian, in order to show the antiquity of the history about which he wrote, entitled his work, *The Jewish Antiquities of Flavius Josephus,* the word 'antiquities' signifying the age of the history. Diodorus, your most famous historian, spent thirty years in summarizing various collections of books, and, to gain the exact truth of events, he traveled (as he states) over Asia and Europe. After he thus saw many things with his own eyes, he composed forty books on history. In the first of these books he affirmed that he learned from the Egyptian priests that Moses was the oldest, in fact, the first, legislator. Here are the words of Diodorus: 'After the legendary period of Egyptian social life which the gods and heroes are alleged to have molded, they say that Moses[1] first induced the people to use written laws; and he is depicted as a man of great spirit and a great authority on social matters.' Then, further on, when Diodorus lists the ancient legislators, he places Moses at the top of the list. Here are his exact words: 'It is the tradition among the Jews that Moses attributed his laws to the God who is called Jahve,[2] either because these laws were considered the result of a wonderfully divine plan which would benefit very many men, or because it was thought that the people would more readily obey these laws when they contemplated the dignity and power of the alleged lawmakers. They say that Sasunchis, a very intelligent man, was the second Egyptian lawgiver. The third was King Sesonchosis, who was not only

---
1 Justin here confused Moses with Menes.
2 Cf. Migne, *PG* 6.259, n. 97. The text here must be reconstructed from the context of Diodorus.

Egypt's most famous military genius, but he also restrained that warlike nation with wise laws. The fourth legislator was King Bocchoris, a wise and extremely capable man. King Amasis, who succeeded him, is said to have laid down the regulations for the provincial governors and for the general administration of the Egyptian government. Darius, the father of Xerxes, is said to have been the sixth lawmaker of the Egyptians.'

Chapter 10

You see, my Greek friends, that the testimony of Moses' antiquity was written by those who do not belong to our religion. Furthermore, these writers affirmed that their information was gathered from the Egyptian priests, among whom Moses was born and educated; in fact, he was given a very thorough Egyptian education, since he was the adopted son of the king's daughter. For this very reason, much attention was centered on him, as those wisest of historians (Philo and Josephus) relate in their biography of Moses, in which they record his genealogy and deeds. For, in their *History of the Jews,* these historians state that Moses was of the Chaldaean race, that he was born in Egypt after his forefathers had migrated from Phoenicia to that country because of a famine, and that because of his rare virtue God wished to honor him by making him the leader and lawmaker of his own people at that time when God deemed it opportune for the Hebrews to leave Egypt and return to their own land. God first gave Moses that divine and prophetic gift with which holy men of those days were endowed, and He made him our first religious instructor. Then, after him, God bestowed the same gift upon the rest of the Prophets, who taught us the same doctrines on the same topics. These are the men whom we claim as our teachers. Everything they taught us was through that God-given gift, and nothing came from their own intellect.

Chapter 11

Since you are unwilling to cast off your ancestors' old error and to accept the doctrine of your teachers, I ask you: What credible religious teachers have you? As I have frequently said, they who have not received an understanding of these great divine matters from those who know them cannot have a personal knowledge of these truths, nor can they direct others to a true knowledge of them. As you rejected your poets as religious teachers, you probably have renounced your philosophers, also, since it has been proved beyond all doubt that their pronouncements are fraught with ignorance and chicanery. I have been told that as a last resort you will, perhaps, turn to the sophistry of the oracles. It is proper for me to relate, therefore, what I once heard from your people about the oracular answers. They tell how a man once asked your oracle who were the really religious men. The oracle is said to have replied: 'The only ones who have acquired true wisdom are the Chaldaeans and the Hebrews, who worship God Himself, the self-begotten King.'[1]

Since you are convinced that you can attain truth by means of your oracles, when you read over the historical writings and recall what has been written about Moses by those outside our religion, and when you realize that Moses and the other Prophets were of the Chaldaean and Hebrew race, do not think it incredible that a man, who descended from a God-fearing people and who followed the piety of his forefathers, should be picked by God as the recipient of this great gift, and become known as the first of all the Prophets.

---

1 Eusebius (*Praeparatio* 9.10) states that Porphyrius had recorded this oracle in his *De philosophia ex oraculis*.

Chapter 12

The next point that should be considered is the period during which your philosophers lived, in order that you may realize how recent and brief that period was. The antiquity of Moses will thus be very evident from a comparison to the age of your philosophers. But, lest I appear too profuse by a lengthy discussion of this period and by producing too great a number of proofs, I propose the following arguments as sufficient evidence. Socrates was the teacher of Plato; Plato, in turn, was the teacher of Aristotle. These men were contemporaries of Philip, and Alexander of Macedon, and of the Athenian orators, as the *Philippics* of Demosthenes indicate. Alexander's biographers clearly prove that during his reign he was friendly with Aristotle. From this it is evident that the history of Moses is by far older than all the profane histories. You should also keep in mind that there is no recorded Greek history prior to the beginning of the Olympiad era, nor is there a really ancient work which records the deeds of the Greeks or barbarians. Before that time there existed only the history of the Prophet Moses, which he was divinely inspired to write in Hebrew letters. Indeed, Greek letters were not yet used, for philologists point out that Cadmus first brought the alphabet to the Greeks from Phoenicia. Even Plato, your foremost philosopher, refers to the alphabet as a recent discovery. He stated in his *Timaeus* that Solon, the wisest of the sages, told Critias that on a recent trip to Egypt a very old Egyptian priest said to him: 'O Solon, Solon, you Greeks are always children; there is not an old Greek among you.' Then he continued: 'In spirit you are all young, for you have no sayings passed down to you as an ancient tradition, nor any age-old doctrine. You remain in ignorance, because, generation after generation, the posterity of those days died without expressing themselves, for they had no alphabet.'[1] You should therefore realize that all your histories have been written in this recently-invented Greek alphabet, and, if you take the time to investigate, you will find that all your ancient poets, lawmakers, historians, philosophers, and orators composed their works with Greek letters.

Chapter 13

If, however, anyone should object that the Mosaic and other prophetic writings were also written in Greek, he ought to consult the history texts of those who are not of our people. He will find that when Ptolemy,[1] the Egyptian king, had constructed his library at Alexandria and had filled it with books collected from every land, he learned of the existence of those carefully treasured and very ancient historical works written in Hebrew. So that he might become acquainted with their contents, he sent to Jerusalem for seventy scholars who were versed in both Greek and Hebrew, and he set them to the task of translating the books. Lest this work be interrupted and delayed by outside interference, he ordered the construction of individual rooms for each translator, not in the city itself, but about a mile[2] away (where the Pharos stood). Another reason for this was to have each scholar make his own translation. Accordingly, attendants were assigned to care for their needs and to prevent one from communicating with another, in order that the accuracy of the work might become more apparent by the uniformity of the translations. When the king learned that the seventy scholars in their re-

---

1 Cf. Maran in Migne, *PG* 6.265, n.12.

---

1 I.e., Ptolomeus Philadelphus (286 B.C.). According to St. Jerome (*Praef. in Pent.*), the *Seventy* translated only the Pentateuch.
2 Literally, 'seven stadia.'

spective translations had not only conveyed the same meaning, but had done so with the same words, and had not contradicted one another in a single instance, but had described the same things in the same way, he was so astonished that he concluded that the translation had been made by divine power, and he considered the men to be justly worthy of praise, since they were so dear to God. Thus, when he sent them back to their own land, he conferred many gifts upon them. And when he naturally marvelled at these books and concluded that they must be divine, he set them apart in his library and declared them sacred. It is not fiction or fable that we recount to you, O Greeks, for we have been in Alexandria and have seen the remains of the little rooms which are still preserved at the Pharos, and we relate to you what we have heard from the lips of the inhabitants as part of the tradition of their country. You can learn the same thing from others, also, especially from those two learned and venerable men who have recorded this happening, Philo and Josephus,[3] and many others besides. If anyone should object that these books belong to the Jews (since they are even now preserved in their synagogues), and not to us [Christians], and that it would be useless for us to say that we learned our religion from them, he should know from an examination of those books that their doctrinal content refers to us [Christians], and not to the Jews.[4] The fact that these books containing our religious doctrines are preserved among the Jews even to this day is but the work of Divine Providence on our behalf. If we were to produce these books out of the Church, they who are ever eager to slander us would have a chance to accuse us of deception. Instead, we ask that they be produced from the synagogue of the Jews, so that from these

---
3 Cf. Josephus, *Antiquitates* 12.2, and Philo, *De vita Moysis*.
4 Cf. Eusebius, *Demonstratio* 1.6.

very books still preserved among them it might be clearly and manifestly shown that the laws which the holy men wrote to instruct really belong to us [Christians].

Chapter 14

You Greeks should therefore think of the future and of the future judgment, foretold not only by the godly, but also the ungodly, so that you might not, without realizing it, fall into the error of your forefathers, nor begin to think that the doctrine which they in their error handed down to you is true. Realizing how dangerous such a mistake would be, you should inquire and study intently the doctrines of those whom you call your teachers. For, by Divine Providence, they were forced against their will to relate many things in our favor, especially those writers who visited Egypt and profited from the religiousness of Moses and his ancestors. I am sure that from a casual reading of the historical works of Diodorus, and of others who wrote on this same topic, some of you will be obliged to admit that Orpheus, Homer, Solon (who wrote the Athenian laws), Pythagoras, Plato, and others, after they had visited Egypt and had made use of the history of Moses, began to circulate doctrines concerning the deities very different from the unfavorable opinions they had previously held.

Chapter 15

For example, I must call to mind what Orpheus, who was the first teacher of what I might call your polytheism, later said to his son,[1] Musaeus, and other closely-associated listeners concerning the one and only God. Here are his words:

---

[1] Musaeus was the son of Eumolpi, not of Orpheus. Justin probably uses the word loosely to indicate a disciple or pupil.

'I speak to those who lawfully may hear:
All others, ye profane, now close the doors,
And, O Musaeus! hearken thou to me,
Who offspring art of the light-bringing moon:
The words I utter now are true indeed:
And if thou former thoughts of mine hast seen,
Let them not rob thee of the blessed life,
But rather turn the depths of thine own heart
Unto the place where light and knowledge dwell.
Take thou the word divine to guide thy steps,
And walking well in the straight certain path,
Look to the one and universal King—
One, self-begotten, and the only One,
Of whom all things and we ourselves are sprung.
All things are open to His piercing gaze,
While He Himself is still invisible.
Present in all His works, though still unseen,
He gives to mortals evil out of good,
Sending both chilling wars and tearful griefs;
And other than the great King there is none.
The clouds forever settle round His throne,
And mortal eyeballs in mere mortal eyes
Are weak, to see Jove reigning over all.
He sits established in the brazen heavens
Upon His golden throne; under His feet
He treads the earth, and stretches His right hand
To all the ends of ocean, and around
Tremble the mountain ranges and the streams,
The depths, too, of the blue and hoary sea.'

In another passage he wrote:

'There is one Zeus alone, one sun, one hell,
One Bacchus; and in all things but one God;

Nor of all these as diverse let me speak.'
And he uttered this oath:
> 'Now I adjure thee by the highest heaven,
> The work of the great God, the only wise;
> And I adjure thee by the Father's voice,
> Which first He uttered when He established
> The whole world by His counsel.'[2]

What does he mean when he writes: 'I adjure thee by the Father's voice, which first He uttered'? By 'the voice' he means the Word of God by whom heaven and earth and every creature were made, as we are taught by the divine prophecies of the holy men. Indeed, after Orpheus himself studied these prophetic sayings in Egypt, he knew that every creature was the work of the Word of God. For this reason, after he says: 'I adjure thee by the Father's voice, which first He uttered,' he adds: 'when He established the whole world by His counsel.' In this verse he calls the Word 'the voice' only for the sake of the poetic metre. This becomes evident from the fact that a few verses later, where the metre permitted, he called Him 'the Word.' Here is the verse: *'Take thou the Word divine to guide thy steps.'*

Chapter 16

I must also remind you of what the very old and ancient Sibyl (whom Plato, Aristophanes, and others, called a prophetess) taught you in her oracles concerning the one and only God. She says:

---

2 For these pseudo-Orphean verses, consult Clement of Alexandria, *Protrep.* 7.74; Eusebius (fragment of Aristobulus), *Praeparatio* 13.12; Theodoret of Cyrus, *De curandis Graec. affect.*, sermo 1; Tatian, *Oratio adv. Graecos* 8. (The translation of the verses is that used by M. Dods in *The Writings of Justin Martyr and Athenagoras*—Roberts and Donaldson's, Ante-Nicene Christian Library, 2. 302f.).

> 'There is one only unbegotten God,
> Omnipotent, invisible, most high,
> All seeing, but Himself seen by no flesh.'[1]

And in another passage:

> 'But we have strayed from the Immortal's ways,
> And worship with a dull and senseless mind
> Idols, the workmanship of our own hands,
> And images and figures of dead men.'[2]

And again:

> 'Blessed shall be those men upon the earth
> Who shall love the great God before all else,
> Blessing Him when they eat and when they drink;
> Trusting in this their piety alone.
> Who shall abjure all shrines which they may see,
> All altars and vain figures of dumb stones,
> Worthless and stained with blood of animals,
> And sacrifice of the four-footed tribes,
> Beholding the great glory of One God.'[3]

Such are the words of the Sibyl.

Chapter 17

The poet Homer, by resorting to poetic license and by emulating Orpheus' original belief in polytheism, makes mention of several gods in a mythical way, lest his poetry should appear to differ from that of Orpheus, which he was so intent on imitating that in the very first verse of his Iliad he expressed his partiality toward him. As Orpheus had exclaimed at the beginning of his poem: *'O goddess, sing the wrath of Demeter, the bearer of fruit,'* Homer began his

---
1 1.8-10. Cf. J. Brettano, *Sibyllina Oracula* (Paris 1607).
2 3.721-722.
3 4.24ff.

Iliad thus: '*O goddess, sing the wrath of Achilles, the son of Peleus.*'[1] It appears to me that Homer here preferred to violate the poetic metre rather than be accused of having omitted from the start the names of the gods. But, shortly afterwards, he clearly and openly expressed his thoughts concerning the One and Only God, when, in one passage, he spoke thus to Achilles through Phoenix: '*Not though God Himself were to promise that He would strip me of my old age and restore me to my youthful strength.*'[2] By means of the pronoun he thus wished to indicate the true God. In another passage he has Ulysses address a Greek mob in this fashion: '*A plurality of rulers is evil; let there be but one ruler.*'[3] Homer then went on to show that rule by many is not a good, but an evil practice, by relating how such rule gave rise to wars, fights, cliques, and various conspiracies. The rule by one, on the other hand, is devoid of all contention.

Thus argued Homer.

Chapter 18

If you think we should prove that monotheism was testified to even by the dramatists, listen to these words of Sophocles:

'*There is one God, in truth there is but one,
Who made the heavens and the broad earth
    beneath,
The glancing waves of ocean and the winds.
But many of us mortals err in heart,
And set up for a solace in our woes
Images of the gods in stone and wood,
Or figures carved in brass or ivory,*

---

[1] *Iliad* 1.1.
[2] Cf. Cowper, *Iliad* 9.551.
[3] *Ibid.* 11.242.

> *And, furnishing for these our handiworks,*
> *Both sacrifice and rite magnificent,*
> *We think that thus we do a pious work.*[1]

Such is the testimony of Sophocles.

Chapter 19

His biographers point out that Pythagoras, son of Mnesarchus, who explained his own philosophical conclusions by means of mystical symbols, seems to have harbored thoughts about the unity of God, which may have been a profitable result of his sojourn in Egypt. He allegorically teaches that there is only one God when he states that unity is the first principle of all things and the cause of all good.[1] This becomes more evident from his statement that unity and one differ greatly from each other. He claims that unity belongs to that class of beings which are perceived by the intellect, whereas one belongs to the class of numbers. Now, if you wish a more explicit proof of the monotheism of Pythagoras, listen to the following quotation: 'God is one. And He is not, as some think, outside the world, but in it, for He is entirely in the whole circle looking over all generations. He is the blending agent of all ages; the executor of His own powers and deeds; the first cause of all things; the light in heaven; the Father of all; the mind and animating force of the universe; the motivating factor of all the heavenly bodies.'[1]

Such is the testimony of Pythagoras.

---

1 For these pseudo-Sophoclean verses, consult Clement of Alexandria, *Protrept.* 7.74; *Strom.* 5.14; Eusebius, *Praeparatio* 13.13; Cyril of Alexandria, *Adversus Julian*, 1; Theodoret of Cyrus, *De curandis Graec. affect.* sermo 7; Athenagoras, *Legat.* 5.

1 Cf. the *Life of Pythagoras*, in Photius, *Biblioth. cod.* 249; and Cyril of Alexandria, *Adv. Julian*.

Chapter 20

Although Plato very probably approved of the teaching of Moses and the other Prophets concerning the One and Only God, which he had learned during his visit to Egypt, yet he was afraid to say so, lest, after what had happened to Socrates, he might cause some Anytus or Meletus to come forward and accuse him before the Athenians in these words: 'Plato is a meddling fool who does much harm, for he does not accept the gods which the state recognizes.' Thus, in fear of the hemlock,[1] Plato composed an artfully ambiguous dissertation on the gods, in which he admitted gods for those who desired them, and denied their existence for the benefit of those who professed no deity. This is evident from an examination of his very words. For, after he stated that every created being is mortal, he affirmed that the gods were created. If, therefore, according to Plato, God and matter are the origin of all things, it must necessarily be concluded that the gods were made of matter. But, if they had their origin from matter, out of which he claims evil also originated, he leaves sound-thinking persons to draw their own conclusions as to the nature of gods who are made of matter. Indeed, to avoid just that conclusion, he taught that matter is uncreated, so he might not appear to affirm that God is the creator of evil. It is also clear that he made the following statement concerning the gods who were created by God: 'Gods of gods, of whom I am the creator.' He also seems to have had accurate knowledge of the existence of the true God. For, after he had heard in Egypt that God had said to Moses, when He was about to send him to the Hebrews:

---

[1] For a similar accusation, see Athenagoras, *Apol.* 2.22; Eusebius, *Praeparatio* 2.6,7; Cyril of Alexandria, *Adv. Julian.*; Theodoret of Cyrus, *Adv. Graecos*; and St. Augustine in the beginning of his *De vera religione.*

'I am who am,'[2] he comprehended that God had not mentioned His own proper name to him.

Chapter 21

No proper name can really be applied to God, for names are used to indicate and distinguish many different subjects. Now, no one existed before God who could have given Him a name, nor did God Himself think it necessary to name Himself, since He is the One and Only God, as He Himself proclaimed through His Prophets when He said: 'I, God, am the first,' and, 'beside Me there is no other God.' Thus, as I stated above, God did not attribute any proper name to Himself when He sent Moses to the rescue of the Hebrews, but by means of a participle He showed in a mystic way that He is the One and Only God. 'For,' He states, 'I am the Being.' He thus openly contrasted Himself, 'the Being,' with the non-beings, in order to convince those who formerly had been deceived that they were not following beings, but those who had no being. God, therefore, knew that the first men still remembered that old trick with which that enemy of mankind, the Devil, tried to deceive their forefathers when he said to them: 'If you obey me in transgressing God's command, you shall become as gods.' He called those gods which had no being, so that men, in the supposition that there were other gods, might even think that they themselves could become gods. God therefore said to Moses: 'I am the Being,' in order to show by the participle 'being' the difference between God who is and those who are not. After they had thus been victimized by the tricky demon and had dared to transgress the command of God, men were driven out of Paradise. They remembered the name of gods, but

---
2 Exod. 3.14.

no longer were they taught by God that there are no other gods. It was not right that they who would not keep such an easy commandment as that first one should continue to be instructed by God; justice required that they should endure suitable punishment. Then, after they had been expelled from Paradise in the belief that this was only because of their disobedience, and not also because they had believed in the existence of gods which really did not exist, they applied the name of gods even to men who were later their own descendants. This first false notion of the gods was due, therefore, to the father of untruth. Realizing that this false knowledge of the gods afflicted the souls of men as a dread disease, God, desiring to remove and wipe it away, first appeared to Moses and said: 'I am He who is.' It was necessary, in my opinion, that the future chief and leader of the Hebrews should be the first to know of the living God. Consequently, having appeared to him first, in so far as it is possible for God to appear to mortals, He said to him: 'I am He who is.' Then, when He was about to send him forth to the Hebrews, He ordered Moses to say also to them: 'He who is has sent me to you.'

Chapter 22

Plato had learned all this in Egypt and he was especially impressed with the doctrine of one God. Yet, because he feared the Areopagus, he did not dare mention to the Athenians the name of Moses, because the latter had taught that there is only one God. But, in his carefully written work, the *Timaeus,* in which he discussed God's nature, he wrote as his own the same opinion as Moses concerning God. He wrote: 'It is my opinion that we must first determine what that is which always exists, but has no generation; and what that is which is always generated, but never really exists.'

My Greek friends, would an intelligent man not realize that
we are here dealing with one and the same thing, with the
sole difference of the article? Moses said: 'He who is,' while
Plato wrote: 'That which is.' Either expression could be
aptly applied to the God who exists forever, since He is the
only one who exists eternally, and has no generation. We
should also study his [Plato's] words carefully to determine
what that other thing is which he contrasted to the eternally-
existent God, and concerning which he wrote: 'And what
that is which is always generated, but never really exists.'
Indeed, we shall see that he clearly and wisely states that
He who is unbegotten is eternal, whereas they who are begotten or created (about whom he claims it was said: 'Gods
of gods, of whom I am the creator') are born and perish.
For he wrote: 'It is my opinion that we must first determine
what that is which always exists, but has no generation, and
what that is which is always generated, but never really
exists. The former, indeed, which is intelligently perceived
by the mind, always exists in the same way, while the latter,
which is based on opinion formed by the perception of the
senses without the aid of reason, never really exists, since it
is always coming into being and perishing.' To the intelligent, these words can only mean the death and destruction
of the gods which have been created. This also should be
noted, that Plato never calls Him the Creator, but the
modeler of the gods, although in Plato's mind there is a
great difference between the two. For the creator, since he
needs nothing else, creates the creature by his own ability
and power; on the contrary, the modeler produces his work
only after he has received from matter the power to do so.

Chapter 23

Some, ever reluctant to renounce polytheism, will object, perhaps, that the creator said to these created gods: 'You are not immortal or indestructible, since you have been created; yet you shall not perish nor shall you be forced to endure death, since you gained my good will which is a greater and stronger bond.' Through fear of the polytheists, Plato here makes his 'creator' utter contradictory expressions. After first stating that he held that every created being is destructible, he now introduces him affirming the opposite. Furthermore, in making such statements, he is totally unaware of the impossibility of eluding the charge of falsehood. Indeed, it is evident that he told an untruth either at first, when he stated that every created being is destructible, or now, when he makes a contradictory statement. If, as he first affirmed, every created thing must be absolutely destructible, how can he reconcile the fact that he makes possible that which is absolutely impossible? It would seem that Plato in vain bestows upon his 'creator' an impossible power, when he claims that they who were once destructible, because created from matter, should, by the creator's power, again become indestructible and everlasting. For it is to be expected that the power of matter, which Plato considered to be uncreated, and therefore contemporaneous and co-existent with the creator, should withstand his will. Since one who has not created has no control over that which is uncreated, it follows that matter, which is free from any external agency, cannot possibly be controlled by it. With this in mind, Plato himself was forced to write: 'We must admit that violence cannot be inflicted upon God.'

Chapter 24

How can Plato justly exclude Homer from his republic

when the poet, in describing the ambassadors sent to Achilles, portrays Phoenix as addressing these words to the great warrior: 'Even the gods themselves may be turned'?[1] Homer did not apply these words to Plato's king and creator of gods, but to those many gods whom the Greeks esteemed as such, which is evident from Plato's expression, 'gods of gods.' Indeed, by his story of the golden chain[2] Homer showed that all power and rule reside in the One and First God. And he considered the rest of the gods so far beneath the First God's divinity that he did not hesitate to place them among the mortals. For instance, he introduces Ulysses speaking of Hector to Achilles in this fashion: *'He rages terribly, trusting in Zeus, nor reverences at all either men or gods.'*[3] To me it appears evident that Homer here betrays that he, like Plato, derived his knowledge of the one God while he was in Egypt, and that he clearly and openly affirmed that he who puts his trust in the really existing God does not give a thought to those non-existent gods. Thus, the poet, in another passage, by using another word with the same meaning, namely, a pronoun, employed the same participle as Plato to indicate the existing God, about whom Plato had written: 'What that is which always exists, but has no generation.' For it appears that the words of Phoenix were not said without a hidden meaning:

'No, not would God Himself
Promise me, reaping smooth this silver beard,
To make me downy-cheek'd as in my youth.'[4]

The pronoun 'Himself' indicates the really existing God. You will find another example of this pronoun in your

---
1 *Iliad* 9.497 (Cowper's translation, verse 616).
2 Cf. *Iliad* 9.18ff.
3 *Iliad* 9.238 (Cowper's translation, verse 294).
4 *Iliad* 9.450 (Cowper's translation, verse 551).

oracle concerning the Chaldaeans and Hebrews. For, when someone had asked what men ever had lived piously, you admit that the oracle replied:

> 'Only the Chaldaeans and Hebrews found wisdom,
> Who worship God Himself, the self-begotten King.'[5]

Chapter 25

With what right, therefore, does Plato censure Homer for his statement that the gods are changeable, for it is evident from the very text that Homer said this for some good reason? They who hope to experience mercy through their prayer and sacrifices must repent of their sins and avoid them in the future. Those persons, however, who believe that God is unchangeable would in no way feel obliged to cease sinning, since in their state of mind they cannot perceive how repentance would help them. How, then, can Plato, the philosopher, condemn Homer, the poet, for his statement that 'even the gods themselves may be turned'? Yet, he himself speaks of the creator of the gods as so changeable that he at one time affirms that the gods are mortal, and at another time that they are immortal. Not only is his teaching concerning the gods contradictory, but also his concept of matter, for matter (from which he believes the created gods have necessarily been produced) he sometimes states is uncreated, and at other times created. Yet, when he teaches that the creator of gods is so easily changeable, he does not realize that he himself is thus guilty of the very errors for which he censured Homer, although Homer said the op-

---

[5] Eusebius (*Praeparatio* 9.10) asserts that Porphyrius had recorded this oracle in his *De philosophia ex oraculis*.

posite about the creator of gods. For he wrote that he spoke thus of himself:

> *'For ne'er my promise shall deceive, or fail,*
> *Or be recalled if with a nod confirmed.'*[1]

But it seems that Plato, against his will and only in deference to the polytheists, made such unusual utterances concerning the gods. Whatever he thought safe to divulge of that knowledge of the One God which he had learned from Moses and the Prophets he alluded to in a crytic way, so that he might reveal his opinion to those who wished to worship the true God. He found great delight in the words which God addressed to Moses, 'I am the existing' [One], and, after pondering over this short participial expression, he realized that God wanted to indicate to Moses His eternity and thus said: 'I am the existing' [One]. For the word 'existing' expresses not only one time, but all three—the past, present, and future. The same must be said of Plato's expression, 'never really existing,' where the participle 'existing' indicates indefinite time. For the word 'never' does not refer to the past, as some think, but to future time. Even profane writers have correctly interpreted this point. Thus, when Plato attempted to decipher, so to speak, for the unenlightened what had been cryptically signified by the participle concerning the eternity of God, he used these words, 'Indeed God, as the old tradition affirms, contains the beginning, the end, and the middle of all things.' By the words, 'the old tradition,' Plato clearly and openly alludes to the law of Moses, but, fearing the hemlock, he did not dare mention him by name whose teaching, he well knew, was hateful to the Greeks. Yet he clearly meant Moses by appealing to the antiquity of the tradition. Now, we have sufficiently shown earlier, from the writings

---

1 *Iliad* 1.526 (Cowper's translation, verse 646).

of Diodorus and the other historians, that the law of Moses is not only old, but also the first. Diodorus himself admits that Moses, the first of all the lawmakers, [lived] before the invention of Greek letters which they used in writing their histories.

Chapter 26

Nor should anyone be surprised to find that Plato adhered to Moses' teaching concerning the eternity of God. You will find that he makes many cryptic references ascribing to the Prophets (who are next to the really existing God) the true knowledge of things. For example, when discussing certain first principles in his *Timaeus,* he wrote: 'We set this as the first principle of fire and of other bodies, proceeding by necessity according to probability. But what the first principles of these again are, God above knows, and those men who are dear to Him.' And what other men would he consider dear to God, except Moses and the other Prophets? Indeed, he read their prophecies and adopted their doctrine of the judgment, which he thus expounds in the first book of his *Republic*: 'When a man first feels that death is approaching, he is filled with fear and begins to worry about things which have never before concerned him. Those stories about how the unjust man will be punished in Hades, which he always laughed at, now begin to torture his soul with doubts that they may be true. Now, either because of the infirmities of old age or because of the proximity of death, he begins to pay more attention to them. Gradually filled with anxiety and fear, he starts to examine his conscience to determine whether he has harmed anyone. That man who then finds that he has committed many iniquities during his life, begins to awaken with a start from his sleep as children do, and he lives in a constant state of hopeless terror. But the man who is conscious of not having sinned has, in the words of Pindar,[1] sweet hope as the constant companion and good nurse of his old age. Pindar expressed this well, Socrates, when he said: "Whoever leads a holy and just life is accompanied by sweet hope, the nurse of old age who soothes the heart and rules the inconstant minds of men."[2] He wrote this in the first book of the *Republic*.

Chapter 27

In the tenth book [of his *Republic*], Plato wrote in no uncertain words what he had learned about the judgment from the Prophets, but, fearing the Greeks, he would not dare admit the real source of his information. Instead, he invented a story of having heard about the judgment from a man who had been killed in battle. He claimed that on the twelfth day, when this man was about to be buried—in fact, when he was already lying on the funeral pyre—he came to life again and began to describe the other world. Here are Plato's own words: 'He said that, when he arrived, another was asked by someone else where the great Aridaeus was. This Aridaeus had been a tyrant in a city of Pamphylia and was said to have murdered both his aged father and his elder brother, besides having committed many other wicked deeds. He then said that the person who had been questioned replied: "He has not, nor will he ever, come to this place. For, among other horrible sights, we saw the following. When we were close to the mouth [of the pit], and were on the point of escaping, after having undergone every possible torment, we suddenly saw Aridaeus and others like him, most of whom had been tyrants. But among them were also some

---
1 This passage is not found in the extant works of Pindar.
2 Cf. Plato, *Republic* 1.

who, as private citizens, had committed detestable crimes. Now, when any of these incorrigible sinners thought that they could escape and tried to do so by ascending before paying the full penalty for their crimes, the mouth would let out a roar and impede them. Then, wild, fiery-looking men stood around and, when they heard the roar, took hold of some and led them away. But, after binding the hands and feet of Aridaeus and the rest, they struck their heads against the ground, beat them soundly, dragged them out on to the road, and lacerated them with thorns, in order to signify to those present the reason for these torments, and that they were going to lead them away to cast them into Tartarus. Thus, he said the greatest of their fears was that the mouth would roar when they ascended, because, if it remained silent, each one would most gladly ascend. He finally pointed out that the punishments and tortures were all of this type, whereas the rewards were the direct opposite."[1] It appears to me that Plato gives evidence of having learned from the Prophets not only the doctrine of the judgment, but also of the resurrection, which the Greeks refuse to believe. For, when he states that the soul is judged together with the body, he surely proves that he believed in the doctrine of the resurrection. Otherwise, how could Aridaeus and the others have undergone such torments in Hades, if they had left [forever] on earth the body, with its head, hands, feet, and skin? They certainly will never affirm that the soul has a head and hands and feet and skin. But Plato, when he became acquainted in Egypt with the teachings of the Prophets, borrowed their doctrine of the resurrection of the body, and taught that the soul is judged along with the body.

---

1 Plato, *Republic* 10.

Chapter 28

Plato was not the only Greek to have become enlightened in Egypt. Homer betrayed a similar debt when he said that Tityus was punished as Aridaeus had been. In explaining to Alcinous his power of divination through the spirits of the dead, Ulysses said:

> 'There Tityus, large and long, in fetters bound,
> O'erspreads nine acres of infernal ground;
> Two ravenous vultures, furious for their food,
> Scream o'er the fiend, and riot in his blood,
> Incessant gore the liver in his breast,
> The immortal liver grows, and gives the immortal feast.'[1]

It is undeniable that it is not the soul, but the body, which has a liver. He likewise stated that both Sisyphus and Tantalus endured torments of the body [after death]. Diodorus, a most famous historian, is our authority that Homer had visited Egypt, and had incorporated into his poetry much of what he had learned there. He stated that when he was in Egypt he had learned that Helen had received from Polydamna, wife of Theon, and carried back to Sparta a drug[2] which 'lulled all sorrow and anger, and caused oblivion of all ills.'[3] Homer affirmed that, by using this drug, Helen was able to end the complaints of Menelaus against the presence of Telemachus. Another result of Homer's visit to Egypt was that he applied the adjective *golden* to Venus, for he had seen the temple which in Egypt is called the temple of *golden* Venus, and the plain called the plain of *golden* Venus. Why do I bring up this point? Simply to prove that the poet bor-

---
1 *Odyssey* 11.576 (Cf. Alexander Pope's translation, verse 709).
2 This drug was probably opium.
3 *Odyssey* 4.221.

rowed much for his own poem from the divine writings of the Prophets. First of all, he borrowed from Moses' account of the beginning of the creation of the world. Here, indeed, are the words of Moses: 'In the beginning God created the heaven and earth, then the sun, the moon, and the stars.'[4] Now, after he became acquainted with the Mosaic writings in Egypt and had been very pleased with what he wrote on the *genesis* of the world, Homer invented a fable about Vulcan, who was supposed to have represented the creation of the world on the shield of Achilles. Here are Homer's words:

> *'There earth, there heaven, there ocean he design'd;*
> *The unwearied sun, the moon completely round;*
> *The starry lights that heaven's high convex crown'd.*[5]

He also pictured the garden of Alcinous as a place forever in bloom and full of every sort of fruit. By this means he tried to make it resemble the [Mosaic] description of Paradise. He thus wrote:

> *'Tall thriving trees confess'd the fruitful mould:*
> *The reddening apple ripens here to gold.*
> *Here the blue fig with luscious juice o'erflows,*
> *With deeper red the full pomegranate glows;*
> *The branch here bends beneath the weighty pear,*
> *And verdant olives flourish round the year.*
> *The balmy spirit of the western gale*
> *Eternal breathes on fruits, untaught to fail:*
> *Each dropping pear a following pear supplies,*
> *On apples apples, figs on figs arise:*
> *The same mild season gives the blooms to blow,*

---

4 Cf. Gen. 1.1.
5 Pope's translation of *Iliad* 18.483.

> *The buds to harden, and the fruits to grow.*
> *Here order'd vines in equal ranks appear,*
> *With all the united labours of the year;*
> *Some to unload the fertile branches run,*
> *Some dry the blackening clusters in the sun,*
> *Others to tread the liquid harvest join:*
> *The groaning presses foam with floods of wine.*
> *Here are the vines in early flower descried,*
> *Here grapes discolour'd on the sunny side,*
> *And there in autumn's richest purple dyed.'*[6]

Does this quotation not prove a clearly positive imitation of what the first Prophet Moses said of Paradise? Furthermore, if anyone would desire a description of the building of that tower[7] by which the men of those times foolishly thought they could reach heaven, he can find a sufficiently accurate, although metaphorical, imitation of the story in the following quotation of Homer, where he ascribes the story to Otus and Ephialtes:

> *'Proud of their strength, and more than mortal size,*
> *The gods they challenge, and affect the skies:*
> *Heaved on Olympus tottering Ossa stood;*
> *On Ossa, Pelion nods with all his wood.'*[8]

This same can be said about the doctrine of the one who was cast out of Heaven, that enemy of mankind, whom the Sacred Scriptures call the Devil,[9] because of his first diabolical persecution of men. On close examination, one would find that, although Homer never uses the name, 'Devil,' yet he

---

6 Pope's translation of *Odyssey* 7.114.
7 Tower of Babel. Cf. Gen. 11.
8 Pope's translation of *Odyssey* 11.312.
9 The calumniator who harms men by lodging false charges against them.

gives him a name from his most wicked crime. The poet calls him Ate[10] and affirms that he was cast from heaven by their god. In this he shows an accurate remembrance of what the Prophet Isaias had said about the Devil. Here are the poet's words:

> '*And, seizing by her glossy locks*
> *The goddess Ate, in his wrath he swore*
> *That never to the starry skies again,*
> *And the Olympian heights, he would permit*
> *The universal mischief to return.*
> *Then whirling her around, he cast her down*
> *To earth. She, mingling with all works of men,*
> [*Caused many a pang to Jove*].'[11]

Chapter 29

Plato states that, next to God and matter, form is the third of the original principles of things. Now, even this doctrine he borrowed from no one else but Moses. He discovered the word *form* in the writings of Moses. Unfortunately, he did not understand the true meaning of the word, for he had no expert to point out to him that it is impossible completely to comprehend the writings of Moses without a certain mystic insight. Moses wrote that God had spoken to him about the tabernacle in these words, 'And you shall make for Me the pattern of the tabernacle according to all that I show you in the mount.'[1] And in the same passage: 'And you shall build the tabernacle according to the pattern of all the vessels for the service thereof; thus you shall make it.' Then again, in a later passage: 'Thus then you shall

---
10 The goddess of mischief.
11 Cowper's translation of *Iliad* 19.126.

---
1 Exod. 25.9.

make it according to the pattern that was shown to you in the mount.'² Now, Plato read these passages and, not comprehending their real meaning, thought that form had some kind of separate existence before that which the senses perceive. Thus, he often calls it the pattern of created things, because Moses in his writings spoke thus of the tabernacle: 'According to the form that has been shown to you in the mount, thus you shall make it.'

Chapter 30

It is obvious that he was likewise misled in his teaching on heaven and earth and man, for he fancies that there are [subsistent] ideas of these. Since Moses wrote: 'In the beginning God created heaven and earth,' and then added: 'And the earth was invisible and unfinished,' he [Plato] thought that the words, 'The earth was,' indicated the pre-existent earth, because Moses had said: 'And the earth was invisible and unfinished.' He also thought that the earth mentioned in the words, 'God created heaven and earth,' was that earth perceived by the senses and made by God according to a pre-existent form. Plato likewise thought that the heaven (also called a firmament) which was created was the heaven which the senses can perceive, whereas the heaven which the mind perceives is the other heaven of which the Prophet said: 'The heaven of heaven is the Lord's, but the earth He has given to the children of men.'[1] The same misunderstanding is evident in his doctrine on man. Moses first mentions the name of man. Later, after describing the creation of many other beings, he returns to man and describes his creation in these

---
2 Exod. 25.40.

---
1 Ps. 113.16.

words, 'And God made man, taking dust from the earth.'² Plato was deceived into believing that the man who was first named [by Moses] existed before the man whose creation was later described, and that the creation of the man formed of the earth was according to the pre-existent form. Even Homer, after having read that ancient and divine history which states: 'Dust thou art, and into dust thou shalt return,'³ and realizing that man was formed from the soil, calls the corpse of Hector dumb clay. In censuring Achilles for dragging the dead body of Hector, he wrote somewhere:
*'On the dumb clay he cast indignity,
Blinded with rage.'*⁴

In another passage, he describes how Menelaus addressed these words to his warriors who were reluctant to accept Hector's challenge to single combat: *'May you all return to earth and water.'*⁵ Thus, in his anger, he wished them to return to their ancient and original formation from the earth.

Both Homer and Plato expressed these opinions in their own writings, after they had learned them in Egypt from the ancient books of history.

Chapter 31

Where else could Plato have picked up the story of Jupiter driving across the heavens in a winged chariot, if not in the prophetic writings? He fabricated such a story from the following description of the cherubim by the Prophet: 'And the glory of the Lord went out from the house and rested on the cherubim; and the cherubim lifted up their wings, and the wheels with them; and the glory of the Lord God of

---
2 Gen. 2.7.
3 Gen. 3.19.
4 Cf. *Iliad* 24.
5 *Iliad* 7.99.

Israel was over them.'¹ Inspired by this, the grandiloquent Plato confidently exclaims: 'The great Jupiter, driving his winged chariot across the heaven.' If not from Moses and the Prophets, from what other source could Plato have learned what he wrote? And what was the origin of his statement that God exists in a fiery substance? Was it not the following passage from the third Book of Kings: 'The Lord is not in the wind; and after the wind an earthquake, but the Lord is not in the earthquake; and after the earthquake a fire, but the Lord is not in the fire; and after the fire a whistling of a gentle air'?² These words must be meditated upon and interpreted by God-fearing men in a spiritual sense. Plato, on the other hand, because he was not able to grasp their higher meaning, understood these words as meaning that God exists in a fiery substance.

Chapter 32

To one who ponders over the gift bestowed upon holy persons by God—a gift which the holy Prophets call the Holy Spirit—it is evident that Plato described it under another name in his dialogue with Meno. Indeed, afraid to call the gift of God the Holy Spirit, lest he be considered an enemy of the Greek people by adhering to the teaching of the Prophets, he admits that this gift descends from God. Yet, refusing to name it the Holy Spirit, he calls it virtue. In his dialogue with Meno on the question of recollection, after a thorough discussion of virtue—whether or not it could be taught, or whether it could be acquired by constant practice, or whether it could be attained neither by practice nor study, but was a natural endowment of man, or whether it

---
1 Ezech. 11.22.
2 3 Kings 19.11-12.

was acquired in some other way—he makes this statement: 'If we have conducted our discussion properly, and have followed the right line of reasoning, we must conclude that virtue is not obtained by study, and that it is not a natural gift, but that the men who have it acquired it through divine providence.' It is my opinion that what Plato learned from the Prophets concerning the Holy Spirit he applied to what he calls virtue. For instance, as the holy Prophets state that the one and same Spirit is divided into seven spirits, so does Plato call it the one and same virtue which is divided into four virtues. In this way, he avoided the use of the name, 'Holy Spirit,' while he allegorically repeated what the Prophets had said of the Holy Spirit. Thus, toward the end of the dialogue with Meno, he said: 'From what we have said, Meno, it appears that they who possess virtue acquired it by divine providence. But we shall have a clearer understanding of how men obtain virtue, if we first investigate independently the very nature of virtue.' You therefore see how he applies the name 'virtue' to the gift which descends from above, yet admits the validity of an inquiry to determine whether that gift should be called by the name 'virtue' or by some other name. Lest he should be accused of following the doctrine of the Prophets, he was afraid openly to call it the Holy Spirit.

Chapter 33

We could also ask where Plato learned that time was created together with the heavens. He wrote: 'Time was therefore created together with the heavens, so that, as they were created together, they might also disintegrate together, if such need be.' Did he not discover this in the sacred history of Moses? He knew that the creation of time was, from the beginning, made up of days, months, and years. Now, since that first day which was created together with the heavens constituted the very beginning of all time (for, after Moses had written: 'In the beginning God created heaven and earth,' he added: 'And one day was made,'[1] as if to designate the whole of time by a part of it), Plato calls the day 'time,' lest, by using the word 'day' he should be charged by the Athenians of having slavishly imitated the expressions of Moses. Where, too, did he learn what he has written about the disintegration of the heavens? Did he not borrow this opinion from the holy Prophets whose writings he interpreted in this fashion?

Chapter 34

Furthermore, if one studies the question of idols, and investigates why the first makers of your gods gave them human forms, he will discover that this, too, owed its origin to the sacred writings. Since Moses, speaking in the name of God, says in his history: 'Let us make man to our image and likeness,'[1] they [erroneously] imagined that men were similar to God in form. Consequently, they began thus to shape their gods, believing that they could make a likeness from another one. But why, my Greek friends, am I led to recall these things? For the sole purpose of convincing you that it is impossible to learn the true religion from those who could not write anything original, even on those topics through which they aroused the admiration of the pagan world, but merely repeated, in allegorical language, what they had borrowed from Moses and the other Prophets.

---
1 Gen. 1.1.5.

---
1 Gen. 1.26.

Chapter 35

Now is the hour, O Greeks, that you (convinced by your own historians that Moses and the other Prophets were far more ancient than any of those whom you honored as sages among you) renounce the ancient error of your ancestors and read the sacred prophetic writings in order to learn from them the true religion. The Prophets do not strive to impress you with a skillful use of words, nor do they resort to specious or persuasive arguments (a device of those who endeavor to rob you of the truth), but with the simple words and phrases that first come to mind they relate to you whatever the Holy Spirit, who descended upon them, wished to transmit through them to those desirous of knowing the true religion. Renounce, therefore, all human respect, and the time-worn error of mankind, and the empty sound of pompous passages (through the use of which you consider yourselves possessed of every advantage), and devote yourselves to truly profitable things. It cannot be said that you will offend your ancestors by embracing a doctrine opposed to their error, since they very probably are now bewailing their lot in Hades and are touched with deep remorse and repentance. Were it possible for them to warn you of what happened to them after their death, you would surely know from what terrible evils they wished you to be saved. But, since it is now impossible in this present life to learn anything from them or from those who here teach an erroneous philosophy, the natural conclusion is that you should renounce the error of your ancestors, read the prophetic writings of the holy men—not expecting from them elegant phrases (for the exercise of our religion rests upon deeds, not words)—and learn from them the means of eternal life. For they who rashly discredit the name of philosophy are obliged unwillingly to admit that they are convicted of knowing nothing, since they not only contradict one another, but even express their own opinions in an inconsistent way.

Chapter 36

Now, if the aim of philosophy, according to them, is the discovery of truth, how can they be called true philosophers who do not have a knowledge of truth? Socrates, indeed, was the wisest of your wise men according to your oracle, which, you say, made the following statement: 'Socrates is the wisest of all men.' Now, if Socrates confesses that he knows nothing, how can they who came after him presume to know even heavenly things? Socrates, indeed, affirmed that he was called wise, because, while others pretended to know what they did not know, he did not hesitate to admit that he knew nothing. For he said: 'I seem to be the wisest because of this one fact, that I do not think that I know what I do not know.' Now, should anyone conclude that Socrates, in a sarcastic way, merely feigned ignorance in this instance, as he did on so many other occasions during his discussions, his last words of self-defense, spoken while he was being led to prison, show how serious and truthful he was in admitting his own ignorance: 'But now is the time for us to part. I go to die, you to live. Only God knows which of us goes to the better state.' After speaking these last words in the Areopagus, Socrates went to prison, testifying to the fact that only God knows the things that are concealed from us. Yet they who came after Socrates profess to know heavenly things as though they had seen them, when they do not even have a knowledge of earthly matters. Thus, Aristotle, as if he had witnessed heavenly things more closely than Plato, affirmed that God did not exist in a fiery substance (Plato's doctrine), but in the air, the fifth element. And he who demanded assent to these theories of his, because of his excellent manner of expression, died in humiliation and dishonor when he could not determine the nature of the Euripus in Chalcis.[1] The intelligent man, therefore, must not prefer the eloquence of these men to his own salvation, but he must stuff his ears with wax, as in the ancient fable, and flee the sweet injury that these sirens would inflict upon him. For the above-mentioned writers, by using their smooth style as a kind of bait, have tried to lure many away from true religion, and in doing so they emulate him who dared to spread polytheism among the first men. I beg you not to listen to such persons, but to read the prophetic writings of the holy men, instead. If laziness or your old ancestral superstition keeps you from reading their prophetic writings which would acquaint you with the One and Only God (which is the first mark of the true religion), at least believe him who, although he at first taught you polytheism, later was obliged to sign a useful and needed recantation—I refer to Orpheus, who said what I mentioned above. Believe those others, too, who wrote in the same fashion about the One God. Indeed, it was for your sake that the providence of God caused them, against their will, to testify to the truth of what the Prophets said concerning the One God, so that, with the universal abandonment of polytheism, you might have a chance to know the truth.

Chapter 37

Nor would it be difficult for you to acquire a partial knowl-

---

[1] This account is now considered to be a fable.

edge of the true religion from the ancient Sibyl,¹ who, through some kind of strong inspiration, issued oracular pronouncements that appeared very similar to the doctrine of the Prophets. It is said that the Sibyl was of Babylonian descent, being the daughter of Berosus, author of the *History of Chaldaea*. After she had traversed the sea and had arrived (I do not know how) in the province of Campania, she began to utter her oracles in Cumae, a city six miles from Baiae, where the hot springs of Campania are located. On a visit to that city we went to a certain place and saw there a very large basilica cut out of one stone—a truly magnificent and admirable work of art.² The inhabitants told us it was a local tradition, handed down from their ancestors, that in this place the Sibyl used to announce her oracles. In the center of the basilica they pointed out three vessels carved from one stone, and told us that she used to bathe in them when they were filled with water, and that, after she again put on her robe, she would enter the basilica's innermost room (which was also cut from that same stone), and there in the middle of that room would sit on a throne over a raised platform and give her oracular answers. Many writers, even Plato himself in his *Phaedrus*, speak of the Sibyl as a prophetess. In fact, I

---

1 Under the name of the *Sibylline Oracles* there circulated, especially in the second and third centuries A.D., a collection of supposed prophecies attributed to the various Sibyls (Varro named ten of them. Cf. Lactantius, *De div. inst.* 50.6). The oracles quoted in this work are supposed to have been uttered by the Cimmerian (or Cumaean) Sibyl in Campania, Italy. In pagan times these oracles were carefully collected and generally venerated by the populace. In order to spread Judaism, some Alexandrian Jews, in the second century B.C., forged some of these oracles. The Christians later did likewise. Consequently, by the second and third centuries A.D. there were several collections of these hexameter oracles of pagan, Jewish, and Christian origin. With the disappearance of paganism, their popularity dwindled, although they were sometimes quoted during the Middle Ages.
2 Tourists may still see this underground building as it was in Justin's time.

think that it was because he read her prophecies that Plato considered Prophets to be divine persons. Since he actually saw happen what she had long before foretold, it was natural for him, as he did in his dialogue with Meno, to express his awe and admiration of the Prophets in these words: 'Those persons whom we now call prophets we should really call divine. Indeed, we would rightly consider them divine and endowed with the gift of ecstasy through the inspiration and possession of God, when they foretell exactly many great events, while they are totally unconscious of what they are saying.' In this passage Plato clearly referred to the Sibylline prophecies. For, unlike the poets who, after they have completed their poems, can correct and polish their metre, the Sibyl had the prophetic gift at the time of inspiration, but when that time ended, she lost all remembrance of what she had said. For this reason, not all the metres of the Sibylline verses have been preserved. On that same visit to the city our guide not only pointed out the places where she used to prophesy, but also a brass casket which was said to have contained her remains. Among the many other old stories they repeated for our benefit was one that the persons who copied down her oracles were not too well educated and quite often did not copy the metre accurately. Consequently, her verses were often without metre, both because she could never recall what she had said, after she came out of her spell (during which she was inspired and possessed by God), and because her reporters, through lack of knowledge, did not copy her metres correctly. It is thus clear that Plato had the Sibylline oracles in mind when he made the following comment on the Prophets: 'When they foretell exactly many great events, they are totally unconscious of what they are saying.'

Chapter 38

But, O citizens of Greece, since the essentials of the true religion are found neither in poetic metres nor in your greatly esteemed culture, you should pay less attention to accuracy of metre and language, and more to the Sibylline utterances, for you will thereby realize what great blessings she will bestow upon you by her unmistakable prediction of the coming of our Savior Jesus Christ.[1] Indeed, this same Jesus Christ, being the Word of God, inseparable from Him in power, assumed the nature of man (who had been made to the image and likeness of God), and restored to us the religion of our ancestors, which their posterity abandoned through the instigation of the envious demon, and turned to the worship of those who were not gods at all. If you are in doubt and find it hard to believe our doctrine of the creation of man, at least listen to those whom, up to this time, you have considered worthy of belief; realize that your own oracle, when requested by someone to utter a hymn in honor of Almighty God, spoke these words in the middle of the hymn: 'Who formed the first man and called him Adam.'[2] Many persons whom we know still keep this hymn at hand to convince those who refuse to believe this truth which is attested to by everyone. If, my Greek friends, you prefer your own salvation to the false rumors of false gods, believe, as I said, the most ancient and venerable Sibyl, whose books are preserved throughout the whole world, and who teaches us by some superhuman inspiration that those beings which are called gods do not really exist at all. She also uttered explicit prophecies about the future coming of our Savior Jesus Christ, and about the things which He would do. A thorough knowl-

---
1 Cf. *Sibylline Oracles* 1.325.
2 Cf., also, *Sibylline Oracles* 1.26.

edge of these things will be a necessary preparation for your study of the writings of the holy Prophets. If, however, any one should object that he has acquired his knowledge of God from the most ancient of the so-called philosophers, let him listen to Ammon and Mercury. The former, in his treatise on God, affirms that He is absolutely hidden from us; while Mercury clearly states that it is very difficult to comprehend God, and that it is impossible for the man who can comprehend God to reveal Him to others. Thus, after considering the question from every angle, we must come to the conclusion that it is impossible to attain a knowledge of God and of the true religion, except through the Prophets who teach us by divine inspiration.

DISCOURSE TO THE GREEKS

INTRODUCTION

THE *Discourse To The Greeks* has come down to us in two manuscripts, the first of which, the Greek *Codex Argentoratensis* (gr. 9, of the thirteenth or fourteenth century), was completely destroyed by fire at Strassburg on August, 24, 1870.[1] The other manuscript, of the seventh century (*Cod. Syr.* Add. 14658, now preserved in the British Museum), contains a Syriac version of the *Discourse* under the name of Ambrosius.[2]

In this short apology of five chapters, the author explains the motives which prompted him to embrace Christianity —motives which were based upon his abhorrence of the immoralities connected with Greek mythology and the pagan festivals. He concludes his *Discourse* by appealing to the Greeks to follow his example and become Christians.

It is doubtful whether it was written by St. Justin.[3] The date of this expose of pagan depravity must rather be placed between the last half of the second century and the first quarter of the third. The style is definitely not Justinian; furthermore, the author gives as the reason for his conversion to Christianity his aversion to heathen immoralities. St. Justin[4] attributes his conversion to an intimate study of the prophets of the Old Testament together with the profound impression made upon him by the constancy of Christians in face of torture and death.

---

1 For a description of this Codex, see Migne, *PG* 6.222.
2 Cf. W. Cureton, *Spicilegium Syriacum* (London 1855) 38-42; 61-69.
3 Cf. W. Smith and H. Wace, *A Dictionary of Christ. Biography* 3.365 for the difference of opinion regarding its genuineness.
4 Cf. *Dial. w. Tr.* 7.

427

The texts used for this translation are those of Migne, *PG* 6.229-240, and of J. C. T. von Otto, *Corpus Apologetarum Christianorum saeculi secundi* (Jena 1879) III 2-18.

CONTENTS

Chapter *Page*

1 Justin's abhorrence of Greek customs 431
2 Evils perpetrated by Greek gods 432
3 Additional evils of the Greek gods 433
4 Sinful customs of the Greeks themselves 435
5 Concluding exhortation to the Greeks 435

DISCOURSE TO THE GREEKS

Chapter 1

DO NOT IMAGINE, my Greek friends, that I am rash and unreasonable in refusing to practice your customs, for I have discovered that they are in no way holy or pleasing to God. Indeed, the very writings of your poets stand as permanent testimonials of madness and perversity. Whoever becomes a pupil of your most learned one[1] encounters more difficulties than any man ever faced. Because, first of all, they[2] affirm that Agamemnon, in assisting his brother's sensuality with great madness and unrestrained passion, did not hesitate to hand over his own daughter[3] to be immolated. Furthermore, to rescue Helen, carried away by the leprous shepherd, he disturbed all Greece. But when captives were taken during the ensuing war, Agamemnon himself was captivated by Chryseis, and because of another girl, Briseis, he became an enemy of Thetis' son.[4] And that great hero of yours, the son of Peleus,[5] who constrained the river, conquered Troy and vanquished Hector, became the slave of Polyxena, and was overcome by a dead Amazon.[6] Replacing his divinely-made armor with a wedding garment, he became a love victim in the temple of Apollo. And the

---
1 Homer.
2 The grammarians who interpreted the Homeric poems.
3 Iphigeneia.
4 Achilles.
5 Achilles. Cf. *Iliad* 21.24ff., 243ff.
6 Achilles was filled with remorse when he perceived the beauty of the Amazon whom he had mortally wounded in battle.

431

Ithacan Ulysses even made evil appear as virtue. Indeed, in sailing by the realm of the Sirens, he showed that he lacked sufficient prudence when he could not trust his own good sense to close his ears.[7] Then there is the example of the son of Telamon, Ajax, that strong man whose shield was covered with seven ox hides, but who, when defeated by Ulysses in the contest for the weapons [of Achilles], went stark mad. I have not the slightest desire to be taught such things. Nor do I aspire to attain such a state of mind that I should believe these Homeric myths. For the whole epic poem, both the beginning and end of the *Iliad* and *Odyssey,* revolves about one theme—woman.

Chapter 2

And as to Hesiod, who, after Homer, wrote his *Works and Days,* who will agree with his futile theogony? For he says that Saturn, the son of heaven, deposed his own father of his reign and took over his sceptre, and that, panic-stricken lest he suffer the same fate, he decided to eat his own children. But Jupiter, through the cunning of Curetes, was taken away and hidden. Later, he returned to take his father prisoner in chains and to divide his kingdom. On this occasion it is said that Jupiter received the air; Neptune, the sea; and Pluto, the portion of Hades. And Pluto carried away Proserpine, while Ceres wandered about in the wilderness, in search of her daughter. Even this myth was exalted by the Eleusinian fire.[1] Not only did Neptune assault Melanippe when she was drawing water, but he also debased a great number of mermaids[2] whose names are too numerous to mention.

---

7 Instead, he had himself bound to the mast of his ship.

---

1 The annual return of Proserpine from the region of the dead was celebrated in the Eleusinian Mysteries.
2 Nereids.

And Jupiter was an adulterer under many guises, for he sinned with Antiope as a satyr, with Danae as [a shower of] gold, with Europa as a bull, and with Leda as a swan. And the love of Semele stimulated both his lewdness and the jealousy of Juno. It is also reported that he carried off the Phrygian Ganymede to serve as his cupbearer. Such were the misdeeds of Saturn's descendants. And your Apollo, that renowned son of Latona, proved himself a liar when he professed to be a soothsayer. For, although he pursued Daphne, he never caught up with her; nor did he warn his beloved Hyacinth, when he pitched the quoit, of his death.[3] And I shall pass over in silence the masculine characteristics of Minerva, the femininity of Bacchus, and the immoral habits of Venus. You Greeks should read aloud to Jupiter the law against parricide, the punishment for adultery, and the stigma of pederasty. Teach Minerva and Diana feminine activities, and show Bacchus how a man should act. What majesty is depicted by the scene of a woman clothed in armor, or of a man in female attire, decorated with cymbals and garlands, and followed by a frenzied mob of female devotees?

Chapter 3

And take the example of Hercules, famous for his three nights[1] and the performance of his labors—Hercules, that son of Jupiter, who killed the lion and the many-headed hydra; who slew the tireless wild boar and scattered the swift man-eating birds; who brought the three-headed dog back from Hades, and cleansed the huge Augean stables of their

---

[3] Apollo killed Hyacinth by accident, when he struck him with a discus.

[1] Perhaps a reference to the legend that he had spent three nights in the stomach of a whale.

dirt; who slew the fire-breathing bulls and stag; who gathered the golden fruit from the tree and killed the poisonous serpent (and he also killed Achelous and Busiris, that murderer of his guests—for what reason it is not right to say); who traversed mountains in order to get water which, it is said, rendered one's speech articulate. Yet, this same Hercules, who performed so many wonderful deeds, was childishly pleased to be fascinated by the cymbals of the satyrs, to be enslaved by the love of woman, and to be slapped on the buttocks by the laughing Lydian.[2] And at length, when he could not take off the robe of Nessus,[3] he died, after first having kindled his own funeral pyre. Let Vulcan desist from his envy and jealousy if he is hated because he is old and lame, while Mars is loved because he is young and handsome. Therefore, O Greeks, since your gods have been proved guilty of intemperance and your heroes of effeminacy, the histories described by your dramatic poets clearly show, for example, the curse of Atreus; the couch of Thyestes;[4] the abominable sins of these descendants of Pelops; Danaus, who, drunk with rage and envious of his brother Egyptus, deprived him of his children by murdering his [fifty] sons; and the Thyestean banquets prepared by the Furies. And Procne, under the form of a bird, even to this day laments, and her Athenian sister chirps as best she can with her tongue torn out. Need we mention the goad[5] of Oedipus,

---

2 Omphale.
3 When Dejaneira, wife of Hercules, heard rumors of his love for Iole, she sent him a robe sprinkled with the poisoned blood of Nessus, whom Hercules had slain. This poison killed Hercules.
4 Thyestes plotted with the wife of his brother, Atreus, to seize the throne from him, but was unsuccessful. After years of exile, Thyestes returned to effect a reconciliation with his brother. Atreus received him kindly, but as revenge he served Thyestes' own son for dinner. This is the so-called Thyestean banquet.
5 This could refer to the means which Oedipus used to blind himself, or to kill his father or it could mean the instrument employed to pierce his ankles when he was a baby.

how he murdered Laius, his father, and married his own mother, and how his sons, who were at the same time his brothers, slaughtered each other?

Chapter 4

I have come to detest even your public festivals. There you indulge in immoderate banquets, listen to finely polished flutes which incite you to lustful actions, and you needlessly submit to elaborate anointings with perfume, while your heads are crowned with flowers. With such an accumulation of evil practices you determine your reverence. With such practices are your minds filled, while your intemperance excites you to Bacchic frenzy, whence you indulge in your customary unholy and mad intercourse. I would like to make another observation. It is this. Why do you, who are Greeks, become angered when your son, in imitation of Jupiter, turns against you and robs you of your own wife? Why do you consider him your enemy, yet worship one [Jupiter] who is like him? Why do you complain of your wife's infidelity, yet honor Venus with temples? If these events had been narrated by others, they could be presumed to have been false and slanderous accusations, but even now your own poets extol them in song, and your histories blatantly describe them.

Chapter 5

Therefore, my Greek friends, come and share in unrivalled wisdom, and receive the teachings of the Divine Word, while you become acquainted with the immortal King; and you will see that they are not heroes who destroy whole nations. For our Leader, the Divine Word, does not demand a strong body and beautiful countenance, or high and noble birth, but a pure soul, well-grounded in holiness. He demands the password of our King, namely, divine deeds, for the power to perform such deeds is transmitted to the soul through the Word. (O trumpet of peace for a soul that is at war! O weapon that drives away dangerous passions! O precept that extinguishes the natural fire of the soul!) This power of the Word does not make us poets, or learned philosophers, or fluent orators, but it does make us immortal; it makes gods of us mortal men, and it transports us from the earth to the regions above Olympus. Come, therefore, and be instructed. Become as I am, for I was once as you. The divinity of the doctrine and the power of the Word have conquered me. Just as an expert snake charmer puts a dreadful snake to flight after luring it from its hole, so does the Word expel the dreadful passions of our sensual nature from the remote recesses of our soul. First, He drives away lust from which every kind of evil originates, for example, enmities, quarrels, jealousy, intrigues, anger, and the like. Once lust is expelled, tranquillity and peace return to the soul. And once the soul is freed of the evils in which it was immersed, it returns to its Creator. For it is necessary that the soul return to the place from which it came.

THE MONARCHY
OR
THE RULE OF GOD

INTRODUCTION

HE GREEK TEXT of the *De Monarchia* is preserved in the *Codex Paris*. gr. 450, of the year 1364, and in the *Codex Claromont*. 82, of 1541. It had also been in the Strassburg manuscript (*Cod. gr.* 9, of the thirteenth century) which was destroyed in the fire of 1870.

The purpose of this short treatise was to prove monotheism from the writings of Greek literature. Consequently, the author quoted the tragedians, Aeschylus, Sophocles, and Euripides; the comic writers, Philemon, Orpheus, and Menander; and the philosophers, Plato and Pythagoras.

The manuscripts list this treatise with the writings of St. Justin, and Eusebius (*Hist. eccl.* 4.18) explicitly attributes it to him. However, Eusebius stated that the *De Monarchia* he had read proved monotheism with arguments taken from both Sacred Scripture and pagan literature. The treatise we now have uses proofs taken *only* from pagan sources. Consequently, there is considerable doubt concerning the authorship of this treatise. It was probably composed in the third century[1] when such great use was made of those falsified verses of Greek poetry.

The texts used for this translation are those of Migne, *PG* 6.312-325, and of J. C. T. von Otto, *Corpus Apologetarum Christianorum saeculi secundi* (Jena 1879) III 126-158.

---

[1] Cf. G. Bardy, 'Justin' *Dict. theol. cath.* 8.2240, and J. M. Semisch, *loc. cit.* 163-167.

CONTENTS

Chapter		Page
1	Plan of the treatise	443
2	Proof of the unity of God	444
3	Future judgment proved from pagan writings	447
4	God is not appeased by pagan libations	448
5	The vanity of false gods	450
6	The One True God alone should be worshipped	454

THE MONARCHY
OR
THE RULE OF GOD

Chapter 1

ALTHOUGH human nature from the beginning was endowed with a twofold gift of intelligence and safety for the purpose of attaining a knowledge of the truth and of the worship due to the One Lord of all, yet envy, appealing to the superiority of man's greatness, induced him to make idols. And, after persisting many years, this superstitious custom passed along the deception to many as though it were natural and correct. Men who have at heart the interest of other men (I should say of God), must remind careless men of what they should know. Indeed, by means of the things under the sky, truth of itself has the power to show the order established by Him who created those things. But men became completely neglectful, and, while God endured all this in patience, they rashly transferred to mortals the name that belongs to the One and Only God. From the few this sinful disease spread until it infected many, who, by this common practice [of idolatry], lost sight of things eternal and immutable. From earliest times men began to practice mystic and public rites in honor of their leaders, and in this way caused their posterity to forget the [original] Catholic faith.[1] But, with a mind filled with love of God, as I stated above, I shall use the language of one who loves man, and set it before intelligent men. For certainly, all

---

[1] Namely, that worship was due only to the one true God.

those who witness the order in this universe should be intelligent enough to know that they ought unchangeably to worship Him who knows all things. And I propose to do this, not by resorting to pretty-sounding phrases, but by producing proofs from the ancient Greek poetry and from writings well know to everyone. In this way their own poets and ballad writers shall reveal the ignorance of those leaders who passed down idolatry to the multitudes as law.

Chapter 2

As a first witness, [let us take] Aeschylus, who, having expounded the different opinions prevalent at his time, expressed the following view of the unity of God:

> *'Afar from mortals place the holy God,*
> *Nor ever think that He, like to thyself,*
> *In fleshly robes is clad; for all unknown*
> *Is the great God to such a worm as thou.*
> *Divers similitudes He bears; at times*
> *He seems as a consuming fire that burns*
> *Unsated; now like water, then again*
> *In sable folds of darkness shrouds Himself.*
> *Nay, even the very beasts of earth reflect*
> *His sacred image; whilst the wind, clouds, rain,*
> *The roll of thunder and the lightning flash,*
> *Reveal to men their great and sovereign Lord.*
> *Before Him sea and rocks, with every fount,*
> *And all the water floods, in reverence bend;*
> *And as they gaze upon His awful face,*
> *Mountains and earth, with the profoundest depths*
> *Of ocean, and the highest peaks of hills,*
> *Tremble: for He is Lord Omnipotent;*

THE MONARCHY OR THE RULE OF GOD 445

And this the glory is of God Most High.'[1]

Nor was Aeschylus the only one well-versed in the knowledge of God, for Sophocles also had this to say of the One and Only God and Creator of all things:

> 'There is one God, in truth there is but one,
> Who made the heavens and the broad earth
>   beneath,
> The glancing waves of ocean, and the winds;
> But many of us mortals err in heart,
> And set up, for a solace in our woes,
> Images of the gods in stone and brass,
> Or figures carved in gold or ivory;
> And, furnishing for these, our handiworks,
> Both sacrifice and rite magnificent,
> We think that thus we do a pious work.'[2]

Philemon, who wrote so much about ancient customs, also gave evidence of knowing something of the truth when he wrote:

> 'Tell me what thoughts of God we should
>   conceive?
> One, all things seeing, yet Himself unseen.'[3]

Even Orpheus, who invented three hundred and sixty gods, is a witness in my favor, for, in his work called *The Testaments*, he seems to repent of his early error when he writes:

> 'I'll speak to those who lawfully may hear;
> All others, ye profane, now close the doors!
> And, O Musaeus, hearken thou to me,

---

1 The translation of the Greek poets is that used by G. Reith in Roberts and Donaldson's *Ante-Nicene Christian Library* 2.330.
2 *Ibid.*, p. 331.
3 *Ibid.*

Who offspring art of the light-bringing moon.
The words I tell thee now are true indeed,
And if thou former thoughts of mine hast seen,
Let them not rob thee of the blessed life;
But rather turn the depths of thine own heart
Unto that place where light and knowledge dwell.
Take thou the word divine to guide thy steps;
And walking well in the straight certain path,
Look to the one and universal King,
One, self-begotten, and the only One
Of whom all things, and we ourselves, are sprung.
All things are open to His piercing gaze,
While He Himself is still invisible;
Present in all His works, though still unseen,
He gives to mortals evil out of good,
Sending both chilling wars and tearful griefs;
And other than the Great King there is none.
The clouds forever settle round His throne;
And mortal eyeballs in mere mortal eyes
Are weak to see Jove, who reigns over all.
He sits established in the brazen heavens
Upon His throne; and underneath His feet
He treads the earth, and stretches His right hand
To all the ends of ocean, and around
Tremble the mountain ranges, and the streams,
The depths, too, of the blue and hoary sea.'[4]

Indeed, he expressed himself as though he had seen the majesty of God with his own eyes.

Pythagoras, too, testified to the same thing when he wrote:

'Should one in boldness say, Lo, I am God!
Besides the One—Eternal—Infinite,

---
[4] *Ibid.*

> *Then let him from the throne he has usurped*
> *Put forth his power and form another globe,*
> *Such as we dwell in, saying, This is mine.*
> *Nor only so, but in this new domain*
> *Forever let him dwell. If this he can,*
> *Then verily he is a god proclaimed.*'[5]

Chapter 3

Furthermore, from your own writers I can produce witnesses to testify that God alone has the power to judge man both for his actions in this life and for his failure to attain a knowledge of the Deity. First, listen to Sophocles, who says:

> *'That time of times shall come, shall surely come,*
> *When from the golden ether down shall fall.*
> *Fire's teeming treasure, and in burning flames*
> *All things of earth and heaven shall be*
>   *consumed;*
> *And then, when all creation is dissolved,*
> *The sea's last wave shall die upon the shore,*
> *The bald earth stript of trees, the burning air*
> *No winged thing upon its breast shall bear.*
> *There are two roads to Hades, well we know;*
> *By this the righteous, and by that the bad,*
> *On to their separate fates shall tend; and He,*
> *Who all things had destroyed, shall all things*
>   *save.'*[1]

And Philemon:[2]
> *'Think'st thou, Nicostratus, the dead, who here*

---

5 *Ibid.*, p. 332.

---

1 *Ibid.*, p. 332.
2 Some critics attribute these verses to Diphilus.

Enjoyed whate'er of good life offers man,
Escape the notice of Divinity,
As if they might forgotten be of Him?
Nay, there's an eye of Justice watching all:
For if the good and bad find the same end,
Then go thou, rob, steal, plunder, at thy will,
Do all the evil that to thee seems good.
Yet be not thou deceived; for underneath
There is a throne and place of judgment set,
Which God the Lord of all shall occupy;
Whose name is terrible, nor shall I dare
To breathe it forth in feeble human speech.'[3]

And Euripides:[4]

'Not grudgingly he gives a lease of life,
That we the holders may be fairly judged;
And if a mortal man doth think to hide
His daily guilt from the keen eye of God,
It is an evil thought; so if perchance
He meets with leisure-taking Justice, she
Demands him as her lawful prisoner:
But many of you hastily commit
A twofold sin, and say there is no God.
But, ah! there is; there is. Then see that he
Who, being wicked, prospers, may redeem
The time so precious, else hereafter waits
For him the due reward of punishment.'[5]

Chapter 4

Philemon[1] again is my witness to prove that God is not

---

[3] Reith, *op. cit.*, p. 333.
[4] Clement of Alexandria ascribes these verses to Diphilus.
[5] Reith, *op. cit.*, p. 333.

---

[1] Clement of Alexandria and Eusebius assign these verses to Menander, while some modern critics think they are spurious.

appeased by the libations and incense of sinners, but justly punishes each one. Here are his words:

> 'If any one should dream, O Pamphilus,
> By sacrifice of bulls or goats—nay, then,
> By Jupiter—of any such like things;
> Or by presenting gold or purple robes,
> Or images of ivory and gems;
> If thus he thinks he may propitiate God,
> He errs, and shows himself a silly one.
> But let him rather useful be, and good,
> Committing neither theft nor lustful deeds,
> Nor murder foul, for earthly riches' sake.
> Let him of no man covet wife or child,
> His splendid house, his wide-spread property,
> His maiden, or his slave born in his house,
> His horses, or his cattle, or his beeves.
> Nay, covet not a pin, O Pamphilus,
> For God, close by you, sees whate'er you do.
> He ever with the wicked man is wroth,
> But in the righteous takes a pleasure still,
> Permitting him to reap fruit of his toil,
> And to enjoy the bread his sweat has won.
> But being righteous, see thou pay thy vows,
> And unto God the giver offer gifts.
> Place thy adorning not in outward shows,
> But in an inward purity of heart;
> Hearing the thunder then, thou shalt not fear,
> Nor shalt thou flee, O master, at its voice,
> For thou art conscious of no evil deed,
> And God, close by you, sees whate'er you do.'[2]

Even Plato, in his *Timaeus*, says: 'But if any one were to

---
2 Reith, *op. cit.*, p. 334.

begin a profound study of these things, he would not be able to learn the distinction between the human and divine nature, for God can mix many things into one, and can return one back into many things (for such is His knowledge and power). But the man does not live, or ever shall live, who is able to perform such deeds.'³

Chapter 5

Menander, in his *Auriga*, speaks thus of those who believe they should be called by the holy and perfect name [of God], which name some have received by a vain tradition, as if they were gods:

> '*If there exists a god who walketh out
> With an old woman, or who enters in
> By stealth to houses through the folding-doors,
> He ne'er can please me; nay, but only he
> Who stays at home, a just and righteous God,
> To give salvation to His worshippers.*'¹

And the same Menander, in his *Sacerdos*, says:

> '*There is no God, O woman, that can save
> One man by another; if indeed a man,
> With sound of tinkling cymbals, charm a god
> Where'er he listeth, then assuredly
> He who doth so is much the greater god.
> But these, O Rhode, are but the cunning schemes
> Which daring men of intrigue, unabashed,
> Invent to earn themselves a livelihood,
> And yield a laughing-stock unto the age.*'²

---
3 *Timaeus* 68D.

---
1 Reith, *op. cit.*, p. 335
2 *Ibid.*

Again, in his *Odiosus*, Menander proved that they who are considered gods are not gods at all:

> 'Yea, if I this beheld, I then should wish
> That back to me again my soul returned.
> For tell me where, O Getas, in the world
> 'Tis possible to find out righteous gods?'[3]

And in his *Depositum*:

> 'There's an unrighteous judgment, as it seems,
> Even with the gods.'[4]

Then there is the testimony of Euripides the tragedian, who says in his *Orestes*:

> 'Apollo having caused by his command
> The murder of the mother, knoweth not
> What honesty and justice signify.
> We serve the gods, whoever they may be;
> But from the central regions of the earth
> You see Apollo plainly gives response
> To mortals, and whate'er he says we do.
> I him obeyed, when she that bore me fell
> Slain by my hand: he is the wicked man.
> Then slay him, for 'twas he that sinned, not I.
> What could I do? Think you not that the god
> Should free me from the blame which I do bear?'[5]

Again, Euripides in the *Hippolytus*: 'But on these points the gods do not judge right.'[6] And in his *Ion* he says:

> 'But in the daughter of Erechtheus
> What interest have I? for that pertains
> Not unto such as me. But when I come

---
3 *Ibid.*
4 *Ibid. p.* 336.
5 *Ibid.*
6 *Ibid.*

> *With golden vessels for libations, I*
> *The dew shall sprinkle, and yet needs must warn*
> *Apollo of his deeds; for when he weds*
> *Maidens by force, the children secretly*
> *Begotten he betrays, and them neglects*
> *When dying. Thus not you; but while you may*
> *Always pursue the virtues, for the gods*
> *Will surely punish men of wickedness.*
> *How is it right that you, who have prescribed*
> *Laws for men's guidance, live unrighteously?*
> *But ye being absent, I shall freely speak,*
> *And ye to men shall satisfaction give*
> *For marriage forced, thou Neptune, Jupiter,*
> *Who over heaven presides. The temples ye*
> *Have emptied, while injustice ye repay.*
> *And though ye laud the prudent to the skies,*
> *Yet have ye filled your hands with wickedness.*
> *No longer is it right to call men ill*
> *If they do imitate the sins[7] of gods;*
> *Nay, evil let their teachers rather be.'*[8]

And in *Archelaus*: 'Full oft, my son, do gods mankind perplex.'[9] And in his *Bellerophon*: 'They are no gods, who do not what is right.'[10] And in another passage of the same play:

> *'Gods reign in heaven most certainly, says one;*
> *But it is false—yea false: and let not him*
> *Who speaks thus, be so foolish as to use*
> *Ancient tradition, or to pay regard*
> *Unto my words: but with unclouded eye*

---
7 The *kald* of the text is amended to the *kakd* of Euripides' text.
8 Reith, *op. cit.*, p. 337.
9 *Ibid.*
10 *Ibid.*

> *Behold the matter in its clearest light.*
> *Power absolute, I say, robs men of life*
> *And property; transgresses plighted faith;*
> *Nor spares even cities, but with cruel hand*
> *Despoils and devastates them ruthlessly.*
> *But they that do these things have more success*
> *Than those who live a gentle pious life;*
> *And cities small, I know, which reverence gods,*
> *Submissive bend before the many spears*
> *Of larger impious ones; yea, and methinks*
> *If any man lounge idly, and abstain*
> *From working with his hands for sustenance,*
> *Yet pray the gods; he very soon will know*
> *If they from him misfortunes will avert.*'[11]

And Menander in *Diphilus*:

> '*Therefore ascribe we praise and honor great*
> *To Him who Father is, and Lord of all:*
> *Sole maker and preserver of mankind,*
> *And who with all good things our earth has stored.*'[12]

Likewise, in his *Piscatores*, Menander says:

> '*For I deem that which nourishes my life*
> *Is God: but he whose custom 'tis to meet*
> *The wants of men—He needs not at our hands*
> *Renewed supplies, Himself being all in all.*'[13]

And in the *Fratres*:

> '*God ever is intelligence to those*
> *Who righteous are: so wisest men have thought.*'[14]

---
11 *Ibid.*
12 Not found in Menander's writings. Clement of Alexandria attributed these verses to Diphilus.
13 Reith, *op. cit.*, p. 338.
14 *Ibid.*

And in his *Tibicinae*:

> 'Good reason finds a temple in all things
> Wherein to worship; for what is the mind,
> But just the voice of God within us placed?'[15]

And the tragedian, in his *Phrixus*, says:

> 'But if the pious and the impious
> Share the same lot, how could we think it just,
> If Jove, the best, judges not uprightly?'[16]

In the *Philoctetes*:

> 'You see how honorable gain is deemed
> Even to the gods; and how he is admired
> Whose shrine is laden most with yellow gold.
> What, then, doth hinder thee, since it is good
> To be like gods, from thus accepting gain?'[17]

In *Hecuba*:

> 'O Jupiter! whoever thou mayest be,
> Of whom except in word all knowledge fails;
> Jupiter, whether thou art indeed
> A great necessity, or the mind of man,
> I worship thee!'[18]

Chapter 6

This, then, is a proof of virtue and of an ever-prudent mind, to return to that twofold gift, namely, to practise prudence unto salvation, to choose the better things according to one's free will, and not to believe that they who have human passions are the masters of all, when they do not

---
[15] *Ibid.*
[16] *Ibid.*
[17] *Ibid.*, p. 339.
[18] *Ibid.*

even seem to be endowed with power that other men possess. Indeed, in Homer, Demodocus claims that he is self-instructed, when he says: *'God inspired me with melodies,'*[1] though he was but a mortal. Aesculapius and Apollo learn the art of healing from Chiron the Centaur—What an innovation, for gods to learn from a man! Need I mention Bacchus, who, the poet claims, is mad? Or Hercules, who, he says, is miserable? Need I mention Mars and Venus, those teachers of adultery, and establish by means of all these the proof of my demonstration? If someone through ignorance should imitate the actions which are said to be divine, he would be labeled an impure man, an outcast of human society. But if one does it knowingly, he will consider it logical to escape punishment by pointing out that it is no sin to imitate bold godlike actions. If one were to censure these deeds, he will remove from them the famous names, and he will not conceal them with plausible and specious explanations. We, therefore, must accept the true and unchangeable Name—the Name announced not only by my voice, but also by that of our first teachers. Yes, we must accept this Name, lest, by leading a slothful life now, we not only remain totally ignorant of the heavenly glory, but also show ourselves to be ingrates— and for this we must answer to the Eternal Judge.

---
[1] *Odyssey* 22.347. Cf. also, 13.30.

INDEX

INDEX

Aaron, rod of, 286, 292
Abdenago, 84 n. 2
Abel, 176
Abraham, 83, 235, 282, 303; name changed from Abram to Abraham, 322; 344f., and *passim*. Cf. Circumcision
Accusations against Christians, atheism, 38; anthropophagy (Thyestean feast), 63, 434; incest (Oedipodean intercourse), 63; infanticide, 63
Achaz, 212
Achelous, 434
Achilles, 61, 395, 402, 408, 413, 431
Acrisius, 58
Acta SS. Justini et Sociorum, 9, 14
Acts, cf. Scriptures, Holy
Adam, 68, 176, 289, 341, 422
Adonis, 60
Adrian, 107f., cf. Hadrian
Adultery, 48
Advents, the two — of Christ, 89, 195, 226f.
Aeschylus, 439; — on unity of God, 444

Aesculapius, 56, 58, 60, 259, 455
Agamemnon, 431
Agrigentum, Empedocles of, 378
Ajax, 432
Alcides, 376
Alcinous, 408
Alcmene, 259, 375
Alexander the Great, 380, 388
Alexander Polyhistor, 385
Alexandria, the famous Septuagint was translated at the museum in, 66 n. 1; 120
Allard, P., 28
Alms, collecting of — at Sunday services, 107
Aloeus, 376
Altaner, B., 10 n.9, 44 n.3
Amalec, 223, 291f.
Amasis, 384, 386
Amath, 180
Amazon, 431
Amen, the meaning of, 105
Ammon, 423
Ammonites, 332
Amos, 179; cf. Scriptures

Amphytrion, 376
Amulets, used by magicians, 283
Ananias, 83
Anastasius, 17 n.52
Anaxagoras of Clazomenae, 378
Anaximander, 378
Anaximenes, 378
Angel, cf. Christ
Angels, bad, 124; free will of, 127, 364; revolt of bad, 274f.
Anger, 50
Annunciation, 305
Anphilochus, 53
Anthropophagy, 24, 63, 132 n.1
Antinous, 65
Antiope, 61, 433
Antoninus Pius, 25, 26, 33 n.1, 57; — s' Epistle to General Assembly of Asia, 109
Apocalypse of John, 278; cf. Scriptures
Apocryphal Gospels, 219 n.2
Apollo, 53, 60, 377, 431, 451, 455
Apollodorus, 378
Apologists, Christian, 9 n.1; 'The triumphal song' of, 47 n.2
Apostle of God, cf. Christ
Apostles, 90, 107; —typified by bells on the priestly robes, 211; and *passim*
Apostolic Fathers, 9
Apotheosis, 57 n.3
Appion, 384
Arabia, 101; the gold of, 199
Arabians, 198
Arbesmann, R., 9 n.1
Archambault, G., 140
Archelaus, 309, 378
Archestratians, 135
Areopagus, 399, 418
Ariadne, 56
Aridaeus, 406f.
Aristeas, 67 n.3
Aristides of Athens, 12 n.20
Aristobulus, 393
Aristophanes, 393
Aristotle, doctrines of, 379ff.; 388, 418
Arithmetic, 153
Arnobius, 58, 66 n.1, 124
Ascalon, 227
Ascension, 56; — of Christ, 61; 82
Ascension of Isaias, 334
Assyrians, 339
Astronomy, 153
Ate, the goddess of mischief, 411
Atheism, 38
Atheists, Christians are not, 38; and *passim*

INDEX 461

Athenagoras, 41 n.1, 63 n.6, 98 n.5, 396 n.1
Atreus, 434
Aubé, B., 19
Augean stables, 433
Augustine, St., 18, 127 n.1, 129 n.1, 397 n.1
Augustus, 57
Auses, Osee, Jesus, Josue, 267
Azarias, 84
Azotus, 352
Baal, 206, 359
Babel, tower of, 307, 410
Babylon, 326
Babylonian Captivity, 276
Bacchius, 23, 33
Bacchus, 56, 58f., 92, 259, 375, 392, 433, 455
Bad angels, revolt of, 274f.
Baptism, Trinitarian formula of, 99; necessity of, 99; the ceremony of, 99; — is regeneration through Christ, 99; effect of, 100; — called *photismós* or illumination, 100; — imitated by demons, 101; Isaias announced, 101
Baptist Pharisees, 276 n.4
Bardenhewer, O., 12, 19, 24, 28
Bardy, G., 15 n.39, 19, 28
Bar Kocheba, 67, 139, 148 n.1
Barnabas, Letter of, 78 n.1
Basilica, cut out of one stone, 420

Basilidians, 201
Batiffol, P., 15 n.42, 19
Bellerophon, 56, 93
Berosus, 420
Bery, A., 19
Bethel, 239
Bethlehem, 172 n.3
Bigamy, 48 n.5
Bihlmeyer, K., 9 n.2
Blood, — of circumcision and — of salvation, 183; — of Christ, figures of, 319f.
Blunt, A.W.F., 27
Boanerges, 313
Bocchoris, 386
Body, human, the resurrection of, 54
Bosor, 186
Branches, fruitbearing — symbol of Christians, 318
Brettano, J., 394 n.1
Briseis, 61, 431
Burning bush, 242
Busiris, 434
Butler, A., 12 n.16, 13 n.22

Caesar, 52, 57
Cain, 303
Caleb, 322
Caligula, 64
Cannibalism, 63 n.6
Capparetaea, 62
Caracalla, 57
Carians, 332
Carmel, the honor of, 260

Carnutum, 110
Carpenter, Christ worked as a, 290
Casamassa, A., 28
Castor, 385
Categories, Aristotelian, 17
Catholicity of Christianity, 23 n.2, 33
Cave, 12 n.17
Cayré, F., 10 n.9, 12 n.17, 14 n.30, 15 n.37, 17 n.50, 18 n.54, 24 n.8, 28
Ceillier, 13
Cerdo the Gnostic, 62 n.5
Ceres, 375, 432
Chalene, 180
Chalice, the Eucharist of the Bread and the, 328
Charito, martyr, 14 n.32
Chariton, martyr, 14 n.32
Charran, 241
Chastity, the virtue of, 47f.; cf. purity
Chevallier, T., 28
Children, pagan sacrifice of, 53
Chiliastic theory of Justin, 275ff.
Chiron the Centaur, 455
Choice, free — of man, 42, 80, 127
Christ, the precepts of, 24; 36; as the Master, 36; 38; as the Logos, 38, 129; 40, 43, 45ff.; as the Son and Apostle of God, 45; — is our Teacher, 45f.; — was not a sophist, 47; — came to call sinners, 48; teachings of, 48ff.; 55ff., 64; the lineage of, 70; — was born of a virgin, 70; called Emmanuel, 70; — our Savior, 71; called Messiah, 72, 201; miracles of, 85; death of — foretold, 85f.; sufferings of —foretold, 86; two advents of, 89, 195f., 226f.; names of, 125; remission of sin through blood of, 166f.; salvation of Jew and Gentile through, 186; — as Mediator, Helper, Redeemer, 192; — as Son of Man, 193; power of — at second advent, 193f.; — is spoken of as a King, a Priest, God, Lord and Angel, a Man, a Leader, a Stone, a Begotten Son, 198; — foretold in psalm 46, 203f.; — foretold in psalm 71, 198f.; foretold in psalm 109, 197; — foretold in psalm "Dixit Dominus", 280; — predicted in twenty-first psalm, 301ff.; — is Lord of all, 202f.; called a Stone, Judge of all men, the Eternal King and Priest, 202; His enemies will be the footstool of, 203; the Lord of Hosts, 203, 282; His Name enlightens us, 207; types of — in Mosaic Law,

208f.; end of Mosaic Law is, 212f.; every one's salvation only through, 214; — not merely of human origin, 220f.; — is distinct from the Father, 234ff.; as the Minister of the Father, 239; as Angel and Lord, 239; — is the beginning of all creatures, 244 n.1; Son, called Wisdom of Solomon, 246; Incarnation of, 247f.; divine Name of, 267; power and majesty of, 268ff.; birth in a cave of, 272; Cross of Christ prefigured in the Old Testament, 285f.; — and the Holy Spirit, 288f.; Crucifixion of — foretold, 291f., 300, 312; — assumed our curse, 298f.; called Wisdom, Day, the East, Sword, Stone, Rod, Jacob, Israel, 304; —'s agony in the garden, 310; resurrection of — forshadowed, 314f.; —'s resurrection rejected by Jews, 315f.; figures of blood of, 319f.; sinless, 319; called the Passover, 319; — prefigured by Josue, 322f.; as Judge of living and dead, 330; various names of, 343f.; — called Glory, 347; power of His name in the Old Testament, 352f.; as King of Israel, 357; Noe a type of, 360; in — all men are free, 362f.; cf. Jesus Christ

Christianity, catholicity of, 23 n.2; — is without revenge, 40; the principle of, 40

Christianoí, chrestós, chrestótatoi, 36 n.1

Christian philosophy, the only sure and useful philosophy, 11

Christians, heavenly kingdom the reward of, 43; — strive for peace, 43f.; accusations against — refuted, 38, 63, 434; — and Jews have the same God, 164; — are a holy people, redeemed by the Just One, 331; — the holy people promised to Abraham, Isaac, Jacob, and Juda, 333; true children of God, 340f.; — pray for obstinate Jews 353f.; fruit-bearing branches symbol of, 318

Chronicon of Eusebius, 26 and *passim*

Chryseis, 431

Church, Eastern, rites of the, 105 n.3; many individuals make up one, 211; Rachel, the symbol of our, 356

Cimmerian land, 97 n.5

Circumcision, 176; Christian, 183f.; — given to Jews as a mark, 171f.; origin of,

174; Abraham received — for a sign, not justification itself, 183; why — is only a sign, 183; — began with Abraham, 217; — of Jews differs from that of Christian, 324; carnal and spiritual, 212; — in the flesh and salutary, 294; instrument used for, 324
Civil authorities, Christians acknowledge and pray for, 52
Civil obedience, Christians observe, 52
Claudius, 57 n.3, 61, 95
Clement of Alexandria, 64 n.3, 124 n.1, 393 n.2, 396 n.1, 448 n.4, 453 n.12
Clement, St., of Rome, 9
Codex, Regius, 26 n.15; *Claromontanus,* 26 n.15; *Paris.* 39 n.1, 369, 455; *Arethas,* 369; *Argentoratensis,* 427;
Commodus, 33, 57
Common sense, the dictates of, 34
Conscience, peace of, 65; sinister, 296
Continency, the virtue of, 65; cf. chastity, purity
Conversion, Christians pray for — of all men, 104f.
Cora, 104 n.1
Corinthians, cf. Scriptures
Corinthus, 147

Cornerstone, Christ as, 324
Covenant, the New, 164; the precepts of the New — fit for all nations, 256
Cowper, William, 374 n.1, 395 n.2, 402 n.1, 404 n.1, 411 n.11
Creatio ex nihilo, 42 n.2
Creation, 42, 62; — of man, 245
Creature, each — has own purpose, 80; Christ is the beginning of all —s,
Crescens, cynic philosopher, 13, 122
Crete, 135 n.2
Critias, 388
Cross, symbols of, 92ff.; figures of, 292; curse of the cross a prediction of what the Jews would do, 299
Crucifixion, 78, 86, 93; — foretold, 291f., 300, 312, how curse of — is to be understood, 297f.; Jews rejected because of, 358
Cumaean Sibyl, 55; cf. Sibyl
Curetes, the cunning, 432
Cureton, W., 427 n.2
Custom—unwritten Law, 355 n.2
Cyril of Alexandria. 396f.

Daimon, the pagan meaning of, 37 n.1; cf. demons
Damascus, 179; the power of, 213

INDEX

Danaë, mother of Perscus, 56, 58, 254, 433
Danaus, 434
Daniel, 192ff., 268; understanding and counsel of, 287; and *passim;* cf. Scriptures
Daphne, 433
Darius, 386
David, psalms of, 46 n.2; 68, 76, 211, and *passim;* cf. Scriptures, Holy
Day, cf. Christ
Deacons, in Eastern and Western Church, 105 n.3
Death, not a state of insensibility, 52; Christians' attitude toward, 132; Eve brought, 305
Debora, 240
Decision, premises for a just, 34
Deeds, righteousness is determined by, 183; divine — the password of our King, 436
Deification (*apothéosis*), 57 n.3
Dejaneira, 434
Demeter, 394
Demodocus, 455
Demoniacal influence, 37 and *passim;* cf. Demons
Demoniacs and madmen, 53
Demons, 38, 57, 59, 61f., 64, 82, 93; — mislead men, 94f.; — instigated heresies, 96; influence on men of, 96; — tried to imitate baptism, 101; — chose their own name, 124; 130; — are gods of Gentiles, 275; exorcism of, 283; — to be destroyed, 353
Demonstratio of Eusebius, 390 n.4
Demosthenes, 388
De philosophia ex oraculis of Porphyrius, 387 n.1
Deucalion, 126
Deuteronomy, cf. Scriptures
Devil, Satan, also called serpent, 64; chief of demons, 64; as serpent deceived Eve, 275; 327, 343, 410f.
De vita Moysis of Philo, 390 n.3
Diana, 377, 433
Diodorus of Tarsus, 16 n.43
Diodorus, 385, 408
Diomede, 375
Dioscuri, the sons of Leda, 56
Diphilus, 447f., 453
Disciplina Arcani, 63, 99
Ditch of Homer, 53
Divination, children used for, 53; Eusebius and Tertullian on, 53
Divine Providence, 390
Divine Word, 43; cf. Word
Divorce, 48

Dixit Dominus, explanation of psalm, 280
Docetists, 310
Doctrine, Christian, true and pure, 200; atheistic and blasphemous, 200
Dodona, 53
Dods, M., 26 n.19
Dove as symbol of the Holy Spirit, 290
Dreams, influence of demons on, 46
Dupuys, J., printer at Paris, 16, 26 n.17

East, the, Christ called, 304
Eastern Church, rites of, 105 n.3
Ebionite Gospel, or *Praedicatio Pauli*, 289 n.1
Ebionites, 276 n.2
Ecclesiastical History of Eusebius, 26; cf. Eusebius
Edom, 186
Edomites, 190
Ehrhard, A., 19, 24
Eleazar, 67 n.2
Elements, the four, 378
Eleusinian mysteries, 432 n.1
Elias, 83, 206, fear of, 287
Elizabeth, mother of John the Baptist, 282
El=power, 342
Emmanuel, Christ called, 70
Empedocles, 53, 378

Endor, witch of, 53 n.3
Enemies, Christian love and pray for their, 47ff., and *passim*
Enoch, 68 n.6
Ephialtes, 376, 410
Ephraim, 180
Epicureans, 135
Epicurus, 127, 378
Epiphanius, St., 9, 12, 172 n.4
Erebos—darkness, 97 n.5
Erechtheus, 451
Esdras, passages deleted from, 263; 334
Eternal life, free will the basis for, 42
Ethics, Stoic, 127
Ethiopians, 198
Eucharist, description of Eucharistic assembly, 105; words of consecration of, 105f,; — after Sunday assembly carried to absentees by deacons, 105; figures of, 209f.; — foretold by Malachias, 328
Euelpistus, martyr, 14 n.32
Eumolpi, the father of Musaeus, 391 n.1
Eunuchs, difference of, 48
Euripides, 76 n.2, 439; — on future judgment, 448; — on vanity of false gods, 451
Euripus in Chalcis, 419
Europa, 433

INDEX

Eusebius, 12, 13 n.24, 14 n.29, 15, 25, 26; — on divination, 53 n.2; 62 n.3, 108 n.1, 105 n.1, 115, 147 n.1, 173 n.1, 387 n.1, 390 n.4, 393 n.2, 396 n.1, 397 n.1, 403 n.5, 439, 448 n.1
Eve, death brought to this world by, 305; 341
Exodus, cf. Scriptures
Exorcism, 283
Exorcists, the instruments used by, 283
Exposure of children, pagan — is murder, 65
Ezechias, 197
Ezechiel, cf. Scriptures

Fables, pagan, 259
False Christs, 279
False Christians, Christ should not be judged by, 279
Fasting, the real meaning of, 170f.
Fatalism of Stoics, 79 n.1, 148 n.5
Father, the Ineffable, 345
Fathers, Latin, 264 n.1
Felix, Prefect of Alexandria, 65
Final conflagration of world, 65
Flavia Neapolis, 9, 10, 23, 33
Flavius Josephus, *The Jewish Antiquities* of, 385

Fool, Gentiles like a, 228
Form, human erect — symbol of the cross, 94
Fornication, 48
Fortunatus, 264 n.1
Fortune-teller, ignorant, 161
Free will, man has, 80, 120; men and angels have, 364
Freppel, Ch.E., 19
Frühchristliche Apologeten, 12 n.18
Fumigation, used by magicians, 283
Funk, F.X., 16 n.43
Furies, 434

Gabriel, the angel, 305
Galatians, cf. Scriptures
Galileans, 276 n.4
Ganymede, 57, 61, 433
Geffcken, J., 28
Genesis, cf. Scriptures
Genistae, 276 n.4
Gentiles, Jews and, 90f.; the crimes of, 298; conversion foretold, 313, 349; gentile converts more faithful than Jews, 350
Geóras=stranger, 336 n.1
Geth, 180
Ghost, Holy, 154; gifts of, 287; and *passim*
Gitta, Simon of, 61
Glimm, F.X., 9 n.3

468 INDEX

Glory, Christ called, 347
Gnosticism, 17, 61 n.2
Gnostics, 62; Valentinian, 201 n.6; 276; antinomian, 364 n.2
Gobarus, Stephen, 369
God, — is cause of existence of all, 10 n.10; — is always the same, 10 n.10; to form a perfect idea of —, Justins' only ambition, 10; — is the Father of justice, 39; — has an ineffable form, 41; — governs all, 47; nothing impossible with, 54; the compassion of, 65; — is indescribable, 154; according to Plato man's mind can see, 154; there is only one, 163; Christians and Jews have the same, 164; sacrifices not needed by, 255; — the Lord, the Holy One of Israel, 264; unity of — proved from pagan writings 144ff.
Gods, men are makers and helpers of their, 41f.; pagan, evils of, 432ff.; vanity of, 450ff.
Gomorrah, 91, 176, 236
Good, — and evil the same to everyone everywhere, 295
Gospels of Hebrews, 219 n.2
Grabe, 46 n.2, 67 n.2, 79 n.1, 92 n.4
Grace, God's — needed to understand Scriptures, 294, 331

Hades, 97 n.5, 303
Hadrian, 33, 40, 57, 65; Rescript of, 108
Hands, outstretched, symbol of the Cross, 292
Harnack, A., 16 n.43, 19, 26
Hate, power of separation, 378
Heart, lamentation of the, 90; circumcision of the 294f.
Hebrews, cf. Scriptures
Hebrew Scriptures, translated into Greek, 66 n.1
Hector, 374, 402, 413, 431
Helen, 408, 431
Helena, 62
Hell, 55, 57, 64; the eternal fires of, 215
Hellanicus, 385
Hellenians, 276 n.4
Hemero-Baptists, 276 n.4
Henoch, 176
Heracles, bishop of Alexandria, 12 n.20
Heraclitus, 83, 127f., 378
Hercules, 56, 58, 93; — on the crossroads, 131; 259, 375, 433f., 455
Heretics, Simon Magus patriarch of, 61 n.2; Ebionites and Gnostics are, 200f.
Hermaphrodites, 64
Hermes, 52 n.1
Herod, 67, 76, 272, 309
Herodians, 276 n.4

Hesiod, 377, 432
Hezekiah, 213, 258, 270, 280
Hierax, martyr, 14 n.32
Hippasus of Metapontus, 378
Historia ecclesiastica, 53 n.2; cf. Eusebius
History of Appion, 384
History of Attica of Philochorus, 385
History of Egypt of Ptolemy, 384
History of the Greeks, Polemon's, 384
History of Chaldaea of Berosus, 420
Holy Family, flight into Egypt of, 272
Holy Land, 332
Holy Name of Christ, 207
Holy Writ, 303, cf. Scriptures
Homer, ditch of, 53; 58, 374ff., 380f., 391; monotheism of, 394f., 402; —'s debt to the Prophets, 408ff.; —'s debt to Moses, 412f., 431f., 455
Horace, 56
Horeb, Mount, 164, 255
Hubík, K., 25 n.12, 28
Hur, 292
Hyacinth, 433
Hystaspes, 55

Ideas, Platonic theory of, 10f.
Idle worship, 41
Idolatry, the sins of, 179
Idumaeans, 332
Ignatius, St., of Antioch, 9
Illumination, baptism called, 100
Immortality, of soul, 53; — of the body, 54
Inachus, 384
Incarnation, 247
Incest, 63
India, 153
Infanticide, 63
Innocents, holy — slain at Bethlehem, 309
Interpretation of Scriptures, 274
Iole, Hercules' love for, 434 n.3
Irenaeus, St., 15, 62 n.3, 264 n.3; — and the millennium, 277 n.5
Ismael, 332
Isaias, 69; knowledge of, 287; cf. Scriptures
Israel, significance and etymology of the name, 341f.
Ixion, 375

Jacob, the Patriarch, 226; 240ff.; — and the ladder, 285; his marriages a figure of the Church, 355f.
Japheth, 361ff.
Jahve, 385

Jeremias, 91 n.3, 180; passages deleted from 263; cf. Scriptures

Jerome, St., 10, 172 n.4, 389 n.1

Jerusalem, Christ and Christians will joyfully congregate with Patriarchs, Prophets and the Saints of old at, 275; and *passim*

Jesus, name of an alleged priest in Babylon, 326

Jesus, cf. Christ

Jews, misconception of, 67; persecution of Christians by, 67; Gentiles and, 90f.; — and Christian have the same God, 164; calumnies of — against Christians, 173f.; 188; —'s hatred of Christians, 206f.; — after conversion, called kinsmen, 219; — rejected because of crucifixion, 358; Justin exhorts — to repent, 359

Job, 310, cf. Scriptures

Joel, cf. Scriptures

John, cf. Scriptures

John the Baptist, precursor of Christ, 221f.; a Prophet, the forerunner, the herald of Christ, 224; foretold by Isaias, 224; Elizabeth, mother of, 282; 288f.

John of Damascus, 17 n.52

Jonas, resurrection foreshadowed by, 314f.; cf. Scriptures

Jordan, H., 19

Jordan River, 288 and *passim*

Joseph, 180

Josephus, 67, 385f.; 390

Josue, — son of Nun, 222; 246; — a figure of Christ, 322f.; at prayer of — the sun stood still, 352; cf. Scriptures

Judaea, a Roman province, 33 n.5

Judaizers, 218f.

Judge, the, cf. Christ

Judgment, should be based on truth, and truth alone, 23; fair, 35; future — proved from pagan writings, 477f.

Julian the Apostate, 106 n.3

Julius Caesar, 57

Juno, 375ff., 433

Jupiter, the licentiousness of, 37; 55, 57f., 70, 92f., 104; Latiaris, 132 n.3; 259, 374f., 413, 432ff., 454

Jupiter Capitolinus, seat of Cumaean Sibyl, 55 n.1

Justice, a mighty torrent, 179; — is concerned with God and man, 296

Justification, not by Jewish rites but by repentance in baptism is, 168ff.; only through Christ one will attain, 189f.

INDEX

Justin, St., — is the outstanding apologist in the second century, 9; as fearless defender of faith, 9; date of birth of, 9; — of Greco-Roman ancestry, 10; excellent education of, 10; thirst for knowledge of, 10; reasons of — for leaving the Pythagoreans, 10 n.11; the travels of, 10; Platonic ideas, their influence on, 11; practical reasons for conversion of, 11f.; — not a priest, nor deacon, but layman, 12f.; probable reason for decapitation of, 14; the works of, 15f.; original edition of the works of, 16; first Latin translation of the works of, 16; — as a trustworthy witness, 16f.; the literary form of the works of, 17; the terminology of, 17; reconciliation of faith with reason attempted by, 17; title Doctor of the Church merited by, 17 n.50; Photius' appraisal of, 17 n.52; virtues of the Apostles and, 18; addressees of First Apology of, 33; — identifies himself as a Christian, 33; — states his genealogy, 33; — demands just hearing for accused Christians, 34f.; — denies that Christians should be condemned only because of their name, 36; — refutes accusation of atheism, 38ff.; — explains why Christians do not offer sacrifices to the gods, 41f.; — explains Christian worship of God, 42, 45; — explains that Christians expect not a human kingdom, 43; — warns Romans not to be misled by the demons, 46f.; — explains Christ's teaching concerning chastity, 47ff.; — speaks of marriage, bigamy, adultery, 48; — speaks of Christian virtue of patience, 50f.; — states that Christians respect civil authority, 52; — refers to Christians' payment of taxes, 52; — speaks of immortality of the soul and refers to the oracles of Amphilochus, Dodona, Apollo, to the writings of Empedocles, Pythagoras, Plato, Socrates, the ditch of Homer, the descent of Ulysses, 53; — avers the future destruction of the world by fire as foretold by the Sibyl, Hystaspes, and the Stoics, 55; — explains the virgin-birth of Christ, 56; — states that the Word was begotten of the Father, 58, — avers that the Word is distinct from Him, 347f.; — condemns pagan idolatries, 60; — accuses Romans of honoring demons as gods, 61f.;

— explains why Christians condemn the exposure of children, 63ff.; — refutes the accusations of incest and anthropophagy, 63; — describes Satan as the chief of demons, 64; — proves the divinity of Christ from the Messianic prophecies, 66ff., 231ff.; — claims that the demons urged on the heretics, 96; — proves that Plato borrowed from the Prophets, 97; —'s explanation of the Sacrament of Baptism, 99f.; — speaks of the Eucharistic assembly, 104ff.; — accuses Urbicus of injustice, and Crescens of ignorance, 119ff.; —'s teaching on suicide, 123; — claims that God is deferring day of doom because of the Christians, 126; — expounds Christian doctrine on Hell, 128f.; — calls Christ the Perfect Logos, 129f.; —'s teaching on the seminal word, 133f.; —'s meeting with Trypho, 147; — continues to wear philosopher's robe after his conversion, 147; — describes his philosophical studies, and the beginning of his conversion, 149ff.; —'s conversation with the old man at the seashore, 151ff.; — answers Trypho's complaint that Christians do not observe the Mosaic Law, 162f.;—claims that the New Testament abrogated the Old, 163ff.; — teaches that justification is gained by repentance and baptism, 168ff.; — states man can only be saved through Christ, 189f.; — describes true fasting, 170f.; — complains the Jews spread calumnies against the Christians, 173f.; — says the Jews hate the Christians, 206f.; —'s tracing the origin of circumcision and of the Mosaic Law, 175f., — speaks of the law of meats, 177; — discusses the sabbath, 178; — speaks of sacrifices and oblations, 179ff.; explains Christian (spiritual) circumcision, 183f.; — tells of the two advents of Christ, 195f.; — proves that Christ fulfilled the prophecies of the Psalms, 198ff.; — points out types of Christ in the Mosaic Law, 208f.; — shows how the offering of flour was a figure of the Eucharist, 209f.; — states that the saints of the Old Testament were saved through Christ, 215; — says that pagan fables imitated Christian truths and the Mithraic mysteries were imitations of the prophecies, 259ff.; — complains of Jewish deletions from the Sacred Text, 264ff.; — while speaking with Trypho promises to write down later their conversation, 276; —'s view of the millennium, 275ff.; — enumerates the various figures of the Cross, 292f.; — defends the resurrection of Christ against the Jews, 314ff.; — pleads with Trypho and his Jewish friends to repent, 359f.

Works (genuine, doubtful):
 Against Marcion, 15; mentioned by St. Irenaeus, 15
 Answers to the Orthodox, 15
 Christian Questions to the Gentiles, 15f.
 Dialogue with Trypho translated, 147-366; and *passim*
 Discourse to the Greeks, translated, 427-436,
 Exhortation to the Greeks, translated, 369-423
 Exposition of True Faith, 15
 First Apology, translated, 33-111; purpose of, 23; exposition of, 24f.; place and date of origin of, 25f.; — is preceded by Second Apology in MSS, original ed. and first Latin translation, 26; 334 n.6; 264 n.1

Letter to Zena and Serenius, 15 n.42
Monarchy or *Rule of God,* translated, 439-455; introduction to, 437; not from the pen of Justin, 437
On the Resurrection, fragments, 15 n.37
On the Soul, 15f.; lost, 15
Questions to the Gentiles, 16
Refutation of Some Aristotelian Dogmas, 15
Second Apology, translated, 119-135; date of origin of, 115; reason for composition of 15; addressees of, 15; precedes the *First Apology* in MSS, 26; 334 n.6
Syntagma against all Heresies, 15; lost, 15
The Psalmist, 15f.; lost, 15
Justinian, 64 n.4

King, Christ the, 198 and *passim*
Kings, cf. Scriptures
Kiss of peace, 63, 105 n.1
Knowledge, sense, 153; — of the mind, 153f.
Kruger, G., 26, 27, 28, 35 n.1

Laban, 239, 355f.
Lactantius, 36 n.1, 37 n.1, 92 132, 263 n.1, 420
Lagrange, M.J., 17 n.50, 18 n.57, 19, 28
Laius, 434
Lamb, the mystery of, 208; cf. Christ

Lamentations, cf. Scriptures
Latin Fathers, 264 n.1
Latona, 60, 375, 377
Law, divine, the world ruled by, 124; a new —, another testament, 183; Mosaic, 198f.; unwritten — and custom, 355 n.2; the first written, 385
Leader, cf. Christ
Leblanc, J., 19
Lebreton, J., 19
Leda, 56, 433
Letter to Diognetus, not from Justin, 15 n.37; 126 n.1
Leviticus, cf. Scriptures
Lia, symbol of the synagogue, 355f.
Libanus, 199; the glory of, 260
Liberianus, martyr, 14 n.32
Life, sinful, monotony of, 95
Logos, 38, 47, 69; Christ, 120; 130f.; divine generation of, 244; — is distinct from the Father, 347f.; — is enkindled from Father as *lumen de lumine,* 244, 348
Lógos spermatikós and *Ho Pâs Lógos,* 38 n.3
Lord, — of Sabaoth, 195; — of Hosts, 317
Love, power of union, 378
Lot, a Chaldaean, 91; 176
Lucius Ceionius Commodus, 33 n.2
Lucius, a Christian martyr, 121f.

Luke, cf. Scriptures
Lumen de lumine, 244
Luza, 240

Magi, 271ff., 288
Magic, tricks of, 46; miracles and, 260 n.5
Magical Arts, 58f.
Magicians, 53
Malachias, 190; — announced Eucharist of the Christians, 328; cf. Scriptures
Mamre, the oak of, 231ff.; 286
Man, the endowments of, 65; the free will of, 289
Manna, 178
Marah, 285
Maran, Prud., 12, 13, 15, 35 n.1, 39 n.1, 46 n.2, 48 n.5, 56 n.2, 59 n.2, 60 n.3, 67 n.2, 71 n.3, 92 n.4, 94 n.4, 98 n.2, 101 n.1, 105 n.3, 122 n.1, 125 n.1, 389 n.1
Marcion of Pontus, 62, 96; teacher of Markianoi, 201
Marcus Annius Verus (Marcus Aurelius), 33 n.1
Marcus Aurelius, 25, 57; epistle to the senate, 115, 121
Marcus Pompeius, 139, 160, 365
Mark, cf. Scriptures
Markianoí, not disciple of Mark, 201
Marique, J.-F., 9 n.3

Marpessus, Sibyl of, 55 n.1
Marriage, second, 48 n.5; procreation the purpose of, 65
Mars, 375f.; young and handsome, 434; 435, 455
Martindale, C.C., 19
Martyrdom of Isaias, 334
Mary, Virgin, Annunciation of the Birth of Christ to, 304
Matter, shapeless, 42
Matthew, cf. Scriptures
Meats, the law of, 177
Melanippe, 432
Melchisedech, 176, 196ff., 323, 329
Melito of Sardis, 109 n.1
'Memoirs of the Apostles,' 304, 311ff.
Menander, the magician, 56; the teachings of 62, 95, 439, 448; vanity of false gods, 450ff.
Menelaus, 408
Menes, Justin confuses here Moses with, 385 n.1
Meno, 414f.
Mercury, 56, 423
Meristae, 276 n.4
Mesopotamia, 240
Messiah, Christ called, 72, 201 and *passim;* the Son of Man, 194
Messianic prophecy, 68ff.

Meton, 378
Micheas, — foretold conversion of Gentiles, 313; cf. Scriptures
Middle Ages, 420 n.1
Migne, 46 n.2, 59 n.2, 369, 427, 439
Millennium, opinion of Justin not universally shared by Christians, 276; — proved by Isaias and St. John, 277f., 361
Mind, the Supreme, 154
Minerva, — considered as first conception of God is ridiculous, 104; 375, 433
Minister, Christ called the — of the Father, 239
Minos, 40, 375
Minucius Felix, 63 n.3
Minucius Fundanus, 108
Miracles, performed to show that Jesus is the Messiah, 207
Misach, 84 n.2
Misael, 84
Mithras, mysteries of, 106; imitations of prophecies, 261, 272
Mnaseas, 284
Mnesarchus, 378
Moabites, 190
Moeller, W., 25 n.12
Moloch, 179
Monarchians, 347
Monarchy, the rule of God, 443ff.

Monogamy, 355 n. 1
Monotheism, in writings of Orpheus, 391ff.; in oracles of the Sibyl, 393ff.; in *Iliad* of Homer, 394f.; in writings of Sophocles, 395f.; in writings of Pythagoras, 396; in writings of Plato, 397, 402
Mosaic Law, why Christians do not observe, 175; origin of, 176; 198; now useless for salvation, 216f.
Moses, first of the Prophets, 68, 176; 71, 92, 98; God appeared to, 101ff.; strength and piety of, 287; — and the brazen serpent, 297; antiquity of — testified to by Greek writers, 384ff.; pagan oracles attested, 387; — is older than pagan philosophers, 388; Plato's debt to, 411ff.; 415; Homer's debt to, 412f.
Mountain, the holy — of God, 186
Munacius Felix, 83
Murder, exposing children is, 65
Musaeus, 391, 445
Music, skill in, 153
Musonius, 128

Nablous, 33
Name, without deeds a — is an empty shell, 24; the — of Christ enlightens us, 207
Nathan, 330
National Library of Paris, *Codex Regius* is at, 26 n.15
Navigation, skill in, 153
Neptune, 124, 375, 377, 432
Neocles, 378
Nereids, 432
Nero, 36 n.2
Nerva, 57, 65 n.1
Nessus, 434
New-born, exposing of, 63 n.6
Nicene Creed, 244 n.2
Nicostratus, 447
Nile River, 65 n.2
Nineve, 315
Ninevites, 314
Noe, 126; the father of our race, 176; a type of Christ, 360
Noetus, 347 n.2
Numbers, cf. Scriptures
Oak of Mourning, 240
Oath, the well of, 240f.
Oblations, origin of, 179ff.
Oedipodean intercourse, 63
Oedipus, 434
Ogyges, 384
Olives, Mount of, 303, Mount Olivet, 309
Omphale, 434
One, the number, 378
Oracles of Sibyls, 420 f; cf. Sibyl
Origen, 18, 130, 190

INDEX 477

Orpheus, 391, 394, 439; unity of God, 445
Osee, 176, Josue, Jesus, 267 n.2; cf. Scriptures
Ossa, 410
Otto, J.C.T., von, 15, 16 n.47, 17 n.51, 27, 35 n.1, 39 n.1, 92 n.4, 369, 427, 439
Otto, R., 19
Otus, 376, 410

Paeon, martyr, 14 n.32
Pagan Idolatries, 60
Pagan immoralities, 64
Pagan mythology, origin of, 91f.
Pallas, 377
Pallium of the Philosophers, 147 n.2
Pamphilus, 449
Papias of Hierapolis, belief of — in millennium, 277 n.5
Parchment, sacred letters upon, 217
Passion, unreasonable, 36f.; slaves of, 91
Passover, truly a type of Christ, 208; Christ called the, 319
Patriarchs — and Prophets and the Saints of old will congregate joyfully with Christ and His followers, 275
Patroclus, 374

Patience, virtue of Christian, 50
Paul of Samosata, 347 n.2
Pautigny, L., 28
Peace, kiss of, 105 n.1; abundance of, 198
Pegasus, 56, 93
Peleus, 393, 431
Pelion, 410
Pelops, 434
Penance, importance of
Perionius, Joach., O.S.B., 13 n.25, 16, 26 n.17
Peripatetics, 10, 149
Perseus, 56, 58, 93, 254, 262, 375
Peter, St., 61
Pfattisch, J.M., 17 n.53, 19, 24 n.7, 26 n.21, 27, 28, 37 n.1
Phares, 333
Pharisees, 307
Pharos, 389
Philaemidians, 135
Philaenis, 135 n.3
Philaenidians, 135
Philemon, 439; — on unity of God 445; — on future judgment, 447; 448
Philip the Deacon, 61
Philo, 67, 347, 385f., 390
Philochorus, 385
Philology, different meaning of, 151 n.1
Phoebus, 377

Philópsophos, philókompos, philósophos, 122 n.3

Philosophers, called pious men, 34; — borrowed from the Prophets, 81; holy men are the philosophers, 149

Philosophy, one's greatest possession is, 10 n.10, 149; Justin's inclination for, 10; the only sure and useful — is the Christian, 11; — most precious in sight of God, 149; the study of, 150; every man should study, 152; — alone produces happiness, 152; — as a clear understanding of, truth, 152

Phoenix, 375, 395

Photismós, illumination, baptism, 100 n.5

Photius, 17 n.52, 18 n.58, 369 n.1, 396 n.1

Phrygians, 433

Pindar, 56, 406

Pirithoüs, 375

Place of Christ's Birth, 71

Plato, 13 n.27, 17, 25, 35, 38, 40f., 53, 55, 81; — borrowed from Moses, 97f.; doctrine of the cross in, 98; 123, 125, 130, 132, 154; destruction of world according to, 157; — a bulwark of philosophy, 158; doctrines of, 379ff.; 388, 391, 393; monotheism of, 397, 402; — ambiguous through fear, 399; — contradicts himself, 401; the opinion of Creator and creation of, 401ff.; — read the Prophets, 405, 413; —'s opinion of the judgment, 406; —'s debt to Moses, 411f., 415; — knew of the Holy Spirit, 414f., 418, 420f., 439, 449

Platonists, 148 n.6, 149

Pluto, 376, 432

Poets, Greek, not reliable teachers, 374ff.

Polemon, 384

Polycarp, St., 9

Polydamna, 408

Polygamy, 355 n.1

Polytheism, 400f.

Polyxena, 431

Pompeius, 365

Pontius Pilate, 46, 76, 83; Acts of, 85; 100, 269, 307 and *passim*

Pope, Alexander, 408 n.1, 409 n.5, 410 n.6

Porphyrius, 387 n.1, 403 n.5

Posidonius, 384

Potérion, 105 n.2

Powers of the Prophets, 287f.

Praedicatio Pauli, 289 n.1

Praeparatio of Eusebius, 387 n.1

Prayer, Christians pray for friend and foe, 201; Justin's — for enlightenment, 373

INDEX 479

Praxeas, 347 n.2
Precepts, Mosaic, 211
Priest, Christ called, 198
Priscus, 33
Procne, 434
Prodicus, 131 n.1
Prophecy, gifts of prophecy transferred to Christians, 278f.
Prophets, — blessed by God, 11; 66ff., 159; holy and false, 278f.; the gift of, 287; Plato's debt to, 406, 413; Homer's debt to, 408ff.; — should be heeded, 422
Proselytes, 275, 336 n.1
Proserpine, 60, 104 n.1, 432
Prostitution, 63; taxes for, 64 n.4
Proverbs, cf. Scriptures
Providence, God's, 65, 148
Psalm, twenty-first psalm foretold Christ, 301ff.
Psalms, cf. Scriptures
Ptolemaeus, a Christian martyr, 121f.
Ptolemy Philadelphus, King of Egypt, Septuagint prepared through, 66f., 262; 389f.
Ptolemy the Mendesian, 384
Purity, the virtue of, 48; cf. chastity
Pythagoras, 10, 53, 149f., 378, 391; monotheism of, 396, 446, 439

Quirinius, 71, 272
Rabbis, Jewish, polygamy and, 355 n.1
Rachel, 273; a symbol of our Church is, 356
Rahab, the harlot of Jericho, 320
Rama, 273
Raphan, 179
Rauschen, G., 12, 15 n.37, 16 n.46, 24, 26 n.21, 26, 28, 35 n.1, 37 n.1, 39 n.1, 44 n.1
Reality, virtue as well as vice is a, 65
Reason, faith and, 17; demands of sane, 23f.; all is ruled by, 152
Rebecca, 240
Regeneration, baptism is — through Christ, 99
Relations, sexual, washing after, 216
Reincarnation, 155f.
Reith, G., 445 n.1, 448 n.3, 449 n.2, 450 n.6, 451 n.3, 452 n.8, 453 n.13
Repentance, necessary for salvation, 365
Resurrection of Christ, 53ff.; — of human body, 54; — foreshadowed by history of Jonas, 314f.; — rejected by Jews, 315f.
Revelation, 38 n.3
Revenge, Christians don't take, 40

Rhadamanthus, 40, 375
Rite, wicked and atheistic, 201
Rivière, G., 28
Robe, His, symbolic meaning of, 69
Roberts and Donaldson, 445 n.1
Rock of living water, 325
Rod, Christ called, 304
Romans, cf. Scriptures
Romulus, 57
Ruben, 333
Rufinus, 108 n.1
Rulers, the duty of righteous, 44
Rusticus, 14

Saba, 198
Sabbath, purpose of, 176; origin of, 178
Sachunchis, Egyptian lawgiver, 385
Sacrament, — of Baptism, 99f; the Eucharist, 105f.
Sacrifice, God does not need any, 179
Sadducees, denied resurrection of the body from the dead, 276 n.4
Salvation, man's only — through Christ, cf. Christ
Samaria, the spoil, 213
Samuel, 53, 282
Sara, 232, 235; name changed, 322; 344
Sardanapalus, 127
Satan, 64; the etymology of the word Satanas, 310
Saturn, 132 n.2, 432
Saturnilians, 201
Satires, the, the cymals of, 434
Scapegoat, the practice of using a, 209
Scriptures, the tremendous majesty of the words of the, 13; — understood by grace of God, 294; Jewish interpretations of — are incorrect, 338ff.
Scriptures, Holy,
Quotations from or references to Biblical writers or Biblical books
Acts, 42 n.1
Amos, 180 n.1
Apocalypse, 278 n.4
Corinthians, 200 n.2
Daniel, 84 n.2, 88 n.3, 170 n.3, 194 n.1, 195 n.2, 261 n.2, 268 n.1, 268 n.2, 274 n.1, 317 n.2, 331 n.1
Deuteronomy, 80 n.1, 99 n.6, 172 n.1, 177 n.2, 178 n.5, 217 n.2, 223 n.6, 230 n.1, 230 n.2, 267 n.3, 290 n.1, 293 n.1, 293 n.2, 295 n.2, 298 n.1, 299 n.1, 332 n.6, 335 n.2, 338 n.2, 345 n.9, 349 n.1, 350 n.1, 351 n.2, 363 n.4

INDEX

Exodus, 101 n.2, 102 n.4, 103 n.8, 177 n.1, 191 n.1, 210 n.1, 217 n.2, 223 n.8, 242 n.2, 242 n.3, 243 n.1, 267 n.1, 267 n.3, 285 n.1, 291 n.1, 344 n.1, 345 n.2, 398 n.2, 411 n.1, 412 n.2

Ezechiel, 89 n.1, 177 n.4, 179 n.1, 214 n.3, 215 n.1, 219 n.1, 219 n.2, 271 n.2, 279 n.1, 330 n.5, 331 n.2, 339 n.7, 363 n.4, 414 n.1

Galatians, 298 n.1

Genesis, 68 n.1, 92 n.3, 97 n.3, 98 n.4, 104 n.2, 163 n.2, 176 n.2, 177 n.3, 177 n.4, 183 n.2, 227 n.1, 227 n.4, 228 n.1, 229 n.1, 231 n.1, 231 n.2, 232 n.3, 233 n.4, 233 n.5, 234 n.6, 235 n.9, 235 n.10, 236 n.11, 236 n.12, 236 n.13, 237 n.14, 237 n.15, 239 n.1, 240 n.2, 240 n.3, 241 n.4, 243 n.2, 246 n.1, 246 n.2, 247 n.2, 268 n.4, 278 n.2, 285 n.1, 286 n.4, 294 n.1, 307 n.2, 307 n.3, 321 n.2, 333 n.1, 333 n.2, 333 n.3, 344 n.2, 344 n.3, 344 n.4, 344 n.5, 344 n.6, 344 n.7, 345 n.1, 345 n.3, 345 n.4, 346 n.5, 348 n.1, 348 n.2, 355 n.3, 356 n.4, 356 n.5, 356 n.6, 356 n.7, 356 n.8, 361 n.2, 361 n.1, 362 n.3, 409 n.4, 410 n.7, 413 n.2, 413 n.3, 416 n.1

Hebrews, 45 n.1, 334 n.4

Isaias, 70 n.1, 72 n.1, 72 n.2, 72 n.3, 74 n.1, 74 n.2, 74 n.3, 74 n.4, 74 n.1, 75 n.2, 75 n.1, 81 n.2, 84 n.1, 85 n.2, 85 n.1, 85 n.2, 86 n.1, 86 n.2, 86 n.1, 87 n.2, 87 n.3, 88 n.1, 89 n.2, 89 n.3, 90 n.4, 91 n.1, 91 n.2, 100 n.4, 102 n.1, 103 n.6, 164 n.2, 165 n.1, 165 n.2, 168 n.2, 170 n.1, 171 n.2, 173 n.5, 173 n.2, 173 n.3, 174 n.4, 175 n.1, 182 n.4, 184 n.2, 184 n.3, 186 n.2, 186 n.1, 187 n.2, 187 n.1, 188 n.2, 188 n.4, 196 n.3, 207 n.3, 209 n.2, 211 n.3, 212 n.1, 213 n.2, 214 n.4, 220 n.1, 225 n.1, 227 n.3, 247 n.1, 251 n.1, 252 n.2, 253 n.1, 257 n.1, 260 n.4, 262 n.1, 268 n.4, 268 n.3, 269 n.5, 270 n.1, 273 n.4, 274 n.5, 275 n.2, 278 n.1, 279 n.2, 281 n.1, 285 n.3, 287 n.1, 289 n.2, 300 n.2, 300 n.3, 300 n.4, 308 n.4, 308 n.5, 319 n.5, 320 n.2, 321 n.1, 324 n.1, 324 n.2, 324 n.3, 329 n.3, 330 n.6, 331 n.4, 332 n.5, 336 n.3, 336 n.4, 337 n.5, 337 n.6, 338 n.1, 338 n.3, 339 n.4, 339 n.6, 340 n.8, 349 n.3, 354 n.1, 354 n.2, 356 n.1, 357 n.2, 357 n.3, 357 n.4, 358 n.5, 358 n.1, 258 n.2, 358 n.3, 360 n.3, 360 n.1, 363 n.2, 363 n.3, 363 n.5

482 INDEX

Jeremias, 91 n.3, 164 n.3, 175 n.1, 181 n.2, 189 n.1, 190 n.2, 202 n.1, 263 n.2, 273 n.3, 325 n.5, 325 n.6, 339 n.5, 363 n.1

Job, 214 n.2, 275 n.4

Joel, 90 n.4, 288 n.3

John, 99 n.3, 289 n.2, 309 n.2, 312 n.1

Jonas, 315 n.4

Josue, 247 n.3, 323 n.2, 352 n.1

Kings, 206 n.1, 286 n.5, 330 n.4, 353 n.2, 414 n.2

Lamentations, 94 n.3

Leviticus, 172 n.2, 209 n.1, 355 n.2

Luke, 49 n.8, 49 n.10, 49 n.12, 49 n.14, 52 n.2, 69 n.2, 71 n.2, 102 n.3, 106 n.2, 165 n.3, 174 n.6, 174 n.7, 209 n.2, 222 n.2, 226 n.1, 269 n.9, 278 n.5, 290 n.3, 300 n.2, 304 n.2, 305 n.4, 306 n.2, 310 n.6, 312 n.2, 355 n.3

Malachias, 190 n.4, 210 n.3, 221 n.1, 328 n.1

Mark, 51 n.6, 69 n.2, 106 n.2, 229 n.3, 270 n.10, 304 n.2

Matthew, 48 n.1, 48 n.2, 48 n.3, 48 n.4, 48 n.5, 48 n.6, 49 n.7, 49 n.9, 49 n.11, 49 n.13, 49 n.15, 50 n.16, 50 n.17, 50 n.18, 50 n.1, 50 n.2, 50 n.3, 50 n.4, 51 n.5, 51 n.7, 51 n.9, 51 n.10, 51 n.11, 52 n.1, 55 n.1, 55 n.2, 69 n.2, 70 n.1, 71 n.1, 72 n.5, 75 n.6, 99 n.2, 102 n.2, 103 n.7, 106 n.2, 165 n.3, 174 n.5, 174 n.6, 200 n.1, 200 n.3, 200 n.4, 222 n.2, 222 n.4, 222 n.5, 226 n.1, 269 n.6, 269 n.7, 269 n.8, 271 n.1, 271 n.2, 296 n.1, 300 n.3, 303 n.1, 303 n.2, 304 n.1, 304 n.2, 304 n.3, 305 n.1, 306 n.2, 307 n.1, 310 n.5, 312 n.3, 314 n.3, 314 n.1, 321 n.3, 326 n.2, 334 n.5, 336 n.2, 342 n.1, 342 n.2, 343 n.3, 355 n.3, 364 n.6

Micheas, 71 n.1, 271 n.2, 317 n.1, 318 n.4

Numbers, 69 n.4, 98 n.2, 98 n.3, 217 n.1, 223 n.6, 267 n.2, 313 n.1, 345 n.8

Osee, 170 n.2, 176 n.3, 309 n.3, 331 n.2

Proverbs, 245 n.3, 348 n.3

Psalms, 72 n.4, 75 n.3, 75 n.4, 75 n.5, 76 n.1, 77 n.2, 78 n.3, 78 n.1, 83 n.1, 88 n.2, 93 n.5, 181 n.3, 190 n.5, 192 n.2, 196 n.5, 197 n.1, 197 n.2, 198 n.1, 198 n.2, 199 n.3, 203 n.2, 203 n.3, 204 n.1, 204 n.2, 206 n.1, 207 n.2, 211 n.2, 230 n.3, 234 n.7, 234 n.8, 237 n.1, 248 n.3, 248 n.4, 248 n.5, 250 n.1, 250 n.2, 250 n.3, 251 n.4, 259 n.3, 264 n.1, 265

INDEX 483

n.3, 266 n.1, 275 n.5, 278 n.3, 280 n.1, 280 n.2, 281 n.3, 281 n.4, 282 n.1, 284 n.2, 286 n.2, 286 n.3, 288 n.2, 290 n.4, 295 n.2, 300 n.1, 301 n.5, 302 n.1, 310 n.4, 311 n.1, 318 n.3, 324 n.4, 329 n.2, 335 n.1, 335 n.3, 338 n.7, 341 n.1, 364 n.1, 412 n.1

Romans, 188 n.3

Thessalonians, 317 n.1

Timothy, 130 n.4

Wisdom, 361 n.4

Zacharias, 73 n.6, 90 n.4, 170 n.2, 195 n.1, 221 n.1, 228 n.2, 229 n.4, 275 n.3, 313 n.2, 325 n.1, 327 n.1, 327 n.2, 331 n.3, 335 n.4, 335 n.5, 346 n.6, 346 n.7, 359 n.1

Segor, 236

Sem, 362

Semele, 60, 259, 433

Semisch, C., 19

Semites, 361

Seneca, 57 n.4

Septimius Severus, 57

Septuagint, 66 n.1, 78 n.1, 258, 262, 314; composition of, 389f.

Serenius Granianus, 108

Serpent, — as a symbol, 64; curse of, 275; 297 n.1

Sesonchosis, King, 385

Sexual relations, washing after, 216

Shell, a name without deeds an empty, 24

Sibyl, the most famous Greek — at Marpessus near Troy, 55; the Roman — was the Cumaean at Rome, 55; monotheism in oracles of, 393ff.; oracles of, 420f.

Sibylline Oracles, Roman Senate consulted the, 55 n.1; 420f.; nature of, 420f.; should be heeded, 422

Sichem, capital of Samaria, 9; 33

Sidon, 199

Sidrach, 84 n.2

Sign, Jewish circumcision only a, cf. circumcision

Simon Magus, 61f., 95, 134; — considered patriarch of heretics, 61 n.2

Simony, the sin of, 61; why called, 61 n.2

Sin, a reality, 80

Sinners, Christ came to call, 48

Sinope in Pontus, 62 n.5

Sion, 180

Sirens, 432

Sisinnius, 15 n.42

Sisyphus, 408

Skeptics, 149 n.1

Smith and Wace, 10 n.9, 25 n.11, 26 n.14, and n.19

Social life, Egyptian, 385
Socrates, 13; — falsely put to death as an atheist, 38; 53, 83, 123; — and Christ, 129f., 388, 418
Sodom, 91 176, 236
Solomon, 197, 250; Christ called wisdom of, 246; the spirit of wisdom of, 287
Solon, 388, 391
Sophist, Christ not a, 47
Sophocles, monotheism of, 395f., 439; unity of God, 445; future judgment, 447
Sophonias, 72, 73 n.6
Sotades, 135 n.2
Sotadists, 135
Soul, immortality of — believed in by pagans, 53f., 312; the affinity of — to God, 154; man's — different from all other souls, 154; if — not immortal, sinner would benefit, 157; Aristotle's and Plato's teachings on, 382f.
Spiritism, 53
Spiritistic seances, 53
Springl, J., 19
Stephanus, H., 16, 26 n.16, 177 n.3
Stoics, 55, 79 n.1, 126, 149
Stone, Christ called, 198, 304
Strabo, 135
Strategy, military, skill in, 153
Subordinationism, 44 n.3

Suetonius, 57 n.4, 64 n.4
Suffering, mental and physical, 343
Suicide, illicit and forbidden by God, 123
Sun and light, the Father and the Son are inseparable as, 347
Sunday assembly, description of Christian service at, 106f.
Swearing, 50
Sword, Christ called, 304
Sylburg, 55 n.2, 93 n.4
Synoptics, 69 n.2
Syria-Palestine, 33, 71 n.2
Syro-Phoenicia, 273

Tanis, 274
Tantulus, 408
Tarphon, Jewish Rabbi, 12 n.19, 139, 147 n.3
Tatian, 13, 64, 393
Taxes, Christ teaches to pay — to civil authorities, 52
Teacher, Christ our, 45f.
Telamon, 432
Telemachus, 408
Temple in Jerusalem, 182
Tertullian, — the *Writings of Tertullian* in translation, 9 n.1; — on divination, 37 n.1; 53 n.2, 56 n.1, 57 n.4, 62 n.3, 63 n.6, 78 n.1, 93 n.1, 106 n.3, 108 n.2, 119 n.3, 124 n.2, 125 n.2, 127 n.1, 132 n.3, 135 n.4, 172 n.3, 244 n.2

Tethys, 374
Thales of Miletus, 377, 380
Thallus, 385
Thamar, 286
Tharsis, 198
Theodoret of Cyrus, 16 n.43, 393 n.2, 396 n.1
Theon, 408
Theophilus of Antioch, 36 n.1
Theoretics, 149 n.1
Thessalonians, cf. Scriptures
Thetis, 61
Timothy, cf. Scriptures
Thirlby, 35 n.1, 92 n.4, 101 n.1
Thomas Aquinas, St., 18
Thought, word should cover, 275
Thrace, 135
Thümer, J., 17 n.53, 19
Thyestes, 434
Thyestean feasts, 63, 434
Tiberius Caesar, 46
Tillemont, 26
Titus, 10, 57
Tixeront, J., 16 n. 43, 19
Trajan, 57
Trinitarian formula of baptism, 99 n.2
Trojans, 374
Trollope, 39, 92
Troy, 55
Truth, man must be less honored than, 13f.; lover of, 16, 34; self-evident, 90

Trypho, 12 n.19, 13, 139; — meets Justin, 147; — blames Christians for not observing Mosaic law, 162f.; objections of, 187; — demands proof of Messiahship of Jesus, 220; — demands clear proof of Christ's divinity, 230; — denies need of Christ, 249f.; — compares Jesus with Perseus, 254f.; — shows anger, 274; — is scandalized at crucifixion, 290f.
Two, symbolism of number, 378 n.1

Ulmmans, before called Bethel, 241
Ulysses, 53, 395, 402, 432
Urbicus, 115, 119, — condemns Christians to death, 121

Valentinians, 201
Venus, 60, 374f., 408, 433, 435, 455
Verbum, cf. Word
Verbum perfectum and *verbum seminale,* 18 n.55
Verissimus, 33
Vespasian, 9 n.5, 10, 33, 57
Vice, a reality, 65; 131
Virgin, Isaias foretold Christ's birth by a, 253
Virgin Mary, Abraham the ancestor of, 333

Virtue, the reality of, 65; 131, 192
Vishtaspa, 55
Vitrasius Pollio, 111
Vulcan, 434

Walsh, G.G., 9 n.3
Weapons, conversion of — of war into those of peace, 318
Wehofer, T. H., 24, 28
Weizsäcker, C., 17 n.53
Western Church, the rite of the Eucharist in, 105 n.3
Will, free, the basis for eternal life is man's, 42; angels', 127, 364; cf. choice, free
Wisdom, the spirit of, 287 and *passim,* Christ called, 304
Wisdom, cf. Scriptures
Witch of Endor, 53
Word, Divine, 43; His — the power of God, 47; Son of God, not born as result of sexual relations, 56, 70; the seminal, 69, 133f.; the Perfect, 69 n.3

Word-concept of Holy Scripture, Son of God, 17
Words, not the — but the spirit of — is of importance, 320
World, — created by the Word, 104; — created for man's sake, 124
Worship, difference between pagan and Christian, 45ff.; — only due to God, 52; observance of, 105f.; — with lips different from that with the heart, 201

X, the letter — as symbol, 97f.
Xenophon, 131
Xerxes, 386

Zacharias, prophecy concerning Christians, 325; cf. Scriptures
Zahn, Th., 12 n.19, 26
Zebedec, 313
Zeus, 60, 254, 402
Zoroaster, 55 n.5

www.ingramcontent.com/pod-product-compliance
Lightning Source LLC
Chambersburg PA
CBHW032021290426
44110CB00012B/626